A BOOK for COOKS

A BOOK for COOKs

101 CLASSIC COOKBOOKS

Leslie Geddes-Brown

MERRELL

LONDON · NEW YORK

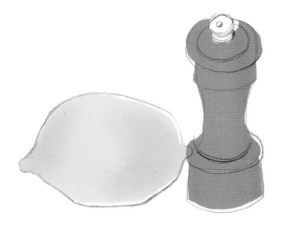

Introduction

First, this is a personal selection, a list of my favourite cookery books. There won't be a cook alive who would choose the same books, because cooking is a personal business. Although it is often considered a chore, like dusting or bed-making – that is, women's work – cooking is truly creative, an art that needs all five senses: taste and smell, of course, but also touch, hearing and sight. Think of a loaf of bread: the flavour and scent of a newly baked slice; the warm, squashy feel of kneading the dough (very calming, too); the sound of its crackly crust as the first slice is cut; and the look of something beautiful made from four ordinary ingredients. If nothing else, the 'shouty' chefs have certainly done one thing for cooking: they have made it serious.

People have been recording their recipes for as long as they have been able to write. The ancient Egyptians inscribed recipes on clay tablets; in Pompeii (that preserved sample of Roman life as it really was), recipes can be seen scribbled on the lintels of kitchen doors; and Marcus Gavius Apicius, a first-century Roman gourmet, is credited (probably wrongly) with compiling a book of recipes, the *Apicius*, during the reign of Tiberius. The first printed cookery book, a version of *Apicius* titled *De re coquinaria* (On the subject of cooking), was produced by Guillermus Le Signerre in Milan in 1498. In London, *The Boke of Cokery* was printed in 1500 by a Norman, Richard Pynson, an apprentice to William Caxton. Eight years later, Wynkyn de Worde produced his *Boke of Kervynge* (a copy from 1513 can be found in the British Library, so it was clearly popular enough to have appeared in several editions). Carving in those days was more than just cutting up roast beef: it involved deer, cranes, swans, herons and peacocks, along with hens, mallard and even fish.

I began collecting cookery books in my twenties, inspired by the lengthy bibliographies in Elizabeth David's books. So I bought Lady Clark of Tillypronie's cookery book (page 50), published posthumously, from a dreary upstairs second-hand bookshop in Darlington, County Durham, along with Lady Jekyll's romp through the aristocracy's kitchens (page 128) and – much later, after much searching – Colonel Kenney-Herbert's jottings from Madras, published under the pseudonym of Wyvern (page 212). To be honest, I have never used any of them for recipes, but I do enjoy their period feel. My mother, on the other hand, got me cooking by introducing me to the nineteenth-century writer Eliza Acton (page 14), probably the first modern cookery writer, and her Fried Chicken à la Malabar – chicken breasts rolled in curry powder and served with fried onions. I cannot imagine anyone using the ponderous Mrs Beeton (page 32). Perhaps it owes its huge sales to mothers buying it for newly married daughters as chunky wedding presents. Most young women, I think, learn to cook from their mothers, as I did.

By now I must own hundreds of cookery books. Not only do I review them, which is a minor adventure, but also I buy them by the shelf-load. Because I have so many, I never tire of them; there's always something new to learn from a book I had forgotten I owned. Recently, I found I possessed two copies of *Japanese Cooking: A Simple Art* (page 198), which is perfectly unusable. As a one-time judge for the Guild of Food Writers award for best book on food and travel, I have also been sent a pile of books to decide a shortlist and a winner. Terrific fun: I like being a critic.

If I were asked to list my top-ten cookery books, just as we have asked some experts to do for this book (page 216), the result would vary from week to week. In the autumn

I would go for books on foraging and wild mushrooms; in summer, Spanish tapas and Provençal salads (you will note how often *salade niçoise* appears in this book, and in how many variations); and, in winter, North American and Scandinavian warmers featuring venison and berries. There's always room for a bit of South East Asian food – inauthentic, probably – such as a much-loved noodle soup, the broth enlivened with nam pla, chilli and soy sauce; and, equally inauthentic, kedgeree, taken from Elizabeth David. Most weeks, I try a new recipe from whichever book takes my fancy. My problem is that, because I'm always reading cookery books (before lunch is the best time), if I'm not careful I forget from which one I got the idea. My shopping list may say 'dark chocolate, asparagus and goat's cheese', but I've no idea why, or where to find the original recipe. Like Julian Barnes in *The Pedant in the Kitchen* (2003), I do like to follow recipes. Otherwise, I forget whether *pytt i panna* includes onions as well as fried potatoes and cubes of beef (it does), or whether it's burrata cheese that should be eaten with rocket and olive oil or bresaola (it's both).

T he cookery writers I researched for this book are a surprising bunch. Where you imagine them to be commonsensical cooks in the vein of Delia Smith, Mary Berry and Marguerite Patten, they turn out to be much more fun. Best of all is the Royalist ('Wrong but Wromantic', as *1066 and All That* avers) Sir Kenelm Digby (page 76), who killed a French nobleman in a duel, was a successful privateer and spent much time in mainland Europe, sometimes as a courtier, sometimes as an exile. But, 300 years later, who would have imagined that Robert Carrier (page 44), the suave owner of Carrier's restaurant in Islington,

This is my modernized kitchen featuring salvaged quarry tiles and Victorian cupboards from a local corn market. The table was made specially from old floorboards.

London, was, before that, a juvenile lead in musicals, a cryptographer for Charles de Gaulle and a publicist for vegetarian dog food? Another American, Craig Claiborne (page 48), saw action in the US Navy during both the Second World War and the conflict in Korea that followed it. The Norwegian Roald Dahl (page 64), aged twenty-three at the outbreak of war, commanded a corps of askaris and joined the RAF, only to crash in the desert, breaking his skull. Later, he spied for Britain in Washington, D.C., alongside Ian Fleming. Chocolate, one of Dahl's other great loves, is tame by comparison.

Another notable trait is that many cookery writers travel. It's obvious, really: it's much easier to become interested and involved in a new cuisine than in the boring old stuff you ate as a child. At the age of twenty-one, Stephanie Alexander (page 16) escaped being a librarian in Australia by travelling to France; Eliza Acton also spent time in France – ostensibly because she had tuberculosis, but rumour suggests it was to have an illegitimate baby instead. Patience Gray (page 96) learned many of her recipes while following her sculptor husband around Europe in his search for a decent piece of marble. The husband of Marika Hanbury Tenison (page 112) was an explorer, going up the Amazon and to remote chunks of Indonesia. Len Deighton (page 72) went to Hollywood.

Elizabeth David, deciding at the age of twenty-six that she should not become an actress, set sail in a yacht with her lover and was stranded in the South of France by the outbreak of the Second World War. She later spent time in prison, lived on a Greek island (being evacuated just before the Germans invaded) and, for the last three years of the war, was librarian for the Ministry of Information in Egypt. For twenty years, Jane Grigson (page 102) and her poet husband, Geoffrey, lived three months a year in a cave in Trôo, central France, with neither running water nor electricity. Sam and Sam Clark of Moro (page 52) spent their honeymoon in a camper van, driving around Spain and Morocco. Great revelations came to the River Café chefs (page 100) in Tuscany (Janet Ross, page 176, was another Tuscan enthusiast), while Colman Andrews (page 24) and Richard Olney (page 156) experienced theirs in, respectively, Catalonia and Provence.

Others of the cookery clan were either diplomats or part of a diplomatic family. Alan Davidson, who wrote the marvellous *Oxford Companion to Food* (1999; not included here because it contains no recipes), was the British ambassador to Laos, and had previously been posted to Egypt and the United States; Lady Clark of Tillypronie was married to a diplomat who was posted all over Europe. A century later, Josceline Dimbleby (page 78) lived in Turkey, Peru and Syria. Lady Maclean (page 142), married to Sir Fitzroy (a possible inspiration for James Bond), was in Moscow during the Stalinist years, although I don't suppose there were many interesting recipes to be had despite the gallons of caviar Stalin served to Churchill and Roosevelt. Elisabeth Luard (page 138), the stepdaughter of a diplomat, spent time in Madrid, Paris and Mexico before living in, variously, Spain (again), Languedoc and Mull.

Next there are such expats as Australian Skye Gyngell (page 106), who set up a restaurant in a plant nursery in outer London, and New Zealander Glynn Christian (page 46), who became a deli expert in Britain. Claudia Roden (page 168), forced to leave Cairo because of the Suez Crisis of 1956, felt so nostalgic for the food there that she set out to recreate it in London. Marcella Hazan (page 114) left Italy for New York.

Cooks become interesting through the genius of their mentors: Rose Gray and Ruth Rogers have inspired, among others, Sam and Sam Clark, Jamie Oliver (page 154) and Hugh Fearnley-Whittingstall; Alice Waters (page 200), enthused by Elizabeth David, passed on her ideas to Sally Clarke (page 54), Bruce Cost (page 58) and David Tanis (page 194). And note, the original input here all came from women, perhaps less competitive and more encouraging to newcomers than men.

The 'shouty' chefs do not have the same record of finding the culinary equivalent of the Road to Damascus. As the acerbic Julian Barnes says in *The Pedant in the Kitchen* (essential reading for cookery enthusiasts), 'remember that cookery writers are no different from other writers: many have

An entire cupboard is given over to cookery books in my kitchen, although this is just a small portion of my collection. The butcher's block was a second-hand purchase.

A Book for Cooks

only one book in them (and some shouldn't have let it out in the first place):

I was recently asked to consider whether the future of cookery books lies in 'apps'. I was persuaded by a friend, who tried to teach me how to work my smartphone, that I should get one or two for cooking. He told me that whenever he found cauliflower, ham and pimentos in his fridge, an app would come up with a suitable recipe. For me, it doesn't work at all, especially as a collector. I don't want lots of apps cluttering up my phone (and is there such a thing as a first-edition app?). Also, I remember the days when media moguls told us that, in the shake of an oxtail, we would henceforth work in the 'paperless office'. Twenty years later, this hasn't happened. If anything, there is even more paper about, even if it is printed emails. It may happen that the cookery book will vanish. Like what, though? Radio, movies, telephone calls, horse riding, lawnmowers and food? All once on the condemned list. I recall a time when it was predicted that we would all be eating energy pills and have robots to do the housework. We are further from those dreary energy pills now than when they were first suggested. Those foreseeing the future got it completely wrong. Backwards, in fact.

Most modern cookery writers now stress the importance of good ingredients: meat that is humanely reared, vegetables that are grown seasonally near by, flour that is carefully ground, and eggs that come from free-range hens. As a result, the quality of our food is starting to improve. Cookery writers have become so powerful that ingredients or products promoted by them sell out: remember Nigella Lawson promoting goose fat for roast potatoes, Heston Blumenthal a supermarket-branded Christmas pudding that ended up changing hands on eBay for ten times its original price? More recently, Swedish cookery writer Leila Lindholm apparently denuded her country of butter. At cookery writers' prompting, governments ensure that nasty additives and such practices as the one that produced BSE are forbidden, and empowered shoppers ensure that good food is chosen more often than bad. Add to this the enormous rise in the popularity of farmers' markets, farm shops and food festivals dedicated to authors' demonstrations and producers' stalls. The art of cookery is clearly in the ascendant. It just needs to avoid being sidetracked by television programmes, unworkable gastro-porn cookery books and clueless celebs. No, models and actresses rarely make ideal cooks; Jane Grigson, whose writing was warm and friendly with plenty of scholarship discreetly hidden, should be the model. Her books have been called 'charming' by food writer Nicola Humble, and Julian Barnes, clearly smitten, finds she suffuses her work like 'some familiar and warming herb in a stew'.

So, I remain a book person, for the sheer pleasure of opening the pages again and again (although the indices are often infuriating) to find them stuck together with unmentionable gobbets, and then to discover some completely new idea to cope with seasonal gluts – fresh tomato pasta, say, or couscous with spiced plums; for the delight when the post arrives, with another stretch of shelving lost but new writers found; for the discovery in a car boot sale or second-hand bookshop of a dog-eared, handwritten notebook by some amateur cook gone by – female, undoubtedly, writing a diary punctuated by cakes and buns and pies. I love it all. And, to quote wise Mrs Berry in George Meredith's *The Ordeal of Richard Feverel* (1859), 'Kissing don't last: cookery do!'

My Aga dates from around 1960 and uses solid fuel – just like the one my mother once had. It is an old if temperamental friend; I think of it as a pet dog that never obeys orders.

101 CLASSIC COOKBOOKS

Eliza Acton
Modern Cookery for Private Families

Stephanie Alexander
The Cook's Companion

Darina Allen
A Year at Ballymaloe Cookery School

Dorothy Allhusen
A Book of Scents and Dishes

Amateurs

Colman Andrews
Catalan Cuisine

Lindsey Bareham
The Big Red Book of Tomatoes

Michael Bauer and Fran Irwin, editors
The San Francisco Chronicle Cookbook

James Beard
James Beard's American Cookery

Isabella Beeton
Mrs Beeton's Household Management

Hilaire Belloc
Advice

Richard Bertinet
Dough

Raymond Blanc
Blanc Vite

X. Marcel Boulestin
Simple French Cooking for English Homes

Arabella Boxer
First Slice Your Cookbook

Robert Carrier
Carrier International Cookery Cards

Glynn Christian
Real Flavours

Craig Claiborne
The New York Times Cook Book

Lady Clark
The Cookery Book of Lady Clark
of Tillypronie

Sam and Sam Clark
Moro

Sally Clarke
Sally Clarke's Book

Sir Francis Colchester-Wemyss
The Pleasures of the Table

Bruce Cost
Asian Ingredients

Margaret Costa
Four Seasons Cookery Book

Culinaria Spain

Felicity and Roald Dahl
Roald Dahl's Cookbook

Elizabeth David
Italian Food

Alan Davidson
North Atlantic Seafood

Tamasin Day-Lewis
Simply the Best

Len Deighton
Action Cook Book

Anthony Demetre
Today's Special

Sir Kenelm Digby
The Closet of Sir Kenelm Digby
Knight Opened

Josceline Dimbleby
Favourite Food

Anne Dolamore
The Essential Olive Oil Companion

Dorling Kindersley
The Cook's Book of Ingredients

Terry Durack
Noodle

David Eyre and the Eagle Chefs
The Eagle Cookbook

Fannie Farmer
The Boston Cooking-School Cook Book

Michael Fennelly
East Meets Southwest

M.F.K. Fisher
With Bold Knife and Fork

Hannah Glasse
The Art of Cookery Made Plain and Easy

Patience Gray
Honey from a Weed

Patience Gray and Primrose Boyd
Plats du Jour

Rose Gray and Ruth Rogers
The River Café Cook Book

Jane Grigson
Jane Grigson's Vegetable Book

Michel Guérard
Cuisine Minceur

Skye Gyngell
A Year in My Kitchen

Trina Hahnemann
The Scandinavian Cookbook

Nathalie Hambro
Particular Delights

Marika Hanbury Tenison
Left Over for Tomorrow

Marcella Hazan
The Classic Italian Cookbook

Ambrose Heath
Good Food

David Herbert
The Perfect Cookbook

Shaun Hill
How to Cook Better

Lucas Hollweg
Good Things to Eat

**Simon Hopkinson with
Lindsey Bareham**
Roast Chicken and Other Stories

Madhur Jaffrey
Madhur Jaffrey's Indian Cookery

Lady Jekyll, DBE
Kitchen Essays

Sybil Kapoor
Taste: A New Way to Cook

Nigella Lawson
How to be a Domestic Goddess

Mrs C.F. Leyel and Miss Olga Hartley
The Gentle Art of Cookery

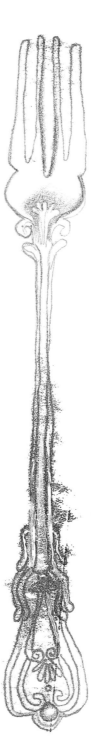

Eliza Acton

Modern Cookery for Private Families

Elek, London, 1966
(reprint; first published 1845)
720 pages
183 x 122 mm (7¼ x 4¾ in.)

It's a happy alphabetical accident that this book begins with Eliza Acton, considered by many to be the first modern cookery writer. Born in 1799 in Battle, East Sussex, she was sent as a young woman to the South of France for her health (or was it to have a baby?). She was originally a poet, but was advised to do something more practical. In addition to producing crisp prose, Acton was the first cookery writer to specify separately the ingredients' quantities and for how long a dish should be cooked.

Elizabeth David claimed that Acton was 'unbeatable' for fruit recipes. If you can get past the archaic language, many recipes are still worth trying. Buttered cherries, either Kentish or 'morella', for example, come with bread fried in butter; stewed fresh figs with port and lemon sound delicious. My mother used to make Fried Chicken à la Malabar, described as an Indian dish – a provenance I very much doubt. But chicken fillets rolled in curry powder and served with onion rings fried 'for a long time gently in a little clarified butter until they have gradually dried up and are a delicate yellow-brown' is a dish worth knowing. Serve with lemon pieces.

'Eat to live' is the motto by which all writers on cookery should be guided, says Acton, primly. The writer Penelope Farmer, in her introduction to the reprint of 1966, calls her 'a most formidable lady – a kind of Florence Nightingale of the kitchen ... . Mrs Beeton by comparison reads like a priggish little girl castigating her dolls.' Acton should have the recognition she deserves. The first American edition, which was published in 1845, is highly sought after.

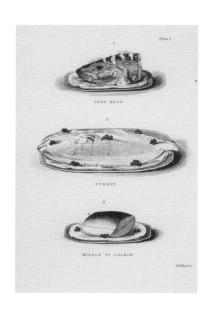

My copy of *Modern Cookery* is a reproduction of the first edition with original illustrations, which are decorative but not particularly helpful. The book had been out of print for a century.

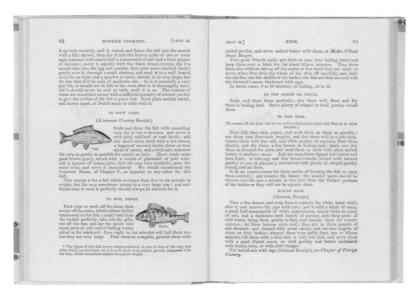

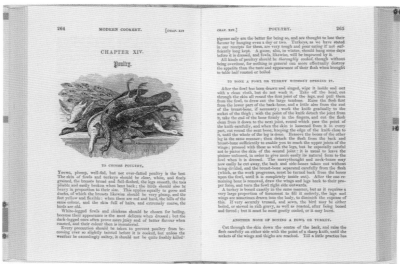

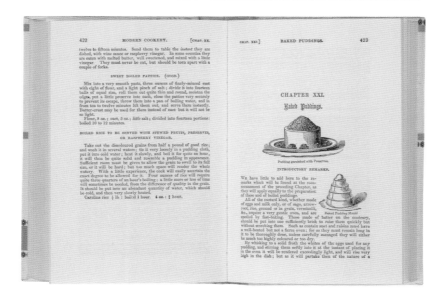

Stephanie Alexander

The Cook's Companion

Viking, Melbourne, 1996
824 pages
244 x 182 mm (9⁵/₈ x 7¹/₈ in.)

It's hard to keep the reader interested over 800-plus pages. The book's design, by Sandy Cull, uses photos of ingredients, by Earl Carter, rather than of finished dishes. Sidebars provide more information, and there are delicate drawings by Jacqui Young.

Stephanie Alexander trained as a librarian, and her magnum opus certainly has all the clarity and care you would expect from someone with a background in books. However, at the age of twenty-one she left her native Australia and travelled to France, an experience that widened her horizons, especially in cookery.

In 1964 Alexander opened her first restaurant (which broke her first marriage); twelve years later she opened Stephanie's Restaurant in Melbourne, which closed in 1997. She claims, with truth, that she and it were 'at the heart of everything culinary in Australia'. If Australia ranks high in producing cookery writers and chefs – and it does – Alexander can take much of the credit. She also champions the teaching of cooking and gardening to children,

through a project at an inner-city school in Melbourne.

The book is arranged A–Z, starting with anchovies and ending with zucchini. This has the advantage of mixing ingredients and dishes so that cooks don't get hidebound. A short section on thyme, for instance, suggests varieties, how to make a bouquet garni and how to roast yabbies in thyme oil. Lamb is treated carefully, and the problem of having a separate section for, say, kidneys is addressed with a list of allied recipes at the end of each section. Sidebars of simpler recipes are a common feature. 'While writing it, I have pretended that you, the reader, have been at my side as I shop and select, store, chop, laugh, taste and, above all, enjoy the heady world of great food', Alexander confides. She succeeds spectacularly.

recipes

glaze for baked ham

ham paste
Work minced ham with Dijon mustard to taste and add about half its volume of unsalted butter to make a potted paste. Spread on hot toast and serve as hot triangles with a vegetable soup, or top with cooked mushrooms or grilled tomato halves.

ham omelette
Warm chopped ham in a spoonful of home-made tomato sauce or chutney as an omelette filling.

beans with ham
Toss warm, boiled green beans with cubes or shreds of ham, fresh herbs and crisp croutons.

1 orange
2 tablespoons Dijon mustard
3 tablespoons brown sugar
1 leg cooked ham
cloves
½ cup white wine

Preheat oven to 180°C. Grate zest from orange, then juice orange. Mix zest, juice, mustard and sugar together. Remove skin from ham and score fat in a diamond pattern. Press a clove into middle of each diamond. Spread glaze over ham. Place ham in a baking dish and pour in wine to prevent ham sticking. Bake for 20 minutes until a rich shiny colour.

southern-style greens and ham   SERVES 6

This is my version of a dish I tasted in New Orleans that was cooked by one of America's best-known exponents of soul cooking, Edna Lewis. It is served with grilled pork chops or good sausages, although I sometimes serve it with lots of crusty bread instead. Cornbread would be traditional in the southern States. Grilled triangles of polenta would be good, too, although not a bit traditional. The long-cooked greens are traditional and a crisp savoy cabbage is by far the best green to use.

1 tablespoon olive oil
3 smoked ham hocks
2 onions, diced
6 large cloves garlic, sliced
1 bay leaf
1 teaspoon fresh thyme leaves
12 black peppercorns
1 fresh red chilli, seeded
6 whole allspice
3 cloves
2.5 litres water
1 savoy cabbage, cut into 6 wedges (attached at stem end)
6 red-skinned potatoes
salt
freshly ground black pepper
red-wine vinegar

Heat oil in a stockpot and brown hocks, then remove them to a plate. Reduce heat and cook onion and garlic for about 10 minutes until soft, then add bay leaf. Tie rest of herbs and spices in a square of muslin and add to pot with hocks and water. Bring to a boil, then skim and simmer, uncovered, for 1½ hours.
   Remove spice bag. Add cabbage and potatoes, then cover and simmer for 30 minutes. Remove cabbage and potatoes with a skimmer and reserve. Test if hocks are quite tender. Remove hocks and cut meat and some of the skin into bite-sized pieces. Increase heat and boil liquid until well reduced and very flavoursome. Cut potatoes into quarters or chunks. Return cabbage, potato and meat to pot to reheat. Taste for salt and pepper. Sprinkle with a few drops of red-wine vinegar. Serve the meat and cabbage with some of the 'potlikker' in deep bowls. Pork chops or sausages are served on top.

---

quinces baked in honey   SERVES 3–6

This recipe was originally published in 1960 by my mother, Mary Burchett, in her cookery book Through My Kitchen Door. The dish has been a favourite in my restaurant for many years.

quince cream
Stir a little melted quince jelly into mascarpone to serve with a quince, apple or walnut tart.

3 quinces, washed well
80 g butter
4 tablespoons light honey
¼ cup water

Preheat oven to 150°C. Halve but do not peel quinces, then remove pips and core from each with a spoon to make a neat hollow. Select a gratin dish that will hold quince halves snugly and grease with a third of the butter. Arrange quince halves hollows uppermost. Divide remaining butter and honey between hollows and pour water gently around sides. Cover with foil and bake for at least 3 hours until quinces are soft and a rich red. (Turn quinces over after 1½ hours.) Serve hot or warm with hollows filled with honey juices and offer thick or clotted cream.

quince and nut cake

This cake can be made using walnuts, almonds or pecans, or a mixture.

375 g plain flour
2 teaspoons bicarbonate of soda
2 teaspoons ground cinnamon
2 teaspoons ground allspice
pinch of salt
1 cup roughly crushed nuts
2 cups Poached Quince (see p. 612) or quince pulp
1 cup brown sugar
2 eggs
250 g unsalted butter, melted and cooled
pure icing sugar (optional)

Preheat oven to 180°C, then butter a 23 cm ring tin and dust it with flour. Sift flour, bicarbonate of soda, spices and salt and stir in nuts. Combine quince and sugar in a large bowl. Whisk eggs into butter and gently stir into quince mixture. Gently stir in flour mixture and mix well. Spoon into prepared tin. Bake for 55–60 minutes or until a skewer inserted in middle comes out clean. Cool cake in tin. Unmould and scatter with icing sugar, if desired, to serve.

other recipes

moroccan tagine with quince *see* LAMB

r a b b i t   The wild or European rabbit (*Oryctolagus cuniculus*) is Public Enemy Number One in Australia today. Imported from Europe in the mid-1800s to provide food, the rabbit, left to breed in the wild without sufficient predators to help redress the ecological imbalance, quickly became (and still remains) a rampant pest. Its burrowing erodes the soil and, along with its feeding habits, has left thousands of hectares denuded and countless native plants and animals extinct. It is said that the rabbit costs the Australian wool industry alone $115 million annually. The introduced virus myxomatosis decimated the rabbit population briefly in the 1950s, but rabbits have since developed immunity and their numbers have grown again to plague proportions. | It is no wonder, then, that the escape in October 1995 of the CSIRO-tested rabbit calicivirus from South Australia's Wardang Island was greeted with measured delight. Its effectiveness became very apparent as reports of dying rabbits were related daily in the newspapers. As hyperbole took over from fact, I contacted the CSIRO to learn more about the calicivirus and what it means to Australia, and especially to Australian cooks. ›

Darina Allen

A Year at Ballymaloe Cookery School

Kyle Cathie, London, 1997
192 pages
278 x 240 mm (11 x 9½ in.)

Although Darina Allen has written many cookery books, at least two of which are grander in scale, I've chosen this one because it is full of the joys of cooking. Few other books' introductions feature views of cattle in green Irish fields, flocks of hens ready to lay free-range eggs and ornamental Muscovy ducks keeping the snails at bay. Cooking is shown in an idealized landscape, where daffodils and fritillaries throng the gardens, and asparagus is for sale in the entrance hall of Allen's cookery school.

What could be a better introduction to spring (the order is seasonal) than a bright-green wild-garlic soup studded with garlic flowers, or dawn in the nearby harbour above a recipe for Pan-Fried Scallops with Beurre Blanc? The recipes and their photographs (by Melanie Eclare, Michelle Garrett and the author's husband, Timmy) are designed to make the mouth water, but are inherently simple. The former are also based on traditional Irish food (the subject of an earlier book by Allen). So there's Easter lamb from Mr Cuddigan; cottier's kale, thought to have been cultivated for 2000 years (the cuttings for the Ballymaloe kale had come from Glin Castle in Limerick); and Carrageen Moss Pudding with Crushed Blueberries. This last dish, Allen notes, was served with crushed bilberries at her wedding. All the guests' gums turned purple.

Other influences include Chinese chef Deh-ta Hsiung (he taught at the school) and, of course, Alice Waters (page 200) of Chez Panisse. A broth of a book.

Left: it is a joy to watch the ducks on the pond at the end of Lydia's garden.

Below: we decorate the Bay tree with chillies to cheer us up in the winter.

INTRODUCTION

In the flower garden, the winter sweet and the mahonia in the part we call the pleasure garden, near the potting shed, smell intoxicatingly delicious, as does the *Daphne odorata* by the garden gate. Under the office and the larder windows in front of the School there are winter-flowering rhododendrons which burst into flower each year, rewarding me when little else is in flower. The crop from our vegetable garden is reduced to sprouting broccoli and kale, still producing abundantly throughout January, and then we have lots of lambs lettuce and mysticana to liven up our winter salads.

As the New Year is ushered in, I start to think about our plans for the coming months. There's time to try out new ideas at home in my own kitchen, and to develop themes for new courses to run at the School. I will always want to expand the range of courses we offer. Of course there are some of the old favourites but it is important to be able to put in new ones and whatever takes my fancy that particular year.

146

147

SUMMER

Honey Lavender Ice-cream

SERVES 8–10
250ml (8¹/₂ fl oz) milk
450ml (³/₄ pint) cream
40 sprigs fresh lavender or less of dried (use the blossom end only)
6 free-range egg yolks
175ml (6fl oz) pure Irish honey – we use our own apple blossom honey, although Provençal lavender honey would also be wonderful

DECORATION
Sprigs of lavender

I make this richly scented ice-cream in June when the lavender flowers in the kitchen garden bloom. Lavender is at its most aromatic just before the flowers open. Serve it on its own on chilled plates and savour every mouthful.

Put the milk and cream into a heavy-bottomed saucepan with the lavender sprigs, bring slowly to the boil and leave to infuse for 15–20 minutes. This will both flavour and perfume the liquid deliciously. Whisk the egg yolks, add a little of the lavender-flavoured liquid and then mix the two together. Cook over a low heat until the mixture barely thickens and lightly coats the back of a spoon (be careful it does not curdle). Melt the honey gently – just to liquefy – and whisk into the custard. Strain out the lavender heads. Chill thoroughly and freeze, preferably in an ice-cream maker or sorbetière.

Serve decorated with sprigs of lavender.

Carrageen Moss Pudding with Crushed Blueberries

SERVES 4–6
8g (¹/₄oz) cleaned, well dried carrageen moss (1 semi-closed fistful)
850ml (28fl oz) milk
¹/₂ teaspoon pure vanilla essence or a vanilla pod
1 egg, preferably free-range
1 tablespoon caster sugar
Blueberries or, better still, wild bilberries or *fraughans*
Caster sugar
Softly whipped cream
Soft brown (Barbados) sugar

Carrageen moss is bursting with goodness. I ate it as a child but never liked it as it was always too stiff and unpalatable. Myrtle Allen changed my opinion! Hers was always so light and fluffy. I even had it for our wedding feast, made with fraughans (bilberries). Alas, the dye from the fraughans dyed all the guests' gums purple, to the consternation of our photographer.

Soak the carrageen in tepid water for 10 minutes. Strain off the water and put the carrageen into a saucepan with the milk and vanilla pod, if used. Bring to the boil and simmer very gently with the lid on for 20 minutes. At that point and not before separate the egg, put the yolk into a bowl, add the sugar and vanilla essence and whisk together for a few seconds; then pour the milk and carrageen moss through a strainer on to the egg yolk mixture, whisking all the time. The carrageen will now be swollen and exuding jelly. Rub all this jelly through the strainer and beat it into the flavoured milk. Test for a set in a saucer as one would gelatine. If it is a little soft, add back a little milk and push more carrageen through the sieve.

Whisk the egg white stiffly and fold it in gently with a whisk. It will rise to make a fluffy top. Leave to cool, then chill until set. Just before serving, crush the blueberries slightly with a potato masher, sprinkle generously with caster sugar and mix well. Serve the carrageen with the berries and cream and a sprinkle of soft brown sugar for a divine combination of flavours.

88

89

Darina Allen

19

Dorothy Allhusen

A Book of Scents and Dishes

Williams and Norgate, London, 1926
256 pages
194 x 142 mm (7⅝ x 5⅝ in.)

Allhusen was a British grande dame, a cousin of Winston Churchill's wife, Clementine, so this book is a typical aristocratic publication of the period. The author (address: Stoke Court, Stoke Poges, Buckinghamshire) lists recipes culled from other aristocratic friends – although chances are it was actually the cook who did the work. Another curiosity is that, although there's space for menus from the Winter Palace, St Petersburg, before 'a terrible cataclysm overtook Russia', there is no index.

Among the contributors are Mrs Thomas Hardy, with Christmas Pudding, and Mrs John Galsworthy, with Egg Nogg. Lady Redesdale (mother of the Mitford sisters) provides Indian Chutney and Boodles Club, a salad dressing. Lady Betty Trafford of Wroxham Hall, Norfolk, supplies 'How to Roast a Fat Cygnet' (now illegal in the UK), and Mrs Geoffrey Congreve of Government House, Malta, suggests a Turkish Pilaff. For real show-offs, the Duke of Marlborough, Blenheim Palace, offers Devonshire Cream. It should have come from the Duke of Devonshire.

Allhusen is not flattering about English cooks, who she believes are wasteful of leftovers and grumble about adding such luxuries as cream: 'The Germans use far more butter than we do, the French more eggs and dozens of flavourings seldom seen in our kitchens.' Despite this, many of the recipes are simple and well worth following. The book itself is nicely made, with a blue-and-gold design covering the front and back and gold blocking on the spine. There are a few black-and-white illustrations, by Elizabeth Murray, which tend, inexplicably, to feature crinolined ladies. I look forward next Christmas to a pudding from Thomas Hardy's wife.

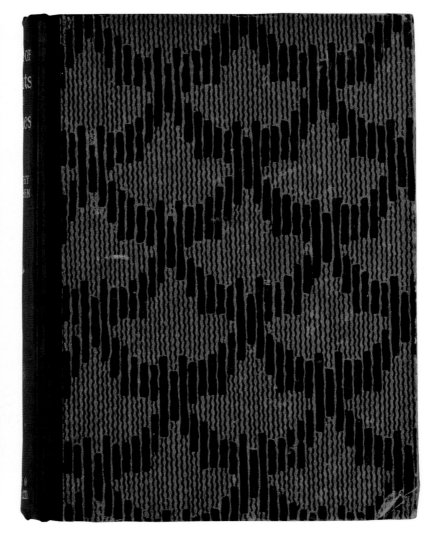

POULTRY & GAME

Canard aux Oranges (Duck with Oranges).

MADAME EUSTACHE, Le Chasnay, Fourchambault, Nevers.

Truss and singe a fat duck and brown it with butter in a saucepan. When it is thoroughly browned, cover it hermetically by interposing a greased paper under the lid. Let it cook over a slow fire for 1½ hours. When the duck is cooked put it on a dish, taking care to keep it warm. For the sauce, pour through a strainer the gravy left in the pan in which the duck was cooked. In another pan melt a piece of fresh butter, and squeeze into this the juice of an orange. Add to this the pulp of a section of orange and of lemon, and a pinch of flour. Add this to the gravy. Let it boil for a few minutes. Get ready some fried croûtons and lay these round the duck, alternated with orange rings. Pour the gravy over the duck and garnishings.

63

CAKES

American Porter Cake.

1 lb. moist sugar, 1 lb. currants, 1 lb. flour, 1 lb. stoned raisins, 4 oz. chopped blanched almonds, 4 oz. mixed peel, two-pennyworth of spice, ½ lb. butter, 4 eggs, 1 teaspoonful carbonate of soda, 2 gills of porter warmed.

Rub the butter into the flour, adding the other ingredients. Mix the eggs with the warm porter and add the soda. When these are well blended, bake.

Burnt-Sugar Cake.

½ lb. sultanas, ½ lb. brown sugar, 1 lb. flour, ½ lb. butter, 1 teaspoonful carbonate of soda, a little nutmeg, peel and salt.

Beat the butter into a cream, then add the sugar, and beat well, sprinkling in the other ingredients. When this is done, add 2 beaten eggs, or a gill of warm milk and some burnt-sugar colouring. When these ingredients have been thoroughly welded, bake in a moderate oven.

193   13

A BOOK OF SCENTS AND DISHES

Norwegian Cream (No. 2).

RHODA, COUNTESS OF CARLISLE, Sandhills, Holmrook, Cumberland.

Whip 1 pint of cream. Add 5 sheets of gelatine dissolved and mix in the stiffly whipped whites of 2 eggs and a little sugar. Put in small moulds till required. Serve with a purée of raspberries or black currants in a sauce-boat.

Orange Compôte.

3 or 4 oranges, ½ lb. loaf sugar, cochineal, maraschino.

Peel the oranges very clean so that no white is left on, holding them over a plate to preserve the juice. Then cut the fleshy parts out of the divisions and put into a basin. Make a thick syrup with the sugar and ¼ pint of water. Add a drop or so of cochineal and a few drops of maraschino. Pour the hot syrup over the oranges and let the whole get cold. The oranges should on no account be boiled.

[For *mixed compôtes*, apples, pears, figs, and French plums should be boiled in syrup separately before mixing. Bananas, strawberries, currants, grapes, raspberries should never be boiled for compôtes—the hot syrup should be poured over them. Stone fruit, such as peaches, plums, apricots, and greengages (and gooseberries also), must simmer gently till soft before they are added.]

134

PUDDINGS

Boodle's Orange Fool.

Boodle's Club, St James's Street, London.

4 oranges, 2 lemons, 1 pint of cream, sponge cakes.

Take the juice of the 4 oranges and the 2 lemons, and the grated rind of 1 lemon and 2 oranges. Sweeten to taste, then add 1 pint of cream. Fill a bowl with the sponge cakes, cut in four pieces each, and pour the mixture over the cakes. This dish should be made some hours before it is served, to allow the juice of the fruit to penetrate into the cakes.

Pain aux Framboises.

This dish is composed of raspberries set in syrup. The raspberries may be set whole, but if they are at all mashy they should be passed through a sieve before being placed in the syrup.

Pain Perdu.

5 eggs, 1 quart of milk, 2 spoonfuls powdered sugar, slices of bread.

Cut the slices of bread very thin. Mix the other ingredients well together in a tureen. Soak the bread thoroughly in this mixture. Plunge it in hot frying grease, not too hot and very clean. The bread is cooked when it is a golden colour on both sides. Take it out and sprinkle with powdered sugar.

135

Amateurs

Where would we be without those scrappy little notebooks, stained with gravy and scratchy with dried flour, handed down by our mothers? The amateur cookbook. I have one, bought who knows where, entitled 'My Favorite Resipes' (*sic*). Mrs Phyllis Pye of Preston, Lancashire, was its proud owner. The notebook itself is a promotional item from Red Star Baler and Binder Twine. Like many amateur cookery books, all the recipes are for cakes or puddings; there's not a stew or shepherd's pie in sight.

Christmas cake, royal icing, almond paste, malt loaf and orange dribble (shouldn't that be 'drizzle'?) cake are all detailed, as are a couple of local dishes: Goosnargh cakes (buttery biscuits flavoured with caraway seeds) and Lardy cakes.

My father, a GP in York, left me nineteen recipes chronicling his efforts to create the perfect sausage. Most are written on the back of pink cards entitled 'The Maternity Hospital, York, Request for Booking in Ward 3'. There are ten for English sausages and six for Cumberland. On the last Cumberland version he comments, 'Very good. Probably no need to go further along this line. To be entered in card-index. On this occasion the sausages were fried'. Nothing could remind me more of his obsessive search for perfection.

When I worked at the *Sunday Times*, I held a competition for the best amateur cookery book, sponsored by British Gas. We received hundreds of entries. The winner was 'A Mull Home Companion', very 1970s, very Celtic. Fifty locals contributed, including six men and five MacDonalds. Fish, understandably, was predominant. We ran into only one difficulty: there was no gas on Mull, much to the annoyance of our sponsor.

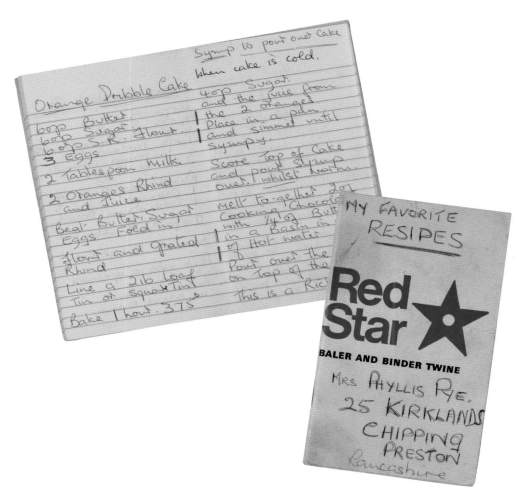

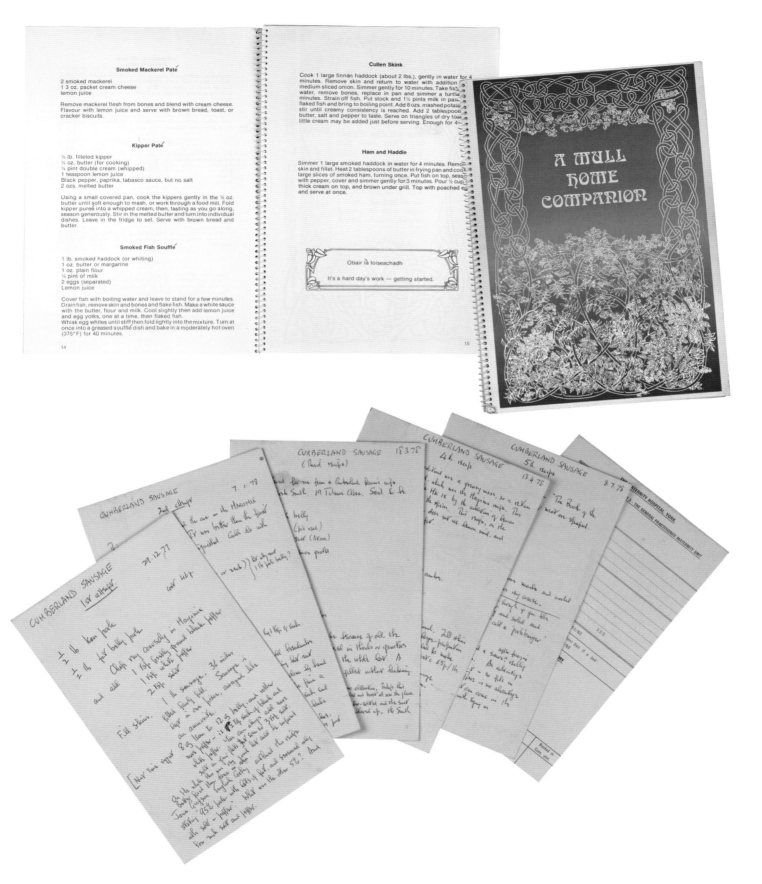

Colman Andrews

Catalan Cuisine: Europe's Last Great Culinary Secret

Grub Street, London, 1997 (first published
1989)
340 pages
234 x 156 mm (9¼ x 6⅛ in.)

Andrews, the founder of American foodie
magazine *Saveur*, has been writing about
food for more than forty years. Between
1984 and 1987 he spent time in Catalonia,
eating and researching the region's fare. In
his note to this edition of the resulting book,
he says that, since then, some of the best
Catalonian restaurants have closed, and
several of the area's notable cooks and
writers have died. However, 'Catalan cuisine
– both traditional and contemporary – is still
as exciting and seductive as it ever was …
the recipes herein, whatever the condition
of their progenitor, still produce exciting,
delicious, often (pleasantly) surprising food.'

While I might argue with the book's
subtitle, it's hard to disagree with Andrews's
findings that Catalonian food has its roots
in the food of the Roman Empire. The region
is well placed for this, being on the east
coast of Spain, bordering France and close
to Italy, Sardinia and Corsica. Andrews
elucidates further: 'Catalan cuisine is
a caldron full of prawns and monkfish
simmering in rich broth on a butane stove
in the galley of a fishing boat off the Costa
Brava port of Palamos; it's a brace of
rabbits roasting on an open fire beside
a slate-roofed field-stone farmhouse in the
eastern Pyrenees … it's an elegant salad of
white beans, celery leaves and marinated
salt cod posed on a cool black plate in
a restaurant dining room in Barcelona.' Or
fresh green figs with anisette and toasted
hazelnuts, the latter still warm from the
oven. And who can resist it?

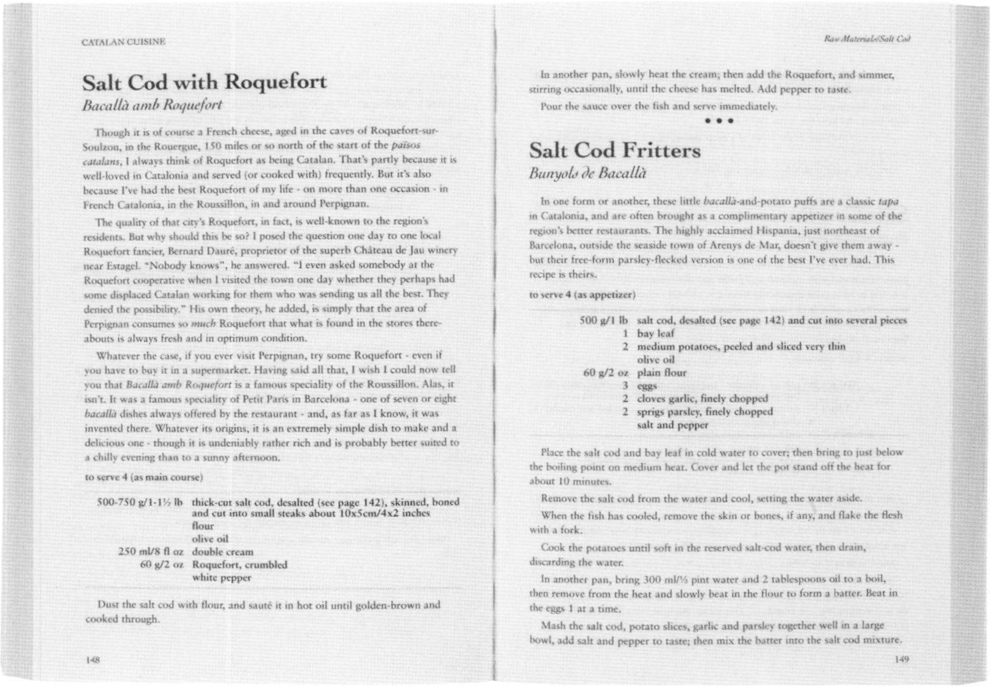

Salt Cod with Roquefort
Bacallà amb Roquefort

Though it is of course a French cheese, aged in the caves of Roquefort-sur-
Soulzon, in the Rouergue, 150 miles or so north of the start of the *països
catalans*, I always think of Roquefort as being Catalan. That's partly because it is
well-loved in Catalonia and served (or cooked with) frequently. But it's also
because I've had the best Roquefort of my life - on more than one occasion - in
French Catalonia, in the Roussillon, in and around Perpignan.

The quality of that city's Roquefort, in fact, is well-known to the region's
residents. But why should this be so? I posed the question one day to one local
Roquefort fancier, Bernard Dauré, proprietor of the superb Château de Jau winery
near Estagel. "Nobody knows", he answered. "I even asked somebody at the
Roquefort cooperative when I visited the town one day whether they perhaps had
some displaced Catalan working for them who was sending us all the best. They
denied the possibility." His own theory, he added, is simply that the area of
Perpignan consumes so *much* Roquefort that what is found in the stores there-
abouts is always fresh and in optimum condition.

Whatever the case, if you ever visit Perpignan, try some Roquefort - even if
you have to buy it in a supermarket. Having said all that, I wish I could now tell
you that *Bacallà amb Roquefort* is a famous speciality of the Roussillon. Alas, it
isn't. It was a famous speciality of Petit Paris in Barcelona - one of seven or eight
bacallà dishes always offered by the restaurant - and, as far as I know, it was
invented there. Whatever its origins, it is an extremely simple dish to make and a
delicious one - though it is undeniably rather rich and is probably better suited to
a chilly evening than to a sunny afternoon.

to serve 4 (as main course)

500-750 g/1-1½ lb	thick-cut salt cod, desalted (see page 142), skinned, boned and cut into small steaks about 10x5cm/4x2 inches	
	flour	
	olive oil	
250 ml/8 fl oz	double cream	
60 g/2 oz	Roquefort, crumbled	
	white pepper	

Dust the salt cod with flour, and sauté it in hot oil until golden-brown and
cooked through.

In another pan, slowly heat the cream; then add the Roquefort, and simmer,
stirring occasionally, until the cheese has melted. Add pepper to taste.

Pour the sauce over the fish and serve immediately.

• • •

Salt Cod Fritters
Bunyols de Bacallà

In one form or another, these little *bacallà*-and-potato puffs are a classic *tapa*
in Catalonia, and are often brought as a complimentary appetizer in some of the
region's better restaurants. The highly acclaimed Hispania, just northeast of
Barcelona, outside the seaside town of Arenys de Mar, doesn't give them away -
but their free-form parsley-flecked version is one of the best I've ever had. This
recipe is theirs.

to serve 4 (as appetizer)

500 g/1 lb	salt cod, desalted (see page 142) and cut into several pieces	
1	bay leaf	
2	medium potatoes, peeled and sliced very thin	
	olive oil	
60 g/2 oz	plain flour	
3	eggs	
2	cloves garlic, finely chopped	
2	sprigs parsley, finely chopped	
	salt and pepper	

Place the salt cod and bay leaf in cold water to cover; then bring to just below
the boiling point on medium heat. Cover and let the pot stand off the heat for
about 10 minutes.

Remove the salt cod from the water and cool, setting the water aside.

When the fish has cooled, remove the skin or bones, if any, and flake the flesh
with a fork.

Cook the potatoes until soft in the reserved salt-cod water, then drain,
discarding the water.

In another pan, bring 300 ml/½ pint water and 2 tablespoons oil to a boil,
then remove from the heat and slowly beat in the flour to form a batter. Beat in
the eggs 1 at a time.

Mash the salt cod, potato slices, garlic and parsley together well in a large
bowl, add salt and pepper to taste; then mix the batter into the salt cod mixture.

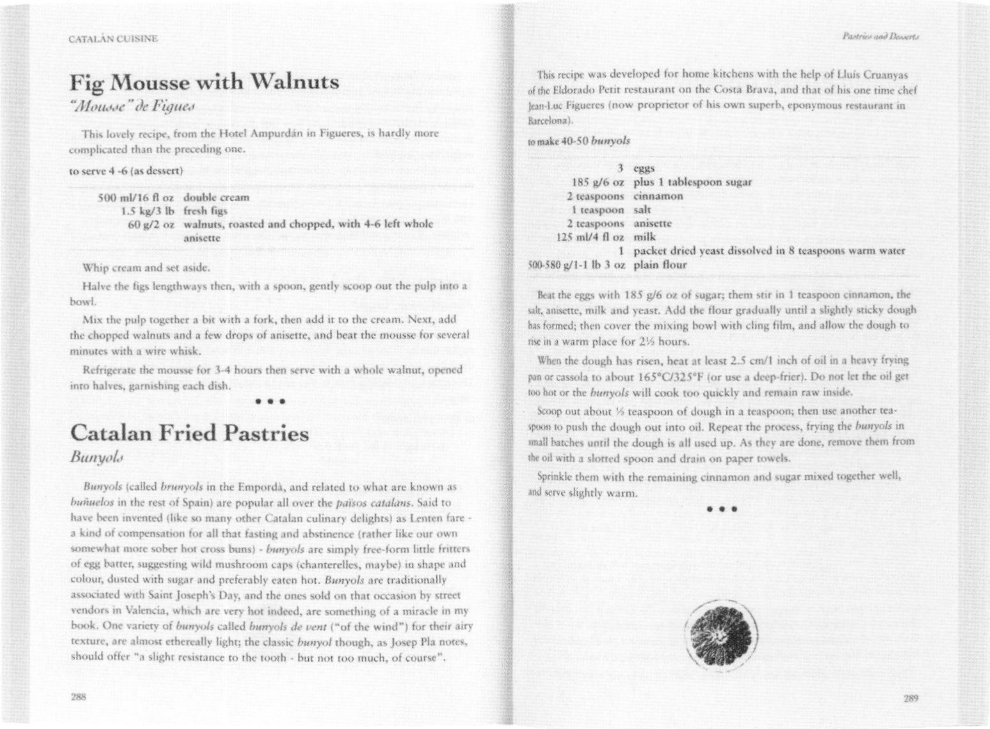

Fig Mousse with Walnuts
"Mousse" de Figues

This lovely recipe, from the Hotel Ampurdán in Figueres, is hardly more
complicated than the preceding one.

to serve 4 -6 (as dessert)

500 ml/16 fl oz	double cream	
1.5 kg/3 lb	fresh figs	
60 g/2 oz	walnuts, roasted and chopped, with 4-6 left whole	
	anisette	

Whip cream and set aside.

Halve the figs lengthways then, with a spoon, gently scoop out the pulp into a
bowl.

Mix the pulp together a bit with a fork, then add it to the cream. Next, add
the chopped walnuts and a few drops of anisette, and beat the mousse for several
minutes with a wire whisk.

Refrigerate the mousse for 3-4 hours then serve with a whole walnut, opened
into halves, garnishing each dish.

• • •

Catalan Fried Pastries
Bunyols

Bunyols (called *brunyols* in the Empordà, and related to what are known as
buñuelos in the rest of Spain) are popular all over the *països catalans*. Said to
have been invented (like so many other Catalan culinary delights) as Lenten fare -
a kind of compensation for all that fasting and abstinence (rather like our own
somewhat more sober hot cross buns) - *bunyols* are simply free-form little fritters
of egg batter, suggesting wild mushroom caps (chanterelles, maybe) in shape and
colour, dusted with sugar and preferably eaten hot. *Bunyols* are traditionally
associated with Saint Joseph's Day, and the ones sold on that occasion by street
vendors in Valencia, which are very hot indeed, are something of a miracle in my
book. One variety of *bunyols* called *bunyols de vent* ("of the wind") for their airy
texture, are almost ethereally light; the classic *bunyol* though, as Josep Pla notes,
should offer "a slight resistance to the tooth - but not too much, of course".

This recipe was developed for home kitchens with the help of Lluís Cruanyas
of the Eldorado Petit restaurant on the Costa Brava, and that of his one time chef
Jean-Luc Figueres (now proprietor of his own superb, eponymous restaurant in
Barcelona).

to make 40-50 *bunyols*

3	eggs	
185 g/6 oz	plus 1 tablespoon sugar	
2 teaspoons	cinnamon	
1 teaspoon	salt	
2 teaspoons	anisette	
125 ml/4 fl oz	milk	
1	packet dried yeast dissolved in 8 teaspoons warm water	
500-580 g/1-1 lb 3 oz	plain flour	

Beat the eggs with 185 g/6 oz of sugar; them stir in 1 teaspoon cinnamon, the
salt, anisette, milk and yeast. Add the flour gradually until a slightly sticky dough
has formed; then cover the mixing bowl with cling film, and allow the dough to
rise in a warm place for 2½ hours.

When the dough has risen, heat at least 2.5 cm/1 inch of oil in a heavy frying
pan or cassola to about 165°C/325°F (or use a deep-frier). Do not let the oil get
too hot or the *bunyols* will cook too quickly and remain raw inside.

Scoop out about ½ teaspoon of dough in a teaspoon; then use another teaspoon to push the dough out into oil. Repeat the process, frying the *bunyols* in
small batches until the dough is all used up. As they are done, remove them from
the oil with a slotted spoon and drain on paper towels.

Sprinkle them with the remaining cinnamon and sugar mixed together well,
and serve slightly warm.

• • •

A Book for Cooks

Cookery books don't need table-candy photographs to look desirable. Adam Denchfield's design for *Catalan Cuisine* is both striking and seductive.

Lindsey Bareham

The Big Red Book of Tomatoes

Michael Joseph, London, 1999
374 pages
233 x 151 mm (9 1/8 x 6 in.)

I was startled to discover that my copy of this book, a first edition, has become quite valuable. I imagine that the publishers printed too few, which shows that first editions are worth buying. Bareham, who writes daily in *The Times* and co-wrote many of Simon Hopkinson's books (see, for example, page 124), has made a speciality of single-food cookbooks, including *In Praise of the Potato* (1989), *A Celebration of Soup* (1993) and *Onions without Tears* (1995).

Bareham quotes Elizabeth David, who wrote that 'A world devoid of tomato soup, tomato sauce, tomato ketchup and tomato paste is hard to visualise.' She then goes on to prove it, discussing everything from the tomato's early history in the Andes to the popular varieties you can buy in the supermarket. She finds that tomatoes may combat cancer and heart disease; the British Tomato Growers' Association, she adds, says that tomatoes are good for the skin. She follows this with a huge selection of recipes from all over the world, so anyone who grows tomatoes and, consequently, has a glut should look out for a copy (or buy a more recent edition). The extensive bibliography takes up three pages.

Because virtually every country in the world has incorporated tomatoes into its cuisine, and since we all cook with them at least once a week, this is an invaluable book, one worth collecting if that's your passion. The only illustration is of a crumpled tomato ('Costoluto Fiorentino'?) in monochrome, which seems a pity for such a colourful fruit.

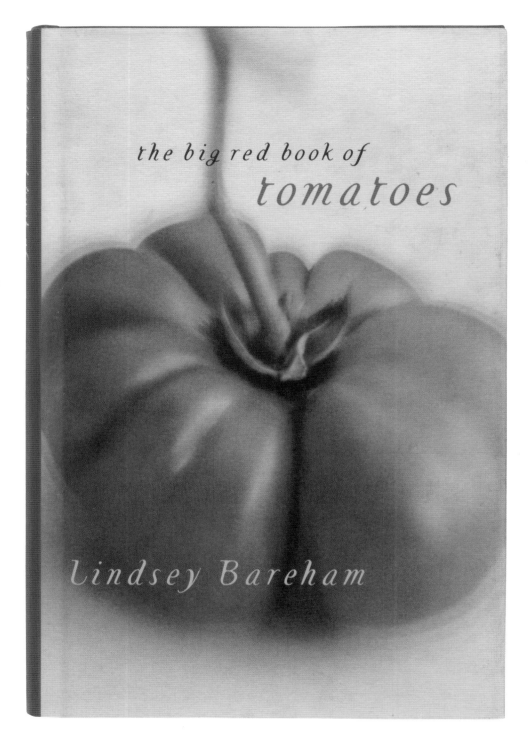

the white membrane. Chop the softened flesh, pour any juices through a sieve into a large bowl and add the chopped pepper.

Meanwhile, place a sieve over a second bowl and quarter the tomatoes over it, scraping the seeds and jelly into it. Finely chop the tomato flesh. Press against the seeds and jelly with the back of a spoon to release as much juice as possible. You should have about 300 ml. Stir the ketchup, vinegar, Tabasco and a good seasoning of salt and pepper into the juice. Whisk in the olive oil. Taste and adjust the flavour with sugar if you think it needs it. Sprinkle over the gelatine and stir to disperse. Pour this mixture into the chopped peppers and their juices. Stir the tomato flesh into the mixture with the basil. The mixture should be thick and dense with tomato and pepper.

Cut the slices of bread in half lengthways. Use them to line a 900 ml–1.2 litre pudding basin. Begin by cutting a disc to place at the bottom of the bowl. Then arrange overlapping slices (or half-slices) working your way round the bowl, thus leaving no gaps. Cut a second, larger, disc to fit the top. This way of lining the bowl means that when the pudding is turned out, you end up with a pretty ridged pattern.

Place the bread-lined bowl in a dish that is roomy enough to catch any over-spill. Spoon in the prepared tomato mixture, completely filling the bowl. Position the lid disc. Now ladle the tomato juice or Rustica carefully between the bowl and the bread, taking care not to disturb it. Pour more tomato juice over the top bread disc.

Lay a saucer on top and cover the pudding with clingfilm and chill overnight. Remove the clingfilm and the saucer, place a dinner-plate over the top of the dish and invert it quickly. Pour extra tomato juice over the top (paying special attention to any white spots). Decorate the top with Grilled Cherry Tomatoes (see page 31) and serve.

Also see:
Tomato Soup Cake (page 343)
Roast Tomato Butter (page 45)
Salad Mechouia (pages 135–6)

'One tomato, skinned and chopped small, cooked hardly more than a minute in butter, with salt and pepper, is added to the eggs already in the pan.'

Elizabeth David, on tomato omelette in *French Provincial Cooking*, 1960

Tomatoes and Eggs

It is hard to imagine an egg dish that would not be complemented by tomato. Creamy eggs and sweet-sour tomatoes are made for each other. This combination of opposites works in many different ways. You have only to think of egg and tomato sandwiches, or something as mundane as a perfectly fried egg and a squirt of tomato ketchup. How about a tomato omelette filled with fresh tomato purée that oozes between the eggy folds as your fork slices into it? My particular weakness is for poached eggs with fresh tomato sauce. And if the sauce has been spiced up, Mexican-style, with a little chilli, then I'm in heaven. I love that moment when the egg is first cut and the yolk gushes forth, making its oleaginous path through the watery tomato. I cannot eat this lovely mess politely. I like to scoop it up greedily, almost as if someone else is trying to beat me to it.

There is a similar but different alchemy with omelettes, soufflés and roulades, when the egg is cooked on the wobbly side of just set so that the tomato can almost, but not quite, melt into it. But it is the combination of scrambled eggs with tomatoes, particularly when the eggs are very fresh and carefully cooked, and the tomatoes very ripe, that is the universally popular way of serving eggs and tomato together. There is something about that combination of creamy soft scrambled eggs and

---

a clean pan and add the unpuréed soup. Reheat the soup and adjust the seasoning as necessary, sharpening it up with a squeeze of lemon.

Make the garnish. Mix together the avocado, lemon juice and tomato. Serve the soup topped with a scoop of cream, a tablespoonful of the avocado mixture and the coriander.

CREAM OF TOMATO SOUP
Serves 4

The Real Thing. It might look like Heinz Cream of Tomato but try it and spot the difference.

50 g butter	salt and freshly ground black
2 medium onions, finely chopped	pepper
2 celery sticks, finely diced	750 ml light chicken or vegetable
2 cloves of garlic, finely chopped	stock
700 g very ripe tomatoes, cored,	10 basil leaves
scalded, peeled and chopped	125 ml whipping cream
a pinch of sugar	

Heat the butter in a spacious heavy-bottomed pan and soften the onion and celery, allowing about 20 minutes for this, adding the garlic towards the end. Add the tomatoes with a little sugar, salt and pepper, let them melt and reduce a little, then add the stock. Cook for 15 minutes, adding the basil for the last few minutes, then liquidize.

Pass through a fine sieve into a clean pan. Stir in the cream and gently reheat, taking care not to let it boil. Taste and adjust the seasoning and, if liked, serve with buttery croutons.

INDIAN CREAM OF TOMATO SOUP
Serves 4–6

I came across this soup when I was researching *A Celebration of Soup* in what I consider to be Madhur Jaffrey's finest book: *Eastern Vegetarian Cooking*. Its spicy-hot, sweet-sour flavour remains a great favourite. I leave out the butter and flour emulsion.

700 g ripe tomatoes, chopped	4 tbsp unsalted butter (optional)
1 tbsp finely chopped lemon grass	2 tbsp flour (optional)
heart	100 ml single cream
1–2 curry leaves	570 ml milk
5 cm piece fresh ginger, peeled and	½ tsp ground roasted cumin seeds
chopped	⅛ tsp cayenne pepper
100 ml water	2 tsp lime or lemon juice
salt and freshly ground black	1 tbsp chopped coriander leaves
pepper	

Put the tomatoes, lemon grass, curry leaves, ginger and water in a pan.

Season generously with salt and bring to the boil. Lower the heat, cover, and simmer gently for 15 minutes. Uncover, increase the heat and simmer more aggressively for 15 minutes. Purée and sieve: you should end up with about 400 ml of thick tomato juice.

Meanwhile, if you are including the butter and flour liaison, heat the butter, stir in the flour and cook on a low heat for a couple of minutes. Pour in the hot tomato juice, stirring all the time. If not, proceed directly to adding the cream, milk, cumin seeds, cayenne pepper and lime or lemon juice. Season generously with black pepper. Stir thoroughly and reheat without boiling. Serve sprinkled with the freshly chopped coriander.

THAI CREAM OF TOMATO SOUP
Serves 4–6

On this occasion, cream means coconut milk and bean curd. An unusual take on tomato soup with Thai seasonings.

1 kg tomatoes, roughly chopped	1 tbsp lemon juice
700 ml coconut milk	2 tbsp chopped coriander leaves
1 tsp red curry paste	salt and freshly ground black
300 g bean curd, cubed	pepper
2 tbsp soy sauce	pinch of sugar

Blitz the tomatoes to a purée. Pass through a sieve directly into a saucepan. Add the coconut milk, red curry paste, bean curd, soy sauce and lemon juice.

Over a gentle heat, bring slowly to the boil. Reduce the heat and cook very gently for 20 minutes. Taste and adjust the seasonings, adding a little sugar if necessary. Stir in the coriander and serve.

LOBSTER BISQUE
Serves 4

Tomatoes are as vital to bisques as the shells of the seafood that qualify a soup to be called a bisque. This particularly fine version, inspired after a visit to the Carved Angel restaurant in Dartmouth, comes from *The Prawn Cocktail Years*, which I wrote with Simon Hopkinson. The flavour in the soup is the very essence of lobster: sweet and deep, rich and fragrant, and lifted by a whisper of Cognac.

**Michael Bauer and
Fran Irwin, editors**

**The San Francisco
Chronicle Cookbook**

Chronicle Books, San Francisco, 1997
432 pages
231 x 203 mm (9¹/₈ x 8 in.)

American cookery books manage
to be elegant without costing
the photographic earth. Here,
designer Pamela Geismar has
used delicate nineteenth-century
engravings, both inside and out.

San Francisco is one of the foodiest places
on Earth. I know, because I was sent there
by *Country Life* to sample its cuisine. Even
the immigration officers (not usually known
for their levity) were enthused. Whether the
general lusty appetites are boosted by the
city's newspaper, or whether the *Chronicle*
is well aware of its readers' interests, I don't
know. But this is a paper that can give its
readers a four-page pull-out on chillies.

Michael Bauer, when the book appeared,
had been editor of the food section for
more than a decade; Fran Irwin had worked
on it for two. The section's columnists, 'the
best … in the country', have contributed
recipes from the paper that represent a
'metropolis of diversity … it's second nature
for local cooks to mix and match ethnic

flavours. Here, a rosemary-accented
roast chicken might be served with a Thai
cucumber salad; the Thanksgiving turkey may
get tandoori treatment with a pomegranate-
juice marinade.' The recipes have also been
chosen for their time–value ratio: if they
take ages, they better be worth it.

Because many of the book's once
obscure ingredients are now generally
available, most of the recipes come within
the range of the home cook, but their
Californian invention makes them exciting.
Recipes take up two-thirds of a page, often
with a sidebar offering advice on, say, easy
garnishes for soup or how to chop garlic.
There are no photos, however, just pretty
sepia drawings. This book, with its diversity,
should provide masses of new ideas.

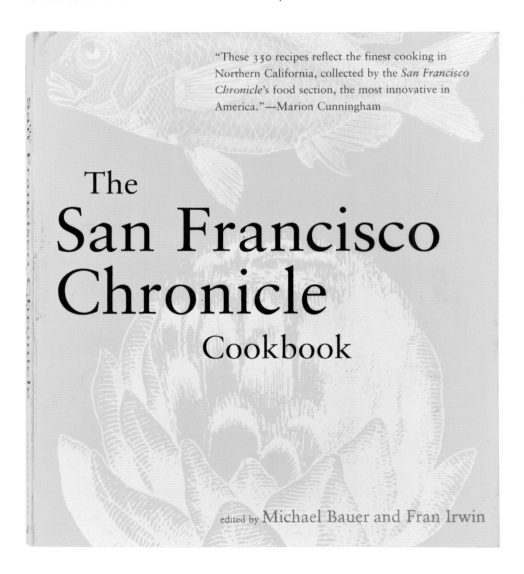

"These 350 recipes reflect the finest cooking in
Northern California, collected by the *San Francisco
Chronicle*'s food section, the most innovative in
America."—Marion Cunningham

The
San Francisco
Chronicle
Cookbook

edited by Michael Bauer and Fran Irwin

A Book for Cooks

Baby Artichokes à la Castroville

Maria Cianci took the classic preparation of fried artichokes as prepared in Castroville, where the majority of the U.S. artichoke crop is produced, and punched them up with powdered onion and garlic. Instead of the traditional mayonnaise dipping sauce, she prefers them plain with only a squeeze of lemon.

16 baby artichokes (1 ounce each or less)

2 cups water mixed with 1 tablespoon lemon juice or vinegar

½ cup all-purpose flour

1¼ teaspoons powdered garlic

¾ teaspoon powdered onion

½ teaspoon salt, plus more to taste

½ teaspoon ground pepper, plus more to taste

Oil for deep-frying

2 eggs, beaten

Lemon wedges

❧ To prepare baby artichokes for cooking, rinse them, trim the stem ends and snip off or pull off the outside, tougher leaves. When you come to the inner pale yellow-green cone, cut off the top quarter using a serrated knife. There is no choke to remove. Cut the artichokes in half lengthwise and drop into the acidulated water.

Thoroughly combine the flour, garlic powder, onion powder, salt and pepper.

Pour 3 inches of oil in a heavy medium saucepan and heat to 360 degrees.

Drain the artichokes and pat dry. Dip into egg, letting the excess drip off. Coat with the flour mixture, tapping off excess.

Fry the artichokes in batches until they are golden brown, turning once, 5 to 7 minutes. Drain on paper towels. Sprinkle with additional salt and pepper, if desired. Serve immediately with lemon wedges.

SERVES 4 AS AN APPETIZER

Artichoke Fact

More than 90 percent of the artichokes in the nation are produced in Monterey County, south of San Francisco.

Storing Artichokes

Sprinkle the artichokes with a little water, place in plastic bag and refrigerate. Although they'll keep for a week, they are best prepared as soon as possible.

Buying Baby Artichokes

When buying baby artichokes, choose the smallest, most compact buds available. A pound contains about 16 to 19. They should have a true "artichoke green" color and appear moist, with no sign of dry, woody exterior bracts (leaves). Superficial brown spotting can occur in winter buds. Fall, winter and spring buds are round or globe-shaped; summer buds flare slightly.

To prepare baby artichokes for cooking, rinse them, trim the stem ends and completely snip off or pull off the outside tougher leaves. When you come to the inner pale yellow-green cone, cut off the top quarter using a serrated knife. There is no choke to remove. Leave buds whole or cut them in half lengthwise, depending on the recipe. Drop trimmed buds into acidulated water (2 cups water mixed with 1 tablespoon lemon juice or vinegar) to retard discoloration. Drain artichokes just before cooking.

Baby Artichoke Puttanesca

Here, Maria Cianci pairs a classic spicy Italian tomato sauce with tiny fresh artichokes. They may be served as a side dish, or tossed with cooked penne or macaroni as a light main course.

20 baby artichokes (1 ounce each or less)

2 cups water mixed with 1 tablespoon lemon juice or vinegar

2 tablespoons olive oil

1 medium onion, diced

2 large garlic cloves, minced

4 anchovy fillets, mashed

2 cups crushed tomatoes

10 kalamata olives, pitted and coarsely chopped

2 teaspoons capers

Salt and pepper to taste

Tabasco sauce to taste

❧ Rinse the artichokes, trim the stem ends and remove the outside, tougher leaves. When you come to the inner pale yellow-green cone, cut off the top quarter using a serrated knife. Cut the artichokes in half lengthwise and drop into the acidulated water.

Heat the olive oil in a saucepan over medium-high heat. Add the onion and garlic and sauté, stirring frequently, until the onion begins to color, about 5 minutes. Add the anchovies and sauté 1 minute. Add the tomatoes, bring to a boil, reduce heat and simmer until the sauce thickens slightly, 8 to 10 minutes. Stir in the olives, capers, salt, pepper and Tabasco sauce. Simmer for 3 minutes. Remove from heat and let stand, covered, for 15 minutes.

Drain the artichokes. Boil in salted water until they are just tender, about 5 minutes. Drain. Add to the sauce and toss thoroughly over medium heat until well coated and heated through.

SERVES 6

To steam: Fit a steaming rack into a wok. Pour boiling water into the wok to come within 1 inch of the rack. Return the water to a boil. Pour off the excess marinade around the duck. Put the duck, in its dish, on the rack. Cover and steam over medium-high heat for 30 minutes. Drain. Let cool for 2 hours or better, refrigerate for several hours or overnight.

To smoke: Line the inside of the wok with enough heavy-duty foil to extend generously over the rim. Mix together the smoking ingredients and distribute over the bottom of the wok. Place a wire cake rack in the wok, cover the wok and set over medium-high heat. When the mixture begins to smoke, put the duck on the rack. Cover. Bring the excess foil up over rim of the lid; press to seal. Smoke for 15 to 20 minutes. The duck should be light golden brown.

To crisp the skin: Preheat the oven to 425 degrees. Place the duck breasts on a baking sheet and roast for 5 to 8 minutes. Pat off grease with paper towels.

SERVES 4

Wild Ragout of Duck

Duck is often on the menu at the Bay Wolf restaurant in Oakland. Here, chef/owner Michael Wild has brought together duck breasts, Pinot Noir, bacon and a few simple vegetables in a rich, robust stew.

½ bottle Pinot Noir

1 pint duck stock (or chicken, turkey or veal stock)

4 duck breasts

1 leek (white and light green part only), well washed and julienned

¼ pound mushrooms, sliced

2 shallots, minced

¼ pound bacon, cubed

Salt and pepper to taste

1 tablespoon to ½ cup heavy cream (optional)

1 cup shelled peas, blanched

❧ Combine the wine and stock and place in a pot large enough to hold a steaming rack for the duck. Bring to a simmer and place the duck breasts on

Skimming the Fat

An easy and effective way to degrease stocks, soups and stews is to let the food cool, then refrigerate overnight, or until the fat rises to the top and solidifies. Simply lift off the layer of chilled fat and discard.

a steaming rack in the pot. Cover and steam until the duck is three quarters cooked, about 10 minutes. (The legs also may be used, but they need to steam about 25 minutes, or until a skewer passes easily through the flesh.)

Slowly sauté the leek, mushrooms, shallots and bacon for 10 minutes, until cooked through. Pour off the bacon fat.

Let the duck cool slightly, then pull off the skin. Cut each breast into 6 to 8 pieces. Reduce the wine mixture to one third of its original volume. Add the cooked vegetables and bacon. Season with salt and pepper. Whisk in a bit of cream if the sauce tastes sharp. Add the duck to the sauce and simmer until cooked through.

Serve the stew in soup plates, sprinkling on the peas to garnish.

SERVES 4 TO 6

Salt-Seared Duck Legs with Fresh Apricots

Fresh apricots, with their natural sweetness, pair beautifully with the sturdy flavor of duck. If fresh fruit isn't available, dried apricots work just fine. Georgeanne Brennan usually slices the meat off the legs, then serves it atop a mound of bitter greens, with the juices poured over the top. It also goes well with creamy mashed potatoes and braised spinach.

½ teaspoon salt

2 duck legs

½ cup Riesling or other fruity white wine

2 tablespoons fresh lemon juice

1 tablespoon minced onion

1 tablespoon finely grated fresh ginger

2 tablespoons packed brown sugar

8 apricots, halved and pitted (see Note)

❧ Sprinkle the salt in a nonstick skillet just large enough to hold the duck legs. Heat the salt over high heat, then add the duck legs and sear 2 to 3 minutes on each side, or until the skin is crisp and browned. Remove the duck. Reduce the heat to low; add the wine and lemon juice, scraping the pan

James Beard

James Beard's American Cookery

Little, Brown, Boston and Toronto, 1972
896 pages
250 x 176 mm (10 x 6⅞ in.)

James Beard was the grand old man of American cookery, with fourteen books to his credit when this tour de force appeared. It is the major work on American cookery, as opposed to books about cookery written by Americans. You can bet that, in its pages, you will find cioppino, a Californian fish stew; the po'boy, a sandwich from New Orleans consisting of French bread filled with anything from fish to cheese; and the Caesar salad, created in Tijuana, Mexico, in the 1920s. And everything else American you can think of.

For me, it is the essential encyclopedia of American recipes. So, around thirty years ago, when I learned that my husband would be visiting New York, I asked him to bring back a copy for my collection. Because British and American cookery have much in common, in technique if not ingredients, I have used it a lot. Rich Chicken Pie with Tabasco is a favourite, as is the retro Ham with Pineapple. Just because dishes were fashionable in unfashionable times should not put us off.

What I particularly like about this book is its elegant design – something many American books have in common, unlike their British counterparts. The cover is genuine buckram, in yellow, with an orange cartouche on the spine. The endpapers are bright orange, and virtually every page features an illustration in black and sepia by US artist Earl Thollander. The ingredients for each recipe are in a sidebar, with the method, crisp and concise, in the main text. If anyone wants to collect American cookery books, they should start by looking at the bibliography.

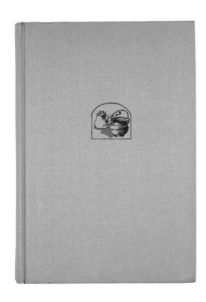

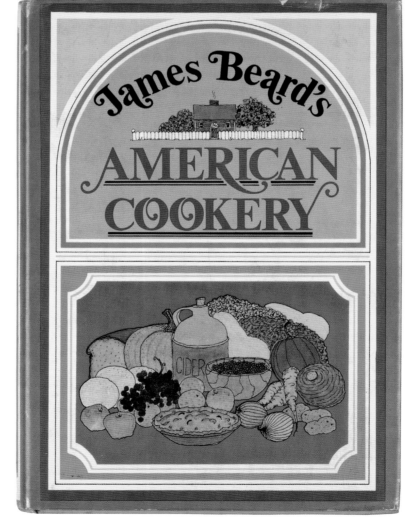

This was my first American cookery book. The publisher used real buckram for the yellow cover – unlike British publishers, which often use textured paper instead.

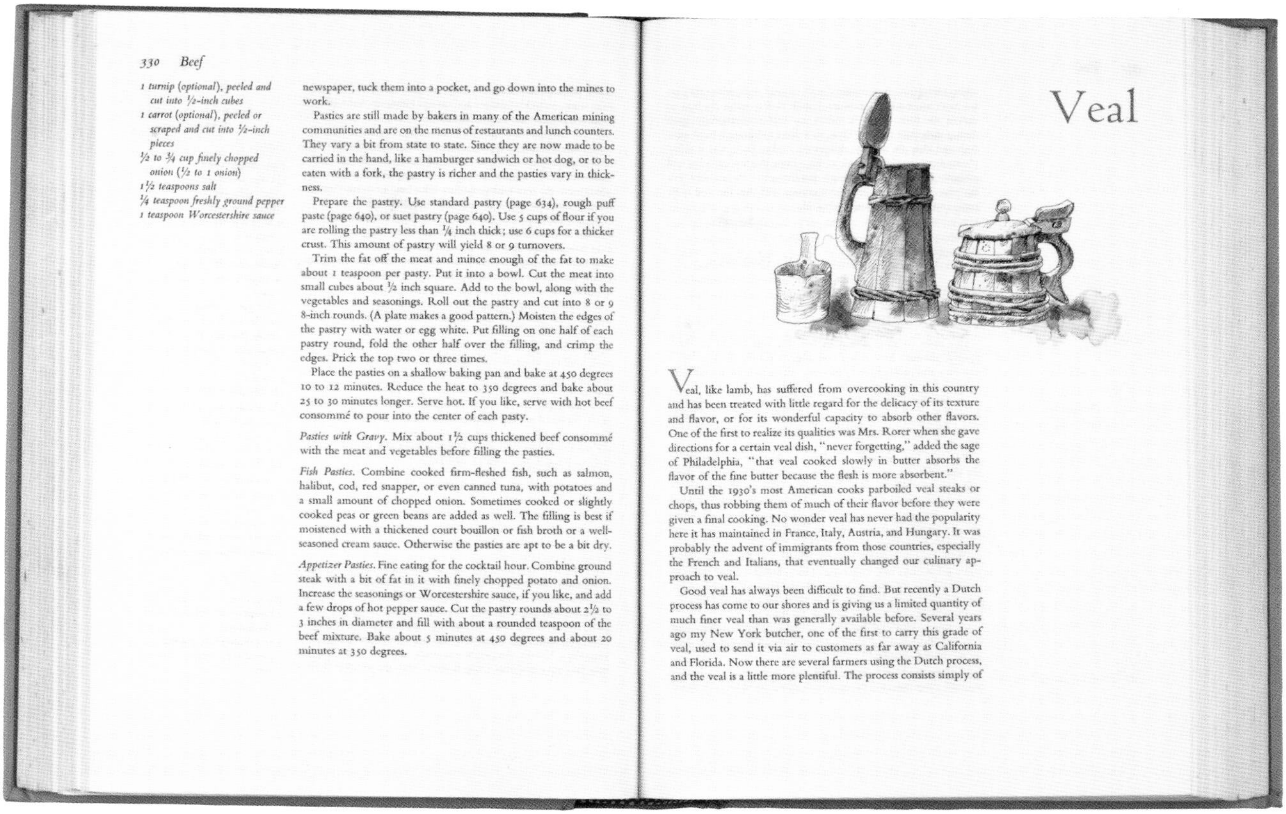

1 turnip (optional), peeled and
cut into ½-inch cubes
1 carrot (optional), peeled or
scraped and cut into ½-inch
pieces
½ to ¾ cup finely chopped
onion (½ to 1 onion)
1½ teaspoons salt
¼ teaspoon freshly ground pepper
1 teaspoon Worcestershire sauce

newspaper, tuck them into a pocket, and go down into the mines to work.

Pasties are still made by bakers in many of the American mining communities and are on the menus of restaurants and lunch counters. They vary a bit from state to state. Since they are now made to be carried in the hand, like a hamburger sandwich or hot dog, or to be eaten with a fork, the pastry is richer and the pasties vary in thickness.

Prepare the pastry. Use standard pastry (page 634), rough puff paste (page 640), or suet pastry (page 640). Use 5 cups of flour if you are rolling the pastry less than ¼ inch thick; use 6 cups for a thicker crust. This amount of pastry will yield 8 or 9 turnovers.

Trim the fat off the meat and mince enough of the fat to make about 1 teaspoon per pasty. Put it into a bowl. Cut the meat into small cubes about ½ inch square. Add to the bowl, along with the vegetables and seasonings. Roll out the pastry and cut into 8 or 9 8-inch rounds. (A plate makes a good pattern.) Moisten the edges of the pastry with water or egg white. Put filling on one half of each pastry round, fold the other half over the filling, and crimp the edges. Prick the top two or three times.

Place the pasties on a shallow baking pan and bake at 450 degrees 10 to 12 minutes. Reduce the heat to 350 degrees and bake about 25 to 30 minutes longer. Serve hot. If you like, serve with hot beef consommé to pour into the center of each pasty.

Pasties with Gravy. Mix about 1½ cups thickened beef consommé with the meat and vegetables before filling the pasties.

Fish Pasties. Combine cooked firm-fleshed fish, such as salmon, halibut, cod, red snapper, or even canned tuna, with potatoes and a small amount of chopped onion. Sometimes cooked or slightly cooked peas or green beans are added as well. The filling is best if moistened with a thickened court bouillon or fish broth or a well-seasoned cream sauce. Otherwise the pasties are apt to be a bit dry.

Appetizer Pasties. Fine eating for the cocktail hour. Combine ground steak with a bit of fat in it with finely chopped potato and onion. Increase the seasonings or Worcestershire sauce, if you like, and add a few drops of hot pepper sauce. Cut the pastry rounds about 2½ to 3 inches in diameter and fill with about a rounded teaspoon of the beef mixture. Bake about 5 minutes at 450 degrees and about 20 minutes at 350 degrees.

Veal

Veal, like lamb, has suffered from overcooking in this country and has been treated with little regard for the delicacy of its texture and flavor, or for its wonderful capacity to absorb other flavors. One of the first to realize its qualities was Mrs. Rorer when she gave directions for a certain veal dish, "never forgetting," added the sage of Philadelphia, "that veal cooked slowly in butter absorbs the flavor of the fine butter because the flesh is more absorbent."

Until the 1930's most American cooks parboiled veal steaks or chops, thus robbing them of much of their flavor before they were given a final cooking. No wonder veal has never had the popularity here it has maintained in France, Italy, Austria, and Hungary. It was probably the advent of immigrants from those countries, especially the French and Italians, that eventually changed our culinary approach to veal.

Good veal has always been difficult to find. But recently a Dutch process has come to our shores and is giving us a limited quantity of much finer veal than was generally available before. Several years ago my New York butcher, one of the first to carry this grade of veal, used to send it via air to customers as far away as California and Florida. Now there are several farmers using the Dutch process, and the veal is a little more plentiful. The process consists simply of

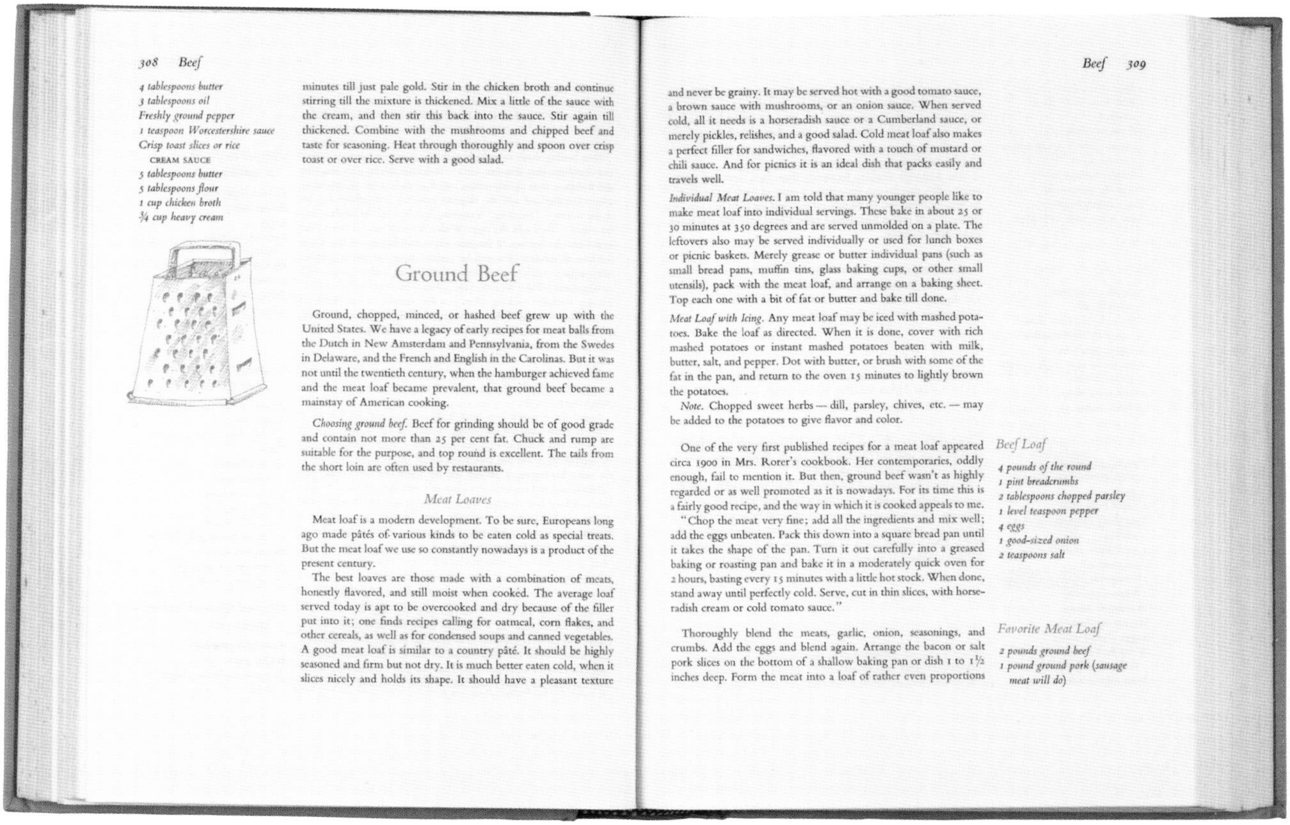

---

4 tablespoons butter
3 tablespoons oil
Freshly ground pepper
1 teaspoon Worcestershire sauce
Crisp toast slices or rice
CREAM SAUCE
5 tablespoons butter
5 tablespoons flour
1 cup chicken broth
¾ cup heavy cream

minutes till just pale gold. Stir in the chicken broth and continue stirring till the mixture is thickened. Mix a little of the sauce with the cream, and then stir this back into the sauce. Stir again till thickened. Combine with the mushrooms and chipped beef and taste for seasoning. Heat through thoroughly and spoon over crisp toast or over rice. Serve with a good salad.

Ground Beef

Ground, chopped, minced, or hashed beef grew up with the United States. We have a legacy of early recipes for meat balls from the Dutch in New Amsterdam and Pennsylvania, from the Swedes in Delaware, and the French and English in the Carolinas. But it was not until the twentieth century, when the hamburger achieved fame and the meat loaf became prevalent, that ground beef became a mainstay of American cooking.

Choosing ground beef. Beef for grinding should be of good grade and contain not more than 25 per cent fat. Chuck and rump are suitable for the purpose, and top round is excellent. The tails from the short loin are often used by restaurants.

Meat Loaves

Meat loaf is a modern development. To be sure, Europeans long ago made pâtés of various kinds to be eaten cold as special treats. But the meat loaf we use so constantly nowadays is a product of the present century.

The best loaves are those made with a combination of meats, honestly flavored, and still moist when cooked. The average loaf served today is apt to be overcooked and dry because of the filler put into it; one finds recipes calling for oatmeal, corn flakes, and other cereals, as well as for condensed soups and canned vegetables. A good meat loaf is similar to a country pâté. It should be highly seasoned and firm but not dry. It is much better eaten cold, when it slices nicely and holds its shape. It should have a pleasant texture

and never be grainy. It may be served hot with a good tomato sauce, a brown sauce with mushrooms, or an onion sauce. When served cold, all it needs is a horseradish sauce or a Cumberland sauce, or merely pickles, relishes, and a good salad. Cold meat loaf also makes a perfect filler for sandwiches, flavored with a touch of mustard or chili sauce. And for picnics it is an ideal dish that packs easily and travels well.

Individual Meat Loaves. I am told that many younger people like to make meat loaf into individual servings. These bake in about 25 or 30 minutes at 350 degrees and are served unmolded on a plate. The leftovers also may be served individually or used for lunch boxes or picnic baskets. Merely grease or butter individual pans (such as small bread pans, muffin tins, glass baking cups, or other small utensils), pack with the meat loaf, and arrange on a baking sheet. Top each one with a bit of fat or butter and bake till done.

Meat Loaf with Icing. Any meat loaf may be iced with mashed potatoes. Bake the loaf as directed. When it is done, cover with rich mashed potatoes or instant mashed potatoes beaten with milk, butter, salt, and pepper. Dot with butter, or brush with some of the fat in the pan, and return to the oven 15 minutes to lightly brown the potatoes.

Note. Chopped sweet herbs — dill, parsley, chives, etc. — may be added to the potatoes to give flavor and color.

One of the very first published recipes for a meat loaf appeared circa 1900 in Mrs. Rorer's cookbook. Her contemporaries, oddly enough, fail to mention it. But then, ground beef wasn't as highly regarded or as well promoted as it is nowadays. For its time this is a fairly good recipe, and the way in which it is cooked appeals to me.

"Chop the meat very fine; add all the ingredients and mix well; add the eggs unbeaten. Pack this down into a square bread pan until it takes the shape of the pan. Turn it out carefully into a greased baking or roasting pan and bake it in a moderately quick oven for 2 hours, basting every 15 minutes with a little hot stock. When done, stand away until perfectly cold. Serve, cut in thin slices, with horseradish cream or cold tomato sauce."

Thoroughly blend the meats, garlic, onion, seasonings, and crumbs. Add the eggs and blend again. Arrange the bacon or salt pork slices on the bottom of a shallow baking pan or dish 1 to 1½ inches deep. Form the meat into a loaf of rather even proportions

Beef Loaf

4 pounds of the round
1 pint breadcrumbs
2 tablespoons chopped parsley
1 level teaspoon pepper
4 eggs
1 good-sized onion
2 teaspoons salt

Favorite Meat Loaf

2 pounds ground beef
1 pound ground pork (sausage
meat will do)

Isabella Beeton

Mrs Beeton's Household Management

Ward, Lock & Co., London, 1888
(revised edition; first published 1861)
1728 pages
188 x 125 mm (7 3/8 x 4 7/8 in.)

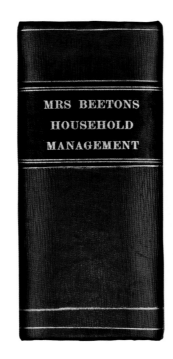
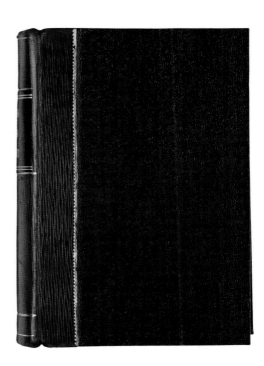

If you were asked to pick a cookery writer whose life was far removed from their legend, you'd choose Mrs B. Poor woman. She came from a complex family of twenty-one. She married the boy next door, Sam Beeton. Two of her children died in infancy, and when she had her fourth boy, it killed her. She was twenty-eight years old. Most readers know nothing of this, for her fame dehumanized her.

My edition is the third, with a solemn leather spine signifying its importance. The first was published in 1861, with a preface by Mrs B. stating, 'I must frankly own that, if I had known beforehand that this book would have cost me the labour which it has, I should never have been courageous enough to commence it.' The second, brought out in 1869, four years after her death, includes a short note from Sam explaining that he has made a few improvements, but that 'My late wife's writing was so clear, and her directions were so practical, that only the slightest alterations and corrections were needed.' My edition, the first under Ward, Lock & Co's control, is little altered; gradually, however, the publishers departed so much from the original that later versions are hardly recognizable (and not worth collecting). First editions command high prices.

In between advertisements, there are more than 900 recipes, along with colour plates and neat drawings of fish, jellies and pickles in jars. There is an astonishing menu for a wedding breakfast that makes modern versions look paltry, together with advice on servants, artificial respiration and cramp in horses.

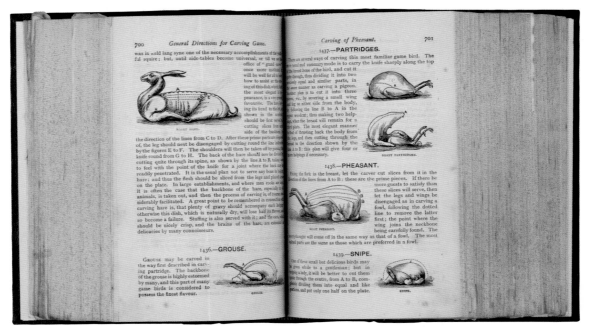

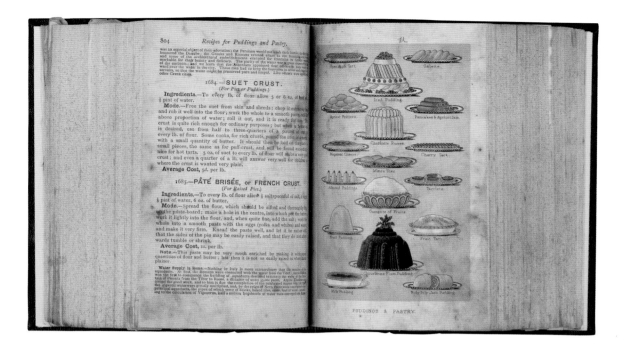

PUDDINGS & PASTRY.

was an especial object of their adoration: the Persians would not wash their hands...
honoured the Danube; the Greeks and Romans erected altars to the fountains...
and some of the architectural embellishments executed for fountains in their...
markable for their beauty and delicacy. The purity of the water was of great moment...
of the ancients; and we learn that the Athenians appointed four officers to survey...
ward-slant the water in the city. These men had to keep the fountains in order, and to see...
servoirs, so that the water might be preserved pure and limpid. Like officers were appointed...
other Greek cities.

1684.—SUET CRUST.
(For Pies or Puddings.)

Ingredients.—To every lb. of flour allow 5 or 6 oz. of beef...
½ pint of water.

Mode.—Free the suet from skin and shreds; chop it extremely...
and rub it well into the flour; work the whole to a smooth paste, with...
above proportion of water; roll it out, and it is ready for use...
crust is quite rich enough for ordinary purposes; but when a better...
is desired, use from half to three-quarters of a pound of suet to...
every lb. of flour. Some cooks, for rich crusts, pound the suet in a mortar...
with a small quantity of butter. It should then be laid on the paste in...
small pieces, the same as for puff-crust, and will be found exceedingly...
nice for hot tarts. 5 oz. of suet to every lb. of flour will make a very...
crust; and even a quarter of a lb. of flour will answer very well for children...
where the crust is wanted very plain.

Average Cost, 5*d.* per lb.

1685.—PÂTÉ BRISÉE, or FRENCH CRUST.
(For Raised Pies.)

Ingredients.—To every lb. of flour allow ½ saltspoonful of salt, 2 eggs...
½ pint of water, 6 oz. of butter.

Mode.—Spread the flour, which should be sifted and thoroughly...
on the paste-board; make a hole in the centre, into which put the butter...
work it lightly into the flour, and, when quite fine, add the salt; work...
whole into a smooth paste with the eggs (yolks and whites) and warm...
and make it very firm. Knead the paste well, and let it be rather stiff...
that the sides of the pie may be easily raised, and that they do not afterwards tumble or shrink.

Average Cost, 1*s.* per lb.

Note.—This paste may be very much enriched by making it with more...
quantities of flour and butter; but then it is not so easily raised as when more plainer.

Water Supply in Rome.—Nothing in Italy is more extraordinary than the results of...

1. VENETIAN VILLA OF PÂTE D'OFFICE AND NOUGAT.

2361.—NOUILLES PASTE.
(For Timbales and Ornaments.)

Ingredients.—½ lb. of flour, ¼ oz. of butter, a saltspoonful of salt,
2 yolks of eggs, 1 whole egg.

Mode.—Put the flour on the board, make a hole in the centre, put in...
the yolks of eggs, butter and salt, and add as many whole eggs as...
needed to make a smooth stiff paste. Probably not more than 1 egg will...
be needed, but different flours absorb different quantities of moisture.

2362.—SWEET PASTE. (Fr.—*Pâte d'Office.*)

Ingredients.—2 lbs. of flour, 1 lb. of pounded sugar, 1 pint of water.

Mode.—Melt the sugar in the water over the fire, put the fire to a...

hard, cutting a hole in the centre; pour in the syrup, and work into a
smooth paste.

2363.—SPINACH GREEN.

Mode.—Pound some spinach in a mortar, press it through a coarse
cloth into a pan, and boil for a few minutes, stirring the while; drain on
a sieve, and squeeze out as much of the juice as possible, then rub the
pulp through a sieve.

2364.—VENETIAN VILLA.

This illustrates most of the processes that are necessary for the con-

2. THE FOUNDATION (PÂTE D'OFFICE).

struction of all ornamental stands, and for it most of the materials made
for this purpose are required.

The plans for this, showing the different parts, are all drawn *to scale,* so
that having determined the size of the model, which might be four, six, or
eight times as large as it is represented, it will be easy to enlarge each
section to the desired size.

2365. **The Foundation** (Illustration No. 2).—The first part to be made
is the rockwork or pathway upon which the villa stands. This is composed of pâte d'office, No. 2362. It is cut in two rounds, the upper one

Hilaire Belloc

Advice: Hilaire Belloc's Advice on Wine, Food and Other Matters

Harvill, London, 1960
40 pages
267 x 169 mm (10½ x 6⅝ in.)

This book started as advice to 'Miss Bridget Herbert on the occasion of her marriage' in 1935. Years later, Mrs Grant, as she became, published the book with a foreword by Evelyn Waugh. When Miss Herbert married, Waugh wrote, 'Belloc was sixty-five years old and approaching the long silence in which his literary life ended. He gave her as a wedding present the manuscript book of advice. His surviving friends will recognize the precepts which were often in one form or another, on his lips.' His views, added Waugh, were 'strong and idiosyncratic to the verge of perversity'.

ADVICE

Never warm Red wine. This deleterious practice is called by the vulgar 'taking the chill off'. Wine—Red wine—can be just as good with the chill on: especially in early Autumn when the weather is fine. Rabelais, who knew more about wine than Dionysos and Noah put together thought that, nay, affirmed it that, in Summer wine should come cool out of a cellar, and he was right. He spoke of *Chinon* wine, known also as the *Fausse Maigre*, for it has more body than the first and superficial acquaintance allows to it.

About Wine
Warming it

But if you *must* warm Red wine do this: Take it out some six hours before drinking it; put it on a sideboard far from any fire—but in a room with a fire, or other heat. Take the cork out a little before drinking it—say half an hour before—to give it air after this slow warming. Then drink it.

To put red wine into warm water (I mean, to put the bottle into warm water) or to put it near the fire turns it into vinegar. This is not so true of Port, which is not a wine: but it is God's truth of Claret and Burgundy, Touraine, the Rhône, the Etruscan, the Spanish and indeed the Algerian. The Rhine. All Red wines.

9

Well, that's as maybe, but with hindsight Belloc's dictum that one should use only sea salt ground at the table is now accepted: 'It is worth the trouble. For cooking sea salt is utterly different from ordinary salt and a million times better. You use processed salt at your peril.'

Belloc believed that there are two kinds of cooking: 'hot and warm. They are quite distinct, and the mixing of them ruins life.' Eggs should be timed from the point the water boils; salad servers should be horn or wood, never metal; and vinegar should be scattered, not poured. He has views on coffee, and is certain that you should always eat off silver.

This slim volume, the cover of which features a 1930s-style pattern, is in a fine, clear typeface with occasional Belloc drawings of wine funnels and corkscrews that prove he was a better writer than artist.

A Book for Cooks

Cooling it Do not cool white wine too much. All white wine is the better for cooling, but beyond a certain point, it kills the taste.

An excellent way of cooling white wine is this: Get a Bath oliver biscuit tin—2 or 3 is better than one, for you may want to have several bottles cooled, and to wait for cooling when one has begun drinking is damnable. These Biscuit tins are just the height of a bottle or a little more, and, *what is their special point*, a *little* wider. Put the bottle into the tin and pour water in till it reaches about one inch or less below the top. There is then a jacket of water all round the bottle. Put broken ice—not much—into the water at the top: not so much as to choke it, but only so much as can float in the water. This ice gradually melts, the cold melted ice sinks, and therefore very soon the whole water jacket is at 32° Fahrenheit, and, being a thin layer doesn't freeze the wine.

A good permanent instrument to have about the place is a leaden roll of this shape and size well fastened, and with handles fixed on. See that it is wide enough for champagne.

Baptizing it All—or nearly all—Red wine is the better for having just one or two drops of water poured into the *first* glass only. Why this should be so I know not, but so it is. It introduces it. This admirable and little known custom is called 'Baptizing' wine.

10

Some also, on seeing a little wine left in a glass throw it on the ground or ashes of the fire, crying 'Cottabus', KOTT and BUS; this is a superstition, but not to be despised. It is said to placate the Gods.

It is strange that the clear and necessary doctrine on Uncorking it the uncorking of wine should be so little known. Get it firmly in early wine-drinking and it will make all your life the easier.

It is this. Always uncork wine with a *Lazy-Tongs*.

Like this

You screw in the screw with the Lazy-Tongs, flat like this

11

Of knives and Never allow Stainless Steel knives. Servants like them forks because they give less trouble to clean. But then, it would be even less trouble to have no knives at all and to eat with one's fingers like the Grand Mogul. Stainless steel doesn't cut, and a knife that doesn't cut is a curse.

I now come to the last, most necessary, and hardest-to-keep piece of advice.

Always get silver—never plate: whether you are buying, or choosing for yourself a present given to you, or stealing *always* buy silver.

Plate does not last—especially electro plate—modern plate powders destroy it; it never looks right and it doesn't pawn or sell or make a gift for your descendants. At all sacrifices have silver: all silver, and the thicker and heavier the better.

And this I say having myself sinned horribly the other way a thousand times, but, now, converted in age I know the truth. Silver is good to eat off and to look at and to drink out of. Plate is a fraud. You will never regret the silver you will accumulate in a long life. It goes with white hairs.

Also silver is going to become more valuable. (1) Because whatever happens to Gold currencies the Orient will never give up silver. (2) Because sooner or later

36

people will wake up to the truth that it is lovely, satisfying and permanent.

It is a by-product of lead—and therefore people think it will become cheap. But it won't.

POST SCRIPT
To make good old Brandy out of Vile Stuff

(1) Pour it through the air into a large receptacle, e.g. from the top of the stairs into a bath below.

(2) Put it into bottles, with a plum in each bottle.

(3) Stand it up *with no corks in the bottles*, for some 2 or 3 days, even a week—or 3 weeks.

(4) Put in a *drop* of Maraschino into each bottle.

The bottles are now old Brandy, and you can give them funny names and drink the stuff out of big glasses and roll it around, warming it with your hands and smelling at it like a dog.

FINIS   *November* 1935

All this is illegible, because I wrote with a full mind. But when I write coldly I can be as legible
AS THIS

Richard Bertinet

Dough: Simple Contemporary Bread

Kyle Cathie, London, 2005
160 pages
254 x 224 mm (10 x 8⁷/₈ in.)

There are plenty of books that aim to teach you how to make bread, but many seem to obfuscate the process rather than clarify it. After all, while there is magic in the way dough rises, there's no difficulty in it. So I chose a work by Bertinet, a baker from Brittany who now runs baking courses in Bath, as the best bread book.

Dough starts with essential tools – hands, baking stone, tea towels and razor blade – and the ingredients. These (flour, yeast, salt and water) are fetchingly laid out on a rough slate. The message here is that this is simple, basic stuff. Later, series of photographs show how to make the dough and how to work it. Then Bertinet gets to the exciting bit: what can be done with the dough. There are rolls, *pain d'épi*, *fougasse*, baguettes and puff balls, the last behaving something like a showgirl bursting from a cake. A soup bowl is made of flavoured bread to eat once the soup has been finished, and focaccia is studded with rosemary and rock salt. Bread-making is not only deeply satisfying but also fun.

Jean Cazals's photography conveys the same message. The styling includes antique French tea towels, slates and well-used chopping boards. The recipes, when they branch out from the basics, include summer pudding ('I love it so much that Jo and I even served it at our wedding'), croque-monsieur and fruited tea loaf. If this book doesn't make you rush to the mixing bowl, I'll eat my puff ball.

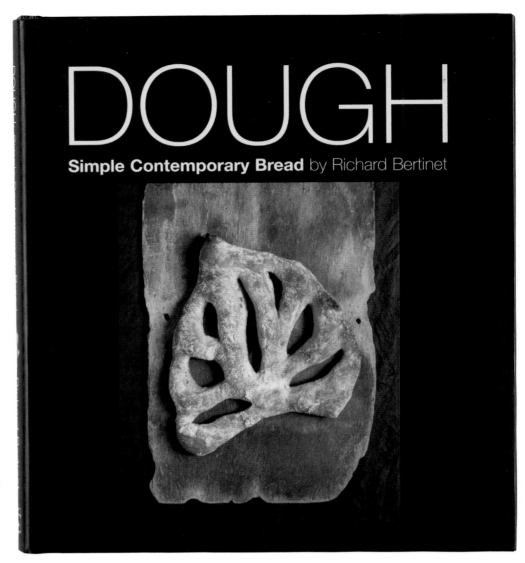

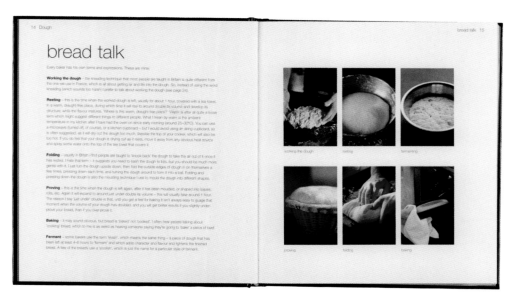

bread talk

Every baker has his own terms and expressions. These are mine.

Working the dough – The kneading technique that most people are taught in Britain is quite different from the one we use in France, which is all about getting air and life into the dough. So, instead of using the word kneading (which sounds too harsh) I prefer to talk about working the dough (see page 24).

Resting – this is the time when the worked dough is left, usually for about 1 hour, covered with a tea towel, in a warm, draught-free place, during which time it will rise to around double its volume and develop its structure, while the flavour matures. Where is this warm, draught-free place? Warm is after all quite a loose term which might suggest different things to different people. What I mean by warm is the ambient temperature in my kitchen after I have had the oven on since early morning (around 20–30°C). You can use a microwave (turned off, of course), or a kitchen cupboard – but I would avoid using an airing cupboard, as is often suggested, as it will dry out the dough too much. Likewise the top of your cooker, which will also be too hot. If you do feel that your dough is drying out as it rests, move it away from any obvious heat source and spray some water onto the top of the tea towel that covers it.

Folding – usually in Britain I find people are taught to 'knock back' the dough to take the air out of it once it has rested. I hate that term – it suggests you need to bash the dough to bits, but you should be much more gentle with it. I just turn the dough upside down, then fold the outside edges of dough in on themselves a few times, pressing down each time, and turning the dough around to form it into a ball. Folding and pressing down the dough is also the moulding technique I use to mould the dough into different shapes.

Proving – this is the time when the dough is left again, after it has been moulded, or shaped into loaves, rolls, etc. Again it will expand to around just under double its volume – this will usually take around 1 hour. The reason I say 'just under' double is that, until you get a feel for baking it isn't always easy to gauge that moment when the volume of your dough has doubled, and you will get better results if you slightly under-prove your bread, than if you over-prove it.

Baking – it may sound obvious, but bread is baked, not 'cooked'. I often hear people talking about 'cooking' bread, which to me is as weird as hearing someone say they're going to 'bake' a piece of beef.

Ferment – some bakers use the term 'leaven', which means the same thing – a piece of dough that has been left at least 4–6 hours to 'ferment' and which adds character and flavour and lightens the finished bread. A few of the breads use a 'poolish', which is just the name for a particular style of ferment.

working the dough   resting   fermenting

proving   folding   baking

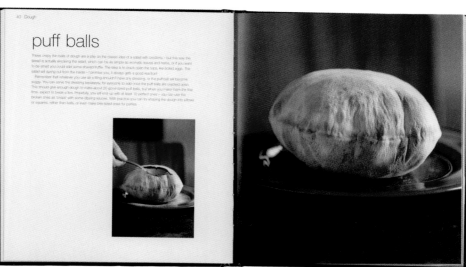

puff balls

These crispy thin balls of dough are a play on the classic idea of a salad with croutons – but this time the bread is actually enclosing the salad, which can be as simple as aromatic leaves and herbs, or if you want to be smart you could add some shaved truffle. The idea is to crack open the tops, like boiled eggs. The salad will spring out from the inside – I promise you, it always gets a good reaction.

Remember that whatever you use as a filling shouldn't have any dressing, or the puff ball will become soggy. You can serve this amazing pendant, for everyone to crack open once the puff balls are cracked open. This should give enough dough to make about 20 good-sized puff balls, but when you make them the first time, expect to break a few. Hopefully, you will end up with at least 10 perfect ones – you can use the broken ones as 'crisps' with some dipping sauces. With practice you can try shaping the dough into pillows or squares, rather than balls, or even make bite-sized ones for parties.

saffron rolls

Saffron (the dried stigma of a particular type of crocus) is another of those luxurious, glamorous ingredients that if you use with too heavy a hand can taste overpowering (and look too yellow) but, used in bread as a background flavour, it gives a lovely warm and delicate note. I love this bread with seafood chowder, or a fish stew like bouillabaisse – or you can use it to make crab or prawn mayonnaise sandwiches. Try to use saffron strands, rather than powder, as they give a smarter appearance to the bread, and a richer flavour.

Quantity:	9 or 10 rolls	**1 Batch** White dough (page 33)
Preparation:	20 minutes	**Pinch** of Saffron strands (if you can't get strands
Resting:	1 hour	powdered saffron will do)
Proving:	45 minutes	**A few** Cumin seeds
Baking:	12 minutes	White flour for dusting

To prepare
When making the dough, divide a few strands of saffron, or powder, in the water before mixing, then carry on as usual, resting for 1 hour.
Line a tray with a tea towel and dust with flour.

To make
• With the help of the rounded end of your scraper, turn out the dough, and with your hand, flatten it into a rectangle. Fold one third of the dough into the centre and press down with your fingertips, fold the opposite side over on top (as if you were folding an A4 letter to put into an envelope). With the flat edge of your scraper cut it into 9 or 10 pieces (weighing about 90–100g each) and mould each one into a ball (page 26). Flour the top of each ball and then place a floured rolling pin across the centre and press down firmly. The dough will rise up either side of the instant you have made, leaving you with a roll that resembles a coffee bean.

• Lay the rolls two abreast on the lined baking tray, making a pleat between each pair of rolls, cover with another tea towel and leave to prove for 45 minutes.

• Sprinkle a few cumin seeds on top of each roll, then slide onto your baking stone/upturned tray in the preheated oven. Mist the inside with a water spray and turn down the heat to 220°C. Bake them for 12 minutes. Cool on a wire rack.

Raymond Blanc

Blanc Vite: Fast, Fresh Food from Raymond Blanc

Headline, London, 1998
320 pages
279 x 210 mm (11 x 8¼ in.)

The Senate's design for Blanc's book is completely different from its more famous work for the River Café books (see, for example, page 100). The effect is calmer and less colourful.

I include Raymond Blanc because two people whose cooking I trust told me that Blanc is their standby. I chose this over *Cooking for Friends* because it is simpler, although I think 'Vite' is a misnomer (his lamb shanks take two and a half hours). These recipes may be quick in the final stages, but an awful lot require lengthy preparations. I am also a bit chary of the nutritional advice (there's a section by the nutritionist Dr Jean Monro), which makes Blanc use fructose instead of sugar and wholemeal pasta instead of white. Blanc insists that all the ingredients can be found in a supermarket. I have never come across fructose.

Anyway, the recipes are what this book is about, and lovely they are too. Rhubarb with Blood Oranges, Opal Basil and Mascarpone deserves its own Chardin still life and gets a double-page spread. The vegetarian main courses are more appetizing than they deserve, especially Pasta with Swiss Chard, Goat's Cheese and Artichokes, even if the pasta is wholemeal. In this recipe, as in many, Blanc provides extra notes – here, that spinach or pak choi can be substituted for chard. Vegetable and Cashew Stir-Fry can be prepared in advance and kept under a damp cloth. Tomato Salsa with Artichoke actually benefits from being made ahead of time.

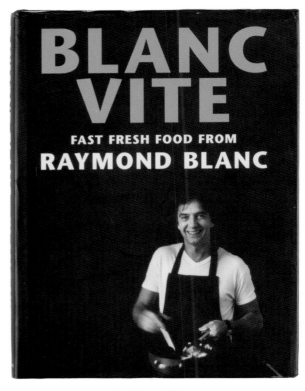

This is a very large book, beautifully photographed by Peter Knab (who deserves a bigger credit), with a good, clear typeface. There are frequent notes, serving tips, variations and comments. It feels trustworthy.

A Book for Cooks

MARINATED SARDINES WITH CHICKPEAS

SERVES 4

Planning ahead
The sardines need to be marinated 12 or so hours in advance, and the chickpeas can either be bought cooked or freshly cooked a day or two before needed.

12 fillets of sardines
100ml olive oil
3 garlic cloves, peeled and crushed
salt and freshly ground black pepper
juice of 2 unsprayed lemons
1 small bunch of fresh fennel herb, chopped

THE CHICKPEAS
200g cooked chickpeas (see page 43), or 1 x 200g tin, well drained and
    rinsed
1 large red onion, peeled and finely chopped
1 small fennel bulb, finely sliced

Method

The fish
Heat the olive oil gently with the garlic and 1 tsp salt until simmering. Place the sardine fillets, skin side up, into a small tray in one layer, then pour the hot oil over along with the lemon juice. Leave to marinate in a cool place for 12 hours.

The chickpeas
Once cooked, strain the chickpeas from their liquid and mix with the onion and the fennel bulb. Set aside.

Serving
Strain the oil off the sardines and mix it with the chickpeas. Season to taste and spoon into four plates. Top these with the fillets of sardine, and sprinkle with the chopped fennel herb and plenty of black pepper. Serve.

LEMON VERBENA CREAMS WITH LEMON SYRUP

Nutritional note
Vegetarians who are not vegans will benefit from the good protein of eggs and milk in this dish. This pudding is excellent because it does not have a high glycaemic index, despite being sweet.

SERVES 4

Planning ahead
The creams need to be made a few hours in advance, and can be made up to a day before serving, as can the syrup.

500ml milk
70g fructose
1 large bunch of fresh lemon verbena, leaves picked and finely sliced
6 free-range egg yolks

THE LEMON SYRUP
2 unsprayed lemons
2 tbsp water
30g fructose

Method
Preheat the oven to 180°C/350°F/Gas 4.

The creams
Mix the milk and fructose together in a saucepan then bring to the boil. Add the sliced lemon verbena, and allow to cool. Mix the fragrant milk with the egg yolks, then strain through your finest sieve.
    Prepare a *bain-marie*, so that the water comes two-thirds of the way up the sides of your ramekins or moulds. Place a piece of kitchen paper over the bottom of this so that the moulds won't slip, then pour the mixture into them. Cover the *bain-marie* with a piece of foil, then place in the preheated oven for 15 minutes. Turn the oven down to 160°C/325°F/Gas 3, remove the foil and allow to cook for a further 20 minutes. They should still be relatively sloppy in the centre. This will give you a much softer and creamier texture once the creams have cooled, and a less obvious taste of egg. Transfer to a container of cold water to cool. Once cold, reserve well clingfilmed until needed.

The lemon syrup and serving
Finely grate the zest of the 2 lemons, then squeeze the juice from 1, and segment the other. Boil together the lemon zest and juice with the water and fructose. When this takes on a syrupy consistency, remove it from the heat and add the lemon segments. Simply spoon the syrup and lemon segments over the tops of the creams in their moulds.

Raymond Blanc

39

X. Marcel Boulestin

Simple French Cooking
for English Homes

Heinemann, London, 1923
132 pages
183 x 120 mm (7¼ x 4¾ in.)

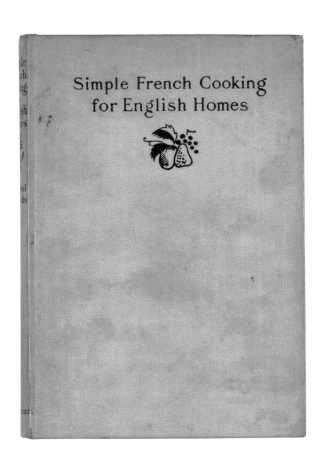

Xavier Marcel Boulestin was the twentieth century's first celebrity chef. A far more appealing figure than, say, Fanny Cradock or Gordon Ramsay, he was also far more of a celebrity. He knew French novelist Colette and her Svengali, 'Willy', in Paris, and opened an interior-design shop in London, which failed. Then Heinemann commissioned him to write this book. In the late 1930s he became the first television chef, while his starry Restaurant Français in London's Leicester Square was designed by English architect Clough Williams-Ellis and French artists Raoul Dufy and Marie Laurencin.

But Boulestin was not really a chef in today's terms. As a child, he loved mint sauce with mutton, a revolutionary combination in France, and this, his first cookery book, is as determinedly simple as its title: 'French cooking is not, as some English people seem to think, complicated, rich and expensive. They must not judge it by the *table d'hôte* dinners they may have eaten … where nondescript dishes boast of pretentious names … . This represents only hotel cooking at its worst.'

However, Boulestin had to lay down some ground rules: no red wine with fish, grind your coffee fresh, use seasonal vegetables and always cook with the best olive oil. The recipes are truly simple: hard-boiled eggs, fried sole and beetroot salad each take up between one and three lines of type. His lemonade (four lines) includes a glass of gin.

I particularly like Boulestin's general observations: 'A good cook is not necessarily a good woman with an even temper. Some allowance should be made for the artistic temperament.'

Right: Cookery books have long had a distinctive style. J.E. Laboureur's frontispiece for *Simple French Cooking* makes a nod to the modernist artists of the day.

husband on his way home from the office looking forward to it. Happiness sits smiling at their table. (Fielding has described that somewhere far better than I can.)

. . .

Do not be unreasonable and suddenly announce at seven o'clock that there will be three extra people for dinner. Cooks are only human beings and cannot work miracles.

. . .

A good cook is not necessarily a good woman with an even temper. Some allowance should be made for the artistic temperament.

. . .

Punctuality should be the first rule, upstairs as well as downstairs.

. . .

Do not be afraid of simplicity. If you have a cold chicken for supper, why cover it with a tasteless white sauce which makes it look like a pretentious dish on the buffet table at some fancy dress ball?

. . .

Do not be too insular, like the Englishman who, discussing with a Frenchman the merits of various birds, said that grey-legged partridges were better than red-legged ones.
"Nonsense!" exclaimed his friend. "We, in Perigord, always use red-legged partridges for our very best *pâtés*, stuffed with *foie gras* and truffles."

"I meant better shooting," said the Englishman.
"Oh, I meant better eating," said the Frenchman.

. . .

One cannot overrate the mellowing influence of good food on civilised beings. Hence the "business luncheons."

. . .

Give your friends "something" to drink—not lemonade, which is worse than nothing, nothing meaning plain water.[1]

. . .

Do not let your servants look after the wines. Do it yourself.

. . .

The man who likes good wines is never a drunkard; his pleasure is the appreciation of quality, not the consumption of quantity, which lowers a human being to the level of a brute.

—AND SPECIAL

Do not use substitutes or essences chemically made; if you want to flavour a cream with vanilla or coffee, use the vanilla pod or make yourself some very strong pure coffee; if you

[1] "Heaven sent us soda water
As a torment for our crimes."
G. K. CHESTERTON.

---

flat dish with the onions, add a claret glass full of *consommé*, a good deal of pepper and salt, and brown in a moderate oven for about one hour and a half.

POMMES DE TERRE AU FROMAGE

Cook some potatoes in salted water, peel them and cut in slices. Prepare a *roux blanc*, to which you add grated cheese. Add the potatoes and mix well. Brown in the oven.

POMMES DE TERRE LYONNAISE

Cook the potatoes in salted water, peel them and cut them in slices. Keep them till they are just warm. Fry them in butter, add salt and pepper. Later add two onions finely sliced, so that potatoes and onions are ready and brown together.

POMMES DE TERRE SAUTÉES

Parboil the potatoes in salt water; peel them; wait till they are just warm and fry them in butter till nicely brown. Add seasoning and chopped parsley just before serving.

POMMES DE TERRE FARCIES

Peel and clean some large potatoes; make a hole in the centre and fill with stuffing made either of sausage meat or of remnants of cold meats, to which you add chopped garlic, a little bacon, parsley, salt and pepper. Put them in a fireproof dish with a piece of butter and a little *consommé*. Cook in a moderate oven, basting often

CROQUETTES DE POMMES DE TERRE

Bake in the oven some large white potatoes. When cooked peel them and pass them through a sieve; add salt and pepper, a little butter and the yolks of two eggs. Work it well over the fire so as to dry it. Let it get half cold. Then make small *croquettes*, about one inch thick and three inches long, roll them in flour, and either bake in the oven or fry in butter.

POMMES DE TERRE NOUVELLES

Wash and scrape some new potatoes; dry them well. Melt some butter in a pan till golden only, put in the potatoes and cook them till lightly brown; put them in a fireproof dish with the butter and finish cooking in the oven. Serve with the butter in which they have cooked. Salt just before serving.

POMMES DE TERRE NOUVELLES MAÎTRE D'HOTEL

Boil your new potatoes in their skins. Drain well. Peel them and cover with a *maître d'hotel* sauce.

CHOUX FARCI
STUFFED CABBAGE

Take a large white cabbage, boil it about a quarter of an hour in salted water. It must be cooked enough for you to open the leaves without breaking them. Remove it, drain it well and open it. Once open, stuff it with either sausage meat or the following mixture: sausage meat,

Arabella Boxer

First Slice Your Cookbook

Nelson, Edinburgh, 1964
170 pages
284 x 180 mm (11 1/8 x 7 1/8 in.)

This beautiful, groundbreaking book appeared at the height of the dinner-party boom that tempted young couples dazed by Elizabeth David's works. It was the idea of the designer and cartoonist Mark Boxer, the author's husband, who thought up the title, designed the book and invented the 'recipe consequences'. Each page is divided into three sections, each of which can be turned individually, enabling the cook to mix and match recipes.

Lady Arabella, youngest daughter of the Earl of Moray, is one of a long line of aristocratic cookery writers (see, for example, Lady Clark of Tillypronie, page 50, and Lady Maclean, page 142), but she had

written nothing before. She went on to write for *Vogue*. Nigel Slater praises the 'calm elegance' of her writing; food writer and journalist Rose Prince admires her 'stylish, practical food'.

The recipes are printed on blocks of colour. Red indicates a rich dish, blue a simple one, grey is intermediate, and green is 'substantial but plain'. Lady Arabella recommends serving not more than one red or green dish per meal.

Each recipe takes up little space and, by today's standards, is straightforward, with aubergines and avocados the most exotic ingredients. The recipes are also typical of the 1960s: iced cucumber soup, moussaka and rice-pudding brûlée ('a far cry from nursery milk puddings').

First Slice, named after the apocryphal instruction 'First catch your hare', often misattributed to the eighteenth-century cookery writer Hannah Glasse (page 94), is not only a period piece but also, in its clarity and simplicity, still ideal for tyro cooks. It sold more than 23,000 copies in six years.

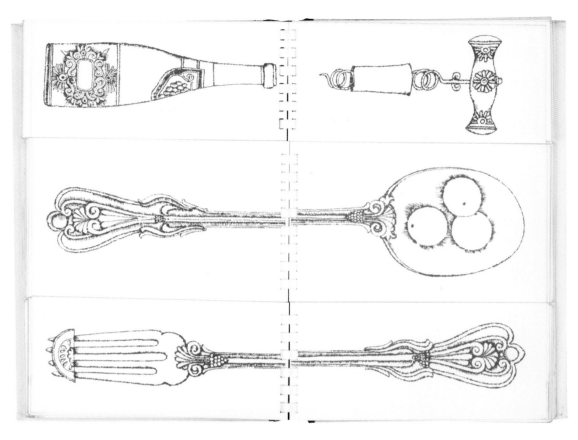

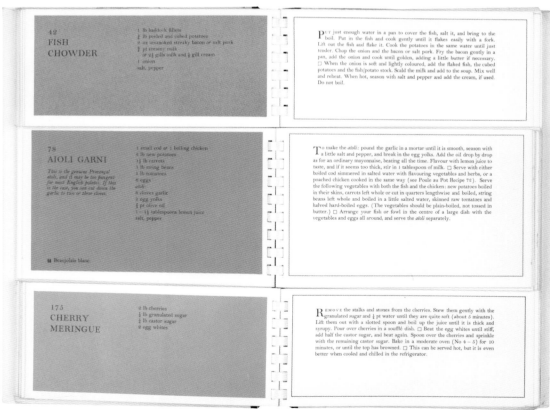

42

FISH CHOWDER

1 lb haddock fillets
½ lb peeled and cubed potatoes
2 oz unsmoked streaky bacon *or* salt pork
½ pt creamy milk
or 2½ gills milk and ½ gill cream
1 onion
salt, pepper

Put just enough water in a pan to cover the fish, salt it, and bring to the boil. Put in the fish and cook gently until it flakes easily with a fork. Lift out the fish and flake it. Cook the potatoes in the same water until just tender. Chop the onion and the bacon or salt pork. Fry the bacon gently in a pan, add the onion and cook until golden, adding a little butter if necessary. □ When the onion is soft and lightly coloured, add the flaked fish, the cubed potatoes and the fish/potato stock. Scald the milk and add to the soup. Mix well and reheat. When hot, season with salt and pepper and add the cream, if used. Do not boil.

78

AIOLI GARNI

This is the genuine Provençal aioli, and it may be too pungent for most English palates. If this is the case, you can cut down the garlic to two or three cloves.

1 small cod *or* 1 boiling chicken
2 lb new potatoes
1½ lb carrots
1 lb string beans
1 lb tomatoes
6 eggs
aioli:
6 cloves garlic
2 egg yolks
½ pt olive oil
1 – 1½ tablespoons lemon juice
salt, pepper

■ Beaujolais blanc.

To make the *aioli*: pound the garlic in a mortar until it is smooth, season with a little salt and pepper, and break in the egg yolks. Add the oil drop by drop as for an ordinary mayonnaise, beating all the time. Flavour with lemon juice to taste, and if it seems too thick, stir in 1 tablespoon of milk. □ Serve with either boiled cod simmered in salted water with flavouring vegetables and herbs, or a poached chicken cooked in the same way (see Poule au Pot Recipe 79). Serve the following vegetables with both the fish and the chicken: new potatoes boiled in their skins, carrots left whole or cut in quarters lengthwise and boiled, string beans left whole and boiled in a little salted water, skimmed raw tomatoes and halved hard-boiled eggs. (The vegetables should be plain-boiled, not tossed in butter.) □ Arrange your fish or fowl in the centre of a large dish with the vegetables and eggs all around, and serve the *aioli* separately.

175

CHERRY MERINGUE

2 lb cherries
¼ lb granulated sugar
¼ pt water
¼ lb castor sugar
2 egg whites

Remove the stalks and stones from the cherries. Stew them gently with the granulated sugar and ¼ pt water until they are quite soft (about 5 minutes). Lift them out with a slotted spoon and boil up the juice until it is thick and syrupy. Pour over cherries in a soufflé dish. □ Beat the egg whites until stiff, add half the castor sugar, and beat again. Spoon over the cherries and sprinkle with the remaining castor sugar. Bake in a moderate oven (No 4 – 5) for 10 minutes, or until the top has browned. □ This can be served hot, but it is even better when cooled and chilled in the refrigerator.

Robert Carrier

Carrier International Cookery Cards: France, Great Britain, Italy

Nelson, London, 1968
20 cards each
145 x 105 mm (5¾ x 4⅛ in.)

Robert Carrier was far more than a chef, even though he was Britain's first modern-day television cook and certainly a celebrity, with his restaurants in Islington, north London, and at the Georgian-fronted mansion of Hintlesham Hall, Suffolk. He played the juvenile lead in American musicals, was a publicist (for vegetarian dog food) and, during the Second World War, worked as a cryptographer at General de Gaulle's headquarters in Paris. His first book, *Great Dishes of the World* (1963), sold more than 10 million copies, despite its high price in today's money. It was also arguably the first cookery book to feature mouth-watering foodie photographs.

Carrier's *International Cookery Cards* – recipes printed on handy, wipe-clean cards, the method on one side and a luscious picture on the other – should have revolutionized the cookbook format. After all, what could be more helpful to the cook than the cuisines of Italy, France, Great Britain, Spain, the United States and China in twenty easy pieces? Take a card to the shops, then keep it next to the mixing bowl. Nonetheless, forty years on, the idea has stalled. It somehow reeks of the 'shameless sixties', when an entire nation's food could be reduced to twenty cards.

Exactly why Carrier decided that cucumber salad and roast pork were integral to the cuisines of France and Italy respectively is not clear. And when you consider Great Britain's offerings – devilled whitebait, old English jellied chicken, cauliflower cheese – it makes you despair of the British table.

9 *Baked Peppers*

2 *Vitello al Herbe*

20 *Cassata alla Siciliana*

BAKED PEPPERS

4 large green peppers	1 tablespoon chopped
Olive oil	fresh basil or tarragon
6 ounces toasted breadcrumbs	2 tablespoons capers,
3 level tablespoons seedless	chopped
raisins	Salt and freshly ground
12 black olives, pitted and	black pepper
cut into pieces	¼ pint tomato sauce
6 anchovy fillets, cut into	Anchovy fillets, to
small pieces	garnish
2 tablespoons chopped parsley	

Wash peppers thoroughly. Trim stem ends of peppers and scoop out seeds and fibres ● Combine 6 to 8 tablespoons olive oil, breadcrumbs, raisins, olives and chopped anchovies, parsley, basil and capers in a large mixing bowl. Add salt and freshly ground black pepper, to taste, and mix well, adding a little more oil if necessary ● Stuff peppers with mixture and place in a heatproof baking dish which you have brushed with olive oil. Sprinkle peppers with olive oil and top each one with 1 tablespoon tomato sauce. Bake in a moderate oven (375°—M4) for 1 hour. Garnish with anchovy fillets and tomato sauce. Excellent hot or cold. Serves 4.

VITELLO AL HERBE

1½ pounds fillet of veal, cut into	Rosemary leaves
thin slices	Juice of 1 lemon
Salt and freshly ground	Rings of lemon
black pepper	
3 ounces butter	

Season thin slices of veal to taste with salt and freshly ground black pepper. Melt the butter in a thick-bottomed frying pan; add the veal, and rosemary leaves to taste, and sauté until golden. Add lemon juice and cook until tender (3 to 5 minutes more). Serve garnished with rings of lemon. Serves 4 to 6.

CASSATA ALLA SICILIANA

1 pint vanilla ice cream	Chopped crystallised fruits
½ pint strawberry or	Chopped nuts
raspberry ice cream	Crystallised fruits for
½ pint pistachio ice cream	decoration

Mould vanilla ice cream around the inside of a 2-pint *bombe* mould or pudding basin, and place a smaller *bombe* mould or basin in the centre to hold the ice cream in position. Freeze. Carefully remove the inner mould. Mould the strawberry ice cream inside the vanilla layer and, as before, place a still smaller mould or basin in the centre. Freeze. Carefully remove the inner mould. ● Stir the chopped crystallised fruits and chopped nuts into the pistachio ice cream. Remove the centre mould and fill with the pistachio ice cream. Freeze once more ● To serve: unmould and decorate with crystallised fruits.

Glynn Christian

Real Flavours: The Handbook of Gourmet and Deli Ingredients

Grub Street, London, 2005
(revised edition; first published 1982)
560 pages
233 x 188 mm (9¹/₈ x 7³/₈ in.)

New Zealander Glynn Christian is the great-great-great-great-grandson of Fletcher Christian, leader in 1789 of the mutiny on the *Bounty*. But, more importantly, he is also a pioneering television chef and co-founder of Mr Christian's, a trailblazing deli that opened in west London in 1974. A life of constant travel and curiosity makes him an expert on ingredients, which is what this book is all about.

Although the book contains enough recipes to justify its inclusion in these pages, it is actually more useful for telling you all – and more than – you need to know about foods. Macadamia nuts have an exceptional protein content; Vietnamese mint is not mint, and 'tastes more like basil in party mood'; and Marco Polo was impressed by sesame seed oil. The author can sometimes be tart (good for him): 'I refuse to listen to one more person telling me how they cook rice.' He then goes on to tell us how he does it. The easiest way is with a microwave: 'utterly reliable and gives amazing results', the best reason yet that might sway me to buy one. He also gets tetchy about sugar/calorie contents being measured in kilojoules: 'What the hell is a kilojoule?'

Real Flavours, an updated, third edition of the author's *Delicatessen Food Handbook* (1982), is a hefty paperback, designed by Lizzie Ballantyne, that has so far not come apart in my hands. The photographs by David Whyte are monochrome and show deli counters rather than portraits of the food. Each ingredient's title is in a demerara brown, which is also used as a background to recipes and sidebars. A cool, cool book in an easy-to-read sans serif typeface.

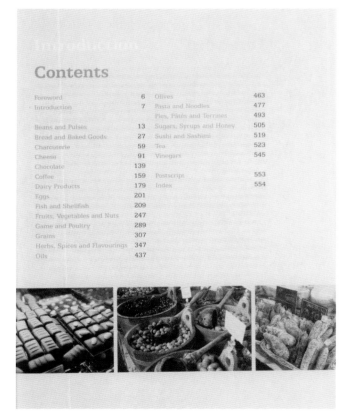

Contents

coated with vegetable oil, gum arabic or glucose after roasting. This encourages much longer life but adds alien flavours and effects.

There is much discussion about storing coffee in the refrigerator but I don't keep coffee long enough to know if this works to any noticeable degree; it is possibly more important that the coffee grounds are kept closely wrapped in foil. Very finely ground coffee, packed tight, lasts longer than coarsely ground coffee, through which air can pass more easily.

Coffee beans can be frozen but after a month the oils go temperamental. If you really have to store coffee for a long time, buy it in vacuum sealed bags or tins. Many shops now buy their bulk-roasted coffee for grinding like this, a great advantage to the customer, especially of the slower moving coffees.

Fair Trade Coffee

Happily this is not one of those apparent advantages that become debased by greed, distortion or treachery. Fair Trade coffee means the growers have been guaranteed a price for their coffee, provided it is of a certain quality. More importantly those who make the agreements actually help coffee farmers improve their land and thus increase both their crop and their family's standard of living. In my experience Fair Trade works, and by buying products with this imprimatur you are helping ensure the system works and that the big conglomerates will one day also face facts: coffee should be a daily comfort for those who grow it, not just for those who trade in it or drink it.

Some independent coffee traders have their own fair-trade equivalent, smaller ones may not even give their policy a name, but all will be proud of it and tell you clearly of their commitment on their web sites and in their brochures. They would be very foolish to risk telling lies.

Dairy Products

Milk must be the world's most important food, even though it is still largely ignored in China and other miscellaneous easterly places.

---

changed out of all recognition. Rather than those hard, small things of yesteryear we have jumbo prunes and soft prunes and ready-soaked prunes and goodness knows what else.

If you must eat them for breakfast, then add a little orange juice or spice to the water you use for cooking, and serve them very cold.

The very finest prunes of all are the French Pruneaux d'Agen and it seems a pity to muck about with them, but people do. Carlsbad plums are actually prunes and, like the best of dried fruits, meant to be eaten at the end of the meal. They are available in wooden boxes but are so expensive they must be eaten instead of a meal. Poles provide us with something even better and even cheaper. They are called plums in chocolate and are stoned small plums (which is to say prunes), filled with a delicious soft toffee and coated with chocolate and decoratively wrapped. They make stunning gifts because everyone expects them to have cost far more than they do.

A purée of cooked prune makes excellent sorbets and ice creams; you can flavour it further with orange or a little praline, add egg in the usual custard-making proportion and then bake it as is or in a pastry flan case.

Prunes are common in stuffings, but you will probably prefer them as an accompaniment when treated this way, something I found in The Guardian over thirty years ago. Take some prunes and cover them with red wine; add cinnamon, mace, a clove or two, a sliver of orange peel and, most important, quite a few bay leaves. Let this cook for a long while, gently, until the prunes are plump and the flavours have blended. Complete the flavour by adding brown sugar or redcurrant jelly if you think sweetness would be an improvement. Remove the prunes and strain the spices from the sauce. Serve hot or cold with game, ham, tongue, duck or goose.

Sweet Ginger

Preserved or stem ginger in syrup is one of the great mysteries of Christmas. Everyone seems to be given it, but almost no one knows what to do with it, other than to slice it onto ice cream. In fact there are many uses. Preserved ginger in slices, or chopped, together with a little of the syrup, is delicious on melon and far better than the silly idea of using powdery ground ginger. It is equally good with fresh or poached pears and can be used for baking in a host of ways, with apples and pears, with peaches, with soft fruits in pies, sponges or crumbles. It is also very good with chocolate sponges; in fact if you put pears and ginger at the bottom of a chocolate sponge mixture you will turn out a memorable pear, chocolate and ginger upside down pudding; this looks better when baked in a ring mould.

Fine slices are a nice addition to any fruit salad, and can be added to homemade ice cream, sliced or chopped, especially when also flavoured with honey. The syrup itself is equally useful for some dribbling onto hot fruit, pancakes or cakes as a moisturizer, or it may be used to mix an icing sugar.

Preserved ginger can rarely be used in savoury cooking, but might be included where there is already a mixture of sweet and sour in the sauce, or where the meat is very fatty, say game,

ham, duck or with goose. But fresh green ginger would probably be better.

See sushi ginger page.

Vine fruits: it is thought the Egyptians discovered they could dry grapes in the sun, and what a good thing that turned out to be. Dried vine fruits have eight times more invert sugar than other types of fruit: as invert sugar is predigested sucrose, ordinary white sugar, the body is able to use it very quickly, hence the usefulness of such fruit as snacks when you are labouring or

Fruit Vinegar Pickled Fruit

A few small bottles of spiced summer fruits, kept chilled in the refrigerator, take little time to make and are an excellent adjunct to meals both simple and super. Although I've specified fruit vinegars in the recipes, wine vinegar would give equally interesting results and cider vinegar is particularly good in this sort of thing. It is important to leave on the skins as they impart colour to the preserving liquid.

500g/1lb firm peaches, plums or pears
1 cinnamon stick
8 dstsp white sugar
2 dstsp pickling spice
300ml/½ pint raspberry or strawberry vinegar

The fruit should be only just ripe and nicely firm. Rinse them under running water. Dry and then cut into four, six or eight segments, according to how big each is.
Put the other ingredients into a pan and bring to the boil very slowly, to extract maximum flavour. Cover and simmer gently for 10 minutes. At this stage you can strain out the spices if you like, but I usually leave them in.
Add the fruit segments and simmer for 5-8 minutes, according to firmness. Spoon the fruit into a sterilised screwtop jar, and then pour over the liquid. Store in the refrigerator for at least three days before eating. I have kept them in perfect condition for four weeks – they may have lasted much longer but by then they were eaten up.
Serve them solo as a fascinating pickle or slice and add to salads or to mayonnaise.

Options: if you want the fruit to last longer, cook them for only three minutes, which keeps them firmer, of course. You will need to wait three weeks before eating them but they will stay firm for some months longer in the refrigerator. Vodka, brandy or peach brandy added to the cool pickle would also prolong the fruit's potential life, but adds so much extra pleasure they may be eaten even sooner.

Craig Claiborne

The New York Times Cook Book

Harper & Row, New York, 1961
734 pages
232 x 164 mm (9¹/₈ x 6½ in.)

Like his fellow American Robert Carrier (page 44), Claiborne had a varied career before he started writing about food. Yes, he trained as a journalist and as a hotelier, but he served in the US Navy in both the Second World War and the Korean War, and was assistant director of publicity for the Midwestern division of US broadcasting company ABC. As well as writing many cookery books, he was food editor of the *New York Times* at a point when American newspapers took food more seriously than those of other English-speaking countries.

This highly popular book is a bible for cooks. It is not especially based on American food: fish dishes include examples from Denmark, Catalonia, Japan, Sweden, Mexico and Tahiti. It makes no attempt at glamour, either. The dull black-and-white photos show dull techniques, such as rolling an omelette on to a plate or filling a fish mould with salmon mousse. Another shows cream puffs in a weird table setting with white porcelain spoons hung on the wall. Yet, in a way, it is rather restful not to have to aspire to the perfect dishes served up by today's food photographers.

The binding is in textured buckram the colour of new blue jeans. Claiborne wastes no time on lengthy introductions. He does, however, quote M.F.K. Fisher (page 92), saying that if France is known for butter, Italy for olive oil and Germany for lard, then America is known for tin cans: 'Fortunately there is reason to believe that America is changing for the better.' How right he was.

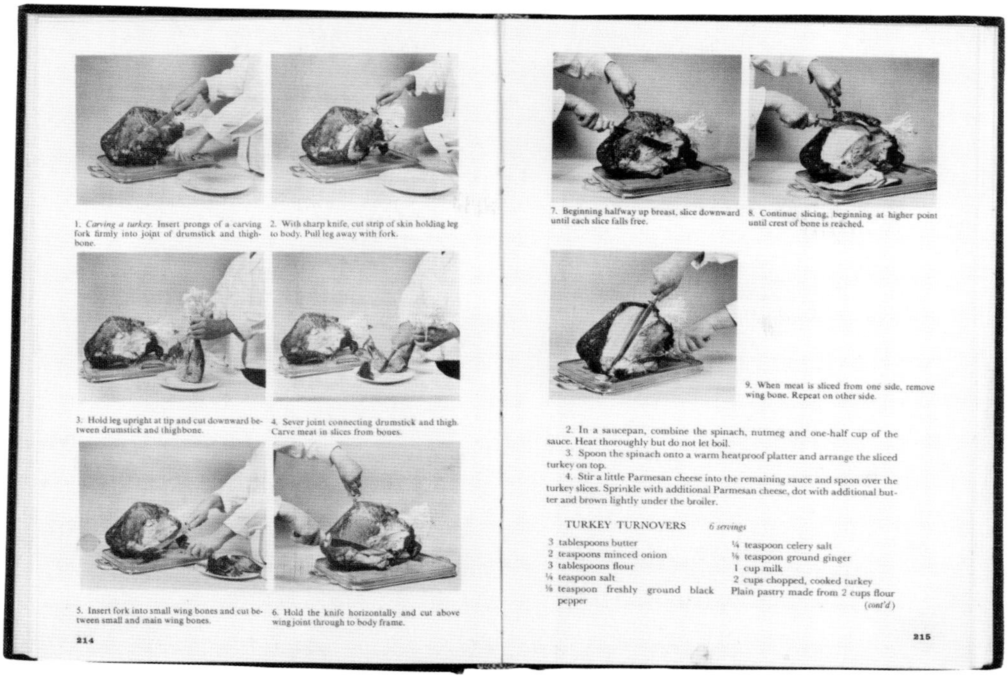

1. *Carving a turkey.* Insert prongs of a carving fork firmly into joint of drumstick and thigh-bone.

2. With sharp knife, cut strip of skin holding leg to body. Pull leg away with fork.

7. Beginning halfway up breast, slice downward until each slice falls free.

8. Continue slicing, beginning at higher point until crest of bone is reached.

3. Hold leg upright at tip and cut downward between drumstick and thighbone.

4. Sever joint connecting drumstick and thigh. Carve meat in slices from bones.

9. When meat is sliced from one side, remove wing bone. Repeat on other side.

5. Insert fork into small wing bones and cut between small and main wing bones.

6. Hold the knife horizontally and cut above wing joint through to body frame.

2. In a saucepan, combine the spinach, nutmeg and one-half cup of the sauce. Heat thoroughly but do not let boil.

3. Spoon the spinach onto a warm heatproof platter and arrange the sliced turkey on top.

4. Stir a little Parmesan cheese into the remaining sauce and spoon over the turkey slices. Sprinkle with additional Parmesan cheese, dot with additional butter and brown lightly under the broiler.

TURKEY TURNOVERS 6 servings

3 tablespoons butter	¼ teaspoon celery salt
2 teaspoons minced onion	⅛ teaspoon ground ginger
3 tablespoons flour	1 cup milk
¼ teaspoon salt	2 cups chopped, cooked turkey
⅛ teaspoon freshly ground black pepper	Plain pastry made from 2 cups flour

(cont'd)

CAKES

AMBROSIA CAKE 12 or more generous servings

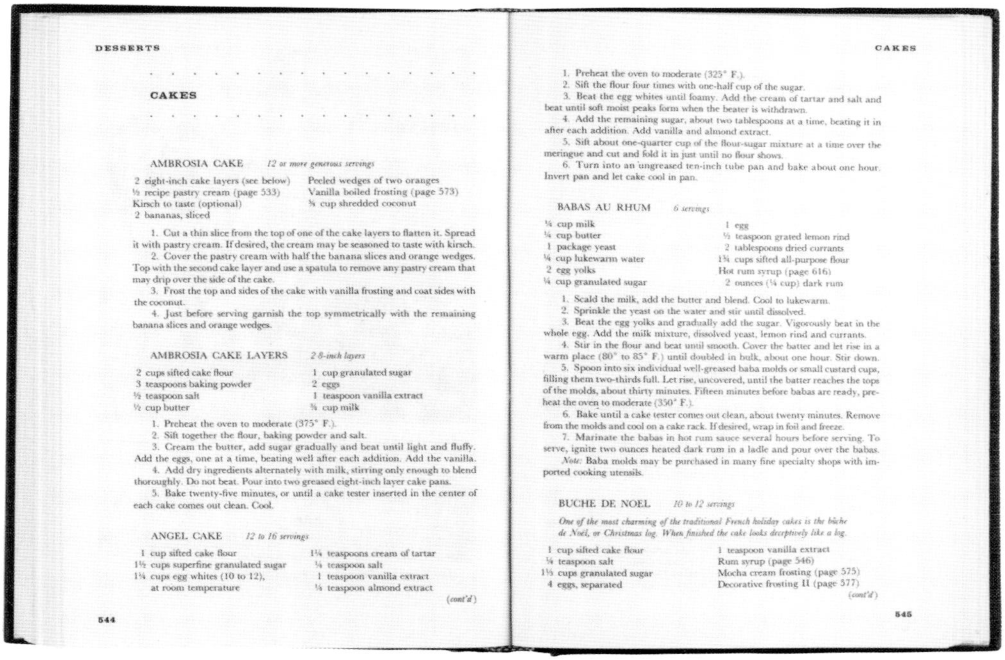

2 eight-inch cake layers (see below)	Peeled wedges of two oranges
½ recipe pastry cream (page 533)	Vanilla boiled frosting (page 573)
Kirsch to taste (optional)	¾ cup shredded coconut
2 bananas, sliced	

1. Cut a thin slice from the top of one of the cake layers to flatten it. Spread it with pastry cream. If desired, the cream may be seasoned to taste with kirsch.

2. Cover the pastry cream with half the banana slices and orange wedges. Top with the second cake layer and use a spatula to remove any pastry cream that may drip over the side of the cake.

3. Frost the top and sides of the cake with vanilla frosting and coat sides with the coconut.

4. Just before serving garnish the top symmetrically with the remaining banana slices and orange wedges.

AMBROSIA CAKE LAYERS 2 8-inch layers

2 cups sifted cake flour	1 cup granulated sugar
3 teaspoons baking powder	2 eggs
½ teaspoon salt	1 teaspoon vanilla extract
½ cup butter	¾ cup milk

1. Preheat the oven to moderate (375° F.).

2. Sift together the flour, baking powder and salt.

3. Cream the butter, add sugar gradually and beat until light and fluffy. Add the eggs, one at a time, beating well after each addition. Add the vanilla.

4. Add dry ingredients alternately with milk, stirring only enough to blend thoroughly. Do not beat. Pour into two greased eight-inch layer cake pans.

5. Bake twenty-five minutes, or until a cake tester inserted in the center of each cake comes out clean. Cool.

ANGEL CAKE 12 to 16 servings

1 cup sifted cake flour	1¼ teaspoons cream of tartar
1½ cups superfine granulated sugar	¼ teaspoon salt
1¼ cups egg whites (10 to 12), at room temperature	1 teaspoon vanilla extract
	¼ teaspoon almond extract

(cont'd)

1. Preheat the oven to moderate (325° F.).

2. Sift the flour four times with one-half cup of the sugar.

3. Beat the egg whites until foamy. Add the cream of tartar and salt and beat until soft moist peaks form when the beater is withdrawn.

4. Add the remaining sugar, about two tablespoons at a time, beating it in after each addition. Add vanilla and almond extract.

5. Sift about one-quarter cup of the flour-sugar mixture at a time over the meringue and cut and fold it in just until no flour shows.

6. Turn into an ungreased ten-inch tube pan and bake about one hour. Invert pan and let cake cool in pan.

BABAS AU RHUM 6 servings

¼ cup milk	1 egg
¼ cup butter	½ teaspoon grated lemon rind
1 package yeast	2 tablespoons dried currants
¼ cup lukewarm water	1¾ cups sifted all-purpose flour
2 egg yolks	Hot rum syrup (page 616)
¼ cup granulated sugar	2 ounces (¼ cup) dark rum

1. Scald the milk, add the butter and blend. Cool to lukewarm.

2. Sprinkle the yeast on the water and stir until dissolved.

3. Beat the egg yolks and gradually add the sugar. Vigorously beat in the whole egg. Add the milk mixture, dissolved yeast, lemon rind and currants.

4. Stir in the flour and beat until smooth. Cover the batter and let rise in a warm place (80° to 85° F.) until doubled in bulk, about one hour. Stir down.

5. Spoon into six individual well-greased baba molds or small custard cups, filling them two-thirds full. Let rise, uncovered, until the batter reaches the tops of the molds, about thirty minutes. Fifteen minutes before babas are ready, preheat the oven to moderate (350° F.).

6. Bake until a cake tester comes out clean, about twenty minutes. Remove from the molds and cool on a cake rack. If desired, wrap in foil and freeze.

7. Marinate the babas in hot rum sauce several hours before serving. To serve, ignite two ounces heated dark rum in a ladle and pour over the babas.

Note: Baba molds may be purchased in many fine specialty shops with imported cooking utensils.

BUCHE DE NOEL 10 to 12 servings

One of the most charming of the traditional French holiday cakes is the bûche de Noël, or Christmas log. When finished the cake looks deceptively like a log.

1 cup sifted cake flour	1 teaspoon vanilla extract
¼ teaspoon salt	Rum syrup (page 546)
1½ cups granulated sugar	Mocha cream frosting (page 575)
4 eggs, separated	Decorative frosting II (page 577)

(cont'd)

THE
NEW YORK
TIMES
COOK BOOK
Craig Claiborne

Harper & Row

Lady Clark

The Cookery Book of Lady Clark of Tillypronie

Edited by Catherine Frances Frere
Constable & Co., London, 1909
604 pages
212 x 135 mm (8³⁄₈ x 5³⁄₈ in.)

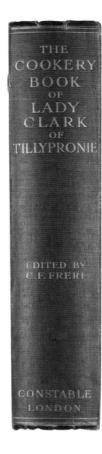

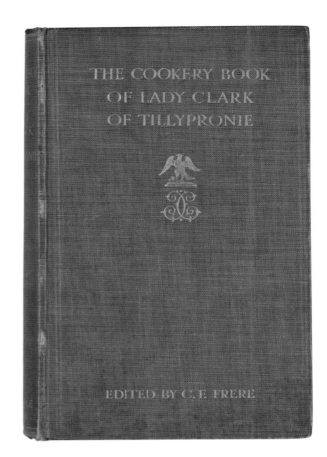

This famous book was published posthumously at the request of Lady Clark's husband. Catherine Frances Frere had to wade through notebooks and loose sheets of paper amounting to 3000 manuscripts in order to refine her recipes into this large, packed book. The index alone takes up thirty-one pages. Lady Clark, the daughter of a judge and the wife of a diplomat, travelled all over Europe – Paris, Turin, Brussels – and her recipes follow her journeys. Many are credited to servants, and many to friends: Mrs Jamieson, Edinburgh; Princess von Reuss; Mrs Hunting, New York; the Duke of Devonshire. Florence Nightingale's father provides Ginger Yeast, for breakfast buns; Sir George Birdwood, of the India Office, adds a note on Bombay Duck, 'a gelatinous and most vicious little fish'. Cooks include 'Bate', a maid in the Austrian embassy in London, and Cataldi, the Clarks' Milanese chef.

The recipes are often repeated, each containing slight variations and from a different origin. There are four for bread sauce (none of which I recognize), five for mulligatawny soup, and seven for rice pudding. And, unlike in modern recipe books, the chapters are in alphabetical order, from 'Baking Powder, Barm and Yeast' to 'Vegetables'. Unusually for the period, there is also advice from the RSPCA on the humane slaughter of animals.

Lady Clark had an extraordinary memory, a brilliant wit and as much passion for her library as for her meals. The cover, featuring her entwined initials below her husband's crest, is of fine golden-brown buckram, its colour 'taken from the tint of a beech leaf picked in autumn from the hedges in the garden at Tillypronie'.

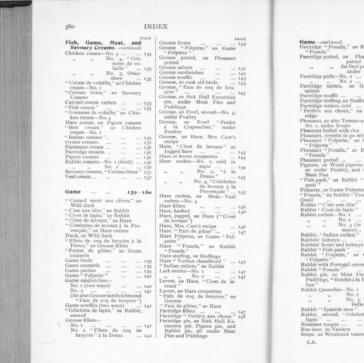

MEAT PIES, PUDDINGS AND SOUFFLES

INCLUDING SOME GAME AND POULTRY PIES AND PUDDINGS.

For other Soufflés and Pies, *see* Game.

For paste and crust for meat and game pies *see* also Paste and Pastry.

Beef and Oyster Pie, a Cornish Dish. (*Mrs. Backhouse.* 1881.)

This is merely the addition of an oyster rolled up in each little piece of beef. It gives an excellent flavour, and the oysters themselves cook most agreeably in their beef blankets.

For good crust *see* Paste and Pastry for Recipes.

The beef must be carefully trimmed from fat, which does not suit with the oysters.

Beef Pies.

N.B.—For servants' hall pies or puddings, ask for beef "skirt," as more tender than any other part, except the rump, and free from gristle. (A "skirt and kidney pie" is a favourite dish in the country.)

Beefsteak Pudding. No. 1. For Two People. (*Isa. Emslie.* 1892.)

Ingredients: The trimmings and parings of rump steak fillets. ¼ lb. suet, 2 tablespoonfuls of flour, and a pinch of salt, with enough water to mix lightly into a paste. Beat the meat well, shred a small onion fine, put it and meat in basin with a little pepper and salt, add a teacupful of stock, and put paste lid over and for one inch down sides of basin, *not more*. Tie a floured cloth over, boil 5 hours. Take off cloth and serve in the basin.

Before sending to table open the paste at the side to see if the pudding wants more hot stock added; it very rarely does.

Beefsteak Pudding. No. 2. "Our Beefsteak Pudding." (*Mrs. Sherwood.*)

1 lb. flour to ½ lb. beef or mutton suet minced fine. Mix well, and add a pinch of salt and as much cold water as is wanted to make it into a stiff paste. Roll it out and line a basin with it. Have 2½ or 3½ lbs. of tender beefsteak (a very little fat, but no skin or gristle). Cut it up neatly, and pack it in layers in the paste-lined basin with a little chopped parsley leaf and plenty of sliced onion. Season with a little pepper

and salt, add a teacupful of good stock, and dredge a small spoonful of flour over all. Cover with a paste lid, and tie tight over all a cloth floured on the inside. Boil for fully 3 or 4 hours, and serve up in the basin. Add more hot stock or hot beef gravy free from fat, at the last, as much as it will take. Ham and bacon improve the pudding.

Mrs. Wellington's beefsteak pudding is similar to above, but she always adds ham—½ lb. ham fat and lean, but no skin—to 2 lbs. steak without fat or gristle, both ham and steak cut in slices. Her paste is ½ lb. flour to 5 ozs. suet, and she fringes the inside of top of basin with it for 1½ or 2 in., no lower, "or it will suck up the gravy." She omits all onion and uses a little shallot instead, and mushroom peelings, or, failing latter, ½ teaspoonful of mushroom catsup, and adds a teacupful of good stock.

Beef and Oyster Pudding.

2 lbs. of fillet from underside of sirloin, 4 doz. oysters with their liquor, but no "beards" or horny part, a wineglassful sherry, the same of catsup, shallot and pepper to taste.

Paste same as for Beefsteak Pudding, No. 2.

"Birk Hall Excursion Pie."

A cold Game pie.

This requires 4 grouse or 6 partridge to make a very good pie. If you take grouse, use the *fillets* only, and as large as you can get without bones. Make clear or thick soup of the rest of the birds. Lay the grouse or partridge fillets in the pie-dish with a sliced onion and some chopped truffles; season, and cover with first stock; then add the paste and remember to make a hole as "chimney" in the centre of the paste under the centre ornament or "rose," to let out unwholesome steam.

For the paste take ½ lb. flour, 4 ozs. butter or some dripping, 1 egg, a little salt, and as much water as will make it into a stiff paste; work it well. Prepare the crust of this, and put it on.

Put the pie to bake in the oven. In 1½ hours the paste will be a nice brown. If it is so, the pastry is done enough, but the birds will require ½ hour's additional simmering to make them tender (*i.e.*, 2 hours in all); so cover the paste quickly with paper to prevent its catching, and if the oven bottom is cool, as it is at Birk Hall, put the pie on that, but if it is hot (as in many ovens), then put the pie on the top of the hot plate, or wherever it *is* cool, to simmer the meat the additional ½ hour. Take off the paper and replace the "rose." Serve cold for an excursion or for breakfast.

For another pie use grouse fillets and thigh only, drawing down the carcase and drumsticks with a slice of lean ham, 2 or 3 sliced onions, 1 sliced carrot, a stick of celery, a little parsley, very little pepper, *no* salt; let there be 1 pt. when strained. Put half into the dish with the fillets and a little chopped shallot, or onion if shallot cannot be got. The pastry and baking to be the same as for the Birk Hall pie, but when the pie is taken out of the oven,

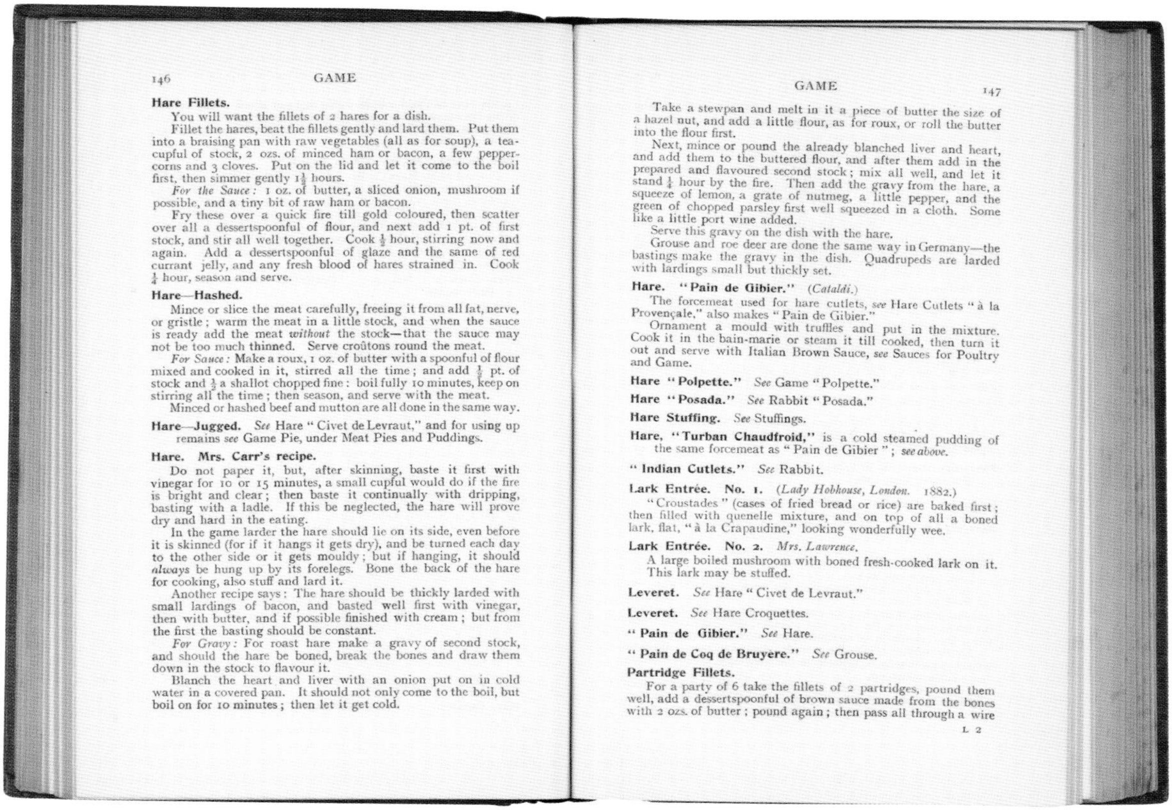

Hare Fillets.

You will want the fillets of 2 hares for a dish.

Fillet the hares, beat the fillets gently and lard them. Put them into a braising pan with raw vegetables (all as for soup), a teacupful of stock, 2 ozs. of minced ham or bacon, a few peppercorns and 3 cloves. Put on the lid and let it come to the boil first, then simmer gently 1½ hours.

For the Sauce: 1 oz. of butter, a sliced onion, mushroom if possible, and a tiny bit of raw ham or bacon.

Fry these over a quick fire till gold coloured, then scatter over all a dessertspoonful of flour, and keep over till first stock, and stir all well together. Cook ½ hour, stirring now and again. Add a dessertspoonful of glaze and the same of red currant jelly, and any fresh blood of hares strained in. Cook ¼ hour, season and serve.

Hare—Hashed.

Mince or slice the meat carefully, freeing it from all fat, nerve, or gristle; warm the meat in a little stock, and when the sauce is ready add the meat *without* the stock—that the sauce may not be too much thinned. Serve croûtons round the meat.

For Sauce: Make a roux, 1 oz. of butter with a spoonful of flour mixed and cooked in it, stirred all the time; and add ½ pt. of stock and ½ a shallot chopped fine: boil fully 10 minutes, keep on stirring all the time; then season, and serve with the meat.

Minced or hashed beef and mutton are all done in the same way.

Hare—Jugged. *See* Hare "Civet de Levraut," and for using up remains *see* Game Pie, under Meat Pies and Puddings.

Hare. Mrs. Carr's recipe.

Do not paper it, but, after skinning, baste it first with vinegar for 10 or 15 minutes, a small cupful would do if the fire is bright and clear; then baste it continually with dripping, basting with a ladle. If this be neglected, the hare will prove dry and hard in the eating.

In the game larder the hare should lie on its side, even before it is skinned (for if it hangs it gets dry), and be turned each day to the other side or it gets mouldy; but if hanging, it should *always* be hung up by its forelegs. Bone the back of the hare for cooking, also stuff and lard it.

Another recipe says: The hare should be thickly larded with small lardings of bacon, and basted well first with vinegar, then with butter, and if possible finished with cream; but from the first the basting should be constant.

For Gravy: For roast make a gravy of second stock, and should the hare be boned, break the bones and draw them down in the stock to flavour it.

Blanch the heart and liver with an onion put on in cold water in a covered pan. It should not only come to the boil, but boil on for 10 minutes; then let it get cold.

Take a stewpan and melt in it a piece of butter the size of a hazel nut, and add a little flour, as for roux, or roll the butter into the flour first.

Next, mince or pound the already blanched liver and heart, and add them to the buttered flour, and after them add in the prepared and flavoured second stock; mix all well, and let it stand ¼ hour by the fire. Then add the gravy from the hare, a squeeze of lemon, a grate of nutmeg, a little pepper, and the green of chopped parsley first well squeezed in a cloth. Some like a little port wine added.

Serve this gravy on the first dish with the hare.

Grouse and roe deer are done the same way in Germany—the bastings make the gravy in the dish. Quadrupeds are larded with lardings small but thickly set.

Hare. "Pain de Gibier." (*Cataldi.*)

The forcemeat used for hare cutlets, *see* Hare Cutlets "à la Provençale," also makes "Pain de Gibier."

Ornament a mould with truffles and put in the mixture. Cook it in the bain-marie or steam it till cooked, then turn it out and serve with Italian Brown Sauce, *see* Sauces for Poultry and Game.

Hare. "Polpette." *See* Game "Polpette."

Hare. "Posada." *See* Rabbit "Posada."

Hare Stuffing. *See* Stuffings.

Hare. "Turban Chaudfroid," is a cold steamed pudding of the same forcemeat as "Pain de Gibier"; *see above*.

"Indian Cutlets." *See* Rabbit.

Lark Entrée. No. 1. (*Lady Hobhouse, London.* 1882.)

"Croustades" (cases of fried bread or rice) are baked first; then filled with quenelle mixture, and on top of all a boned lark, flat, "à la Crapaudine," looking wonderfully wee.

Lark Entrée. No. 2. *Mrs. Lawrence.*

A large boiled mushroom with boned fresh-cooked lark on it. This lark may be stuffed.

Leveret. *See* Hare "Civet de Levraut."

Leveret. *See* Hare Croquettes.

"Pain de Gibier." *See* Hare.

"Pain de Coq de Bruyere." *See* Grouse.

Partridge Fillets.

For a party of 6 take the fillets of 2 partridges, pound them well, add a dessertspoonful of brown sauce made from the bones with 2 ozs. of butter; pound again; then pass all through a wire

L 2

Sam and Sam Clark
Moro: The Cookbook

Ebury Press, London, 2001
288 pages
251 x 188 mm (9⅞ x 7⅜ in.)

This book came out to such excellent
reviews that I bought it immediately –
and have never regretted my decision.
The husband-and-wife team of Sam and
Sam Clark spent their honeymoon driving
around Morocco and Spain in a camper van.
They first met while working in the Eagle
gastropub (see page 86) and went on,
like so many, to work at the River Café in
west London. Next came the opening of
Moro, their Moorish-ish restaurant in London,
in 1997. This, in turn, led to two awards for
best new restaurant, and, a few years later,
this publication.

One of the many things that make this
book special is its fine design, from the
endpapers showing an early map of the
Mediterranean to the Arabic characters
behind the recipe names. The photographs,
by Pia Tryde, are excellent, as is the use
of occasional archive shots of old Spain
and Morocco.

The recipes, while being exotic, are
deliberately 'simple to put together'. It's
important, the authors add, that the dishes
'should be balanced, complementary and
culturally true'. So, adjacent to the recipes
are explanations about the ingredients, such
as piquillo peppers, salt cod and chorizo.
The tapas/mezze section is inspiring, and
the vegetable dishes enlivening. Even
cauliflower, courgettes and potatoes are
improved, the first two with pine nuts and
raisins, the last with hot bravas sauce.

I met Sam and Sam when writing about
their home kitchen. It was a small corner of
Morocco in London, complete with Moorish
tiles, its very own vinegar mother and a
catering-size stove bought second-hand.

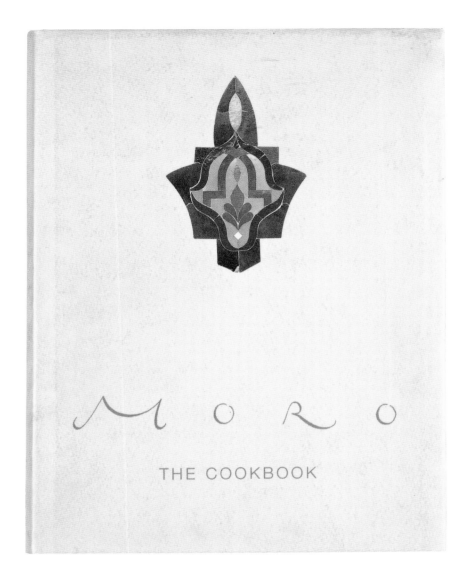

Moroccan bread

Rounds of this bread are served with some of our Moroccan recipes such as Lentil Soup with Cumin (see page 76) or mezze.

Makes 4 breads

300g unbleached strong white bread flour (preferably organic)
1 teaspoon fennel seeds
a good pinch of salt
½ teaspoon dried yeast, dissolved in 1 tablespoon warm water
¾ teaspoon runny honey
225–250ml milk
a little olive oil
1 egg yolk, mixed with 1 tablespoon milk, to glaze

Mix the flour, fennel seeds and salt in a large bowl. Add the dissolved yeast and the honey. Now pour the milk into the flour a bit at a time while mixing. We like to do this by hand, squelching out the lumps as they appear. When all the milk is added, transfer the dough to a floured surface and knead well. If it is still sticky add a little more flour; if it is still crumbly add a little more milk. Continue kneading for about 5 minutes until the dough is a little tacky, but soft, elastic and smooth. Set aside to rest for 1 hour on the floured surface covered by a cloth, until doubled in size.

Preheat the oven to 230°C/450°F/Gas 8.

Divide the dough into four, and roll into balls. On a generously floured surface with a rolling pin, gently roll each ball to approximately 1.5cm thick, making sure the shape is a rough circle about 12–15cm in diameter. Place on an oiled baking tray, and pinch your index around the centre of the bread twelve times, which looks nice and slightly restricts rising. Brush the top with the egg glaze, and bake for about 15–20 minutes or until the dough has risen slightly, is golden in colour and sounds hollow when tapped on the bottom.

TAPAS AND MEZZE

Fatayer

Fatayer are stuffed triangles of flatbread from Lebanon and Syria. The traditional fillings are spinach and labneh (yoghurt cheese). This is our version, using pumpkin, feta and pinenuts. The choice of pumpkin is key, for many can be stringy and insipid. At Moro we make these fatayer in the late summer/early autumn when pumpkins and squashes are in season. We use the Hubbard or Crown Prince varieties which are dense and sweet, but Kabouchi or Butternut work well and are more readily available. Indian/Bengali shops often have good-quality pumpkins.

Serves 4

FATAYER DOUGH

220g strong white bread flour, plus a little extra for dusting
½ teaspoon sea salt
½ teaspoon dried yeast
100ml tepid water
2 tablespoons olive oil

FILLING

800g pumpkin or squash, peeled, seeded and chopped into 5cm
    square chunks
½ garlic clove, crushed to a paste with salt
1 tablespoon olive oil
80g feta cheese, crumbled and mixed with ½ small bunch fresh
    oregano, chopped
1 tablespoon pinenuts, lightly toasted
sea salt and black pepper

To make the fatayer dough, place the flour and salt in a large mixing bowl. Dissolve the yeast in the water and then pour the oil into the water. Now pour the water into the flour a bit at a time while mixing. We like to do this by hand, squelching out the lumps as they appear. When all the water is added, transfer to a floured surface and knead well. If the dough is still sticky add a little more flour; if it is still crumbly add a little more water. Continue kneading for about 5 minutes until the dough is no longer tacky, but soft,

Sally Clarke

Sally Clarke's Book: Recipes from a Restaurant, Shop and Bakery

Macmillan, London, 1999
328 pages
245 x 188 mm (9⅝ x 7⅜ in.)

As I reread these cookery books, I see a whole network opening up. Sally Clarke, at the time an aspiring food writer, was telephoned by the great Elizabeth David (page 66) with advice. Clarke then taught at Prue Leith's cookery school. Alice Waters (page 200) of Chez Panisse, another David fan, provides the foreword to Clarke's book and is clearly a friend. Clarke copied the Chez Panisse no-choice menu with similar happy results. She is also influenced by its seasonal, simple food.

This is an inspiring book. I turn to it regularly but, reading it again, I want to rush off and cook most of the recipes. Clarke's soup of five tomatoes and three beetroots relies on having access to a vegetable garden, a good farmers' market or a wholesale supplier. Elsewhere you will need plenty of different berries, fresh courgette flowers, herbs and excellent cheeses. If you are lucky enough to have such items – all much more obtainable now than when the book was written – the recipes are simple. They need an eye for display and colour but, generally, no complex cooking skills. This is women's cookery. I like, too, her comment on the dreaded *salade niçoise* question about what to include. 'Does it really matter?' she asks. Again, a woman's point of view.

The endpapers show Clarke's forty-plus staff at her London restaurant, while the excellent photographs are by Martin Brigdale. The food is arranged by season, with plenty of advice and the sort of descriptions that make you salivate. But why no captions, and why a cream dust jacket just asking for stains?

A Book for Cooks

THYME & MALDON SALT
BREADSTICKS

Makes 24 breadsticks

300g flour
½ tsp salt
approximately 180ml warm water
10g yeast or 5g dried yeast
60ml olive oil, plus a little for brushing
2 tsp chopped thyme
Maldon salt

In a mixing bowl mix the flour and salt. In a small bowl mix half the water with the yeast and olive oil until the yeast is smooth. Pour this into the flour and mix on a slow speed with the dough-hook attachment until the dough is smooth, adding the remaining water when necessary. Alternatively the mixing can be done by hand in a medium-sized bowl and then turned out on to a clean table and kneaded for 5–10 minutes until smooth. Place the dough in a clean bowl and cover with cling film and leave in a warm place for up to 1 hour or until it has doubled in bulk. Preheat the oven to 180°C/350°F/gas mark 4.

Turn the dough out on to a board, sprinkle with the thyme and knead to expel the excess air. Cut the dough into 24 walnut-sized pieces. One at a time, roll them by hand into long thin sticks, placing them on to a well-oiled baking sheet, not touching each other. Gently brush the sticks with olive oil and sprinkle with Maldon salt. Allow to prove for 5–10 minutes in a warm, draught-free place and then bake for 12–15 minutes until crisp and golden.

Preheat the oven to 180°C/350°F/gas mark 4. Wash the pumpkin well, slice off the stalk end approximately a quarter of the way from the top, and retain it. With a strong-handled spoon scoop out the seeds. Place the pumpkin in an ovenproof serving dish just large and deep enough to hold it and to support its lower half. In a pan heat the double and single cream with the garlic, salt, pepper and rosemary. Pour into the cavity and replace the lid.

Bake it in the oven for 1–1½ hours, depending on the density of the flesh. Take it out of the oven and carefully remove the lid. The flesh should feel tender enough to scoop with a spoon. Sprinkle the Gruyère or Cheddar cheese into the cavity and reduce the oven to 160°C/325°F/gas mark 3. Return to the oven with the lid half covering the top and continue cooking for 10 minutes.

Serve at the table in 6 flat soup plates, giving each portion a scoop of the flesh and a ladleful of cream. Garnish with Parmesan shavings and sprigs of rosemary and parsley.

SPICED CORN SOUP WITH CHILIES
& CRÈME FRAICHE

60ml olive oil
2 medium onions, sliced
4 sticks celery, chopped
1 head fennel, chopped
6 heads fresh corn, kernels removed from the cobs
1 tsp salt
3 cloves garlic, chopped
1 chili, chopped
a few coriander stalks, plus 2 tbsp chopped coriander leaves

FOR THE GARNISH
2 heads corn, kernels removed
30ml olive oil
½ chili, very finely chopped
salt
1 tbsp chopped coriander leaves
120ml crème fraiche
6 coriander sprigs

In a heavy-based pan heat the olive oil with the onion, celery and fennel and stir until the vegetables start to absorb the oil. Add the corn, salt, garlic, chili, water to barely cover and coriander stalks and stir until well mixed. Bring to a boil and simmer with the lid on for 30 minutes or until the vegetables are soft. Purée in a food processor or liquidizer until smooth and push through a sieve into a clean pan. Add the chopped coriander leaves and taste for seasoning.

For the garnish, sauté the corn in a small pan with the olive oil and chili. Season with salt and add the chopped coriander. Pour the hot soup into 6 bowls and divide the corn garnish between them, piling it into the centre. Add crème fraiche and finish with a sprig of coriander.

Sir Francis Colchester-Wemyss

The Pleasures of the Table

James Nisbet & Co., London, 1931
276 pages
195 x 131 mm (7⅝ x 5⅛ in.)

This is a lovely period piece. The dust jacket explains that 'this is a *man's* cookery book, which reflects a man's own choice, taste and pleasure'. The dedication is 'To those charming young people at Cheltenham Ladies' College whose amiable reception in November 1929 of a Disquisition on Housekeeping by an Elderly Gentleman set a Ball Rolling which has reached its Goal in this Book'.

Despite being an Elderly Gentleman, Sir Francis writes clearly and prefers his food simple (even if he does call pork 'plebian'). Duck is best with young potatoes and young green peas, 'roasted with a mild stuffing inside him'. He is always dogmatic: 'Here is perhaps the moment to offer the advice not to eat lettuce salad in England or on the Continent unless in some way one knows for certain it is really clean; and never, never, never to venture on it in the East'.

There is, of course, an entire chapter on curries and another on shooting/fishing lunches, but then this is a chap's book by an author who also wrote on cricket and croquet. He goes into rhapsodies over a fishing lunch in New Zealand: 'It was a gorgeous day in February, the sun shining, not a ripple on the lake, and [Mount] Ngaurahoe, forty miles away, with her eternal little jet of smoke mirrored in the glassy water.'

The book itself is without any affectation: cream cover and wrapper, delightful typeface and not a single illustration.

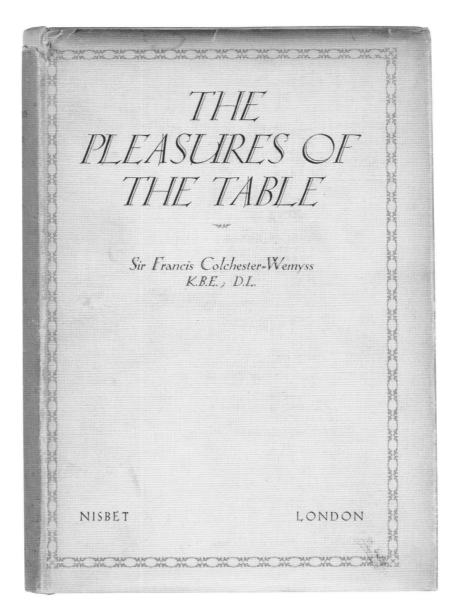

A Book for Cooks

FISH STOCK.—This is chiefly required for fish sauces, but can of course be used for making a fish soup. It is very quickly and simply made.

For 1 quart, put 2 lb. of any good white fish—sole, lemon sole, plaice or whiting for choice—into a pan with a large onion, some parsley, and three or four mushrooms, if available, all chopped, and a squeeze of lemon juice. Add a quart of cold water, and a glass of white wine, salt, and pepper. Boil gently for ½ hour, skimming very carefully. Strain and set aside for use.

The meat stocks described are all that is required to provide, with various additions, the whole range of clear soups, the consommés which appear at the beginning of good dinners all over the world.

Practically all of them are completed by the addition of one or a combination of a whole range of garnitures which include:

Thin pieces of fowl or tongue, vegetables, especially carrots, cut into small dice, diamonds, and discs.

Batter cut into strips or patterns.

Little balls of forcemeat of various kinds.

Strips of Royale. A Royale may be described as a mixture of an egg and two yolks beaten together with one or more of various ingredients—carrots and other vegetables, scraps of meat and game, foie gras or truffles, sometimes with béchamel or cream added. The mixture is cooked in a bain-marie, set to get cold, and cut into small elegant

pieces. A French restaurant chef recognises, and makes, a great variety of Royales.

Sago and tapioca. Vermicelli, and whole small cooked green peas.

Croûtons—small dice of breadcrumbs fried in deep fat till golden just before serving. These are more greatly a concomitant of a thick soup, but occasionally appear with a consommé.

Here are recipes for a selection of well-known consommés. To each should be added an appropriate spot of good pale sherry immediately before serving.

TURTLE SOUP.—For practical purposes this is made of turtle soup bought in a bottle, poured into an equal quantity of very good beef stock, simmered for ½ hour and served very hot.

CONSOMMÉ BELLE FERMIÈRE.—A strong beef consommé completed with cabbage, carrot, French beans, and batter, all cut into thin strips.

CONSOMMÉ COLBERT.—Strong fowl stock completed with fine strips of sorrel, carrot and, for each portion, one poached plover's egg; if not available, use a pigeon's or pheasant's egg.

CONSOMMÉ DEMIDOFF.—Strong poultry stock completed with small cubes of carrot, turnip, and truffle, with green peas and balls of forcemeat made with hare or other game.

CONSOMMÉ DORIA.—Strong poultry stock, finished with little balls of forcemeat made with fowl or rabbit, cubes

---

CHAPTER XIX

DINNER AT HOME

THE late Dr. Johnson is reported to have stated that a man might travel all round the world and never encounter anything more interesting than his dinner; and of the many remarks attributed to him, not one is more wise, though times and tastes have changed, and few people would now take much interest in the meals Dr. Johnson used to enjoy. When he went to a dinner party he expected something like this:

Oysters
Turtle Soup
Fried Sole—Boiled Turbot
Stewed Sweetbreads
Roast Sirloin of Beef
Roast Saddle of Mutton
Boiled Turkey
Roast Pheasant
Plum Pudding
Trifle
Cheese

Most of the guests, Dr. Johnson of course included, would go straight through the programme, turning their heads at nothing.

Everything would, no doubt, be of the best,

and in its Georgian way well cooked—the roasts of course all being actually roasted on a spit, in front of the fire.

No one nowadays wants a meal like this, but dinner is still the chief event of the day, and we owe it to ourselves to make it pleasant and appetising and satisfying, without, if we are wise, attempting the impossible.

The other meals, though just as much care should be taken in their planning and preparation, are simple and of secondary importance. At breakfast, whether we are hearty feeders or of the toast and fruit persuasion, we cheerfully endure monotony—most of us, quite contentedly, eat the same breakfast day after day, month after month.

We may occasionally sit down to a long elaborate lunch, but to do so often would not be desirable or attractive: a couple of courses, of which one at any rate is a light one, are all that most of us want—say an omelette, a slice of grilled ham, and a piece of Camembert; a half-lobster, cold or hot, and a slice of pressed beef; a sole and a cheese omelette; whitebait and a nicely cooked chop or a grilled kidney; half a grouse or partridge, and a cheese soufflé.

For those who take a sweet, stewed fruit or tart and cream, or a caramel custard might take the place of either item in any of these suggested meals, which, though very simple, are good enough for

Bruce Cost

Asian Ingredients: A Guide to the Foodstuffs of China, Japan, Korea, Thailand, and Vietnam

Quill, New York, 2000 (first published 1988)
336 pages
231 x 186 mm (9¹/₈ x 7³/₈ in.)

This book was originally published (as *Bruce Cost's Asian Ingredients*) in 1988, when, as the author says, few people knew where to find Asian ingredients or what to do with them. Today, they are in every supermarket, so this mixture of descriptions of ingredients and recipes for the dishes of China, Japan, Korea, Thailand and Vietnam is extremely useful. The foods of these five countries are becoming mainstream.

In her foreword, Alice Waters (page 200) describes Cost – a former columnist for the *San Francisco Chronicle* and a partner in the Big Bowl restaurants – as 'one of the greatest cooks I've ever known'. Which is praise indeed. I would say that this book takes a complex subject and treats it with charm and humour: knowledge worn lightly. We learn, for example, that there is only one species of coconut, and that because the nuts float they can be found on tropical beaches all over the world. Cost then gives us a recipe for Coconut 'Crème Brûlée' with added water chestnuts, which sounds delicious. I like, too, his idea of rubbing a roast chicken with dark soy sauce, giving the skin a golden sheen.

The book is a large paperback, and while lots of coloured photographs of the various ingredients would be useful, the black-and-white versions are adequate. Cost divides the chapters into classes of ingredients, such as 'Spices, Sugars, Nuts, and Seeds' and 'Noodles and Wrappers'. Curiously, there is no chapter on fruit (so the appalling durian he cooked for Waters – 'one of the most extreme things I have ever eaten' – doesn't make an appearance).

"Bruce Cost is one of the greatest cooks I've ever known. . . . He truly demystifies many previously forbidding and odd ingredients."—Alice Waters

A Book for Cooks

shoots may be stored for up to two weeks in the refrigerator in a water-filled container if the water is changed every two days.

RECOMMENDED: Ma Ling, from China, available in 16-ounce cans. Companion brand Winter Bamboo Shoots, and Giant Bamboo Shoots.

The Cabbage Family

Cabbages, referred to sometimes as "Brassicas," their family name, take up the lion's share of space on most Asian produce stands. They include various bok choys, celery cabbages, mustard cabbages, and Chinese broccoli, and the similarity in appearance of many of them—various bunches of stems and leaves with white or yellow flowers—is confusing to non-Asians. Over a dozen varieties are grown (mainly in California and Florida) and sold in the United States.

This, however, is a paltry selection compared to the variations available in Asia. The famed Cornell University botanist L. H. Bailey, who authored two volumes on the cultivated Brassicas, encountered hundreds of varieties of these plants and wrote: "The Brassica group is indeed perplexing, . . . the most bewildering I have attempted."

This family of plants, particularly the bok choys, are by far the most popular leafy vegetables in China and Southeast Asia. It's probable that they were first cultivated for the edible oil in their seeds—the mustards being the earliest—and once cultivated, they were cooked and enjoyed, or at the least, their rich nutritional value was immediately appreciated.

Bok Choy (Brassica chinensis)

Other names:
Chinese white
cabbage

Region of use:
China, Southeast
Asia

Hong Kong farmers alone grow over twenty kinds of bok choy—"horse's tail" bok choy, "horse's ear" bok choy, "soup spoon" bok choy, and so on—of which four or five kinds are regularly available here and are described below. The vegetable we call simply *bok choy*, with its snow-white stalks, slightly bulbous base, and dark green leaves, is, along with *bok choy sum* (see next page) and the celery cabbages, one of the most popular and well-known Chinese leafy vegetables.

Available all year, bok choy is a versatile vegetable that may be simply cut up and cooked, leaves and all; or it's a good foil for stir-fried meats and seafood and is popular when combined this way in noodle dishes. Its stalk has a mild, refreshing flavor, and the leaves are pleasantly tangy and bitter.

Bok Choy Sum or "Choy Sum"

Other names:
Flowering bok choy,
Flowering white
cabbage, Flowering
cabbage, Bok choy

Region of use:
China, Southeast
Asia

Almost identical to bok choy in appearance, *bok choy sum* can be distinguished by its yellow flowers. (The Cantonese *sum* means "younger and flowering" when applied to vegetables; literally it means "heart.") It's also slightly smaller, with narrower stalks and green leaves a shade lighter. Cooked exactly like bok choy, flowers and all, it's at least as popular and commands a slightly higher price. Ask for "choy sum," although some Hong Kong dealers might give you *yow choy* (see page 41).

"Baby" Bok Choy Sum or "Short Legs" Choy Sum. Increasingly available, this is simply a miniature bok choy sum. The advantage of it is that its stalks, with their leaves and flowers, can be cooked whole, which makes for an attractive presentation.

Shanghai Bok Choy

Other names:
Green stem bok choy,
Blue River (Yangtse)
bok choy

Region of use:
China

The leaves of this vegetable are spoon-shaped and the stems are flatter than regular bok choy; leaves and stem are the same light green. Although it grows to a foot or more in height, it's often harvested as a baby plant of 6 inches or less and sold four or five plants to the bunch. This plant is delicious when cooked like bok choy, but it's at its best when just the hearts of the baby vegetables, after a layer or so of outer leaves are stripped away, are stir-fried or steamed briefly. Cooked whole or cut in half lengthwise, the brilliant green of the cooked hearts makes an attractive adornment to a red-cooked meat dish, such as Braised Yangchow Pork and Pine Nut Cake (page 243), or they may be cooked and served by themselves. Shanghai bok choy is available, with occasional lapses, year-round.

*Clockwise from left: Shanghai bok choy,
bok choy, bok choy leaf*

Shredded Pork Stomach and Cucumber Salad with Sesame Dressing

I found this dish by pointing at random to an item in the Chinese part of a dual-language menu at a small restaurant in San Francisco's Chinatown. With its mustard and sesame paste combination, this is a Beijing specialty, rare among the predominantly Cantonese dishes enjoyed in that community. If you've never tried pork stomach, this is a tasty introduction.

Yield: 8 servings

2 pigs' stomachs (about 1 ½ pounds total)
Salt
¼ cup Shaoxing wine
5 thick slices fresh ginger
2 teaspoons powdered mustard
2 tablespoons sesame seed paste
3 tablespoons brewed tea
2 tablespoons light soy sauce
½ teaspoon salt
2 teaspoons sugar
2 tablespoons white rice vinegar
1 teaspoon minced garlic
1 tablespoon sesame oil
2 teaspoons chili oil
½ cucumber, peeled, seeded, and sliced
½ cup coriander leaves

Remove any excess membrane or fat from the stomach lining, rub with coarse salt, and rinse. Simmer in lightly salted water for 5 minutes. Drain, then simmer in new water with the wine and ginger slices for 1 ½ hours, or until tender.

Meanwhile, prepare the sauce: Mix the mustard powder with 2 teaspoons water and let stand for 15 minutes. Stir the tea into the sesame paste until well blended, then stir in the soy sauce, salt, sugar, vinegar, garlic, and oils. After the mustard is set, stir it in.

When the stomachs are done, drain them. When cool enough to handle, slice them thinly. Toss with the mustard-sesame sauce, the cucumber, and the coriander, and serve.

Barbecued Pigs' Tails in Five-Spice Marinade

These are quite tasty and easy to do. If left whole—which is easier for grilling—it's the presentation that's problematical. The 5-inch tail itself can be thought of as a handle to hold on to while you gnaw at the morsels along the section of spinal column it's attached to. For oven roasting, have the butcher cut up the tails.

Yield: 4 to 6 servings

8 pigs' tails (cut up for roasting, left whole for grilling)
3 tablespoons white rice vinegar (5 tablespoons for grilling)
¼ cup light soy sauce
¼ cup hoisin sauce
4 teaspoons red bean curd "cheese" (see page 193)
1 teaspoon five spice powder (see page 220)
2⅔ tablespoons sugar
4 teaspoons bean sauce

TO ROAST: Preheat the oven to 350°F. Score the skin twice lengthwise along each tail part. Put all the meat in a pot with water to cover. Bring to a boil, reduce the heat to medium, and simmer for 5 minutes. Then drain and dry the pieces.

Mix 3 tablespoons vinegar with the light soy sauce, hoisin sauce, red bean curd, five spices, sugar, and bean sauce. Smear the mixture all over the pieces of meat, and spread them out on a foil-lined baking sheet. Bake for 40 minutes. Turn the pieces, brush them with more sauce, and cook for another 20 minutes. Allow the meat to sit for 6 to 7 minutes before eating.

TO GRILL: Score the skin twice along each tail part. Put the tails in a pot with water to cover and bring to a boil. Reduce the heat to medium, add 2 tablespoons vinegar, and simmer uncovered for 45 minutes.

Meanwhile, mix 3 tablespoons vinegar with the light soy sauce, hoisin sauce, red bean curd, five spices, sugar, and bean sauce. Start your charcoal fire.

When the meat is done, drain the pieces, dry them, and smear them with the sauce. Grill over a medium fire, turning the pieces, for 10 to 15 minutes. Baste once. Allow to sit 6 to 7 minutes before eating.

NOTE: For a simpler method, after simmering, dry the pieces and toss them in some dark soy sauce, salt, and pepper before roasting or grilling.

Margaret Costa

Four Seasons Cookery Book

Sphere, London, 1972
(first published 1970)
378 pages
196 x 128 mm (7¾ x 5 in.)

Margaret Costa apparently bribed her mother to teach her how to cook when she was only six. The rest of her life, until her death in 1999 aged eighty-one, was filled with cooking and, sadly, disappointments. Although she was a prolific writer, contributing to *Farmer and Stockbreeder*, the *Sunday Times* and *Gourmet*, this was her only book. In her obituary in *The Guardian* (13 August 1999), Nigel Slater (page 188) notes that she can probably be credited with introducing the British public to garlic butter, mayonnaise and olives. Describing salads, Costa says: 'As for the faint-hearted measure of rubbing a salad bowl with a cut clove of garlic – to those of us who appreciate the flavour of garlic, it is an ignoble compromise, and one that in any case will get you nowhere.' The whole book is studded with such comments.

Costa was married three times: first, to a man who would eat only English food; next, to one who preferred French; and finally, to a chef, Bill Lacy, which must have been a relief. In 1970 Lacy and she opened Lacy's, a wildly popular restaurant in central London that eventually fell on hard times and closed. The couple lost most of their money and, at one stage, had to live in their car.

Even so, many (including me) have a tattered and food-stained copy of Costa's book, which attests to its success. Mine is a scuffed paperback with an unlikely Brueghel on the cover and pleasant black-and-white drawings by John Tribe. It was republished in 1996 by Grub Street.

Spring

Pancakes · Easter Teas · Omelettes
Fish Soups · Scallops · Salmon
Pigeons · Lamb
New Potatoes · Sorrel · Asparagus
Salt, Pepper and Mustard
Rhubarb and Green Gooseberries
Pieces of Cake · Part-time Preserves
Cooking with Liqueurs

Summer

Cold Soups · Summer Starters
Crab · Trout and Mackerel
Salad Dressings · Salad Vegetables Hot and Cold
Chicken, Duck and a Small Turkey
Cooking with Cream
Peaches · Strawberries and Other Summer Fruits
Custard Cup Sweets · Ices and Sorbets
Mixed Fruit Jams · Herbs

Autumn

Mushrooms · Olives
Pizza and Savoury Pies
Awful Offal · Game
Mixed Vegetable Dishes
Soufflés · Apples · Plums and Pears
Tea-Breads and Family Cakes
Nuts · Chutneys and Relishes
Cooking with Brandy

Winter

Christmas Classics · Party Pieces
Comforting Breakfasts · Winter Soups
Sardines and an Anchovy · Mussels
Cooking with Wine · Proper Puddings
Baking with Yeast
Marmalade · Spices
Winter Vegetables
Comforting Casseroles

---

218   SOUFFLÉS

Beat the yolks until thick and lemon-coloured. Gradually beat in half the
sugar and add the lemon juice and the grated rind. Lightly fold in the egg
whites, beaten up stiffly with the rest of the sugar. Bake for 40 minutes in a
moderate oven, Mark 4, 350°F.

Serve with an orange compôte: cut up the oranges into little chunks, free
of pith and membrane, and pour over them a syrup made by melting the
granulated sugar in ⅓ cup water and simmering it gently for about 10
minutes. Lace with an orange-flavoured liqueur if you can. And if you have
time, cook 2 tablespoons of very thin slivers of orange rind in the syrup.

CHOCOLATE SOUFFLÉ

3½–4 oz bitter or plain chocolate;
2 tablespoons rum, brandy or strong black coffee;
2 oz caster sugar, vanilla-flavoured if possible; 4 egg yolks;
6 egg whites; icing sugar and cream, to serve.

Melt the broken-up chocolate in the top of a double boiler or in a very heavy
pan with the brandy, rum or coffee and the sugar. When quite melted, beat
until smooth, then stir in the well-beaten egg yolks. Fold in the stiffly beaten
whites, turn into a 2 pint soufflé dish and bake at Mark 6, 400°F., for just
under 30 minutes. Dust with icing sugar and serve immediately with thin,
fresh, cold cream.

APRICOT SOUFFLÉ

4 oz dried apricots; 2 tablespoons vanilla sugar;
2 tablespoons Grand Marnier, Cointreau or other orange-
flavoured liqueur; grated rind of ⅓ orange; 3 egg whites;
butter and sugar, for soufflé dish.

Soak the apricots overnight or for at least several hours in enough water to
cover them. Stew with the vanilla sugar in a moderate oven, Mark 4, 350°F.,
for about 40 minutes, or until tender. Drain well and put the fruit through a
sieve or an electric blender with the liqueur. Stir in the orange rind. Whip up
the egg whites stiffly and fold them gently into the apricot purée. Turn into a
buttered and sugared 1½ pint soufflé dish and bake for about 20 minutes at
Mark 6, 400°F. Serve at once.

Apples

'Every millionaire,' according to Ronald Firbank, 'loves a baked apple.'
Perhaps it would be a good idea to try something richer, sweeter and more
likely to be appreciated by those not yet accustomed to the austerity of
extreme wealth.

DANISH APPLE CAKE

About ¾ pint coarse white breadcrumbs; 3½ oz butter;
1½ lb cooking apples; 3 oz sugar; grated rind of ½ lemon;
redcurrant jelly or raspberry jam; icing sugar.

Pull day-old bread apart into coarse crumbs, grate it, or make the crumbs
in the electric blender. If they are very fresh and absorbent, dry them out in
the oven. Fry them in 3 oz of the butter until golden brown and really
crisp.

Peel, core and slice the apples, and cook them in a heavy pan with the
sugar, the lemon rind and the rest of the butter – no water – until soft.
Crush to a pulp with a silver fork, and dry out over a low heat if necessary;
the apple purée must not be too wet.

Put a thin layer of jelly or jam in the bottom of a soufflé dish or a glass
bowl. Cover with a layer of crumbs, then with half the apple purée, another
layer of jelly and more crumbs. Finish with a dusting of icing sugar and a

Culinaria Spain

Edited by Marion Trutter
Könemann, Königswinter, 2004
488 pages
310 x 265 mm (12¼ x 10⅜ in.)

Culinaria is a series of books that combine information about a national cuisine with travel photography and essays on the production of typical foods. Other countries in the series include France and the United States. The books are comprehensive and, I believe, the best way to get an overall view of a nation's food from a single volume. They are inspiring and fun, and, if your kitchen table is strong enough to hold a book the size and weight of a family Bible, work as recipe books, too.

Culinaria Spain is divided into regions, a sensible arrangement because each has a distinct character. As editor Marion Trutter writes, the large range of climates in Spain 'is a sure sign that this country has more than just one unified culinary tradition: the cool, damp northwest produces a very different harvest from the constantly mild Mediterranean'. Several authors contribute to the text, while the principal photographer, Günter Beer, is used throughout. This, together with firm art direction from Peter Feierabend, gives the whole cohesion.

The photographs of market stalls straining under the weight of crustaceans, the freshest vegetables and *jamón* remind me of a visit to a Barcelona market where I lusted after a *pata negra* ham (too big for

hand luggage). A section on Iberian pigs includes images of their wooded pastureland, the *dehesa*, and a description of how the ham is cured and carved. This is more than a recipe book or travelogue. It explains, it gets the juices going, it makes you want to go back.

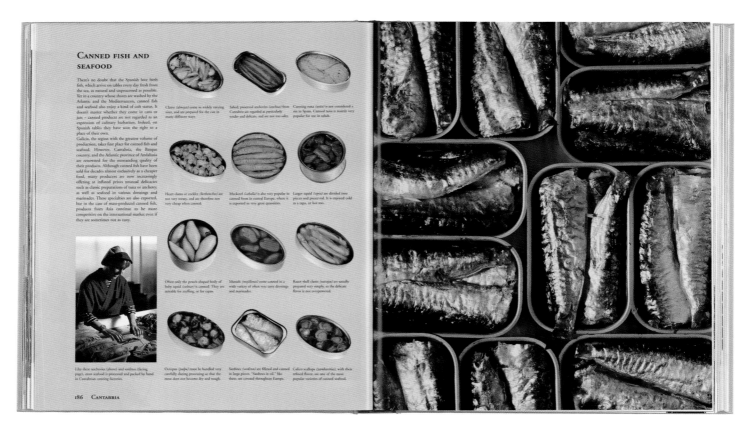

Rice for every day

Arròs a banda
Rice with fish

4½ lbs/2 kg ready-prepared mixed fish,
e.g. red mullet, monkfish, or ray
Salt and pepper
Juice of 1 lemon
1 onion, spiked with a bay leaf and
2 cloves
3 tbsp olive oil
2 cloves of garlic, diced
2 cups/400 g round-grain rice
½ envelope of saffron
½ tsp mild paprika

Wash and pat the fish dry. Cut it up into reasonable size pieces, rub in salt and pepper, and squeeze over the lemon juice. Leave to marinate for 10 minutes.
Meanwhile bring 4 cups/1 liter water to a boil in a pan with the spiked onion. Put the fish in the pan, reduce the heat, and simmer for 15-20 minutes. Then remove the fish from the stock and keep warm.
Heat the olive oil in a deep pan and brown the garlic and rice. Pour in the fish stock and season with saffron, paprika, salt, and pepper. Simmer for about 20 minutes, until the rice has absorbed all the liquid. Traditionally, the rice is served first, and then the fish, accompanied with *alioli* (see recipe page 17).

Arrós negre
Black rice
(Photograph below)

2¼ lbs/1 kg small fresh squid
Salt
½ cup/125 ml olive oil
1 large red bell pepper, sliced
1 clove of garlic, diced
2 ripe tomatoes, skinned and diced
Juice of 1 lemon
2 tbsp chopped parsley
2 cups/400 g round-grain rice
½ cup/125 ml white wine
Pepper

Carefully remove the ink sac from the squid and set it aside. Clean the squid (follow detailed directions on page 375) and boil in salted water for 10 minutes.
Heat 2 tbsp oil in a pan and fry the bell pepper on a gentle heat. Dice the pepper together with the oil, garlic, tomatoes, lemon juice, and parsley in a food processor.
Heat the remaining oil in a pan. Stir in the pepper mixture and then stir the rice in. Pour on 3 cups/750 ml water and bring everything to a boil.
Meanwhile empty the ink sac and mix the ink with the white wine. Pour it through a strainer onto the rice. Then mix in the squid. Season with salt and pepper and cook for 15–20 minutes. Serve with *alioli* (recipe page 17).

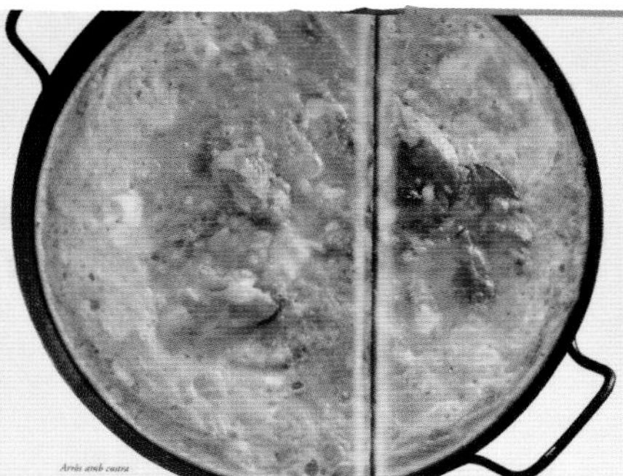

Arròs amb crosta

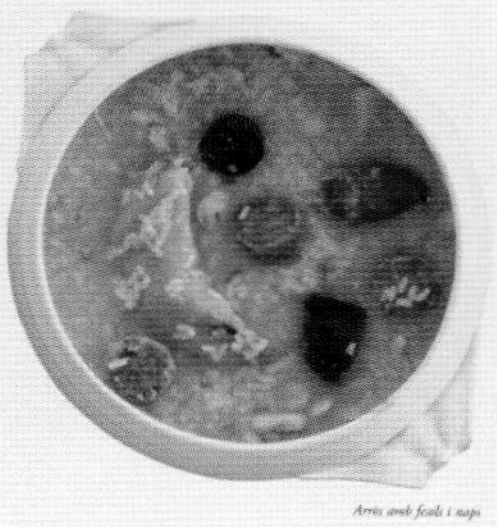

Arròs amb fesols i naps

Below: *arròs negre*

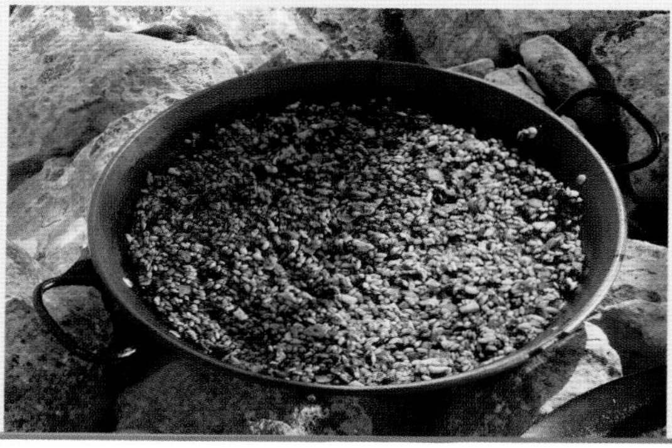

Arròs amb crosta
Rice with a crust (photograph above)

Scant ½ cup/100 g chickpeas
2 cloves of garlic, diced
1 small onion, finely diced
1 bay leaf
1 chicken, cut into 8 portions
5¼ oz/150 g Valencian blood sausage
3 tbsp olive oil
3½ oz/100 g smoked ham cubes
2 cups/400 g rice
Salt and pepper
½ tsp mild paprika
½ envelope of saffron powder
2 eggs
2 tbsp breadcrumbs

Soak the chickpeas overnight. Next day bring them to a boil in a good 6 cups/1.5 liters water with the garlic, onion, and bay leaf. Add the chicken portions and blood sausage; simmer until tender. Take out the chicken portions and blood sausage; discard the bay leaf. Drain the chickpeas, keeping the water. Heat the olive oil in a flameproof casserole and sweat the rice and ham until translucent. Pour in 4 cups/1 liter stock from the chickpeas and season with salt, pepper, paprika, and saffron. Boil for 10 minutes. Slice the blood sausage. Mix the blood sausage and chicken portions into the rice and simmer for another 5 minutes. Beat the eggs and pour over the rice. Sprinkle with the breadcrumbs and then bake in a preheated oven at 435 °F/225 °C until golden brown.

Arròs amb fesols i naps
Rice with navy beans and rutabaga
(Photograph above)

¾ cup/200 g dried navy beans
2 onions, roughly diced
1 pig trotter
9 oz/250 g veal
7 oz/200 g smoked bacon in a piece
Salt and pepper
2 black Valencian blood sausages (negrets)
2 white Valencian blood sausages (blanquets)
4 small rutabagas, peeled and diced
1 cup/250 g round-grain rice
½ envelope of saffron

Soak the beans in cold water overnight. The following day bring the beans to a boil in a good 6 cups/1.5 liters salted water with the onions, pig trotter, veal, and bacon and simmer for 30 minutes. Then add the blood sausages and rutabaga, and simmer for another 30 minutes. Take the pig trotter, veal, bacon, and blood sausages out of the stock. Remove the pork from the bone. Keep everything warm.
Put the rice in the stock and season with saffron, salt, and pepper. Cook for approximately 15 minutes. Meanwhile cut the meat, bacon, and blood sausages into small pieces. Shortly before the end of the cooking time mix the meat into the rice.

Fideua

It does not always have to be rice that is cooked in Valencia's paella pans. *Fideuá* is a type of paella with noodles, and the cooking-crazy Valencians like to disagree as to how the dish actually came about.
In the harbor area of Gandía they insist that fishermen from the village had the idea when they had no rice onboard their cutter. Wanting to eat the fish that they had caught, after the catch they found only noodles in the galley.
In the hinterland, on the other hand, it is said that hungry hikers resorted to noodles because they had left the rice for a proper paella at home.
What is, however, certain is that, like paella, the preparation requires a certain skill to get the paella just right. The proportions of the ingredients and the amount of heat must be correct. There is now even a *Concurso de la Fideuá* which takes place annually in Gandía. Foreign cooks now come to Spain to take part in this competition – and are more than able to hold their own against the Valencians.

Fideua
Valencian noodle paella

Generous 2 lbs/1 kg fish scraps
1 onion, spiked with 1 bay leaf and 1 clove
Salt and pepper
5 black peppercorns
4 tbsp olive oil
2 onions, diced
2 cloves of garlic, diced
1 ripe tomato, skinned and diced
14 oz/400 g monkfish fillet
1 tsp mild paprika
1 tbsp chopped parsley
14 oz/400 g fideos *(short noodles)*
4 langoustines
8 shrimp

Make a rich fish stock out of the fish scraps, 6 cups/1.5 liters water, the spiked onion, salt, and peppercorns.
Heat 2 tbsp oil in a paella pan and sweat the onion and garlic until translucent. Then add the tomatoes and pour in 3¼ cups/800 ml fish stock. Bring to a boil and add the fish. Season with paprika and parsley. Stir in the noodles and then season with salt and pepper. Simmer until the stock has almost all boiled away.
Meanwhile fry the Norway lobsters and shrimp in the remaining oil.
Arrange the seafood over the noodles and finally cook for another 5 minutes in a preheated oven at 345 °F/175 °C.

Saffron

The Greeks of antiquity used saffron as a cosmetic for their beautiful women. The Emperor Nero had the streets of Rome covered with the golden threads before he rode into the city. Wealthy Romans drank a saffron broth at their orgies, so that they could devote themselves more energetically to the service of Venus, the goddess of love. And saffron also gives fabrics a color which ranges from yellow to a deep gold. It was a prized material for the veils of Phoenician brides, and after the death of the Buddha his priests approved the noble spice as the dye for coloring their robes. Saffron has always been one of the world's most valuable products, with a price which could sometimes be higher than that of gold.
Crocus sativus is the name botanists give to this treasure. This type of crocus originally came from Asia Minor, where it has been cultivated since ancient times. The Arabs brought the spice *az-zafaran* (literally, "yellow") to Spain during their tempestuous drive west over a thousand years ago, and today over 70 percent of the world's production is grown on the high Castilian plateau. The miracle happens each year in October. The crocus flowers open up in the dark, and the red light of dawn shines on a purple carpet, the *manto*. From Toledo to Albacete, pure chaos reigns. Safran *(azafrán)* must be gathered within a day. Otherwise, the valuable threads lose their flavor. The harvest period lasts scarcely ten days. The farmers pluck the flowers between their index fingers and thumbs. The women sit at long tables and separate out the reddish stigma with practiced skill, their fingers moving as fast as lightning. Finally, the stigma is roasted on a sieve. In earlier times, this was done over charcoal. Nowadays, gas burners tend to be used. About 200 crocus flowers are needed to obtain a single gram of saffron, and the average harvest obtained by a family enterprise is around 8 Castilian pounds (a Castilian pound equals 460 grams, approximately 1 pound, avoirdupois weight). Since time immemorial, the "red gold of La Mancha," dried and preserved in the closet between layered sheets, has acted as a savings bank for the farming families. Saffron was once accepted as a currency, and even today the Spanish expression for bartering is "to pay in *especie*" ("spice").
The saffron harvest has always brought life to the sleepy, dazzlingly white villages of La Mancha. In the old days, helping out with the harvest was a good opportunity for a young man to visit the home of a farmer's daughter he loved. Perhaps he could steal a kiss unnoticed during the bustle of the harvest. (After all, from olden times love has been connected with the valuable plant: in a Roman fable, a lovesick youth called Crocus is turned into a flower.) The "Saffron Rose Festival" *(Fiesta de la Rosa del Azafrán)* is the highpoint of the year in Consuegra. On the last Sunday in October, at the foot of the white windmills against which Don Quixote once battled, the farmers celebrate with music and dancing, and choose the most captivating local beauty to be crowned as *Dulcinea de La Mancha* in honor of the beloved Don Quixote.

How to handle the noble threads

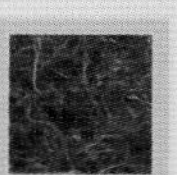

The aroma of saffron is strong, but difficult to define. It has little in common with the unobtrusive perfume of the crocus flower, and even the scent of a roasting stigma is beguiling. Nowadays it is mainly the Italian risotto milanese and the Spanish paella which are colored with saffron. Cheaper substitutes suffice for the color, but those who are in search of the unique taste will not be able to do without the expensive original. For only saffron contains the carotenoids and ethereal oils which create the mysterious aroma, but which can also become bitter in excessive doses. Once roasted, it can be kept for a long time. It should be stored in a dry place away from the light, and for the finest flavor it should be consumed within two to three years. Anyone using the valuable threads in cooking has to be careful. They develop their taste only in hot dishes – but adding them directly to a hot mixture that is already cooked destroys their effect. The threads are crushed between the fingers or in a mortar and are then softened in a little water. A little melted butter fixes the flavor. Crushed saffron can also be stirred into yogurt and can thus be added to a sauce. In cooking, an envelope of powder weighing less than half an ounce (12.5 grams) or a few threads are enough for four to six portions.

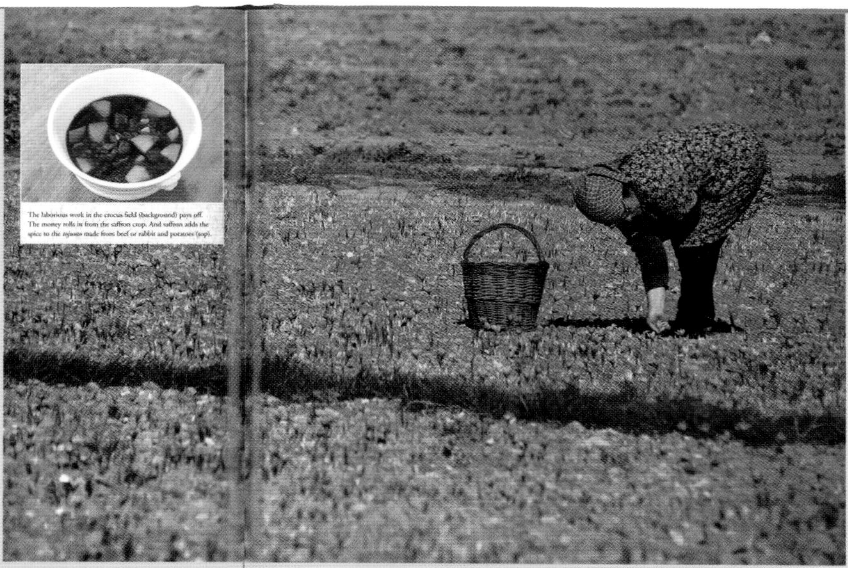

The laborious work in the crocus field (background) pays off. The money rolls in from the saffron crop. And saffron adds the spice to the *tojunto* made from beef or rabbit and potatoes (top).

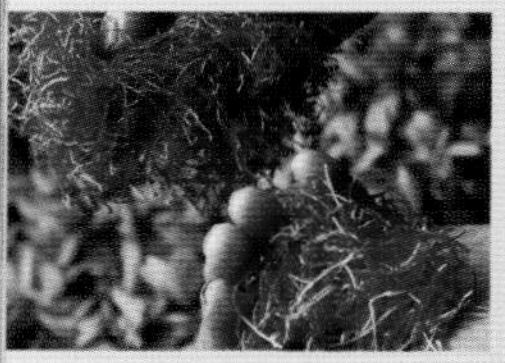

The fresh stigma of the saffron crocus flower (bottom) perishes quickly. If the saffron is to be used as a spice (top), it must be first dried over a fire.

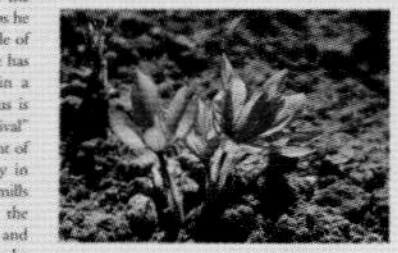

Crocus sativus grows wild on poor soils. The saffron extracted from its stigma has been much sought for thousands of years as a dye, a medicine, and also a spice.

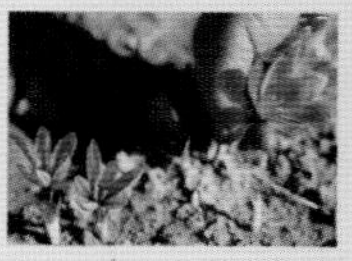

The saffron crocuses are harvested in October. The farmers go out into the fields and use their thumbs and index fingers to pick thousands of flowers.

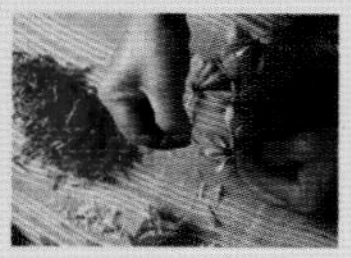

Women pull the reddish threads from the stigma of each individual flower. Around 200 crocus flowers are needed to obtain a single gram of saffron (0.035 oz).

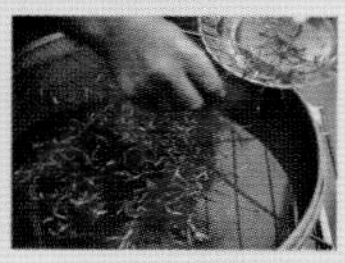

The fresh saffron threads are roasted in a sieve. In earlier times, there was usually a wood or charcoal fire burning underneath. Nowadays, it might also be a gas burner.

Felicity and Roald Dahl
Roald Dahl's Cookbook

Penguin, London, 1996 (first published 1991)
239 pages
245 x 189 mm (9⅝ x 7½ in.)

Food makes a good background to a family saga, and this book, co-authored by Roald Dahl's second wife, tells us a lot about the Dahl family (although to call it an autobiography would be wrong). It starts with a family tree, drawn by illustrator Quentin Blake in his inimitable style. We meet Roald's three sisters, Alfhild, Else and Asta, and his father-in-law, known as 'Pon'. The book's photographer, Jan Baldwin, whose images include much more than food, is celebrated as a tripod-mounted camera. Josie, the cook, appears as a basket of fruit.

I love this book (first published in 1991 as *Memories with Food at Gipsy House*), and children will too: it is slightly threatening. Blake's recipe for Savoury Crocodile consists of a baguette stuffed with 'succulent children (or equivalent as available)' to send shivers down tiny spines. A selection of 'last suppers' reveals what the famous would eat if they were about to be executed. John le Carré opts for nursery food, roast lamb and bread-and-butter pudding 'served by a very young, very pretty nanny'.

Most of the recipes are from family and friends: blackberry meringue from Josie, Else's casseroled ptarmigan, Lou's Norwegian fish pudding. Mr Wells, Felicity's father's First World War batman, photographed with waistcoat and watch chain, contributes cucumber and beetroot salads.

Baldwin's photographs reveal life as it was at Gipsy House – the Dahl family home in Great Missenden, Buckinghamshire – prior to Roald's death in 1990: the author writing on his yellow notepads, clutching his Jack Russell, with grandson Luke and crocodile of food. 'His family meant everything to him', says Felicity.

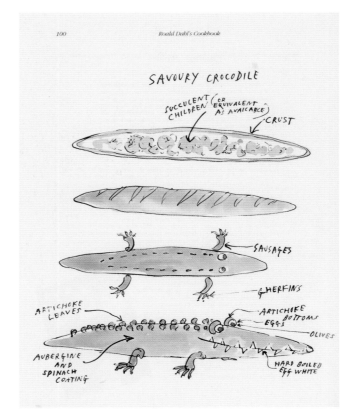

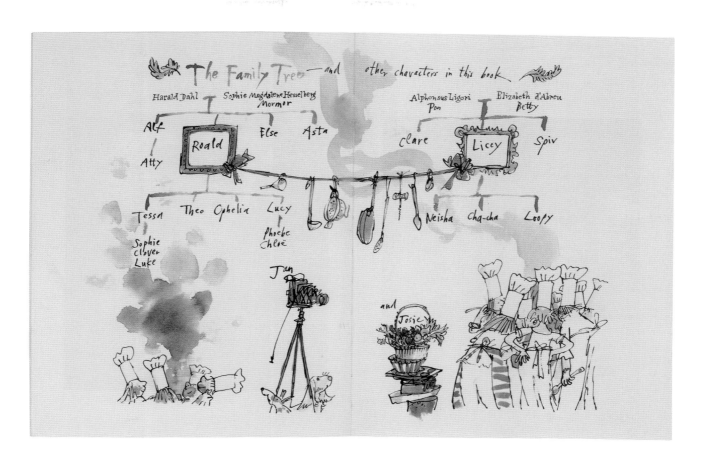

The Family Tree — and other characters in this book

Harald Dahl — Sophie Magdalene Hesselberg
Mormor

Alphonsus Ligori — Elizabeth d'Abreu
Pon   Betty

Alf   Roald   Else   Asta

Atty

Clare   Liccy   Spiv

Tessa   Theo   Ophelia   Lucy

Phoebe
Chloë

Neisha   Cha-cha   Loopy

Sophie
Clover
Luke

Jan

and
Josie

156   *Roald Dahl's Cookbook*

Chocolate St Emilion

Puddings   157

Chocolate St Emilion

Use the best-quality chocolate you can find.

Serves 8

8 oz Amaretti, crushed
2–3 fl oz Cointreau
1 lb Menier chocolate
4 oz butter
2 egg yolks
1 pt double cream

DECORATION
icing sugar

1. Soak the crushed Amaretti in the Cointreau.
2. Melt the chocolate in a *bain-marie*.
3. Remove from the heat and gradually beat in butter and egg yolks. Leave the mixture to cool.
4. Whip the cream until semi-stiff.
5. Gently fold the cream into the chocolate mixture.
6. Place in a lightly greased cake tin (8-in. diameter × 2¼-in. deep) alternate layers of chocolate mixture and Amaretti.
7. Chill for a couple of hours or until set.
8. To decorate, place either a paper doiley or a stencil on to the cake and dust with some icing sugar in a fine sieve. Whatever you use, make sure you can remove it easily without disturbing your design!

Capri Chocolate Cake

LD. When my three daughters entered their teens and life became more sophisticated, this cake became their favourite and they insisted on having it for their birthdays. The recipe was given to me by a large Italian mama at the kitchen door of an hotel in Capri. She spoke no English, I no Italian, but somehow I got it right and it always seems to work. Make the cake the day before, but top it with whipped cream and grated chocolate just before serving.

Serves 10

9 oz sugar
9 oz butter
5 eggs, separated
9 oz ground almonds
4 oz bitter chocolate, grated

DECORATION
10 fl oz whipping cream
grated bitter chocolate

1. Preheat oven to 350°F / 180°C / Gas mark 4.
2. Line shallow sponge tin (11-in. diameter) with buttered greaseproof paper.
3. Cream butter and sugar together until light and fluffy.
4. Gradually add egg yolks. Fold in ground almonds and bitter chocolate.
5. In a separate bowl beat egg whites until stiff, then fold gently into chocolate mixture with metal fork.
6. Pour ingredients into tin and bake for 45–60 minutes till risen.
7. Insert skewer into centre of cake; it should come out a little sticky.
8. Turn out and cool.
9. Cover with softly whipped cream and grated bitter chocolate, and serve.

Felicity and Roald Dahl

65

Elizabeth David

Italian Food

Macdonald, London, 1965 (revised edition;
first published 1954)
364 pages
216 x 136 mm (8½ x 5⅜ in.)

This is the big one. In the 1950s Elizabeth
David, my heroine, set Britain (and probably
the entire English-speaking world) on a
course that has led to the food we eat today.
That said, the reviews of *Italian Food* were
tepid ('Helpfully classified', said *Ideal Home*).
Evelyn Waugh, a sharper reviewer, told the
Sunday Times that it was one of the two
books that had given him the most pleasure
that year. I have chosen *Italian Food* over
the earlier *French Country Cooking* (1951)
because it tackles an entire country, from
Piedmont to Sicily, and because David, who
had an eye for art, commissioned Italian
artist Renato Guttuso to produce the
illustrations. These, especially the one
used on the front cover, are vivid and bold.
A David-owned painting of eggs by Cedric
Morris appears on the cover of David's
An Omelette and a Glass of Wine (1984).

As always, David combines
lyrical descriptions of the food –
the 'vivid scarlet dishes of the
south … contrast strikingly with the
unique green food of central and
northern Italy' – with scholarship.
She traces its origins to Greece,
Rome, Byzantium and the Orient,
and notes that it was the Italians
who taught the cooks of the
French court. The Italians were
'unimpressed' by the French.

As for the recipes, there is
everything here a cook could want,
from the massive Bistecca alla
Fiorentina to five pages on pizza.
I always use David's recipe for
Neapolitan pizza, which needs
fresh tomatoes. She comments
that Italian *salame* is nearly always
good, adding, with characteristic
acerbity, that 'Danish *salame* simply
does not compare; and as for Irish
salame, the less said the better'.
Wonderful; she should have been
made a duchess.

PASTA ASCIUTTA

On 15th November 1930, at a banquet at the restaurant Penna d'Oca in Milan, the famous Italian futurist poet Marinetti launched his much publicised campaign against all established forms of cooking and, in particular, against *pastasciutta*. "Futurist cooking," said Marinetti, "will be liberated from the ancient obsession of weight and volume, and one of its principal aims will be the abolition of *pastasciutta*. *Pastasciutta*, however grateful to the palate, is an obsolete food; it is heavy, brutalising and gross; its nutritive qualities are deceptive; it induces scepticism, sloth and pessimism."

The day after this diatribe was delivered the Italian press broke into an uproar; all classes participated in the dispute which ensued. Every time *pastasciutta* was served either in a restaurant or a private house interminable arguments arose. One of Marinetti's supporters declared that "our *pastasciutta*, like our rhetoric, suffices merely to fill the mouth", Doctors, asked their opinions, were characteristically cautious: "Habitual and exaggerated consumption of *pastasciutta* is definitely fattening." "Heavy consumers of *pastasciutta* have slow and placid characters; meat eaters are quick and aggressive." "A question of taste and of the cost of living. In any case, diet should be varied, and should never consist exclusively of one single element." The Duke of Bovino, Mayor of Naples, plunged into the fight with happy abandon. "The angels in Paradise," he affirmed to a reporter, "eat nothing but *vermicelli al pomodoro*," to which Marinetti replied that this confirmed his suspicions with regard to the monotony of Paradise and of the life led by the angels.

Marinetti and his friends proceeded to divert themselves and outrage the public with the invention and publication of preposterous new dishes. Most of these were founded on the shock

83

ANTIPASTI E INSALATE
HORS D'ŒUVRE AND SALADS

Among Italian *antipasti* (hors d'œuvre) are to be found some of the most successful culinary achievements in European cooking. Most midday meals in Italy start with some small dish of *antipasti*, particularly if the meal is to be without *pasta*. The most common *antipasti* are some kind of *salame* sausage, olives, anchovies, ham, small artichokes in oil, fungi in vinegar (rather tasteless and unsatisfactory, these last), pimientos in oil, raw fennel, raw broad beans.

Of varieties of *salame* sausage there is seemingly no end. Some are garlicky, some not; some are eaten very fresh; others are considered best when they have matured.

Apart from sausages there are a number of interesting pork products which are eaten as *antipasti*. *Lonza*, which is fillet of pork cured in much the same way as ham, served raw in very thin slices, can, if not oversalted, be quite delicious, with its background scent of spices, wine and garlic. *Coppa* is another name for the same sort of product, but this word can be misleading, for in Rome it signifies pig's head brawn, in the Veneto a remarkable kind of loaf comprising whole slices of cooked ham, tongue and *mortadella* sausage. This *mortadella*, most famous although to my mind least alluring of all Italian sausages, is found at its best in Bologna, its own home. As an ingredient of various stuffings and little pastries it is useful, but as an hors d'œuvre frankly dull.

Prosciutto di Parma and *prosciutto di San Daniele* are, at their best, perhaps the most delicious hams in the world and the most perfect hors d'œuvre. Whose was the brilliant idea of

53

---

140   ITALIAN FOOD

it out on a floured board into a large disc about ⅛ in. thick, or divide it in half and make two smaller *pizze*.

Have ready the skinned and coarsely chopped tomatoes, the cheese (in England use *Bel Paese* or good fresh gruyère) and the anchovies. Spread the tomatoes on top of the *pizza*, season with salt and pepper, put halves of the anchovy fillets here and there, and then the cheese cut in thin small slices. Sprinkle a liberal amount of *origano* or basil over the top, moisten with olive oil, pour more oil in a shallow round baking dish which should be large enough to allow the *pizza* to expand during the cooking.

Bake in a hot oven for 20–30 minutes. If *Bel Paese* cheese is used it is best to add it only a few minutes before the *pizza* is ready, as it melts very quickly.

When fresh tomatoes are watery or unripe use peeled tomatoes from a tin, but not concentrated tomato purée. A few stoned black olives are sometimes added to the *pizza*.

The quantities given make a *pizza* of about 8 in. diameter, which is sufficient for two or three people, although in an Italian *pizzeria* a *pizza* of this size constitutes one portion. It should be eaten almost as soon as it comes out of the oven, for it toughens as it gets cold.

This is robust food—to go with a corresponding appetite and plenty of rough red wine.

Pizza alla Casalinga

In private houses it is usual to serve a somewhat more elegant variety of *pizza*, made with a kind of pastry instead of the classic bread dough, which is certainly more suitable when other courses are to follow.

Make a pastry dough with 6 oz. of flour, 2 oz. of butter, 1 egg, ½ oz. of yeast dissolved in a little water, salt, and enough extra water to form a medium stiff dough. Let it rise for 2 hours.

Roll out the pastry, cut it into two rounds, and garnish them with the usual tomatoes, anchovies, *origano* or basil, and cheese, and allowing twice the quantities given for *pizza Napoletana*. Cook the *pizza* in oiled tins or fireproof dishes in a fairly hot oven for 25 minutes, adding the cheese only during the last 5 minutes.

EGGS, CHEESE DISHES, PIZZE, ETC.   141

Pizza al Tegame   FRIED PIZZA

A dish which may be made in a hurry, baking powder instead of yeast being used in the dough, which is therefore cooked as soon as it is prepared, not left to rise.

¼ lb. of flour, 1 good teaspoonful of baking powder, a little water, salt. Tomatoes, cheese, and anchovies as for *pizza Napoletana*. Olive oil for frying.

Put the flour in a mound on the pastry board, make a well in the centre, put in the salt and the baking powder and 2 tablespoonfuls of water. Make into a dough, adding a little more water to make it the right consistency. Knead for a few minutes, then roll out into a thin round, about 7 in. in diameter.

In a heavy frying pan heat enough oil to come level with the top of the disc of dough. When it is hot, but not smoking, put in the ungarnished *pizza* and cook it steadily, but not too fast, for 5 minutes. When the underside is golden, turn it over. Now spread on it the prepared tomatoes, anchovies and *origano* or basil. After 2 minutes add the sliced cheese and cover the pan until the cheese is melted. The entire process of cooking takes about 10 minutes.

An excellent variety of *pizza* if carefully made.

Pizza alla Francescana   FRANCISCAN PIZZA

Make the dough in the same way as for *pizza Napoletana*. The garnish consists of about 2 oz. each of sliced mushrooms previously cooked in oil, 2 oz. of raw or cooked ham cut into strips, 2 or 3 peeled and chopped tomatoes, 3 oz. of cheese. Cook in the same way as *pizza Napoletana*.

Pizza con Cozze   PIZZA WITH MUSSELS

Add a teacupful of cooked and shelled mussels to the garnish for *Pizza Napoletana* and leave out the anchovies.

Pizzette   LITTLE PIZZE

Make the same dough as for the *pizza casalinga*. The amounts

Elizabeth David

67

Alan Davidson
North Atlantic Seafood

Macmillan, London, 1979
512 pages
233 x 155 mm (9¹/₈ x 6¹/₈ in.)

Cookery throws up some unlikely writers, many whose interest is amateur. While serving as British ambassador to Laos, Alan Davidson wrote *Fish and Fish Dishes of Laos* (1975). As a diplomat, he had previously spent time in Washington, D.C., The Hague, Cairo, Tunis and Brussels. Together with the earlier *Mediterranean Seafood* (1972), *North Atlantic Seafood* arose from his travels and obvious interest in fish. It is dedicated to Elizabeth David ('in homage') because she recognized, when she saw one, a scholar cook like herself.

After a series of maps of the Atlantic and of salt levels in the Baltic, a 'Catalogue of Fish' groups the various species by family, from 'The Herring and Its Relations' to 'Miscellaneous Uncouth Fish'; two shorter catalogues deal with crustaceans, molluscs and other edible sea creatures. Most species are accompanied by a line drawing (there are no photographs), as well as their many common names. In the case of the sea trout, these include Portuguese, Icelandic, Russian, Finnish, Welsh and Faroese versions.

Recipes come a definite second, grouped by country – France, Poland, Sweden, the United States and Germany among them – rather than by fish. I get the impression that Davidson is much less interested in the recipes than in the classifications. But, because the Atlantic extends from America to Europe, the recipes vary greatly and, I imagine, were chosen more for the differences from country to country than their taste or the pleasure of making them. Davidson is meticulous in crediting the somewhat obscure volumes from which they were taken. This is a book that every collector should have but few will use.

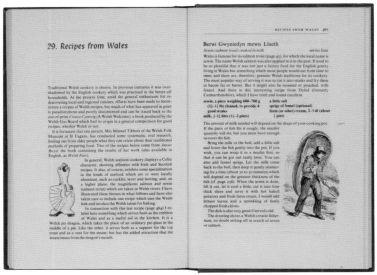

REMARKS

Under this heading I give various pieces of information, including almost always maximum length and colour.

It is usual to measure the length of a fish from its snout to the base of its tail fin, as shown in the diagrammatic drawing below. This is the method which I have tried to follow in giving maximum and normal lengths. But some writers in the past have included projections such as the tail fin at the rear and the sword of the swordfish at the front. Some measurements of this kind may have crept into my text.

However, what I would particularly ask readers to remember is that the maximum length is that of an unusually large adult; and that very many fish are caught before they even attain normal adult length.

Information about colour may also be useful in identifying fish. But many species can modify their own colours to match their habitat; and colours often change when fish are taken out of the water and die. Surer clues to identification are provided by such features as the shape of the fish, the number and position of the various fins and the course of the lateral line along the fish's side. The diagram below explains the technical terms used in the catalogues with regard to such features.

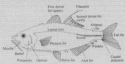

USING THE CATALOGUES

In each catalogue entry the reader will find under the heading 'Cuisine' a summary indication of how the fish or other sea creature can best be cooked or otherwise prepared for eating, and sometimes the outline of a recipe which could not be included in the recipe section. In many catalogue entries a further heading 'Recipes' covers signposts to full recipes which are specifically suitable.

2. Catalogue of Fish

The Herring and Its Relations

The Order *Clupeiformes*, which comprises the herring family and its relations, constitutes what is probably the most important group of food fish in the world.

The clupeoid or herring-like fish all have a single dorsal fin, placed near the middle of the body. They have no lateral line, but a network of sensory canals just under the skin of the head, which seems to fulfil a similar function. Most of them travel in huge shoals.

The family includes some species which spawn in, and are usually taken in, fresh water. These are the shad and their relations. Their abundance, indeed survival, depends on the state of the rivers in which they reproduce themselves. There are now far fewer clued to be had in Europe; but on the American side of the Atlantic they continue to be numerous and important as food.

I should also mention here three fish which are related to the herring and which stray north as far as Cape Cod from the warmer waters where they really belong. These are *Megalops atlantica* Valenciennes, the TARPON, a magnificent sporting fish which is illustrated at the foot of the page; *Elops saurus* Linnaeus, the ten-pounder; and *Albula vulpes* (Linnaeus), the bonefish. The first two belong to the family *Elopidae*, the last to the family *Albulidae*. None of them is important as a food fish in our area, but North American anglers take them from time to time, especially in the summer months.

RED DRUM, CHANNEL BASS   Family *Sciaenidae*

Sciaenops ocellata (Linnaeus)

REMARKS This is a large drum, with maximum length of about 150 cm. However, the large specimens have coarse flesh; and, although they excite the angler (see admiring 'Song of the Old-timer', to be sung to the tune of 'Watermelon Hanging on the Vine'), it is the smaller fish, known as puppy drum, which are good to eat.

The red drum is a well-known fish from Chesapeake Bay southwards. It is not really red in life, although Goode concedes that in adults one may observe 'a tint, an evanescent, metallic reflection of silver from the scales'. But the name channel bass does not seem very appropriate either.

The red drum is generally considered to resemble the striped bass in eating qualities, but to be slightly less good. It may be prepared according to the advice given for the striped bass on page 86.

A short entry is required for the MEAGRE, *Argyrosomus regius* (Asso), a sciaenid fish of the Mediterranean with occasionally ranges up to the English Channel. Its usual adult length is about 1 metre; back silvery brown, fins reddish brown. It is corvina in Portugal, corbina in Spain and maigre in France. Its quality is good, and it too may be prepared like the striped bass.

'Oh, the weakfish are good,
And the kingfish are great,
The striped bass are very, very fine,
But you are, oh, oh, gee me,
Oh, how I wish you would!'
—a channel bass a-hangin' on my line!

NORTHERN KINGFISH   Family *Sciaenidae*

Menticirrhus saxatilis (B. and S.)

REMARKS Maximum length just over 40 cm. The back is leaden in colour or grey, sometimes almost black; the sides are marked irregularly with dark bars; and the underside is whitish. Note the small barbel. The kingfish, by the way, has no air bladder, so cannot make the drumming or creaking noises which other members of the family produce.

This species is most common between Chesapeake Bay and New York, but it occurs up to Cape Cod and down to Florida. In the north it is a summer visitor. In the southern part of its range it is largely replaced by *Menticirrhus americanus* (Linnaeus), the SOUTHERN KINGFISH, shown below, which closely resembles it.

A fantastic wreath of inappropriate common names gathered over the kingfish in the nineteenth century. They were called hake or barb (New Jersey and Delaware), tom-cod (Connecticut), black mullet (Chesapeake), whiting (in the south) and sea-mink (N. Carolina).

CUISINE An excellent table fish. At the beginning of the century it was almost entirely neglected, but then rose swiftly to popularity. It has a low fat content and responds well to being fried, poached or steamed and served with a rich sauce. The flesh is pure white and of a fine texture, which makes it a good fish for salads. One could, for example, use it in making the Swedish Skärbommullad (page 374).

RED CRAB   Family *Geryonidae*

Geryon quinquedens Smith

REMARKS Maximum width about 15 cm. The colour of the carapace is red. This is a deep-sea crab, usually found at depths between 300 and 900 metres. It is an under-explored species, with a range from Nova Scotia to Cuba. There is a small fishery for it in southern New England, which may be expanded in the light of research into its habits.

Another species of the same genus occurs in deep waters on the eastern side of the Atlantic, but seems not have been fished at all, so far.

Canada is fortunate in possessing the excellent QUEEN CRAB or SNOW CRAB. This is shown below. Its scientific name is *Chionoecetes opilio* (Fabricius) and it is found only in cold northerly waters.

CUISINE I ate a quantity of red crab at Gloucester, Mass., and liked the flavour. The legs are thin, but the meat slips out of them readily. Indeed the whole creature is remarkably easy to dismantle and consume.

As for the snow crab, I have only eaten it canned, but found it to be of very high quality.

SPIDER CRAB, SPINY CRAB   Family *Maiidae*

Maia squinado (Herbst)

REMARKS Maximum width 20 cm. The colour of the carapace varies from reddish orange to brown. The arrangement of the legs makes one think of a spider. This species does not occur on the American Atlantic coast, although other spider crabs (not normally eaten) do. They all have a remarkable ability to disguise themselves.

Edward Step, in *A Naturalist's Holiday* (on the Cornish coast before the First World War), devotes a chapter to the spider crab, which was known locally as Grati'l'er Jenkin (or the porwick or the gallet) and says that it usually emerges from winter retirement in May (hence *Maia*, the specific name *squinado*, being taken from the common name of the species in Provence). He describes with charm how Grati'l'er uses his nippers to break off bits of pinkweed or other suitable camouflage and 'plants' these among the prickles and hooked hairs on his back, after 'kissing' the ends to coat them with gummy saliva. In this way, choosing always items which will bear transplanting and which blend with his surroundings, he makes himself all but invisible, looking like a small rock encrusted with natural growths.

CUISINE AND RECIPE A good crab, which is in particularly strong demand in France. It may be prepared according to any crab recipe. Or follow the recipe on page 282, from the Basque country, where this crab is known as txangurro.

Portuguese: Santola
Spanish: Centolla
French: Araignée (de mer)
Dutch: Aequinoeskrab
German: Teufelskrabbe
Swedish: Spindelkrabba
Danish: Troldkrabbe

Tamasin Day-Lewis

Simply the Best: The Art of Seasonal Cooking

Cassell, London, 2001
304 pages
244 x 187 mm (9⅝ x 7⅜ in.)

Tamasin Day-Lewis's famous family has nothing to do with cooking. Her father, Cecil, was the poet laureate; her mother, the actress Jill Balcon. Her brother is Daniel Day-Lewis, also an actor. Tamasin herself was a documentary film-maker when the *Daily Telegraph*, 'out of the azure', asked her to become its weekend cook. She had no doubts: 'We have a renaissance of dedicated and brilliant small producers, artisan craftsmen if you will, who are doing their best to transform our eating habits.' She can write beautifully, too.

Day-Lewis's book is dedicated to George Perry-Smith, 'arguably the finest restaurateur of the last 50 years' – a claim with which I agree, having had a revelatory lunch at his Hole in the Wall restaurant in Bath. He told her, 'The learning has always only just begun', and this book is intended to prove his point.

The publishers here have employed the same look as used for Day-Lewis's other books, with a shiny foam-green cover and endpapers and some luscious peaches on the front. The photographs, by David Loftus, have fine colour and immense charm, while the text, set in Perpetua, is resolutely un-gimmicky. Sections follow the seasons, each opening with a suitable double-page image: a bluebell wood, a buttercup-studded meadow, fallen leaves and snow. Short essays about Day-Lewis's food heroes – including some Irish cheesemakers and Prospect Books, independent publisher of highly regarded food titles co-founded by Alan Davidson (page 68) – change the pace and add to our knowledge. There is, of course, a fine section on producers and their associations, from a small Devon post office to the British Pig Association. Great stuff.

'Doing the season is a constant, one of the chief pleasures of my cooking life. The turning year is about waiting, anticipating, discovering; about picking the first crimson and primrose crab apples, downy quinces and wet walnuts from my trees, eating the tiny embryos of pistachio green broad beans raw from the pod, baking the first gluey-tailed salmon trout from the River Dart.'

Tamasin Day-Lewis

Tamasin Day-Lewis

SIMPLY THE BEST
The Art of Seasonal Cooking

BASIL, TARRAGON, LOVAGE AND THYME

MY FRIEND GALE, SELF-APPOINTED ROVING CULINARY SLEUTH, is on the telephone from wettest Devon, 'I've found an organic herb grower in Tiverton Market.' The following Tuesday I enter the pannier market and am transported, momentarily, to a Ligurian basil field. What I am not prepared for is quite how extensive my ignorance is about this herb, the high priestess of the Mediterranean, whose omni-presence is in danger of eclipsing our cold-climate cuisine. The truth is, food always tastes better eaten where it is indigenous, no amount of modification other than the climatic sort will change that. But here, in a not too far distant small-town market, the heady, nosey pungence of several hundred basil plants is beginning to tell me otherwise.

I introduce myself to the stallholders, Mike and Sylvie, and so beginneth the first lesson. I was aware of only three types of basil, the verdant-leafed ordinary sort we all make pesto with; 'Genovese', the more minimalist bush basil, soft skinned, frail limbed, perfect for strewing over tomato salads; and a wine-dark purple basil, 'Rubin.' Here there are 17 different kinds, including a huge, palm-of-the-hand variety of 'Napolitana' basil with a skin like bubble wrap; the grape-skinned 'Rubin' which I seize in pot loads for my first purple pesto – Sylvie tears it raw into steamed rice – and an intense, rough tasting 'Holy' basil, grown around the Thai temples. My later research tells me that this last was regarded by the Hindus with such reverence, that when the British required them to take an oath in court, it took the place of the Bible. Sylvie says it is best used in combination with other spices, 'It gives an extra kick, it's the same principle as the clove, disgusting on its own, but great in a sauce.' Here in the West, sanctity replaced by fecundity, basil is the symbol of fertility. There is spicy 'Green Globe', brilliant at surviving the cooking process, 'It is extremely strong,' Sylvie says; lime and lemon basils, the lime sharply, astringently sherbetty and citric on the tongue; 'Cinnamon' and 'Anise' basils with echoes of tarragon.

'We're still small enough to have time to talk to people, they can touch and smell the herbs and get hooked.' If there is one thing that sums up the difference between French and English market culture, it is this. In France you touch, squeeze, taste, in England prohibition is an unspoken rule. Sylvie says, 'We also rely on our personalities. Being French, I have to take English taste into consideration.' It is clearly another country to her, 'You don't use tarragon. At home we put a sprig of it in our bottles of oil and vinegar, and we don't cook chicken without it. And the English don't use chervil. We use twice as much of it in salads and with fish as we would parsley. It is a traditional component of our bouquets garnis.' Get Sylvie on the subject of parsley, and there is clearly a La Manche-sized gap between us and them. 'The English want curly parsley, not flat-leaf, and they haven't discovered how to cook with it. I stir-fry it in huge branches until it goes black and crispy, and mix it with rice. It looks like burnt grass to people here.'

Fresh Thyme Soup

This is an intensely flavoured, beautiful soup to make in summer, when the thyme flowers have turned into new growth. It is simple, aromatic, and needs no embellishment.

SERVES 4

a whole handful of thyme, as much as you can wrap your fist around
1 small onion, finely chopped
2 small new potatoes
a knob of butter
olive oil
750ml / 1¼ pint strong chicken stock, i.e. strong enough to jellify in the fridge
450ml / ¾ pint Jersey milk
salt and pepper

Strip half the thyme stalks, about 10 or 12 twigs, of their leaves and chop to release the oils. Melt a knob of butter and a couple of tablespoons of good olive oil in a heavy-bottomed casserole, then add the finely chopped onion, the diced potatoes and the thyme. Stir to coat for a few minutes, then ladle in the stock. Bring to the boil, add the milk, bring to the boil again, turn down to a lazy simmer, adding the rest of the thyme stalks tied in a bundle like a bouquet garni, salt and pepper.

Put the lid on, and continue to simmer for about 20 minutes. Remove the bouquet, check the seasoning, and put the soup through the thinnest of the three discs of a mouli-legumes. The result is utterly white, with tiny flecks of thyme.

Do not add cream, or you will dilute the magical flavour, the essence of the herb.

Lovage and Potato Soup

The Greeks and the Romans used lovage, as did the Tudors and the Stuarts, who also bathed in it. It has a sort of musky flavour redolent of old spice and underscores a dish in just the same way as celery. If you grow some, you will use it – it's good with smoked fish and on salads.

SERVES 4

50g / 2oz lovage leaves after stripping them from their stalks
1 medium onion, finely chopped
3 medium potatoes, diced
1.2 litre / 2 pints chicken stock
a knob of butter and 2 tbsp olive oil

Heat the butter and oil together in a heavy-bottomed casserole, add the onion and potato, and stir to coat. Add the finely chopped lovage, stir for a couple of minutes, season, then add the stock. Bring to the boil, then turn down to a blip of a simmer, and put the lid on the pan for 15 minutes. Liquidize thoroughly, add salt and pepper to taste, and heat to scalding point again. I also ate this soup cold the next day, jellied and straight from the fridge, and it was delicious.

Sugar-Topped Morello Cherry Pie

Morellos are almost impossible to find in England, they obviously all end up bottled or jammed. Use the best-flavoured fresh cherries you can find as an alternative.

SERVES 6

SHORTCRUST PASTRY
225g / 8oz organic white flour
125g / 4oz unsalted butter

FOR THE FILLING:
750g / 1¾lb morello cherries, pre-stoned weight
5 tbsp sour cherry fruit syrup. I bought a bottle of Austrian D'Arbo syrup in the supermarket, worth it to intensify the flavour
1 tbsp Kirsch
2 tbsp cornflour
vanilla sugar to taste
1 egg, separated
1 tbsp demerara sugar

Make a basic shortcrust pastry in the usual way. Refrigerate for half an hour before rolling out a slightly bigger half, and lining your greased pie dish.

Macerate the stoned cherries in the syrup, Kirsch and a couple of tablespoons of vanilla sugar, turning occasionally, until they have released their juices. An hour or two will do. Check the juice for sweetness, and add a bit more if you need to, remember, the cherries are tart.

Preheat the oven to 200°C / 400°F / Gas Mark 6. Brush the base of the pie with the egg white. Spoon a couple of tablespoons of the cherry liquor over the cornflour you have sieved into a small bowl, and stir until completely dissolved. Return it to the cherries, and pour the whole lot into the pie dish. Cover with a pastry lid, crimp the edges, and brush a glaze of beaten egg over the surface. Make a small incision in the middle to let the steam escape, and bake for about 35 minutes. We ate ours warm with clotted cream, the ripe fruit coated in the thickened purple syrup.

Tamasin Day-Lewis

Len Deighton

Action Cook Book: Len Deighton's Guide to Eating

Penguin, London, 1967 (first published 1965)
256 pages
126 x 191 mm (5 x 7½ in.)

Working with fellow RCA graduate Raymond Hawkey, Deighton himself devised this pure 1960s cookery book, which combines James Bond-style covers (the back cover is shown right) with chunky, typographical cartoon strips.

This one takes me right back to the sixties. Its cover, designed by Deighton's fellow Royal College of Art graduate Raymond Hawkey, features a James Bond-ish cook with shoulder holster and an adoring, false-eyelashed woman in Biba broderie. The cartoon 'cookstrips' that make up the recipes, drawn by Deighton, first appeared in the modish *Observer*.

Deighton, although old enough to have done National Service, is a typical product of the sixties. A working-class Londoner – his father was a chauffeur, his mother a cook – he has been, at various times, an art director, illustrator, film producer, novelist (the film of *The Ipcress File* starred a young Michael Caine) and cook. Back in 1960, the world was his oyster and trout.

Despite the gimmickry, the cookstrips – one per recipe – are perfectly clear, but, to suit the format, pretty simple. The recipes themselves tend to be very sixties: chilli con carne, chicken Kiev, steak au poivre and crêpe Suzette. Many, including oxtail, steak-and-kidney pudding, boiled mutton and curry, are also masculine and hearty. There's a lot of added information about seasonal food, cuts of meat and ingredients (ask your wine merchant where to get good olive oil). This is very much a chap's book, with a section

for bachelors and, even more a period piece, a guide to buying and smoking cigars.

This would still make a very useful book for aspiring male home cooks, from students to pensioners, because it's made easy by the illustrations. It's also a book that should be on every collector's bookshelf for its originality. HarperCollins republished it in 1999.

Coquilles St Jacques, or scallops, are in season from October to March, but at no time of the year is this an inexpensive dish to prepare, which is why some restaurants fake the contents of their shells with cod in white sauce. It is quite all right to have the fishmonger open the shells for you for, unlike oysters, there is no precious liquid inside to spill or waste. However, if you wish to open them yourself they will open easily if put in a warm place, e.g. the plate rack. Be sure the rounded part is downward. The sticky part is not eaten, which will leave you with a large white piece and a soft tongue of coral, which is bright orange. The American types do not have this coral content, which is bad luck because this is the most delicate and delicious part. Whenever possible the coral should be less cooked than the harder white part, whether you grill or poach or fry. Scallops can be prepared in any of those ways, and a traditional English way to serve is fried with bacon. Incidentally, it's the way my fishmonger eats them for Sunday breakfast.

You should allow at least two per person, and if it's a main course, more. To make them go a long way chop them finely and use as a filling for pastry turnovers, pancakes or vol-au-vents.

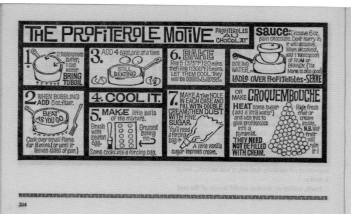

Ramequins: make and bake balls as here (say about the size of an apricot). Brush with egg and roll in finely chopped cheese (Gruyère or similar). Bake ten minutes in a hot oven. Make a hole and fill with a creamy cheese sauce, put them in a warm place so that they can be eaten while still warm. These are served as hot hors d'œuvres.

For Petits Fours try **Carolines**. These are just tiny éclairs (about the size of your little finger) filled with thick cream.

Or try **Salambos**. Make small choux pastry balls. Fill the inside with thick cream. Paint the top with melted sugar (heat it with a little water) so that you can stick lots of chopped pistachio nuts on top.

Tyrolians are covered with chopped almonds in the same way, then put back in the oven so that the almonds scorch a little bit. Then you fill them with almond cream.

Almond cream is very easy to make in a blender. If you don't have one, you must pound the ingredients by hand (using e.g. pestle and mortar).

Put 3 oz. almonds and 3 oz. sugar together and crush them with care. Add two yolks still beating, then a shot of rum, still pounding away. When it is a thick cream, use it, if it hasn't all disappeared in the tasting.

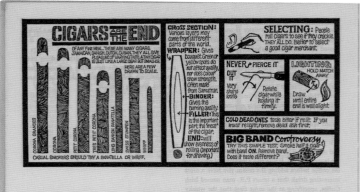

Larousse tells us that professional tasters have to renounce smoking.

Smoking during a meal should be discouraged, but the aroma of cigar smoke at the end of a meal, blending with the aroma of good brandy, gives the host a fine feeling of complacency.

Good drawing depends upon careful, even filling. Buy cigars which are regular in size, shape and colour, for those are likely to have been best filled.

Uneven burning can usually be traced to wrong preparation. Never pierce the end, because this is an inadequate 'flue' and will give several different troubles at once (e.g. heat and tobacco oil in the mouth), so make a large vent in the end.

Provide a cigar cutter if you can. Don't put the open end in the mouth and light the closed end, for although this gives a good draught, it may come unwrapped.

England is the only place where there is a nonsensical tradition of removing the band. Do as you wish,

but don't be upstage about smokers who leave the band on.

1 Never stub a cigar out; it will go out quickly enough.

2 If your cigar goes out before you are finished, relight it immediately. Once it gets cold, it will taste bitter if relit.

3 Don't leave cigar butts in the dining-room overnight. They leave a musty aroma.

4 Lighted candles in a room where cigars are being smoked reduce the smoke and the musty aroma the next day.

Remember that a tiny cigar can be just as good in quality as a large one (or better), and have a few small or slim ones for guests who don't normally smoke cigars.

Anthony Demetre

Today's Special: A New Take on Bistro Food

Quadrille, London, 2008
192 pages
247 x 187 mm (9¾ x 7⅜ in.)

Anthony Demetre is well qualified to be the author of this book. After working with chefs Marco Pierre White, Gary Rhodes, Pierre Koffmann and Bruno Loubet, he set up London restaurants Arbutus and Wild Honey, in 2006 and 2007 respectively. Each venue won an award for best new restaurant and has a Michelin star. His wife, Frédérique, is a Parisienne with family in the Auvergne and Provence.

If all this tends to put you off (too much cheffery), never fear. In his introduction, Demetre writes that 'My early career, working with some of the UK's finest chefs, brought me to the conclusion that simplicity, generosity and hospitality are the crucial elements that make a restaurant great.' The modern bistro concept is built around 'Today's Special', and this is where the title comes from, as do the recipes.

While most of the dishes are inventive, few demand the sorts of ingredients chefs can find but we cannot. So there is halibut with roast baby gem lettuce, roast venison with Swiss chard and, my favourite, *sot-y-laisse*, chicken oysters (although breast will do) with peas, lemon and pasta. And try Slow-Cooked Shoulder of Elwy Valley Lamb (even if your lamb comes from a different valley). Desserts include roast peaches with lemon thyme, warm chocolate soup and, marvellously, old-fashioned rice pudding – 'old-fashioned' because, unlike most restaurant chefs, Demetre lets his bake for 1½ hours.

Filled with excellent photographs by Simon Wheeler, this book could well become a collectable classic.

A Book for Cooks

Braised Jacob's ladder (short rib of organic beef) with shallots à la crème

Short rib of beef is seldom, if ever, served in this country. I discovered it on a recent visit to the USA, in a restaurant serving its own version of modern bistro food.

SERVES 4–6

2 short ribs of beef (Jacob's ladders) or enough for 4–6 people
Flour for coating
A little vegetable oil
2 knobs of butter
1 large onion, chopped
2 large carrots, chopped
1 celery stalk, chopped
6 garlic cloves, finely chopped
4 tablespoons red wine vinegar
375ml port
375ml full-bodied red wine
1 bouquet garni
2 litres chicken stock
Salt and freshly ground black pepper

FOR THE SHALLOTS À LA CRÈME

100g butter
2 garlic cloves
Sprig of thyme
18 medium-sized shallots
150ml Madeira
150ml double cream

Cut the short ribs into individual ribs and coat in flour. Heat a heavy-based casserole with a film of oil and the knob of butter in it. Add the floured ribs and lightly brown on all sides. Reserve.

Add another knob of butter, followed by the vegetables and garlic, and lightly brown them.

Deglaze the pan with the vinegar and reduce by two-thirds. Then add the port and wine, and reduce them by half. Add the ribs, bouquet garni and stock, bring to the boil and skim. Season with salt and pepper, and simmer for about 2 hours, skimming from time to time.

Towards the end of this time, prepare the shallots: melt the butter in a sauté pan, add the garlic and thyme, followed by the shallots, and cook, stirring, until the shallots are golden. Add the Madeira and cook until that is reduced by half. Add the cream with 150ml water and salt and pepper to taste. Bring to the boil and simmer until the shallots are tender.

When the ribs are cooked, carefully take them out of the cooking liquid and reserve. Strain the liquid and vegetables through a fine sieve into a clean pan. Add the ribs, adjust the seasoning and bring back to the boil to serve, together with the shallots.

Walnut and Arbutus honey tart

As with all sweet pastry, speed and a cool environment are crucial to the result. By a stroke of luck I discovered that the added cornflour in the mix helps make the pastry dry, producing a better, crisper result. When baking a tart case blind, I recommend covering the pastry with cling film rather than foil or baking parchment, as these can often puncture the pastry. We get our arbutus honey from La Fromagerie, which also sells it by mail order.

170g fresh wet walnuts
90g caster sugar
70g unsalted butter, softened
3 eggs
70g liquid honey, preferably Arbutus honey
2 tablespoons Oloroso sherry (any other sherry or even rum would do)

FOR THE SWEET PASTRY

80g butter
50g sugar
2 eggs
130g flour
10g cornflour
Pinch of salt

Well ahead, make the sweet pastry: cream the softened butter with the sugar, add the eggs and combine lightly. Then add the sieved flour, cornflour and salt. Knead lightly, wrap in cling film and refrigerate for 2 hours.

Towards the end of this time, preheat the oven to 160°C/gas 3. Roll the dough out to a thickness of about 3mm and use to line a 20cm tart ring. Line with cling film, weight with baking beans and bake blind until golden, about 20 minutes. Allow to cool.

When ready to finish the tart, preheat the oven again to 160°C/gas 3.

Shell the walnuts and crush them coarsely. Whisk together with the rest of the ingredients.

Spoon the mixture into your precooked tart case and bake until the filling is just set, about 20 minutes.

Sir Kenelm Digby

The Closet of Sir Kenelm Digby Knight Opened

Philip Lee Warner, London, 1910
(reprint; first published 1669)
348 pages
204 x 135 mm (8 x 5⅜ in.)

Some cookery writers have led surprisingly adventurous lives, but Sir Kenelm Digby beats them all. His father was executed for involvement in the Gunpowder Plot; he was a privateer, a Royalist and the inventor of the modern wine bottle; and, if his memoirs are to be believed, Marie de' Medici was madly in love with him. During one of his various stays on the Continent (sometimes as a diplomat, sometimes in official exile), he killed a French noble in a duel for his insults to Charles II (as he later became). He was given the monopoly of sealing wax in Wales, almost certainly met Galileo and, before being a cookery writer, was an important scientist.

When did he find the time to write recipes? Although they were published four years after his death by a servant, they are redolent of court life under the Stuarts. In her introduction to my edition, Anne Macdonell says they do not 'reek' of shops but 'of the wood, the garden, the field, the meadow'. The recipes also reek of aristocratic acquaintance: 'Hydromel as I made it weak for the Queen Mother'; 'To make a Pan Cotto, as the Cardinals use in Rome'; 'My Lord of Bristol's Scotch Collops'; 'The Countess of Penalva's Portuguez Eggs'.

The book is bound in handsome brown buckram impressed with a fleur-de-lis,

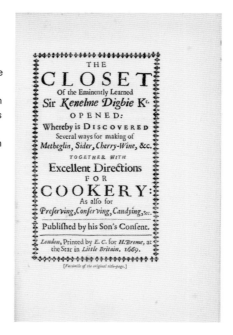

from the Digby coat of arms. His closet reveals a great deal about what people ate in the seventeenth century – gruels, potages, possets, baked venison – none of it very appetizing today. In 2008 an early edition of the book fetched £1188 at auction in London.

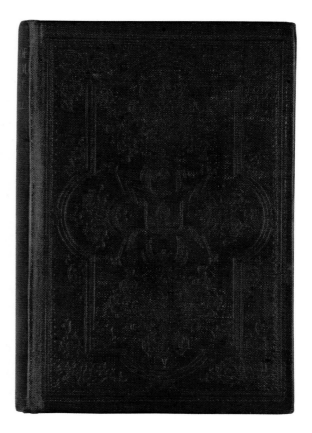

A Book for Cooks

of the Powder of Sympathy in an appendix to his *Natural History*.

In Spain, Kenelm had flirted with some Spanish ladies, notably with the beautiful Donna Anna Maria Manrique, urged thereto by gibes at his coldness ; but Venetia was still the lady of his heart. Her amorous adventures, in the meanwhile, had been more serious and much more notorious. His letters had miscarried, and had been kept back by his mother. Venetia pleaded her belief in his death. Aubrey's account of her is a mass of picturesque scandal. "She was a most beautiful desirable creature. . . . The young eagles had espied her, and she was sanguine and tractable, and of much suavity (which to abuse was great pittie)." Making all allowance for gossip, the truth seems to be that in Kenelm's absence she had been at least the mistress of Sir Edward Sackville, afterwards the fourth Earl of Dorset ; that Dorset tired of her ; and on Digby's return she was more than willing to return to her old love. But, alas ! Sackville had her picture, which seemed to her compromising. Digby, therefore, having accepted her apologies and extenuations, challenged Sackville to a duel ; whereupon the faithless one proved at least magnanimous ; refused to fight, gave up the picture, and swore that Venetia was blameless as she was fair. A private marriage followed ; and it was only on the birth of his second son John that Sir Kenelm acknowledged it to the world. To read nearly all his *Memoirs* is to receive the impression that he looked on his wife as a wronged innocent. To read the whole is to feel he

knew the truth and took the risk, which was not very great after all ; for the lady of the many suitors and several adventures settled down to the mildest domesticity. They say he was jealous ; but no one has said she gave him cause. The tale runs that Dorset visited them once a year, and "only kissed her hand, Sir Kenelm being by."

But Digby was a good lover. All the absurd rhodomontade of his strange *Memoirs* notwithstanding, there are gleams of rare beauty in the story of his passion, which raise him to the level of the great lovers. His *Memoirs* were designed to tell "the beginning, progress, and consummation of that excellent love, which only makes me believe that our pilgrimage in this world is not indifferently laid upon all persons for a curse." And here is a very memorable thing. "Understanding and love are the natural operation of a reasonable creature ; and this last, which is a gift that of his own nature must always be bestowed, *being the only thing that is really in his power to bestow*, it is the worthiest and noblest that can be given."

But, as he naïvely says, "the relations that follow marriage are . . . a clog to an active mind" ; and his kinsman Bristol was ever urging him to show his worth " by some generous action." The result of this urging was Scanderoon. His object, plainly stated, was to ruin Venetian trade in the Levant, to the advantage of English commerce. The aid and rescue of Algerian slaves were afterthoughts. King James promised him a commission ; but Buckingham's secretary, on behalf of his master absent in

---

porate it well with them, by stirring them together. You stew these between two dishes. The quickest Apples are the best.

PORTUGUEZ EGGS

THE way that the Countess de Penalva makes the Portuguez Eggs for the Queen, is this. Take the yolks (clean picked from the whites and germ) of twelve new-laid Eggs. Beat them exceedingly with a little (scarce a spoonful) of Orange-flower-water. When they are exceeding liquid, clear, and uniformly a thin Liquor, put to them one pound of pure double refined Sugar (if it be not so pure, it must be clarified before) and stew them in your dish or bason over a very gentle fire, stirring them continually, whiles they are over it, so that the whole may become one uniform substance, of the consistence of an Electuary (beware they grow not too hard ; for without much caution and attention, that will happen on a sudden) which then you may eat presently, or put into pots to keep. You may dissolve Ambergreece (if you will, ground first very much with Sugar) in Orange-flower or Rose-water, before hand, and put it (warm and dissolved) to the Eggs, when you set them to stew. If you clarifie your Sugar, do it with one of these waters, and whites of Eggs. The flavor of these sweet-waters goeth almost all away with boiling. Therefore half a spoonful put into the composition, when you take it from the fire, seasoneth it more then ten times as much, put in at the first.

TO BOIL EGGS

A CERTAIN and infallible method to boil new-laid Eggs to sup up, and yet that they have the white turned to milk, is thus : Break a very little hole, at the bigger end of the shell, and put it into the water, whiles it boileth. Let it remain boiling, whiles your Pulse beateth two hundred stroaks. Then take it out immediately, and you will find it of an exact temper : others put Eggs into boyling water just as you take it from the fire, and let them remain there, till the water be so cooled, that you may just put in your hand, and take out the Eggs.

Others put the Eggs into cold water, which they set upon the fire, and as soon as the water begins to boil, the Eggs are enough.

TO MAKE CLEAR GELLY OF BRAN

TAKE two pound of the broadest open Bran of the best Wheat, and put it to infuse in a Gallon of Water, during two or three days, that the water may soak into the pure flower, that sticks to the bran. Then boil it three or four walms, and presently take it from the fire, and strain it through some fine strainer. A milky substance will come out, which let stand to settle about half a day. Pour off the clear water, that swimmeth over the starch or flomery, that is in the bottom (which is very good for Pap, &c.) and boil it up to a gelly, as you do Harts-horn gelly or the like, and season it to your taste.

TO BAKE VENISON

BOIL the bones (well broken) and remaining flesh of the Venison, from whence the meat of the Pasty

Josceline Dimbleby

Favourite Food

Penguin, Harmondsworth, 1984
(first published 1983)
176 pages
196 x 128 mm (7¾ x 5 in.)

Josceline Dimbleby, former wife of
broadcaster David, describes the agonies
of a book signing, hating 'the ones who
glanced at my book with a bored look
saying that they had far too many cookery
books at home already. "Ah," I said, "but I
promise you, none of the recipes in any of
those books will be quite like these."'

And they aren't. Take Cucumber and
Green Peppercorns in Aspic, an aromatic
appetite tickler in heart-shaped patty tins,
or Curried Beef Surprise Cake – the
surprise being softly poached eggs in a
herby 'cake' of beef. Inevitably, in the years
since the book's publication, tastes have
caught up with Dimbleby's use of Middle
Eastern spices, chilli powder and coconut,
but here their use is adapted from the
traditional. As a child, Dimbleby lived in
Turkey, Peru and Syria (and was always
saving up for further travel), and her food
is influenced by the world.

The other thing to note about *Favourite
Food* is that a great many of the recipes
are designed to appeal to children, even
though this is emphatically not a children's
cookery book: 'Although my life was now
dominated by the demands of two little
children and a baby I found that creativity
in the kitchen was still possible ... it gave
me a feeling of some independence.' One
of her guests was Jane Grigson (page 102),
to whom she served Ginger Seafood in
Red Pepper and Tomato Sauce with
Lovage. 'She said it was the best dish
she had eaten for a long time.'

Broccoli and Avocado Salad (for 6)

I make this salad over and over again. It is very pretty and combines cooked and raw vegetables and contrasting textures.

12 oz (350 g) calabrese broccoli (this is the green kind with hardly any leaves, thickish stalks and large compact heads)
1 small red pepper, finely sliced in rings

lemon juice
1 large avocado
vinaigrette dressing with French mustard

Cut just the end of the stems off the broccoli. Steam or boil the broccoli for 4–5 minutes until bright green and still crunchy. Rinse under cold water and drain. Put into a salad bowl with the sliced pepper. Squeeze a little lemon juice into a mixing bowl. Cut the avocado in half, scoop out in chunks into the lemon juice and stir around. Add the broccoli, and before serving dress with the vinaigrette dressing.

Jerusalem Salad (for 4)

The mysterious flavour of Jerusalem artichokes makes a delicious alternative to a potato salad. Here they are subtly mixed with skinned broad beans and avocado. A perfect accompaniment to cold meat.

1 lb (450 g) Jerusalem artichokes
8 oz (225 g) packet frozen broad beans

1 avocado
bunch parsley, finely chopped
vinaigrette dressing

Scrub and peel the artichokes as well as you can (don't bother to do it too thoroughly as it takes too much time and a little peel tastes good), and slice thinly. Either steam or boil for only 3–4 minutes until very slightly cooked but still crunchy. Put into a salad bowl. Pour boiling water over the frozen broad beans and leave for a minute. Then pop the beans out of their skins into the salad bowl with the artichokes. Cut the avocado in half, carefully peel off the skin and slice the flesh thinly across in semi-circles. Add to the artichokes and beans and mix in the chopped parsley and some vinaigrette dressing.

Savoury Orange and Onion Salad (for 4–5)

The idea for this salad came from a 1920s recipe book, and it is excellent with duck (hot or cold), ham or pork.

3–4 medium onions
3 oranges
8–10 black olives
paprika

For the dressing
1 tablespoon orange flower water
2 teaspoons lemon juice
3 tablespoons sunflower oil
1–2 pinches cayenne pepper
salt

Peel and slice both the onions and the oranges very thinly in rounds, removing any pips and pith from the oranges. Arrange them in layers in a round dish. Dot the olives on top and sprinkle all over with paprika. Mix the dressing ingredients thoroughly together and pour them over the salad before serving.

Tomato and Kiwi Fruit Salad with Fresh Mint (for 4)

This savoury salad is actually made with fruit, tomatoes being officially a fruit and not a vegetable. It is the simplest mixture but the flavours are perfectly compatible and the combination looks beautiful too. Try it as a first course or between courses.

1 lb (450 g) tomatoes
4–5 kiwi fruit
handful fresh mint leaves, chopped
vinaigrette dressing

Slice the tomatoes across in rounds and put into a glass bowl. Peel the kiwi fruit carefully, slice thinly across in rounds and mix with the tomatoes. Gently mix in the chopped mint. Before serving dress with a simple vinaigrette dressing.

Pour the mixture into a pretty serving bowl or individual glasses and put at once in the bottom of the fridge for 2–3 hours, or longer if possible. Decorate the top of the mousse with chopped nuts or flaked chocolate.

Lovely Lemon Ring (for 5–6)

I have a particular passion for any sweet made with lemons, and this delicately textured ring is truly exquisite. It has a delicious shiny lemon curd top and creamy honeycombed base, and it slips down the throat in the most irresistible way.

1 oz (25 g) self-raising flour, sifted
8 oz (225 g) caster sugar
pinch salt
finely grated rind of 1 lemon
3 tablespoons lemon juice (approx. 1 lemon)

3 large eggs, separated
½ pint (300 ml) single cream
chopped toasted nuts to garnish (optional)

Mix together the sifted flour, the caster sugar and the salt. Sift into a mixing bowl and stir in the lemon rind and juice. In another bowl whisk the egg yolks with an electric whisk until pale and creamy. Stir into the flour, sugar and lemon mixture. Then stir in the single cream gradually. Put a roasting pan full of warm water on the centre shelf of the oven and heat the oven to Gas 3/325°F/170°C. Then whisk the egg whites until they hold soft peaks and fold them gently into the yolk and lemon mixture using a large metal spoon. Pour into a wetted 2 pint (1·1 litre) ring mould tin and set it in the pan of water in the oven. Cook for 1 hour. Allow to cool (it will sink a bit as it cools), and when very cold loosen the edges carefully and turn out, giving a shake, on to a serving plate. If liked, sprinkle the top with chopped toasted nuts. Refrigerate until needed.

Apricot and Guava Tart (for 8)

This is one of our favourite Sunday lunch puddings, especially in winter when the variety of fruit is limited and we are tired of apple pies. Serve hot or warm with plenty of cream.

For the pastry
8 oz (225 g) plain flour
4 oz (100 g) butter
2 oz (50 g) vegetable fat } cold from the fridge
1 egg
1 egg yolk

For the filling
8 oz (225 g) dried apricots, soaked in water for several hours or overnight
14 oz (400 g) can guavas
rind and juice of 1 lemon
4 oz (100 g) pale brown or demerara sugar
1 packet sponge fingers
2 oz (50 g) caster sugar
1 egg white

Remember to soak the apricots for the filling, and then make the pastry. Sift the flour into a bowl. Cut the butter and fat into small pieces and then crumble them into the flour with your fingertips until the mixture looks like breadcrumbs. Whisk the egg and egg yolk (keep the white for glazing the pastry at the end) together and then, using a knife, stir them into the flour mixture until it begins to stick together. Then gather it up into a ball, wrap in cling film, and leave in the fridge for at least 30 minutes.

When the apricots are soaked, drain them and put them in a saucepan with the strained juice from the can of guavas. Coarsely grate the lemon rind and leave on one side. Squeeze the juice and add it to the apricots. Add the brown sugar. Bring the apricots to the boil, stirring until the sugar is dissolved, then cover and simmer gently for 20–30 minutes until the apricots are soft. Then uncover the saucepan and boil over a high heat for 3–5 minutes until they are syrupy and somewhat thickened. Break up the sponge fingers roughly and spread over the bottom of a 9 inch (23 cm) earthenware flan dish. Spoon the apricots and juices over the sponge fingers. Cut the guava halves into 2–3 slices each and arrange them evenly on top of the apricots. Finally, scatter over the grated lemon rind. Put the dish in a cool place to become cold.

Roll out the pastry on a floured surface in a circle slightly larger than the flan dish. Moisten the edges of the dish and place the pastry on top. Cut round the edge neatly, gather up the scraps of pastry and roll out to cut out decorations. Thoroughly mix the caster sugar with the egg white with a small whisk or fork, and brush this glaze all over the pastry.

P.P.—9

Anne Dolamore

The Essential Olive Oil Companion

Macmillan, London, 1988
160 pages
233 x 151 mm (9¹/₈ x 6 in.)

As a once proud owner of a Tuscan olive grove (which I helped to replant), I can testify that this small book is the business. From it I learned which varieties to grow (Frantoio, Leccino and Moraiolo) and how to make green olives edible by brining them. Precisely how the Syrians, the first recorded olive growers 6000 years ago, discovered this process is one of the great mysteries of agriculture.

Anne Dolamore was inspired to research the olive by the Oxford Symposium on Food in 1986. Two years later, after fact-finding in some of the most beautiful places on Earth, she produced exactly what the title of this book says. She delves into the history of the olive, the varieties and flavours, and how it is harvested, ending with a table of world production in 1988: Spain had 193 million olive trees, Italy

Jaen, Andalucia

A Book for Cooks

183 million and the United States, in a very poor twelfth place, 2.2 million.

And then there are the recipes from Spain, Italy, France, Greece, North Africa, the Americas and the rest of the world, from Australia to, as it was then, Yugoslavia. As Dolamore says, it's extraordinary that, when so much has been written about grapes, olives have been virtually ignored.

Madeleine David's colourful and impressionistic drawings, from piles of olives and lemons in a Moroccan market to a near abstract double-page spread of olive groves in Andalucia, bring the whole to life. This is the happiest of books: it glows like a demijohn of oil in the sun, and is as delicious as *imam bayaldi* (translation: the imam fainted), stuffed aubergine cooked in olive oil.

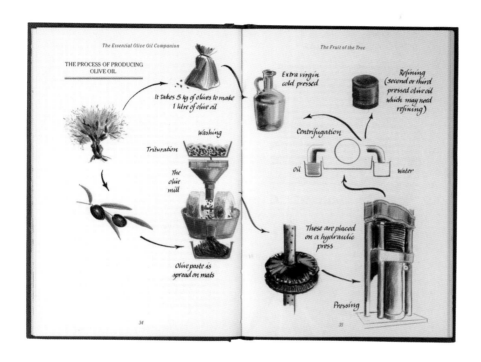

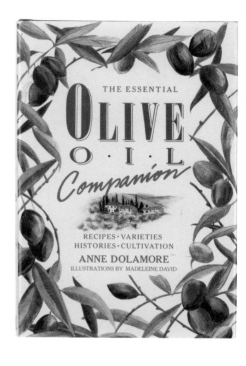

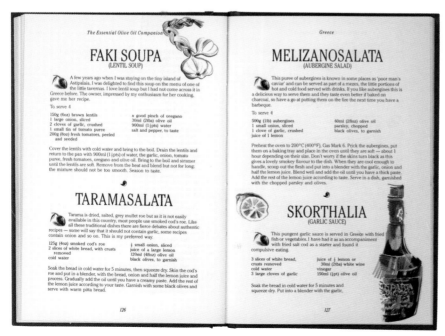

Dorling Kindersley

The Cook's Book of Ingredients

Dorling Kindersley, London, 2010
544 pages
275 x 228 mm (10⅞ x 9 in.)

Unlike many recipe books, dictionaries of ingredients should be kept up to date because ingredients (or the fashions for them) keep changing. This hefty work contains 2500 ingredients, all carefully displayed – in Dorling Kindersley's characteristic style – against a white background. Adjacent to each are details on buying, storing and cooking, and most double-page spreads feature a complementary recipe. Next to photographs of various clams, including the extraordinary geoduck clam (which can live for more than 100 years and has a siphon, or 'trunk', up to 70 centimetres/27½ in. long), there is a recipe for New England Chowder.

I wouldn't be without this book: whenever I'm stuck it's the first thing I reach for. Are the chillies I bought mild or hot, for instance? What do I do with harissa paste? What's the difference between Moroccan, Sardinian and Israeli couscous? (Answer: the size.) In the oil section, glass dishes of each type, from argan to sunflower, demonstrate the varied colours, from transparent to dark brown; the same technique is used for vinegars, honeys, oriental sauces and sugars.

At the back of the book the publisher thanks all the traders who gave both advice and their products for photography, thus providing a handy guide to where to shop. It could be Olives Et Al of Dorset, Billingsgate Market in London, butchers Ramsay of Carluke in Scotland or Sky Sprouts in Devon. I now even know what to do with the Meyer lemons I'm growing in the greenhouse, and what the collard greens I meet in novels set in America's Deep South actually are.

PLUMS

Plums are widely cultivated in temperate zones. There are many varieties, with flesh of orange-red, orange-yellow or golden-green, and purple, red-green, or yellow skin. The types differ in sweetness, tartness, and amount of juice, so some are more suitable for eating fresh than for cooking, although many can be used for both. European varieties tend to be smaller and firmer than plums of oriental origin. Plums are a plum-apricot hybrid, with plum as the dominant parent. Mainly grown in California, they are extremely sweet, juicy, and fragrant.

BUY Buy in midsummer to early autumn for immediate use if possible. They should be firm, yet give slightly when pressed, and have a slight bloom. They should never feel squashy. Avoid hard, wrinkled, or shrivelled plums, and brown patches.

STORE Ripe plums can be kept for several days in an open paper bag in the vegetable drawer of the fridge. Soften fruit that is slightly under-ripe in a paper bag at room temperature. Freeze in syrup, or as a purée.

EAT Cut along the seam and twist the two halves to open the fruit. *Fresh:* Eat as a snack or add to salads. *Cooked:* Leave the skin on for dishes in which they need to keep their shape. Purée for soufflés, mousses, and sauces. Poach or bake in syrup. Use in pies, tarts, crumbles, batter puddings, and quick breads. Enclose in pastry for dumplings. Add to stews. Halve and grill. *Preserved:* Bottle in syrup or brandy. Make into preserves. Dry (as prunes).

FLAVOUR PAIRINGS Lamb, duck, pork, ham, goose, almonds, spices, mascarpone, brandy.

CLASSIC RECIPES Plum jam; plum dumplings; plum and mascarpone tart; potato gnocchi stuffed with plums; damson cheese; tartlet-size mirabelles.

Santa Rosa
A particularly large, round plum, this has firm, zingy, dark red-purple skin and a pleasantly tart flavour. Eat fresh, or use in crumbles and cobblers.

Sloe
These are wild plums, the small, black fruits of the blackthorn, a wild hedgerow bush. They are too sour to eat but make good jam and home-made sloe gin.

Flavor Rich
A Pluot with black skin, crunchy amber flesh, and a medium-sweet taste. This cooks well in tarts and sauces, but is also good to eat fresh.

Damson
Small, dark blue damsons have a large stone and spicy-tart flavour that makes them superb for jam. Their midsummer season is very short, so buy when you see them.

Flavor Queen
A large, green-yellow Pluot, Flavor Queen has sweet, juicy flesh and regular skin. Eat fresh or use in tartlets and cakes.

Coe's Golden Drop
An old English variety, this has clear yellow skin and flesh and a sweet, melting flavour.

Greengage
Distinctively sweet and fragrant, greengages are best eaten fresh, although they also make excellent jam and tarts.

Victoria
The classic English dessert plum, this has an all-too-short summer season. Large, sweet, and pinkish-yellow, Victoria are luscious fresh but also superb for cooking and preserving.

Mirabelle
Small and round, the Mirabelle is an enchanting yellow with a pink blush, often speckled with reddish dots. Intensely sweet, it is mainly used in tarts, preserves, and eaux-de-vie.

PLUM JAM

Most varieties of plum make delicious jam. Jars can be stored in a cool, dark place for up to a year, but once opened keep in the fridge.

MAKES ABOUT 2.5KG (5½LB)

1.5kg (3lb 3oz) firm plums
1.5kg (3lb 3oz) granulated or caster sugar

1 Halve the plums and remove the stones. (If the fruit is too hard to remove them easily, you can cook with the stones in and use a slotted spoon to scoop them out when the jam is boiling.)

2 Put the fruit in a large heavy-based or preserving pan. The pan should not be more than half full to ensure sufficient space for rapid boiling. Add 600ml (1 pint) water and bring to the boil. Reduce the heat and simmer gently for about 30 minutes, or until soft. The exact time will depend on the ripeness of the fruit.

3 Add the sugar and stir until it has completely dissolved, then bring back to the boil. Boil steadily and rapidly for 15–20 minutes, or until setting point is reached.

4 Remove from the heat and skim any froth from the surface of the jam. Let the jam stand for about 5 minutes, then ladle it into warmed, sterilized jars, cover, and seal.

AGED FRESH CHEESES

As the name suggests, these are fresh cheeses that are aged in caves or cellars. Moulds and yeasts grow on the rinds, and the cheeses lose moisture and shrink, causing the rinds to wrinkle. Like all cheeses, each develops its own individual character. Varying in shape, from small rounds and pyramids, to cones, bells, and logs, the cheeses are often covered in herbs, spices, or ash, or wrapped in vine or chestnut leaves, over which the moulds grow. Mostly goat's cheeses, they are moist, creamy, and aromatic when young, gradually becoming more crumbly in texture and nutty tasting, then turning dense, flaky, and brittle with a sharp flavour as they mature. When made with cow's or ewe's milk, the cheeses are typically softer and sweeter.

BUY The best-known aged fresh cheeses are made in the Loire in France – you see them in small straw-lined wooden boxes on rickety tables in French markets – but they are increasingly being produced around the world. They are sold at varying stages of ripeness, depending on the taste and preference of the purchaser: the best way to buy is from a good cheesemonger and take their advice.

STORE Aged fresh cheeses are sold ready to eat, so it is best to enjoy them the same day you buy them or the next. Keep in an airtight container in a cool, moist place or the fridge.

EAT *Fresh:* No cheeseboard is truly complete without one of these attractive, rustic-looking cheeses. *Cooked:* Slice, drizzle with olive oil, and grill or bake on rounds of crisp baguette. An aged fresh cheese, such as Crottin de Chavignol, is wonderfully nutty and aromatic prepared this way.

FLAVOUR PAIRINGS Crusty or fruity bread, peppery salad leaves such as rocket, celery, chicory, dried fruit, walnuts.

CLASSIC RECIPE Chèvre salad.

Fleur de Maquis
The name of this unusual ewe's milk cheese, which means "flower of the maquis", refers to the Corsican landscape. The crunchy, aromatic crust is a perfect partner for the tender cheese and the overall taste is rather honeyed.

Banon AOC
Sold nationally wrapped in chestnut leaves and bound with raffia, the flavour of this French goat's cheese is mild and lactic at first, changing to slightly nutty and then developing a distinct goaty tang.

Bouton-de-Culotte
The smallest of the French cheeses, whose name means "trouser button", is traditionally made in the late summer and stored through autumn for winter use, when it is hard enough to be grated into the pungent local cheese, fromage fort.

Chabichou du Poitou AOC
The attractive, wrinkled white rind dotted with grey, yellow, and blue moulds conceals a French cheese with a firm to dense brittle texture and nutty-to-strong goaty flavours that intensifies as it ages and dries out.

Persil
This French cheese has a less assertive flavour than most ewe's milk cheeses, probably because of its rather short ageing period, but it is still identifiably nutty, with a smooth texture and tender rind. Try it with dried figs and new season's walnuts.

Holy Goat La Luna
From Australia, this very creamy, hand-made goat's cheese has deliciously complex, lingering nutty flavours. Made in a ring shape, a barrel shape, or a small "lobby", it is sometimes wrapped in chestnut leaves.

Boulette d'Avesnes
Made in France with the fresh curds of Maroilles cheese, mashed with herbs and spices, this is a spicy one indeed. A slice of gin will bring out the unusual combination of flavours.

Crottin de Chavignol AOC
This is the classic Loire goat's cheese sold across the world. Known for its piquant taste, it can be eaten at various stages: when young it is tender in texture, becoming harder, crumbly, and sharp as it ages.

Terry Durack
Noodle

Pavilion, London, 1999 (first published 1998)
208 pages
278 x 214 mm (11 x 8³/₈ in.)

Can't tell a soba from a shirataki, a hokkien from a gooksu? This book, with its all-you-need-to-know title, will sort you out. And even after years of eating noodles, you'll probably still need it.

Noodle is the British version of what was originally an Australian publication. Its author, according to the blurb, is Australia's 'most influential food critic'. One, what's more, whose life was saved by Pho Ga, a Vietnamese noodle dish made with fresh rice noodles and chicken; Pho Bo, which appears on the same spread, is made with fillet steak. Both need inordinate quantities of bones, herbs and spices.

The designers and photographer, Geoff Lung, have had huge fun with the subject, from the front cover featuring seventeen different noodles laid out on black to the blown-up portraits of each of the twenty noodles profiled in the book. The portraits are then reduced to postage-stamp size and placed at the bottom of the relevant recipes so we can see which slurpy variety is being used. Each completed dish is photographed, again on a black background, in a fine oriental bowl.

As well as those from China and Japan, Durack covers noodles from South East Asia, India, Korea and Taiwan. The book is dedicated to 'all the people who create the noodles of the world', and Durack pledges to treat their work with respect: 'There is no east meets west, no "oriental pasta", and no garbage.' Noodles prolong life and certainly make it more enjoyable. By the way, a gooksu is a Korean wheat noodle.

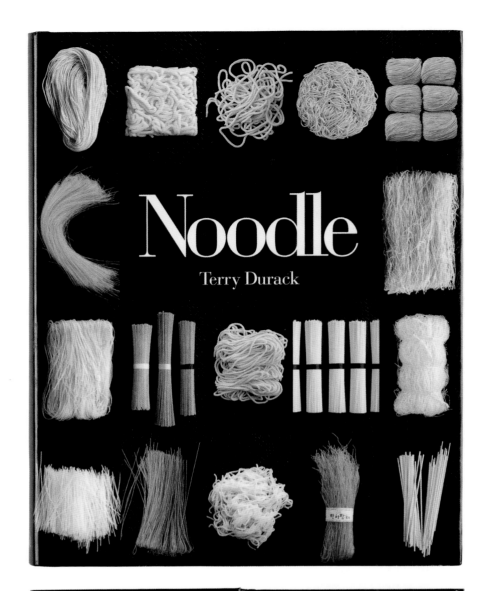

What
Nobody quite knows how an Italian-style fine vermicelli noodle
found its way to India, but nobody is complaining, either. Finer than
angel hair pasta, sevian – also called sev – is enjoyed throughout
India in a milk pudding known as sevian kheer. It is also sometimes
used in soups.

Why
Because these noodles have a pleasant fresh bread smell and a good,
discernible taste that becomes even more pronounced when fried in
ghee. But mainly because of the way they feel in your mouth,
brushing it gently like the bristles of a soft shaving brush.

Where
They are a big favourite of Muslim people, so are found in Sri
Lanka, Pakistan and Malaysia, as well as throughout the length and
breadth of India.

Which
Sevian is always sold dried, normally in protective cardboard boxes,
for it is extremely brittle, and is hard to handle without causing
untold damage. It is usually a pale creamy colour, although there is
a roasted variety that is a distinctive light brown.

How
Generally, sevian is eaten as sevian kheer, and needs only to be
boiled in milk along with the other ingredients for about 15 minutes,
so it absorbs some of the milk and flavourings (see recipe, page 181).

Whatever
For an impressive presentation of sevian kheer, add fresh rose
petals, or a sheet of edible silver or gold leaf, available from Indian
food specialists, just before serving.

Recipes
Sevian kheer (page 181).

15

Nem nuong

The Vietnamese have a happy knack of turning practically any grilled meat
into a complete meal just by serving it on a bed of rice noodles and
accompanying it with a bowl of nuoc cham. Rarely, however, does the idea
work as well as it does with these moist, delicious pork meatballs served on a
bed of rice vermicelli.

1 tbsp jasmine rice
500 g (1 lb) boned pork shoulder or neck
2 tbsp sugar
2 tbsp fish sauce (nuoc mam)
3 cloves of garlic, finely chopped
¼ tsp white pepper
100 g (3 oz) pork fat, chopped into small cubes
1 tsp salt
pinch of baking powder
250 g (8 oz) rice vermicelli
1 cup loosely packed bean sprouts
1 small cucumber, peeled and sliced
½ cup peanuts, roughly chopped
small bunch Asian basil, or fresh mint, picked
1 quantity nuoc cham (see Basics, page 192)

Toast rice in a dry, heavy-bottomed frying pan until lightly golden. Grind or
pound rice to a coarse powder and set aside. Soak 8 wooden skewers in cold
water for 1 hour to stop them from burning on the grill.

Cut pork into thin strips and mix with sugar, fish sauce, garlic and pepper.
Cover and let stand for 30 minutes.

Transfer meat to a food processor with pork fat, ground roasted rice and salt
and whiz until it is a pale, smooth paste. Mix in baking powder with your
hands and, using hands again, roll mixture into balls the size of small plums.
Thread balls onto wooden skewers and char-grill until nice and brown.

Meanwhile, cover noodles in boiling water and leave for 6 to 7 minutes. Drain,
then transfer to a saucepan of boiling water and cook for one more minute.
Rinse in cold water and drain. Put a little vermicelli on each plate and top
with the meatballs. On a separate plate, arrange bean sprouts, cucumber,
peanuts and herbs. The meatballs can also be wrapped in rice paper rounds
and lettuce leaves at the table. Serve with nuoc cham for dipping.

Serves four.

Vietnam   *Noodle i-d 8*   155

David Eyre and the Eagle Chefs

The Eagle Cookbook: Recipes from the Original Gastropub

Absolute Press, Bath, 2009 (revised edition;
first published 2001)
192 pages
254 x 194 mm (10 x 7⅝ in.)

In 1991 Michael Belben and chef David Eyre took an end-of-lease pub on London's Farringdon Road and, on a modest budget, created the first gastropub. The idea behind the Eagle was a simple one: combine the licensing laws of a pub with the output of a quality restaurant and, eureka, a pub with good food. Eyre has described the menu as 'On holiday all around the Mediterranean', adding, 'It is not a dining experience.'

Despite the tiny kitchen spaces – room for only two cooks – the chefs often managed to cater for 120 customers in a single two-hour lunch session. The need for speed meant single courses only: no appetizers, no desserts. The original title of the book (mine is the second edition) was *Big Flavours and Rough Edges*, which tells you all you need to know.

Belben notes that Eyre calls the Eagle a 'stud farm for chefs'. Thus each recipe is credited to the chef who created it. Trish Hilferty provides Spaghettini with Walnut Sauce; Tom Norrington-Davies, Risotto with Sage and Lemon; Sam and Sam Clark, Charmoula Mackerel; and Margot Henderson, Braised Puy Lentils. Eyre has the lion's share, including Salade Niçoise ('skipjack and albacore [tuna] are best left for the cat. Tinned tuna in brine is horrid').

True to the concept of the pub, the book features main meals only, a pioneering idea in itself. The photographs by Lara Holmes, of cooks, diners, shops and the dishes, are fine and moody.

LAMB SHANKS WITH CHICKPEAS
TOM NORRINGTON-DAVIES

SERVES 6

A dish for patient people. The key to tasty lamb shanks and soft chickpeas is time, lots of it. The meat should be cooked until it is almost falling off the bone; the chickpeas should be creamy, with very little bite. This dish is quite brothy – the stock pretty much makes itself, due to the long cooking processes.

5 tablespoons olive oil
6 lamb shanks
2 large onions, roughly chopped
3 garlic cloves, roughly chopped
3 leeks, roughly chopped
3 celery sticks, roughly chopped
about ½ bottle of white wine
1 teaspoon dried mint
a generous pinch of saffron
2 tablespoons tomato purée
about 250g/9oz chickpeas, soaked in cold water overnight, or 2 x 400g/14oz tins of chickpeas (look for a brand that adds nothing but salt and water)
a bunch of parsley or coriander, chopped
salt and freshly ground black pepper

Heat the olive oil in a large frying pan over a fierce heat. Brown the lamb shanks in it and then put them to one side. Pour the fat and juices from the pan into a large casserole and use them to fry the onions, garlic, leeks and celery, adding a little more oil if you need to. When the vegetables have softened but not browned, add the wine, mint and saffron. As soon as it is bubbling, stir in the tomato purée. Add the lamb shanks and turn to coat them with the other ingredients. Add enough water for the shanks to be just about covered, but not swimming. Cover and cook over a low heat for about 2 hours.

Meanwhile, deal with the chickpeas, if you are using dried ones. Drain them of their soaking water, put them in a large pan of unsalted water and bring to the boil. Boil them rapidly for 10 minutes, then drain again. Now cover them with fresh water again and simmer until tender. The best way to get chickpeas right is to keep tasting the odd one. If the water evaporates before the chickpeas are tender, just add more boiling water from the kettle.

When the lamb has been cooking for about 2 hours, add the chickpeas and enough of their cooking liquid to cover. If they look as if they will swamp the stew, don't add them all. Continue cooking until the lamb is tender and the chickpeas are a little overcooked; make sure the stew does not dry out – add a little more liquid if necessary.

Serve in bowls with plenty of liquid, garnished with the parsley or coriander and accompanied by some good bread for mopping up the juices.

SPANISH ROAST VEGETABLE SALAD
ESCALIVADA **KATE LEWIS**

SERVES 4–6

This dish isn't sure if it's a salad or a stew but it is lovely both as an accompaniment to meat or fish and as a dish on its own. If you can cook the vegetables on an open fire or barbecue, so much the better, as the flavour will be much improved. Otherwise, roast them in a hot oven.

2 large baking potatoes
3 aubergines
3 red peppers
2 red onions
extra virgin olive oil
10 basil leaves, torn
2 courgettes, cut into 2cm/¾-inch pieces
sea salt and freshly ground black pepper

Pierce the skin of each potato and aubergine 3 or 4 times with a fork or sharp knife. Place all the vegetables except the courgettes on a baking sheet and roast on the top shelf of an oven preheated to 220°C/gas mark 7, until they are cooked through and the skins are evenly coloured (or, alternatively roast them over a hot fire or barbecue). The peppers and aubergines will need 20–30 minutes and the potatoes and onions up to an hour.

When the vegetables are cool enough to handle, peel them and roughly break them into large chunks. Dress the aubergines and potatoes generously with olive oil, salt, pepper and some of the torn basil and mix together in a serving dish.

Season the courgettes and then fry them in olive oil until lightly coloured and tender. Lay them on top of the aubergine and potatoes with the peppers and onions. Season well, add the remaining basil and dress with more olive oil. Serve hot or at room temperature.

David Eyre and the Eagle Chefs

Fannie Farmer

The Boston Cooking-School Cook Book

Ottenheimer, Baltimore, 2000
(reprint; first published 1896)
624 pages
189 x 122 mm (7½ x 4¾ in.)

This is a story of triumph over adversity. Fannie Farmer, whose cookery book is now so famous that, like Mrs Beeton's grand work, it is simply referred to by the author's name, suffered a stroke when she was sixteen. It left her unable to walk, effectively ending her formal education. However, at the age of thirty, by now walking again but with a severe limp, she enrolled in the Boston Cooking-School, rising to become its principal by 1891.

Five years later, Farmer's cookery book was published. Little, Brown, the publishers, had no faith in her. In addition to limiting the print run to 3000 copies (a big mistake), they made her pay for it. The book contains more than 1800 recipes, along with domestic advice and nutritional information. There is a whole chapter on cooking for the sick – which Farmer must have known a lot about. She died in 1915 aged only fifty-seven.

The recipes are innovative in that amounts of ingredients are given in tablespoons and cups; weighing scales are not needed. Indeed, this is the perfect stand-alone recipe book, and, I imagine, many young American wives had no other. The language is simple, easily understood and highly practical. Truffles, for example, are dismissed as 'too expensive for ordinary use'. Other recipes are period pieces: a plain omelette is accompanied by white sauce, lobsters 'are difficult of digestion' and terrapins, poor things, 'should always be cooked alive'. There are a few simple illustrations and, at the back of the book, some amusing (to the modern reader, at least) advertisements.

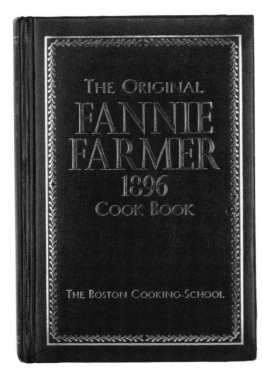

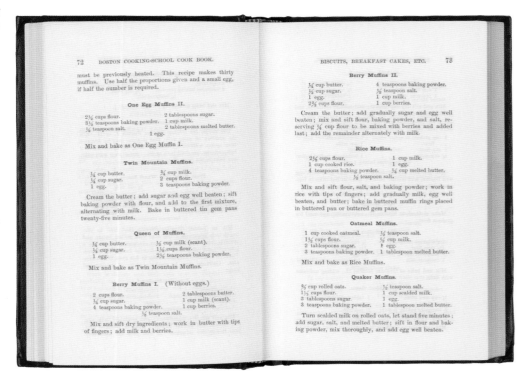

Top, right: Why shouldn't cookery books carry advertising to help with the costs? It's a perfectly logical idea, and perhaps should be copied by struggling publishers today.

DIVISION AND WAYS OF COOKING A SIDE OF BEEF.

HIND-QUARTER.

Divisions.		Ways of Cooking.
Flank (thick and boneless)		Stuffed, rolled and braised, or corned and boiled.
Round	Aitchbone	Cheap roast, beef stew, or braised.
	Top	Steaks, best cuts for beef tea.
	Lower Part	Hamburg steaks, curry of beef, and cecils.
	Vein	Steaks.
Rump	Back	Choicest large roasts and cross-cut steaks.
	Middle	Roasts.
	Face	Inferior roasts and stews.
	Tip	Extra fine roasts.
Loin	Middle	Sirloin and porterhouse steaks.
	First Cut	Steaks and roast.
The Tenderloin	Sold as a Fillet or cut in Steaks	Larded and roasted, or broiled.
Hind-shin		Cheap stew or soup stock.

FORE-QUARTER.

Five Prime Ribs		Good roast
Five Chuck Ribs		Small steaks and stews.
Neck		Hamburg steaks.
Sticking-Piece		Mincemeat.
Rattle Rand	Thick End, Second Cut, Thin End, Navel End	Corned for boiling.
Brisket	Butt End or Fancy Brisket	Finest pieces for corning.
Fore-shin		Soup stock and stews.

Other Parts of Beef Creature used for Food.

BRAINS	Stewed, scalloped dishes, or croquettes.
TONGUE	Boiled or braised, fresh or corned.
HEART	Stuffed and braised.
LIVER	Broiled or fried.
KIDNEYS	Stewed or sautéd.
TAIL	Soup.
SUET (kidney suet is the best).	
TRIPE	Lyonnaise, broiled, or fried in batter.

1. Aitchbone.
2. A rump from which cross-cut steaks have been cut.
3. A loin from which to cut porterhouse steaks.
   a. Sirloin. b. Tenderloin. c. Kidney-suet.

The Effect of Different Temperatures on the Cooking of Meat.

By putting meat in cold water and allowing water to heat gradually, a large amount of juice is extracted and meat is tasteless; and by long cooking the connective tissues are softened and dissolved, which gives to the stock when cold a jelly-like consistency. This principle applies to soup-making.

By putting meat in boiling water, allowing the water to boil for a few minutes, then lowering the temperature, juices in the outer surface are quickly coagulated, and the inner juices are prevented from escaping. This principle applies where nutriment and flavor is desired in meat. Examples : Boiled mutton, fowl.

Clean and pick over clams, reserve liquor, and add to hard part of clams, finely chopped; put aside soft part of clams. Heat slowly to boiling point clams and oysters with liquor from both, strain through cheese cloth. Scald milk with onion, mace, parsley, and bay leaf; remove seasonings, and add milk to stock. Thicken with butter and flour cooked together, add soft part of clams, and cook two minutes. Season with salt and pepper.

Cream of Clam Soup.

Make as French Oyster Soup, using clams in place of oysters.

Lobster Bisque.

2 lb. lobster.	¼ cup butter.
2 cups cold water.	¼ cup flour.
4 cups milk.	1½ teaspoons salt.
Few grains of cayenne.	

Remove meat from lobster shell. Add cold water to body bones and tough end of claws, cut in pieces; bring slowly to boiling point, and cook twenty minutes. Drain, reserve liquor, and thicken with butter and flour cooked together. Scald milk with tail meat of lobster, finely chopped; strain, and add to liquor. Season with salt and cayenne; then add tender claw meat, cut in dice, and body meat. When coral is found in lobster, wash, wipe, force through fine strainer, put in a mortar with butter, work until well blended, then add flour, and stir into soup. If a richer soup is desired, White Stock may be used in place of water.

1. Saucepan, with purée strainer and potato masher.
2. Purée strainer.
3. Soup kettle.

CHAPTER IX.

SOUPS WITHOUT STOCK.

Black Bean Soup.

1 pint black beans.	⅛ teaspoon pepper.
2 quarts cold water.	¼ teaspoon mustard.
1 small onion.	Few grains cayenne.
2 stalks celery, or	3 tablespoons butter.
¼ teaspoon celery salt.	1½ tablespoons flour.
½ tablespoon salt.	2 hard boiled eggs.
1 lemon.	

Soak beans over night; in the morning drain and add cold water. Slice onion, and cook five minutes with half the butter, adding to beans, with celery stalks broken in pieces. Simmer three or four hours, or until beans are soft; add more water as water boils away. Rub through a sieve, reheat to the boiling point, and add salt, pepper, mustard, and cayenne well mixed. Bind with remaining butter and flour cooked together. Cut

Michael Fennelly

East Meets Southwest: Innovative Cuisine from Santacafé

Chronicle Books, San Francisco, 1991
108 pages
244 x 251 mm (9⅝ x 9⅞ in.)

I include this book because it teaches us something very important, a subject most cookery books don't address: that is, how the food looks on the plate. While I know all about dribbling and scattering red chard seedlings, Fennelly (who trained as a designer) takes this further, using coloured plates, boards and stones. I find it quite inspiring, although as a domestic cook you can't be quite so poncey.

In the 1980s Fennelly was the chef at Santacafé in Santa Fe, New Mexico, a restaurant in a nineteenth-century adobe Spanish colonial courtyard house. There he blended Japanese cooking with New Mexican. 'It is my hope that everyone who uses this book will come away with a new vision of food – an understanding of its beauty when it is presented in its purest form.'

From the title page, where Charles Greer's photographs show the seven different Japanese squashes grown specially for the restaurant, the care taken with display is evident. I love the black-dotted rectangular dish for fresh mozzarella with shiitake mushrooms, the oysters with chilli-ginger salsa served

surrounded by pine cuttings, the snake-shaped biscochitos and, with a sudden return to traditional china, the blue-and-white plate for the wild-mushroom enchiladas with red pepper sauce. This book will have you searching the antique shops and jumble sales for wonderful crockery finds, beaches for pebbles and your garden for edible flowers.

EAST MEETS SOUTHWEST

INNOVATIVE CUISINE FROM SANTACAFÉ

BY MICHAEL FENNELLY

WITH A FOREWORD BY JAMES BIRO   PHOTOGRAPHY BY CHARLES GREER

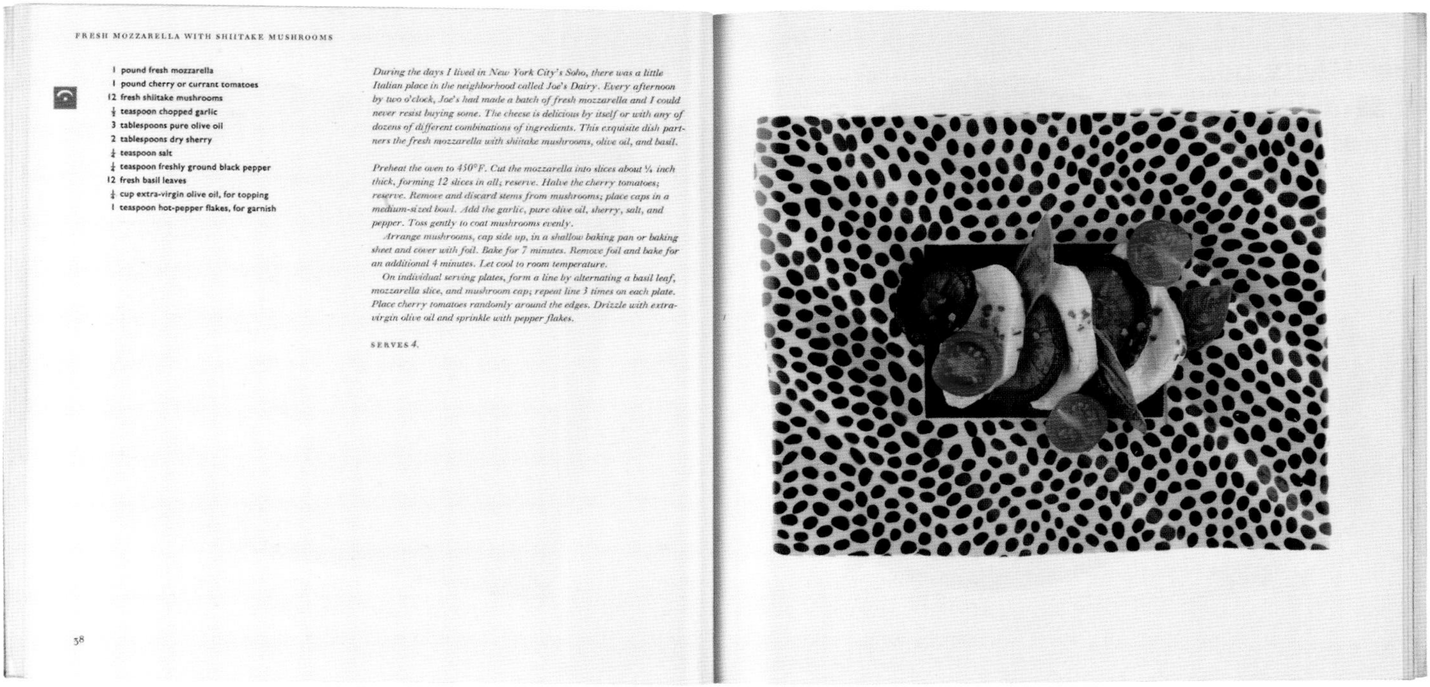

FRESH MOZZARELLA WITH SHIITAKE MUSHROOMS

1 pound fresh mozzarella
1 pound cherry or currant tomatoes
12 fresh shiitake mushrooms
½ teaspoon chopped garlic
3 tablespoons pure olive oil
2 tablespoons dry sherry
½ teaspoon salt
¼ teaspoon freshly ground black pepper
12 fresh basil leaves
¼ cup extra-virgin olive oil, for topping
1 teaspoon hot-pepper flakes, for garnish

During the days I lived in New York City's Soho, there was a little Italian place in the neighborhood called Joe's Dairy. Every afternoon by two o'clock, Joe's had made a batch of fresh mozzarella and I could never resist buying some. The cheese is delicious by itself or with any of dozens of different combinations of ingredients. This exquisite dish partners the fresh mozzarella with shiitake mushrooms, olive oil, and basil.

Preheat the oven to 450°F. Cut the mozzarella into slices about ¼ inch thick, forming 12 slices in all; reserve. Halve the cherry tomatoes; reserve. Remove and discard stems from mushrooms; place caps in a medium-sized bowl. Add the garlic, pure olive oil, sherry, salt, and pepper. Toss gently to coat mushrooms evenly.

Arrange mushrooms, cap side up, in a shallow baking pan or baking sheet and cover with foil. Bake for 7 minutes. Remove foil and bake for an additional 4 minutes. Let cool to room temperature.

On individual serving plates, form a line by alternating a basil leaf, mozzarella slice, and mushroom cap; repeat line 3 times on each plate. Place cherry tomatoes randomly around the edges. Drizzle with extra-virgin olive oil and sprinkle with pepper flakes.

SERVES *4.*

58

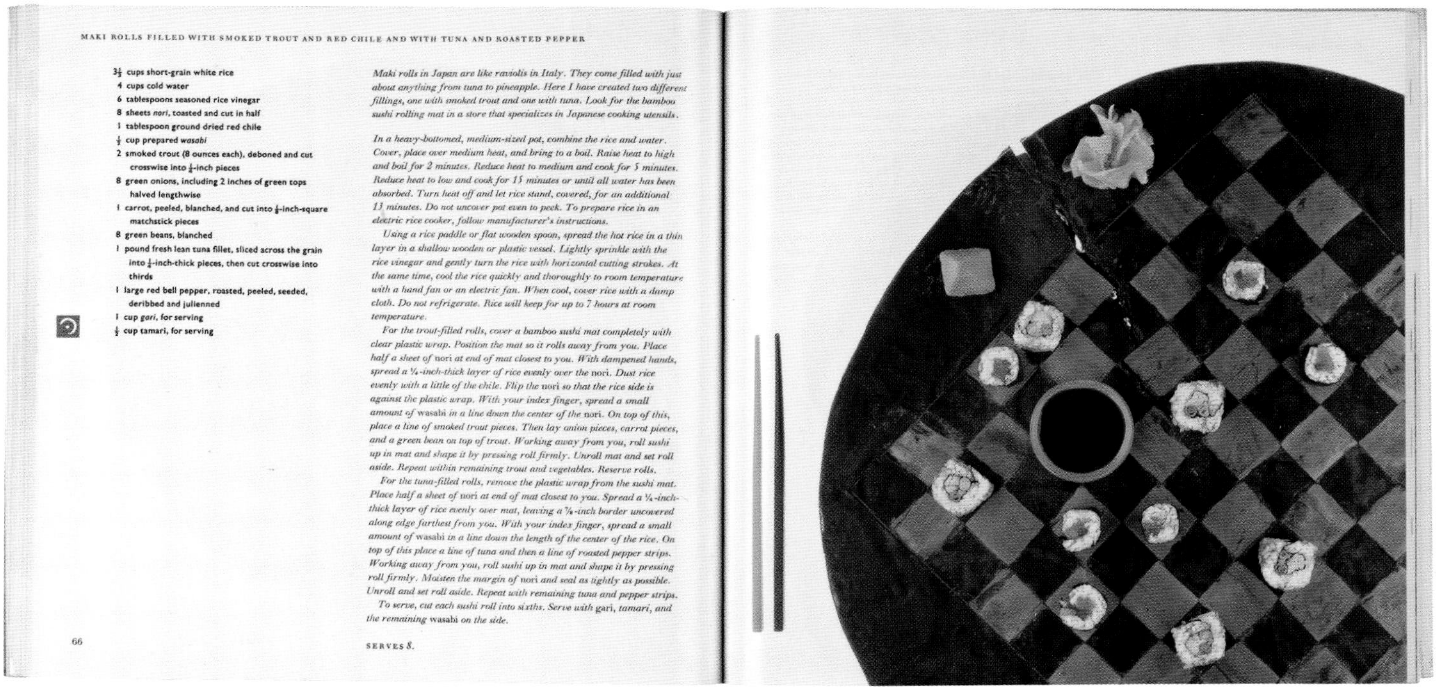

MAKI ROLLS FILLED WITH SMOKED TROUT AND RED CHILE AND WITH TUNA AND ROASTED PEPPER

3½ cups short-grain white rice
4 cups cold water
6 tablespoons seasoned rice vinegar
8 sheets *nori*, toasted and cut in half
1 tablespoon ground dried red chile
½ cup prepared *wasabi*
2 smoked trout (8 ounces each), deboned and cut crosswise into ¼-inch pieces
8 green onions, including 2 inches of green tops halved lengthwise
1 carrot, peeled, blanched, and cut into ⅛-inch-square matchstick pieces
8 green beans, blanched
1 pound fresh lean tuna fillet, sliced across the grain into ½-inch-thick pieces, then cut crosswise into thirds
1 large red bell pepper, roasted, peeled, seeded, deribbed and julienned
1 cup *gari*, for serving
½ cup tamari, for serving

Maki rolls in Japan are like raviolis in Italy. They come filled with just about anything from tuna to pineapple. Here I have created two different fillings, one with smoked trout and one with tuna. Look for the bamboo sushi rolling mat in a store that specializes in Japanese cooking utensils.

In a heavy-bottomed, medium-sized pot, combine the rice and water. Cover, place over medium heat, and bring to a boil. Raise heat to high and boil for 2 minutes. Reduce heat to medium and cook for 5 minutes. Reduce heat to low and cook for 15 minutes or until all water has been absorbed. Turn heat off and let rice stand, covered, for an additional 13 minutes. Do not uncover pot even to peek. To prepare rice in an electric rice cooker, follow manufacturer's instructions.

Using a rice paddle or flat wooden spoon, spread the hot rice in a thin layer in a shallow wooden or plastic vessel. Lightly sprinkle with the rice vinegar and gently turn the rice with horizontal cutting strokes. At the same time, cool the rice quickly and thoroughly to room temperature with a hand fan or an electric fan. When cool, cover rice with a damp cloth. Do not refrigerate. Rice will keep for up to 7 hours at room temperature.

For the trout-filled rolls, cover a bamboo sushi mat completely with clear plastic wrap. Position the mat so it rolls away from you. Place half a sheet of nori *at end of mat closest to you. With dampened hands, spread a ¼-inch-thick layer of rice evenly over the* nori. *Dust rice evenly with a little of the chile. Flip the* nori *so that the rice side is against the plastic wrap. With your index finger, spread a small amount of* wasabi *in a line down the center of the* nori. *On top of this, place a line of smoked trout pieces. Then lay onion pieces, carrot pieces, and a green bean on top of trout. Working away from you, roll sushi up in mat and shape it by pressing roll firmly. Unroll mat and set roll aside. Repeat within remaining trout and vegetables. Reserve rolls.*

For the tuna-filled rolls, remove the plastic wrap from the sushi mat. Place half a sheet of nori *at end of mat closest to you. Spread a ¼-inch-thick layer of rice evenly over mat, leaving a ⅞-inch border uncovered along edge farthest from you. With your index finger, spread a small amount of* wasabi *in a line down the length of the center of the rice. On top of this place a line of tuna and then a line of roasted pepper strips. Working away from you, roll sushi up in mat and shape it by pressing roll firmly. Moisten the margin of* nori *and seal as tightly as possible. Unroll and set roll aside. Repeat with remaining tuna and pepper strips.*

To serve, cut each sushi roll into sixths. Serve with gari, *tamari, and the remaining* wasabi *on the side.*

SERVES *8.*

66

This is what happens when a visual man turns into a cook. The book's design, by Fennelly and Eleanor Caponigro, shows that style can be added to substance.

M.F.K. Fisher
With Bold Knife and Fork

Vintage, London, 2001 (first published 1969)
320 pages
196 x 128 mm (7¾ x 5 in.)

M.F.K. Fisher – although she married three times, she kept the name of her first husband – died in 1992 at the age of eighty-three. It is a tribute to her enduring and elegant writing that my edition of *Knife and Fork* came out nine years later. John Updike described her as 'a poet of the appetites', while W.H. Auden claimed, 'I do not know of anyone in the United States who writes better prose.' What's more, once you dive into her essays on food, the result is uplifting and educational. She clearly had a huge circle of friends, many rich or grand; she also travelled widely and, later (hurrah!), was active in the American civil rights movement.

Every essay in this book is delightful. I love the idea of a famous (but unnamed) Hollywood star – as far from a peasant as you can get – cooking a peasant leek-and-potato soup. In the chapter on rice Fisher includes risotto, jambalaya, curry and a line from a Fats Waller song: 'Swimpses and rice / Are *very* nice!' She also recounts fishermen swapping recipes in a bar in Delaware: 'Then I throw in some goddamn sherry and it makes, man, well ... *good*.' A Life Saver is a soup made from stock, tomato juice or V8, and clam juice. Nothing more.

This is not so much a cookery book as a good read with recipes. What shines through is Fisher's sheer *joie de vivre* and enjoyment of food, whether grand, exotic or basic. It's combined with extraordinary knowledge of food in history and literature. A good first edition to collect.

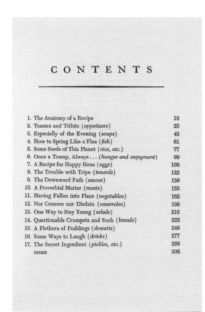

the Russian River grow fewer with the years and because most of the pitiable stuff called by name in the local markets is beneath my stove's contempt. It has been frozen, perhaps when caught and perhaps not, and then thawed again. It does not smell right. It does not feel right to my disdaining but always hopeful finger. Then it does not taste right, once cooked. A pox on it.

But I do use *frozen* fish, which I myself can pick up like bleak logs now and then in the markets. They tease my inventiveness. And of course I use canned and pickled and smoked fish as the spirit moves me, with no feeling of betrayal to my inner standards. Here in my town we can occasionally buy fresh salmon, and more rarely the excellent rex sole, with its blunt taste of iodine. In season, if we are lucky, there are shipments of cooked crab, best eaten cracked in the San Francisco fashion, with lemon juice and a mayonnaise firm in its taste of olive oil. (This calls imperatively for crusty bread, and to my mind none is better than the flat loaves of "sourdough" sold on Fisherman's Wharf, which fortunately can be bought in our whole area if people are insistent and persistent. Any light dry wine will do, but a Grey Riesling from Livermore Valley is traditional in our family.)

There used to be a good fishman in this little town, but he has gone from my scene. He would blow a horn here and there inside the city limits, the way the mobile merchants did when I lived on a farm in Provence. It was fun, forewarned and armed with my wallet and a tray or basket, to meet him at the curb. Neighbors would gather, and of course our cats. He had his own two-legged pets, nice old ladies who had been buying from him for fifty years and got the best of his family's catch before we ever even heard about it. Still, we fared well. I miss him. He used to plunge onto the dark roads up to Napa Valley right from his brothers' boat at the Wharf, and as early morning traffic grew thicker his outdated driving habits failed him, and he and all the freshly caught fish got spilled a few times too many. . . .

I can still fake a lot, thank God. I can make a very decent oyster stew, for instance, with the Western Olympias shucked and packed into glass jars and kept chilled in reputable markets, and even canned ones will do, if one is fortunate with the brand. Often large coarse-seeming oysters, fresh or canned, prove very rewarding in flavor when chopped finely or put through a food

grinder and then added to a basic cream soup. Purists strain most such blends, but at home I like them "rough." And here is a good recipe, unorthodox as All Get Out (a tantalizing comparison from unknown but not too remote ancestral sources), for a kind of stew that might raise eyebrows if not shoulders and hackles of Escoffier et Cie. It is one of those things easy to assemble and serve forth on buttered toast . . . and it is as good made with clams, chopped or whole, fresh or canned!

Sunday Night Oysters

    3 tablespoons butter
    1 small chopped onion
        or
    6 whole scallions, thinly sliced
    1 #2 can tomatoes with juice (2 to 3 cups)
    Salt, pepper
    ½ cup chopped parsley and/or other herbs, to taste
    1 pint canned oysters with juice (about 3 cups)
    4 eggs
    Hot buttered toast

Melt butter. Cook onion slowly until translucent. Add tomatoes and heat until bubbling. Season and add herbs. Simmer 8 to 10 minutes, add oysters, and mix well. Carefully break eggs into bubbling sauce. Cover, remove from stove, and let stand until eggs are set. Serve over and with hot toast.

Once I got caught up in a wild correspondence about how to tell when an oyster is bad. It involved all the old wives' tales, including the trick of seeing if a silver coin would turn black if left with the opened mollusks in a covered dish. One experienced old trencherman/chef advised me to drink copiously of the lowest type of rotgut red wine if ever I suspected that I had downed a potential murderer, and then flush it out of my system in an almost equally lethal flood of tannic acid. And perhaps the most stoical counsel, especially since I had just swallowed the oyster I at once suspected to be bad, and had at least nine more on my plate (they were flown to Berne from Bordeaux that morning, the maître d'hôtel had assured us . . .), was a cool remark which still has almost the ring of an adage to it: "As in certain other forms of physical assault, sit back and enjoy it. You will either be

---

13

One Way to Stay Young

A MAN I COUNT AMONG MY MOST TRUSTED FRIENDS ONCE SAID of a green salad, "I can recommend this dish to all who have confidence in me: salad refreshes without weakening, and comforts without irritating, and I have a habit of saying that it makes us younger." Jean Anthelme Brillat-Savarin was going into his seventies when he published this mild remark in 1825, a few months before his death, but he was and is one of the youngest people I ever met. It could not have been the salads alone . . . but surely his countrymen's habit of following a good dish with some leaves of green lettuces is one of the best ways to stay refreshed and comforted in our pattern of survival.

I much prefer it to a custom which is rapidly spreading into American culture from the West Coast, where I suspect it was a stepchild, spawned by homesick refugees, of the Italian way of eating a few fresh raw things before the *pasta*: the ubiquitous

210

"tossed green salad" served automatically at the beginning of many restaurant meals, and perhaps more private ones. I suppose it is better to eat something from the overfilled bowls of chopped lettuces and radishes and so on, which are put before the diners while they wait for the rare grilled steak with stuffed baked potato to be slapped down, than it is to plunge right into that mechanical blast of proteins. At least it prepares the stomach, if not the tastebuds, for what will soon come sizzling from the infrared grill, and it would throw into chaos the whole routine of not only the waitresses but the kitchen to try to replace it with a small hors d'oeuvre, in an average eating place in America.

As one looks around a public dining room, and if one can see through the deliberately tactful gloom, it is as if above almost every head, at least of the males, a little banner floats, saying bravely: MIGHT AS WELL EAT SOME RABBIT FOOD WHILE THAT T-BONE-TENDERLOIN-FILET-MIGNON GETS CHARRED ON THE OUTSIDE AND BLUE-RARE INSIDE, GOD DAMN IT. And the salads are badly concocted, badly mixed, and decorated with tasteless olives, rounds of overdeveloped radish, now and then a quarter of hard-boiled egg, or a scallion stuck almost sheepishly on one side. I know one place, quasi-Italian, where marinated garbanzos are to be discovered at the bottoms of the awkward little ice-cold bowls. I seek them out.

In general this silly business called "tossed green salad" constitutes what in France is called a hunger-killer, an *abat-faim*, to keep the customer sober enough to see the steak he has ordered, something in place of a couple more vodka martinis from the bar. The dreadful bowls can be assembled hours ahead of time, and pulled out of the salad reefer as needed by the waitresses, who will then douse them with "Russian-Thousand-Island-Roquefort" according to the customer's wish. (It is generally disastrous to say no to this rattle of choices and ask for plain vinegar and olive oil. . . .)

In other words, I deplore the whole caper, and hope it is not creeping too firmly into what I still like to think of as the home kitchen in our country. A green salad, I firmly believe, should *follow* the main course of a meal, at noon or night, and should be made almost always and almost solely of fresh crisp garden lettuces tossed at the last with a plain vinaigrette. "I can recommend

---

a fruit jelly. Top them with butter. Bake them as one would the fruits above.

And so on.

Every plain cook, which means a day-to-day cook enjoying and learning from experience, will have dozens of such easy and generally unwritten maneuvers ready to use. It is good to read classical manuals for both help and pleasure, and to look also at whatever drifts into view from the fastly rolling culinary presses of America and the rest of the world. There are astonishing variations on the old themes. . . .

I feel like a patriot named Pareto, who in 1900 or so exclaimed about a totally opposite subject, "Give me a fruitful error, and time, full of seeds, bursting with its own corrections!" Georgie-Porgie, you may keep your sterile truth for yourself, and let boys and girls too, burst with their own corrections of the stodgy things you stole along with the kisses! There is plenty left. *Fall to, therefore!*

16

Some Ways to Laugh

FOR ANYONE WHO "DRINKS HIS WINE WITH LAUGHTER AND WITH glee," as it says we do in the song about the tavern in the town, it will perhaps seem odd for me to include coffee-tea-milk in a list of potables, and certainly they do not qualify as *apéritifs* or cocktails. But I am putting them here because they are liquid and a part of our life and I want to get them out of the way. Other people have written about them, with greater skill and knowledge, from Brillat-Savarin to Soyer and beyond, and their words are available in most libraries, for those of us whose opinions can accept some embellishing.

In the same way, it is wasteful of me to say much about either spirits or wines, in the face of bad to wonderful books about them which continue to be written after several thousand years of steady praise and some blame. As for beers and their like, I agree with A. E. Housman, who wrote as one who should know,

277

Hannah Glasse

The Art of Cookery Made Plain and Easy

Printed for Alexander Donaldson, Edinburgh, 1786 (sixteenth edition; first published 1746)
492 pages
Modern binding
175 x 100 mm (6⅞ x 3⅞ in.)

Below, right: Innovation can strike at any time. Glasse's wonderful fold-out guide to what to eat when includes 'Larks à la Surprife' (February) and 'Ragoo'd Lobfters' (November).

There is a theory that the best cookery writers all share a tragic past: Mrs Beeton, Elizabeth David, Nigel Slater, Nigella Lawson. Hannah Glasse, likewise. She was an illegitimate child, brought up in her father's household (as was fairly common in the eighteenth century) in Hexham, Northumberland; however, he died when she was sixteen. After that, marriage to a spendthrift Irish soldier, eleven children (five survived) and service in Lord Donegal's household in Essex all followed.

Glasse wrote *The Art of Cookery* anonymously (her authorship was discovered only in 1938). In it was the first British recipe for curry, and recipes that were indeed plain and easy. The writing avoided jargon, the ingredients were available and affordable, the method simplified (although many of the recipes were copied from earlier sources). 'The great cooks have such a high way of expressing themselves, that the poor girls are at a loss to know what they mean', she wrote. It's not that different these days. Her various creations included trifle, and her crayfish soup and venison pasty can still be made today.

Writer and former television chef Clarissa Dickson Wright is a great champion of Glasse and, in *A History of English Food* (2011), suggests she should be better known. She was, Dickson Wright adds, 'the mother of the modern dinner party'. But, thanks to her husband's ways, she went bankrupt in 1745, sold the copyright to her book and was imprisoned in both Fleet and Marshalsea prisons. She died in poverty. Prospect Books has published a facsimile of the first edition.

wine, two shalots shred small, boil them, a[nd]
the dish, with the gravy which comes out o[f]
it eats well. Spit your meat before you [...]
inside.

Another way to force a sirloin.

When it is quite roasted, take it up, [...]
the dish with the inside uppermost, with a [...]
lift up the skin, hack and cut the inside ver[y]
a little pepper and salt over it, with two [...]
it with the skin, and send it to table. Yo[u]
red wine or vinegar, just as you like.

To force the inside of a rump of bee[f.]

You may do it just in the same manner,
the outside skin, take the middle of the mea[t]
as before-directed ; put it into the same plac[e,]
fine skewers put it down close.

A rolled rump of beef.

Cut the meat all off the bone whole, [...]
down from top to bottom, but not throug[h]
spread it open, take the flesh of two fowl[s]
suet, an equal quantity, and as much cold [...]
if you have it, a little pepper, an anchovy, [...]
grated, a little thyme, a good deal of pars[ley]
mushrooms, and chop them all together, be[at]
a mortar, with a half-pint bason full of crumb[s]
mix all these together, with four yolks of eg[gs]
into the meat, cover it up, and roll it roun[d]
skewer in, and tie it with a packthread cro[ss]
to hold it together ; take a pot or large sauce[pan]
will just hold it, lay a layer of bacon and [...]
beef cut in thin slices, a piece of carrot, [some]
pepper, mace, sweet herbs, and a large oni[on]
rolled beef on it, just put water enough to [...]
the beef ; cover it close, and let it stew ver[y]
slow fire for eight or ten hours, but not too f[ast]
you find the beef tender, which you will kno[w by run-]
ning a skewer into the meat, then take it o[ut]
up hot, boil the gravy till it is good, then [...]
and add some mushrooms chopped, some [...]

morels cut small, two spoonfuls of red or white wine,
the yolks of two eggs, and a piece of butter rolled in
flour ; boil it together, set the meat before the fire, baste
it with butter, and throw crumbs of bread all over it ;
when the sauce is enough lay the meat into the dish, and
pour the sauce over it. Take care the eggs do not curd.

To boil a rump of beef the French fashion.

Take a rump of beef, boil it half an hour, take it
up, lay it into a large deep pewter dish or stew-pan, cut
three or four gashes in it all along the side, rub the
gashes with pepper and salt, and pour into the dish a
pint of red wine, as much hot water, two or three large
onions cut small, the hearts of eight or ten lettuces cut
small, and a good piece of butter rolled in a little flour ;
lay the fleshy part of the meat downwards, cover it
close, let it stew an hour and a half over a charcoal fire ;
or a very slow coal fire, Observe that the butcher chops
the bone so close, that the meat may ly as flat as you
can in the dish. When it is enough, take the beef, lay
it in the dish, and pour the sauce over it.

Note, When you do it in a pewter dish, it is best
done over a chafing-dish of hot coals, with a bit or two
of charcoal to keep it alive.

Beef escarlot.

Take a brisket of beef, half a pound of coarse sugar, two ounces of bay salt, a pound of common salt ;
mix all together, and rub the beef, lay it in an earthen
pan, and turn it every day. It may ly a fortnight in
the pickle ; then boil it, and serve it up either with sa-
voys or peas pudding.

Note, It eats much finer cold, cut into slices, and
sent to table.

Beef à la daub.

You may take a buttock or a rump of beef, lard it,
fry it brown in some sweet butter, then put it into a
pot that will just hold it ; put in some broth or gravy
hot, some pepper, cloves, mace, and a bundle of sweet
herbs,

D 2

To stew pears in a sauce-pan.

Put them into a sauce-pan, with the ingredients as
before ; cover them, and do them over a slow fire.
When they are enough, take them off.

To stew pears purple.

Pare four pears, cut them into quarters, core them,
put them into a stew-pan, with a quarter of a pint of
water, a quarter of a pound of sugar, cover them with
a pewter plate, then cover the pan with the lid, and do
them over a slow fire. Look at them often, for fear
of melting the plate ; when they are enough, and the
liquor looks of a fine purple, take them off, and lay
them in your dish with the liquor ; when cold, serve
them up for a side-dish at a second course, or just as
you please.

To stew pippins whole.

Take twelve golden pippins, pare them, put the parings into a sauce-pan with water enough to cover
them, a blade of mace, two or three cloves, a piece of
lemon-peel, let them simmer till there is just enough to
stew the pippins in, then strain it, and put it into the
sauce-pan again, with sugar enough to make it like a
syrup ; then put them in a preserving-pan, or clean stew-
pan, or large sauce-pan, and pour the syrup over them.
Let there be enough to stew them in ; when they are
enough, which you will know by the pippins being soft,
take them up, lay them in a little dish with the syrup ;
when cold, serve them up ; or hot, if you chuse it.

A pretty made-dish.

Take half a pound of almonds blanched and beat
fine with a little rose or orange-flower water, then take
a quart of sweet thick cream, and boil it with a piece
of cinnamon and mace, sweeten it with sugar to your
palate, and mix it with your almonds ; stir it well together, and strain it through a sieve. Let your cream
cool, and thicken it with the yolks of six eggs ; then
garnish a deep dish, and lay paste at the bottom, then
put

put in shred artichoke-bottoms, being first boiled, upon
that a little melted butter, shred citron, and candied
orange ; so do till your dish is near full, then pour in
your cream, and bake it without a lid. When it is baked, scrape sugar over it, and serve it up hot. Half an
hour will bake it.

To make kickshaws.

Make puff-paste, roll it thin, and, if you have any
moulds, work it upon them, make them up with preserved pippins. You may fill some with gooseberries,
some with raspberries, or what you please, then close
them up, and either bake or fry them ; throw grated
sugar over them, and serve them up.

Pain perdu, or cream-toasts.

Having two French rolls, cut them into slices as
thick as your finger, crumb and crust together, lay
them on a dish, put to them a pint of cream, and half
a pint of milk ; strew them over with beaten cinnamon
and sugar, turn them frequently till they are tender,
but take care not to break them ; then take them from
the cream with a slice, break four or five eggs, turn
your slices of bread in the eggs, and fry them in clarified butter. Make them of a good brown colour, but
not black ; scrape a little sugar over them. They
may be served for a second-course dish, but are fittest
for supper.

Salamongundy for a middle dish at supper.

In the top-plate in the middle, which should stand
higher than the rest, take a fine pickled herring, bone
it, take off the head, and mince the rest fine. In the
other plates round, put the following things : in one
pare a cucumber, and cut it very thin ; in another apples pared, and cut small ; in another an onion peeled,
and cut small ; in another two hard eggs chopped
small, the whites in one, and the yolks in another ;
pickled girkins in another, cut small ; in another, celery cut small ; in another, pickled red cabbage chopped fine ; take some water-cresses clean washed and
picked, stick them all about and between every plate or
saucer,

Patience Gray

Honey from a Weed: Fasting and Feasting in Tuscany, Catalonia, the Cyclades and Apulia

Macmillan, London, 1987 (first published 1986)
376 pages
233 x 151 mm (9 1/8 x 6 in.)

One curious fact I have discovered since compiling this book is that an extraordinary number of the featured writers were also travellers. Born in Shackleford, Surrey, Patience Gray was a journalist, the translator of much of *Larousse Gastronomique* and a textile designer before marrying a sculptor. 'From then on,' she says, 'my life was governed by his pursuit of marble.' *Honey from a Weed* is the result of that pursuit.

This is a scholarly book, and it's easy to see why the great Alan Davidson (page 68) – 'a St George in action', says Gray – rescued the typescript from oblivion. The fish section alone includes such rarities (to me) as houting, vopa (or *Boops boops*, to use its scientific name) and one called toadfish or sea devil, which turned out to be monkfish. No wonder the fishmongers needed a different name. A section on edible weeds includes dandelion, fat hen and wild beet, with recipes for elderflower fritters and fried wild asparagus. There's also an exhaustive list of utensils, including an oil drizzler (we get its Italian, Greek and Catalonian names, too).

Especially alluring are the illustrations by Corinna Sargood, who travelled throughout Greece and Italy drawing kitchens, including the author's. I envy her. Later, she learned to paint narrowboats. Her kitchens are filled with giant fireplaces, hanging dented copper pans and vast demijohns, their sides covered with plaited straw. They make me homesick for my Tuscan kitchen and tiny trattorias in hilltop villages.

A Book for Cooks

plants to be cultivated in the royal domains; chickpeas occur in this plant list under the name *cicerum italicum*.

Gathered fresh in May, though no one will believe it, they are a short-lived delicacy, brilliant green, growing two to a pod; eaten raw they have a refreshing taste of lemon. Cooked in a dish of rice they delight the eye. But, as the May sun in southern latitudes quickly dries them, they are imagined, even by Italians, to be born brown and born dry.

In Catalonia this winter staple, valued for its nutty flavour as well as for its nourishment, has mercifully received a preliminary cooking by the market ladies. However, I give the recipe starting from scratch.

½ kg (1 lb 2 oz) chickpeas
bicarbonate of soda, a pinch
olive oil
1 onion, finely hashed
chopped parsley
1 large ripe tomato, peeled
1 teaspoon flour
salt and black pepper

for the picada (all to be finely ground together in the mortar)
8 peeled and pounded almonds
a few pine kernels
sea salt
more chopped parsley
garlic

Soak the chickpeas overnight with a pinch of bicarbonate of soda. Rinse and simmer them in an earthenware pot, adding a little salt. Cook for 3 hours, more if need be, then drain and keep some of the liquor.

Heat some oil in a pan, put in the onion and some chopped parsley. When the onion begins to colour, add the tomato, crushing it. Simmer, then add the flour and stir while it thickens. Dilute with a few spoonfuls of chickpea liquor. Put in the chickpeas, some black pepper, and add the *picada*. Simmer on a low flame for 10 minutes. Serve for lunch.

In northern Italy, chickpea flour is used to make appetizing *pizze*, thin as flannel, in Carrara called *Calda! Calda!* The name arose from boys carrying them in covered baskets, shouting their piping hot wares, along the rocky torrent of the Carrione, down which the famished quarrymen returned at evening on foot from the marble mountains.

In the market, a thick pancake called *panizza*, the size of little crumpets, were sold to be taken home to grill or fry. Made like *polenta* but with chickpea flour instead of maize flour, then poured to a specific thickness on a board and punched into rounds when cold.

In the Salento, chickpeas are often soaked overnight, then roasted in the bread-oven on a metal tray before bread-making. Crunched hot as a *passatempo* while waiting for the bread to come out. A neolithic way of dealing with recalcitrant grains, seeds, legumes.

'FAVA E FOGLIA'
purée of dried broad beans with wild chicory

½ kg (1 lb 2 oz) broad beans · olive oil · onion shoots · mint
wild chicory · strips of *pancetta* (salt belly of pork)

Cook the dried broad beans in the usual way in the hearth in the *pignata*, or on the stove in an earthenware pot. Strain when tender, reserving the liquor. Slip off the outer skins.

Cover the bottom of a pan with olive oil and cook in it some finely sliced *sprunzale* (onion shoots, p 164) or wild leeks, then add some leaves of mint and the beans, with a little of their liquor. Cook on a gentle heat till they dissolve, then beat to a purée with a fork. Season.

Serve the purée, which should be rather stiff, with wild chicory which has been washed, boiled, drained, then tossed in a frying pan in which you have first fried some little strips of *pancetta*.

NOTE. Dried beans minus their outer skins exist in commerce. Oddly enough one cannot achieve a smooth purée with these packaged beans. Just a warning.

'PISCIMMARE' · 'fish at sea'

Ironic Salentine name for a fish-less breakfast.

The labourer the night before has supped on a dish of *piselli secchi* (p 67), cooked in the *pignata*, and a dish of rape (p 163). When he rises at dawn in autumn to go fishing or shooting before starting work at 7, his wife hastily puts a pan on the fire, heats some olive oil, then throws in some dried chilli peppers, 2 or 3 tomatoes (*pomodori appesi*, p 324) and then the remaining peas followed by the rape.

He eats it with some home-baked bread and knocks back a glass of wine. (For a quarryman's breakfast, see *Pista e Coza*, p 145).

Feasting

For de la bella caiba
fugge lo lusignolo

Out from the fine cage
flies the nightingale

AND then they went on to Harddlech, and they sat them down and began to regale them with meat and drink; and even as they began to eat and drink there came three birds and began to sing them a certain song, and of all the songs they had ever heard each one was unlovely compared with that. And far must they look out over the deep, yet was it as clear to them as if they were close to them; and at that feasting they were seven years.'

These birds were the immortal birds of Rhiannon.

The passage comes from 'Branwen daughter of Llyr', one of the Four Branches of the *Mabinogion*. It belongs to the episode of the Wondrous Head, and marries feasting with poetry for all time. It is close in spirit to the antique Mediterranean world of which we have perceived the shadow. A feasting is marvellously evoked. We do not see the materials of the feast, we do not hear the birds, we only know all songs were unlovely compared with that and that it lasted seven years. This underlines the transition from common transient time to timelessness of which real feasts are the instrument; their essence also involves the intrusion of the unpredictable. And this is why I am not going to describe feasting; I shall name some feasts.

The feast that began with the May Day bean feast at La Barozza was a feast of a company of friends and relations of the vine grower, a friendship that had long been cemented by successive wine harvests. It started a whole week of feasting – there were excuses enough, May Day being, that year, immediately followed by the Feast of the Ascension. The wonderful month of May flowered in matchless *stornelli*. The vine-yard was full of flowers, nightingales, cuckoos, four-leaved clovers, laughter and the scent of acacia flowers drifting from nearby woods.

The company only reached the imperishable heights of song through perfect familiarity with celebration, of which this week in May was the apogee; the wine had also reached perfection just as the vines were sprouting. Kilos of raw broad beans brought from the market at Sarzana in a sack were consumed, and quantities of *tordelli* and grilled chickens, at a long trestle table on the terrace.

Patience Gray and Primrose Boyd

Plats du Jour

Persephone Books, London, 2006
(reprint; first published 1957)
304 pages
192 x 137 mm (7½ x 5⅜ in.)

This is the exception to my rule that each author is allowed only one book, because while Gray is already represented (page 96), Primrose Boyd is not. It seemed unfair to exclude her masterwork, especially as the book was her idea. The crucial point about *Plats du Jour* is that when it was published in 1957, it sold 50,000 copies in a year, far outstripping Elizabeth David's early books (*Mediterranean Food* first appeared in 1950).

One reason for the book's success must have been the charming cover of a Mediterranean family – grandmother with cat, father about to uncork a bottle – all seated around a table against a rhubarb-pink background. This and the book's black-and-white illustrations were by a young David Gentleman.

Another reason was that, unlike those in David's books, the recipes were adapted to suit English meals: 'We have tried to set down the recipes for a number of dishes of foreign origin, in the belief that English people may be stimulated to interpret them.' Like this sentiment, much of the book is pleasantly old-fashioned, but it's worth remembering that in 1957 English cooks reacted to garlic much as Dracula did, and that there were about three shops in the country where you could get Parmesan and a mezzaluna. Moussaka is explained as 'a Balkan version of shepherd's pie', while *soupe de poisson* 'is particularly relevant on a seaside holiday'.

Unlike David's books, *Plats du Jour* travels widely across Europe, taking in such countries as Hungary, Germany, The Netherlands and even Britain (Mrs Cule's Pickled Tongue), albeit rather half-heartedly.

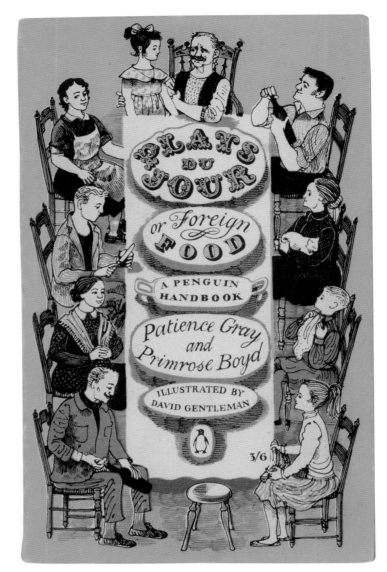

PLATS DU JOUR

VENISON STEW

Cuts of venison unsuitable for roasting can be stewed after a period of hanging. In such a case the piece is divided into suitable joints, rubbed with a mixture of powdered wholespice, ground black peppers, and a little salt, sautéd in mutton fat, and transferred to an earthenware casserole in the oven. When the meat is thoroughly browned, two glasses of red wine or port should be poured over the meat and reduced by rapid boiling. A pint and a half of good stock is heated and added to the casserole, the lid is put on, and the cooking is proceeded with in a moderate oven for a long time, at least 3 hours. The venison is served straight from the hot casserole with red currant jelly or cranberry sauce.

Cranberry Sauce

½ lb cranberries, a slice of lemon peel, the juice of a lemon, a tablespoonful of sugar and a little butter.

Put the cranberries in a pan with only sufficient water to moisten the bottom, put in the lemon peel and the sugar, and simmer very slowly with the lid on for about 40 minutes, by which time the fruit will be pulpy. Beat in the butter, squeeze over the lemon juice, and once it has cooled the sauce is ready.

236

Cheeses

PLATS DU JOUR

Gruyère is made from cows' milk and is a hard cheese with a small proportion of small holes in it. It is made in a circular shape about 6 inches in depth and about 2 feet in diameter. It is one of the finest of all eating cheeses, sweet in flavour and with a wholesome smell. Its only disability is that when cut the outside surface tends to become varnished and very hard. If it has to be kept for a day or two put it in a loosely woven cloth and store in an airy but not too cold place.

250

Fungi

Rose Gray and Ruth Rogers
The River Café Cook Book

Ebury Press, London, 1995
320 pages
245 x 188 mm (9⅝ x 7⅜ in.)

'This is a seminal book from a seminal restaurant', wrote Nigella Lawson (page 132) in a review for *The Times*. What she didn't say is that the design, too, is seminal. Today, it may be hard to appreciate how innovative the design was because so many later cookery books have copied it (as, indeed, chefs have copied the Tuscan cooking).

Designed by the Senate, the book uses colour to brilliant effect, the ultramarine dust jacket leading to intense lemon-yellow endpapers. Coloured pages, their text in clear white type, are scattered throughout the book, as are photographs, by Jean Pigozzi and Martyn Thompson, showing the London cafe's cooks (including such now-famous graduates as Sam and Sam Clark, page 52; Jamie Oliver, page 154; and Hugh Fearnley-Whittingstall) at work or doing such mundane tasks as cleaning the cookers.

Although this is clearly a restaurant cookbook, the recipes, being Tuscan, are quite achievable at home. What they emphasize is the authors' insistence on the best ingredients: 'We were overwhelmed by the enormous variety of produce available in Italian food shops – the local pecorinos … the smoked and salted pancettas, olive oils made by local farms … . In the vegetable markets we found tiny fennel bulbs … stalls that sold only herbs, or garlic or wild leaves.' You can hear their excitement in every word. At first, they grew their own *cavolo nero* from seed brought back from Italy. Now, in Britain, thanks to the River Café, you can buy the Tuscan black cabbage in most major supermarkets.

Penne alla Carbonara

For us the two most important ingredients are excellent free-range eggs, and pancetta stesa.

Serves 6

200 g (7 oz) pancetta, cut into matchsticks

1 tablespoon olive oil

sea salt and freshly ground black pepper

6 egg yolks

120 ml (4 fl oz) double cream

150 g (5 oz) Parmesan, freshly grated

250 g (9 oz) penne rigate

In a large pan fry the pancetta in the olive oil slowly, so that it releases its own fat before becoming crisp. Add some black pepper.

Beat the egg yolks with the cream and season with salt and pepper. Add half the Parmesan.

Meanwhile, cook the penne in a generous amount of boiling salted water, then drain thoroughly. Combine immediately with the hot pancetta and the oil, and then pour in the cream mixture. Stir to coat each pasta piece; the heat from the pasta will cook the egg slightly. Finally add the remaining Parmesan and serve.

Variation

Asparagus: instead of the pancetta, cut 675 g (1.1/2 lb) blanched asparagus into short pieces and fry briefly in oil with a handful of basil leaves. Add to the pasta before combining with the egg sauce.

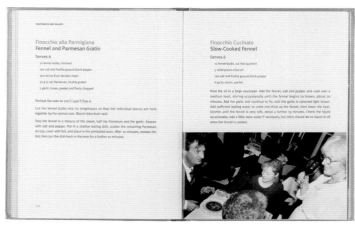

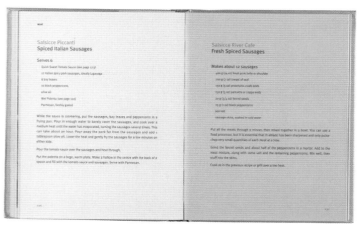

Jane Grigson

Jane Grigson's Vegetable Book

Michael Joseph, London, 1978
608 pages
230 x 154 mm (9 x 6 in.)

Like her mentor, Elizabeth David (page 66), Jane Grigson poses something of a dilemma: which book to pick? I chose this one because I find it the most helpful and use it often. It is dedicated to her husband, Geoffrey, the poet, botanist and author of *The Englishman's Flora* (1955), and is full of his learning. What you get along with the delightful recipes is a huge amount of knowledge about each vegetable.

The book is also idiosyncratic. In her acknowledgements, Grigson thanks 'Mrs Agnes Short who tried to convert me to kale', an obviously unsuccessful endeavour as the vegetable isn't featured. Grigson is pretty unenthusiastic about cabbage, too. The format – vegetables listed alphabetically, from artichoke to yams – doesn't allow for such mixed dishes as minestrone, and garlic has no section to itself.

Grigson writes beautifully, with sly wit: 'The Roman Emperor Tiberius ... had a remarkable partiality for cucumbers, one of his enthusiasms that we can, I think, feel happy to share.' Unlike many others. She blames the disappearance of leeks from the British table between the sixteenth and twentieth century on worries about smelly breath, which also inhibited British use of onions and, especially, garlic. In her introduction, she foresees (wrongly, I fear) high-rise flats where Marmande tomatoes grow on balconies and courgettes trail round the doors.

My copy, a first edition, is set in VIP Times. It features simple illustrations, by Yvonne Skargon, to introduce each vegetable, and, on its jacket, an early use of an eighteenth-century oil painting. In this case it is Antoine Raspal's *Cuisine Provençale*, held by the Musée Réattu in Arles. A book to be used and treasured.

A Book for Cooks

Celtuce is not mentioned in Chinese cookery books published in England, but is an obvious candidate, both leaves and stalk, for Chinese dishes in which spinach or celery figure.

To stir-fry celtuce stalks, heat through two slices of fresh ginger, a small chopped onion and one chopped clove of garlic in three or four spoons of oil. Use a large light frying pan. When it is very hot, after a minute, add the celtuce and stir about until the pieces are coated with oil. Pour in 125 ml (4 fl oz) chicken stock, two tablespoons soya sauce, a teaspoon of sugar and ¼ teaspoon salt. Continue to stir until the celtuce is tender but still slightly crisp. You can, if you want to make a change, cream the sauce by stirring in at the end a teaspoon of cornflour slaked with two tablespoons of water.

If you are using this method for the leaves you may have to raise the heat to maximum to evaporate any wateriness.

CHARD see SWISS CHARD

CHAYOTE

Although the chayote grows on a vine, it does not look much like the gourds we know well, such as courgette or pumpkin. It is more of a ridged green pear in shape, a pear-cucumber to look at, and the vine that seems so tender does not lie submissively on the ground, but scales roofs and trees. The harvesting of chayotes can involve incredible gymnastics, unless you take care to plant them at the foot of a trellis and train the ramping growth sedately on strings across a courtyard or terrace. Then the fruit becomes a deliciously precise crop, hanging down evenly spaced like Christmas decorations. You have only to reach up to pick them and can see why the Chinese call them Buddha's hand gourd.

A friend of mine in Australia, where chokos as they are known there now run wild, will preserve the last fruit of the season so that she can plant a more manageable crop. One year she took into her kitchen an enormous fruit weighing well over a kilo (the ideal eating size is from about 175 g or 6 oz). It soon started to wander. A long pale stem with rudimentary leaves and clinging tendrils burst through the choko from the single flat seed, and explored every cranny of the room, a trellis of a plant, until it found the door. Then she disentangled it carefully and cradled the shrunken parent to a hollow she had made by the trellis, where it could take root and rampage fruitfully. She mostly picks her chokos when they are only a few days old and about 8 cm (3¼ in) long. Then they can be cooked, skin and all, like courgettes, and served as a salad with an olive oil and lemon dressing. Some are left to grow larger, up to about 20 cm (8 in); they go into chutneys, or they are simmered in a red wine syrup like pears and eaten for pudding. You will judge from this that the taste is not pronounced, delicate according to some people, insipid according to others. It is more of a texture and substance than a flavour, though it has its devotees, especially in Mexico and the Caribbean islands. This you might expect, as the chayote is a native of tropical and sub-tropical America (the name comes from the Aztec chayotl).

NETTLES

Young nettles in the spring, when they shoot with fierce bright leaves, are good to eat. Not as good as spinach, whatever some people may claim, but not to be despised especially at a season of the year when greenery is scarce. There was a folk belief that nettles taken in April and May purified the blood. After a winter of stodgy storable foods, one would have welcomed the lighter flavour, and felt better for the vitamins, less stuffy, and so in a sense purified.

Wear gloves and use scissors to snip off nettle leaves, and, as Florence Irwin remarks in *Irish Country Recipes*, choose them from a field in preference to a dusty road. Wash them well, cook them in their own juices and use the well drained purée like spinach. Naturally the sting goes with heat, so that is no worry. Delicious on fried bread with a topping of poached egg or egg mollet, or brains with a creamy sauce.

There is a story about St Columba and nettle soup, that Miss Irwin quotes from Joyce's *Lives of the Saints*. One day the saint met an old woman gathering nettles near his monastery in Ireland, and he asked her why. She replied that with her cow in calf she was deprived of her usual diet of milk and white meats and was making do with nettle soup. The ascetic Columba reflected that if she could keep going on such poor nourishment, with the uncertain prospect of the cow having a healthy calf, he should be able to survive on it even better, as his hopes were for the certain prospect of heaven. His monks were dismayed at Columba's decision, but he seemed to thrive on the soup which he had ordered to be made without milk or butter. After a while Columba too became puzzled at feeling so well. Being a sensible man, he didn't assume a miracle, but sent for the cook. 'There's nothing in your soup but what might have come from the iron pot, or the wooden pot-stick I stir it with.' An evasive answer. Columba went to look at the pot. That was all right. Then he picked up the pot-stick and found that the cook had hollowed it out like a reed, so that he could fill the channel with milk and enrich the soup without anyone noticing. If you have a mind to try St Columba's soup, in either version, here is the recipe.

IRISH NETTLE POTTAGE OR SOUP

½ litre (1 pt) water, or milk, or milk and water, or meat or vegetable stock
30 g (1 oz) butter
30 g (1 oz) rolled oats
½ litre (½ pt) chopped young nettles
pepper, salt
1 good teaspoon chopped parsley

Bring the liquid and butter to boiling point, then stir in the oats. When the pan returns to the boil, add the nettles and seasoning. Cover and simmer for 30 to 45 minutes, stirring occasionally. Taste and correct the seasoning, add the parsley, and leave for another two minutes. Then serve.

IRISH NETTLE BROTH

When the broth is half done, a separate pot of potatoes would be prepared, to be ready at the same time. The meat was taken out and cut up, with a piece or two put into each bowl along with some of the broth and potatoes. Everyone mashed up his bowlful to his own liking, and ate it with a spoon.

1 kg (2 lb) shin or any boiling beef or lamb tied in a piece
2½ litres (4 pt) water
1 teacup pearl barley
bunch of spring onions
1 litre (½ pt) chopped young nettles
pepper, salt, flour

Simmer the first three ingredients for two hours. Add the greenery and give it another hour. Finally add seasoning - this should not be done until the beef is tender, as salt can toughen it. If you like an even thicker soup, mix some of the broth into a tablespoon of flour, then stir this mixture when smooth into the soup, and leave to simmer for a further 15 minutes.

OTHER SUGGESTIONS

Nettle champ, see the recipe for potato champ on page 405, and substitute a teacupful of young chopped nettles for the spring onions.

JOHN EVELYN'S SALAD CALENDAR

Michel Guérard

Cuisine Minceur

Translated and adapted by Caroline Conran
Macmillan, London, 1977 (first published
1976)
416 pages
234 x 156 mm (9¼ x 6⅛ in.)

This is the book that swept through the restaurants and kitchens of Britain in the 1980s, bringing with it tiny portions exquisitely positioned on white hexagonal plates and waiters theatrically flourishing large silver domes as though a rare and beautiful treasure lay beneath – which it usually didn't.

Of course, it's easy now to laugh at the pretension, which had many of us in its grip, but it all began when the restaurateur/author was told by his wife that he was getting portly. When grated carrots drove Guérard to despair, he decided 'to try and fight back … and to do it by modifying some of the fundamental rules of gourmet cooking that have been handed down to us'. One could reasonably suggest that Guérard's need to diet led, in three decades, to the demise of the traditional French cream-and-butter haute cuisine that, until then, had been considered the gourmet's delight.

Guérard explains that the book should not be used as a normal recipe book, but, instead, should be dusted down periodically for a week devoted to *cuisine minceur*. In it he prescribes no more than a single glass of light table wine at each meal, as well as regular consumption of his Eugénie Tisane, an unexciting mix of heather, maize, horsetail, bearberry and cherry stalks. It has to be said that, these rules aside, the recipes, including tomato tarts (without pastry), grilled guinea fowl with limes and plaice cooked with cider, are distinctly appetizing. Of course, given the date of publication, the type is printed in brown; Guérard's drawings, meanwhile, prove that he's better as a chef. The photographs are by Didier Blanchat.

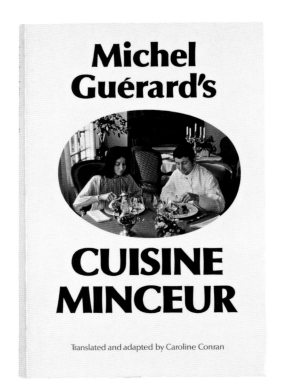

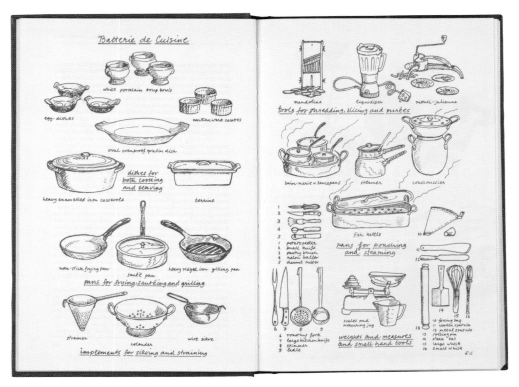

No 106 Veal kidney 'in a green waistcoat'—braised in spinach and lettuce leaves (*Rognon de veau 'en habit vert'*)

No 107 Steamed calf's liver with sweet-sour leeks (*Foie de veau à la vapeur aux blancs de poireaux en aigre-doux*)

135 Watercress Purée

Purée-mousse de cresson

For three or four people

Main ingredients	4 bunches watercress 1·5 litres (2½ pints) water 3 heaped teaspoons coarse salt ½ teaspoon lemon juice 1 teaspoon crème fraîche
Equipment	1 stainless-steel saucepan 1 liquidiser

1 Remove the coarser stalks from the watercress. You will have about 250 g (9 oz) left.

2 Bring the water to the boil, add the salt and plunge in the watercress, blanching for three minutes.

3 Drain the cress and plunge immediately into iced water to prevent it cooking any further.

4 Drain it and purée in the mixer.

5 Pour the resulting purée into the stainless-steel pan and reheat, adding lemon juice and cream.

Served immediately, this purée is a beautiful delicate green, but after a few hours it fades and turns a yellowish-green.

338

136 Onions Cooked in Sherry Vinegar

Marmelade d'oignons au jerez

For four people

Main ingredients	1 kg (2¼ lb) onions sugar substitute equivalent to 2 teaspoons of sugar salt ½ teaspoon pepper 1 teaspoon olive oil 4 tablespoons sherry vinegar
Equipment	1 heavy-based saucepan with a lid

1 Peel the onions and slice them finely.

2 Heat the olive oil in the heavy-based pan, add the onions, sugar substitute, salt and pepper.

3 Cover the pan and allow the onions to brown slowly, stirring from time to time with a wooden spoon.

4 After three-quarters of an hour, pour in the sherry vinegar and allow to cook gently for a further three-quarters of an hour, stirring occasionally. The onions slowly turn into a transparent 'jam'.

Dried fruit (muscatel raisins, prunes, apricots, etc.), previously washed, soaked and plumped in water can be added with the vinegar.

Editor's note This can be eaten on its own as a first course or with grilled or roast pork, beef or lamb.

339

Skye Gyngell
A Year in My Kitchen

Quadrille, London, 2006
256 pages
227 x 164 mm (8⅞ x 6½ in.)

Faced with three excellent books by the former head chef at Petersham Nurseries Cafe in south-west London, I have plumped for her first. Some writers begin slowly and get better (Nigel Slater, for example; page 188); others produce a masterpiece first time. This book is unusual in that Gyngell begins by describing her philosophy and basic ingredients before going on to list the recipes. And it explains why a relatively unknown chef from Australia has won two awards and wide acclaim.

I like the idea of being given a 'toolbox' with base notes, from roasted spices to stock, and top notes, such as lemon zest and chilli-infused oil, because it helps me create my own dishes: the base notes provide the foundation, and the top notes make the dish 'sing'. It is, Gyngell says, 'the way people have cooked in the East forever'. The next few pages list recipes for stock, tea-smoking and chilli oil, among others, and advice is given on such activities as roasting spices, toasting nuts and making sourdough breadcrumbs (something I do every month since I found the recipe). At the back of the book she describes her 'dessert toolbox', again with the intention of encouraging the cook to develop his or her own dishes and combinations.

The photography by Jason Lowe is enticing, a combination of actual dishes and portraits of herbs, the nursery and the chef. The food itself is simple, sophisticated and seductive.

Skye Gyngell's books are written with a personal touch, and so the designer, Lawrence Morton, has perfected a style that immediately identifies the author.

Roasted spice mix

I use this combination of spices a great deal, because their flavours work particularly well together, lending a depth and sensory aroma to many purées and slow-cooked dishes. They definitely belong at the earth end of the scale and must be used in conjunction with other flavours in order to balance and pad them out. The spice mix is a foundation that only really works if the heat of chilli is added, plus the sweetness of palm sugar or maple syrup, and the sourness of tamarind, lemon or lime. The saltiness of soy or fish sauce is also needed to underpin the spice mix flavour.

Buy whole spices for this – ready-ground spices will already have lost their freshness and give dishes a dull, musty taste. And for optimum flavour, use a pestle and mortar or spice grinder rather than a food processor to grind the mix. You can keep the roasted spice mix in a sealed container up to a month, but no longer.

for the roasted spice mix

1–2 cinnamon sticks
50g coriander seeds
50g cumin seeds
50g fennel seeds
50g mustard seeds
50g fenugreek seeds
5 cardamom pods
2–3 star anise (or cloves)

Place a dry, heavy-based frying pan (preferably non-stick) over a low heat. Break the cinnamon stick in half. Once a clear smoke begins to rise from your pan, add all the spices and cook, stirring frequently, to toast them. Be careful not to burn them though, as this would give a bitter taste. Once the seeds begin to pop, they are ready. Remove from the heat and grind to a fine powder. Store in an airtight container until ready to use.

Blood orange and rosemary jelly

A lovely, light, palate-cleansing dessert, this is jelly as it should be... wobbly, cool and not too sweet. Blood oranges are one of my favourite things. These beautiful, blackberry-scented jewels are usually around from December to March, but they are at their best during January and February – just when winter seems almost too barren to bear. You will need about 10 oranges to obtain the amount of juice you need, depending on their size. As the flesh of blood oranges varies in colour and pattern, so will the depth of colour of this jelly.

Serves 4
600ml freshly squeezed blood orange juice
100g caster sugar
3 rosemary sprigs
3½ sheets of leaf gelatine (or 11g sachet powdered gelatine, see toolbox, page 246)
sunflower (or other neutral-flavoured) oil, to oil

To serve
blood orange slices and a little freshly squeezed juice

Put the orange juice and sugar into a saucepan. Lay the rosemary sprigs on a board and bruise to release their flavour by pressing them firmly with the handle of your knife, then add to the saucepan. Immerse the gelatine sheets in a bowl of cold water and leave to soften for about 5 minutes.

In the meantime, place the saucepan over a gentle heat to dissolve the sugar. As the juice begins to warm through, it will take on the flavour of the rosemary. When the sugar has completely dissolved and the juice comes just to the boil, take off the heat. Remove the gelatine from the cold water and squeeze to remove excess liquid, then add to the hot orange juice and stir to dissolve. Strain through a sieve into a bowl, to remove any pithy bits and the rosemary.

Lightly oil 4 individual pudding bowls and pour in the jelly. Allow to cool completely, then place in the fridge to set – this will only take 1 or 2 hours. I like to serve these jellies on the day they are made, as they continue to set if you leave them in the fridge for longer and can become too firm.

To serve, place a slice of blood orange on each serving plate and squeeze over a little more juice. To unmould each jelly, briefly dip the base of the mould into warm water, then run a little knife around the rim and invert on to the plate. Serve straight away.

As leaf gelatine varies in potency, you may need to adjust the quantity depending on the brand you are using. My quantity relates to medium-strength gelatine.

Skye Gyngell

Trina Hahnemann

The Scandinavian Cookbook

Quadrille, London, 2010 (first published 2008)
224 pages
279 x 215 mm (11 x 8½ in.)

It's curious that as Mediterranean cuisine, once wildly evocative of romance, has become mainstream, we've started to turn to Scandinavia for our romantic foods. Perhaps it's the combination of the world's top restaurant – Copenhagen's Noma, where foraged foods are favourites – and the ubiquity of Ikea (there's one on the outskirts of Florence, providing an interesting clash of cultures). Of the several Scandinavian cookbooks published in recent years, I chose this one because Lars Ranek's photographs emphasize the romance of these cold lands and our curiosity about them.

Hahnemann's book is organized by month. February's chapter opens with a dead-still snowbound landscape, March's with a steely seascape, and May's with a precipitous street of colourful clapboard houses. Other landscapes remind us of the 'exotic' northern ingredients: moose and reindeer, lingon- and cloudberries, rye bread and smørrebrød.

The recipes possess the essential fashionable freshness. Flavours are not contrived, but allowed to speak for themselves, with a little help from many herbs: lovage, dill, caraway, mustard. One of my favourite recipes here is Biff Lindström, a kind of cooked steak tartare. Easy to make using easy ingredients, this dish manages to be both homely and utterly foreign. As did the salted, marinated and smoked herring on offer at a buffet I enjoyed on the shores of Sweden's Lake Vänern.

If other ingredients are hard to come by, the book provides some handy websites both for learning more about Scandinavian cuisine and for buying its more obscure ingredients. Although I reckon you can find quite a few of them at Ikea.

Herrings live in the chill waters that surround the Scandinavian coast. Some people have them for lunch daily; they are an important part of meals at special occasions such as Easter, too. Serve three or four different kinds of herrings at one meal and eat them on rye bread with sliced raw onion and dill on top.

Marinated fried herrings (Serves 4)

BRINE
500ml spirit vinegar
300g caster sugar
1 tbsp whole peppercorns
4 bay leaves

COMBINE ALL THE INGREDIENTS for the brine in a saucepan and bring to the boil, then reduce the heat and leave to simmer for 30 minutes. Remove from the heat and set aside to cool.

HERRING
12 fresh herring fillets
4 tbsp Dijon mustard
1 bunch dill, chopped
200g rye flour
75g butter
2 onions, sliced

TO PREPARE THE HERRING, cut off the little fin on the back side of each fillet. In a small bowl, mix the Dijon mustard and dill together. Spread out the rye flour on a tray or large plate.

PLACE THE HERRING FILLETS SKIN-SIDE DOWN in the flour, pressing them down a bit so that the flour sticks to them. Spread 1 teaspoon of the mustard mixture over each herring and fold them over so that the fillets form a square sandwich. Make sure the skin is covered in rye flour.

HEAT THE BUTTER in a frying pan and cook the herring for 3–5 minutes on each side, depending on size.

PLACE THE COOKED HERRINGS in a large plastic box, laying them side by side. Scatter the sliced onions over the herrings, then cover with the brine and leave to marinate for 2 hours, or overnight in the refrigerator. They will keep for up to a week in the refrigerator.

Homemade white herrings (Serves 12)

12 salted herring fillets
1 red onion, sliced
2 carrots, thinly sliced
2 dill sprigs, fronds picked off

COVER THE SALTED HERRING FILLETS with cold water and leave them to soak for 6 hours.

COMBINE ALL THE INGREDIENTS for the brine in a saucepan and bring to the boil, then reduce the heat and leave to simmer for 30 minutes. Remove from the heat and set aside to cool.

BRINE
400ml water
250ml caster sugar
2 bay leaves
2 tbsp whole peppercorns
1 tbsp coriander seeds
2 tbsp mustard seeds
10 whole cloves
400ml vinegar
15 allspice

DRAIN THE HERRING FILLETS and cut them into 3cm slices. Place them in a sterilized preserving jar with the sliced onion, carrots and dill fronds. Pour over the cold brine, seal tightly and leave in the refrigerator for a week before eating. Then simply fish out the pieces of herring and any parts of the brine as desired. Stored in the refrigerator, the herrings will last for up to 3 months.

Moose is eaten during the hunting season. The meat is darkly red and can be used for various dishes such as hamburgers, stews and tournedos. Traditional cowberry compote (see page 84) is a perfect match. If you can't buy moose, venison is a good substitute.

Moose tournedos with kale salad and cowberry compote (Serves 4)

30g butter
4 tbsp olive oil
4 moose tournedos
100g chanterelles or other mushrooms
cowberry compote (page 84), to serve

TO START THE SALAD, mix the kale, carrots and apples in a bowl.

TOAST THE ALMONDS IN A HOT DRY FRYING PAN, stirring constantly so that they do not burn. When lightly browned and fragrant, add the honey and let it caramelize. Add the balsamic vinegar and simmer until the liquid has evaporated. Set the almonds aside to cool on a piece of baking paper, then chop them and add to the kale salad together with the oil and the balsamic vinegar. Season the salad with salt and freshly ground pepper.

SALAD
200g fresh kale, finely shredded
2 carrots, peeled and cut into thin batons
2 dessert apples, peeled, cored and cubed
2 tbsp walnut oil or vegetable oil
2 tbsp balsamic vinegar
salt and pepper

IN A FRYING PAN, heat the butter and 2 tablespoons of the olive oil and fry the tournedos for 5–6 minutes on each side. Meanwhile, clean the chanterelles with a dry brush. Remove the tournedos from the frying pan and set aside to rest. Add the remaining oil to the frying pan and cook the mushrooms for 5 minutes.

SERVE WITH MOOSE TOURNEDOS WITH THE CHANTERELLES ON TOP and the salad and cowberry compote on the side.

BALSAMIC ALMONDS
100g blanched almonds
1 tbsp honey
2 tbsp balsamic vinegar

Nathalie Hambro

Particular Delights: Cooking for All the Senses

Jill Norman & Hobhouse, London, 1981
206 pages
216 x 133 mm (8½ x 5¼ in.)

As a publisher, Jill Norman (page 152) has a fine reputation: she created the Penguin cookery list and worked with Elizabeth David (page 66). So, when she published this first book by a relatively unknown cookery writer, reviewers took notice. Rightly, it won a Glenfiddich Food and Drink Award.

Nathalie Hambro is a Renaissance woman: interior and fashion designer, photographer and art consultant. She asserts that cookery should be attractive to all the senses, not just taste; smell, for example, is intimately connected to eating, and the one sense that is hard to control. Hambro is particularly inventive with salads: grape and radish, rhubarb and mint; puddings include geranium or juniper jelly.

A final chapter on drinks features one called Aphrodisiac. An ironic title, says Hambro, as it's a reliable soporific, a mixture of rosemary, thyme, boiling water and honey served in delicate china cups. 'I make it often after our holidays in Provence. The hillsides around the house there are covered with wild thyme and rosemary.' The honey, she says, should be lavender.

As you would expect from this publisher, the book is elegant. The drawings are by Thao Soun Vannithone, a Laotian artist who went on to illustrate Alan Davidson's *Oxford Companion to Food* (1999) and to open a restaurant in Hythe, Kent. They are detailed and careful, but have an instinctive oriental sense of place and space.

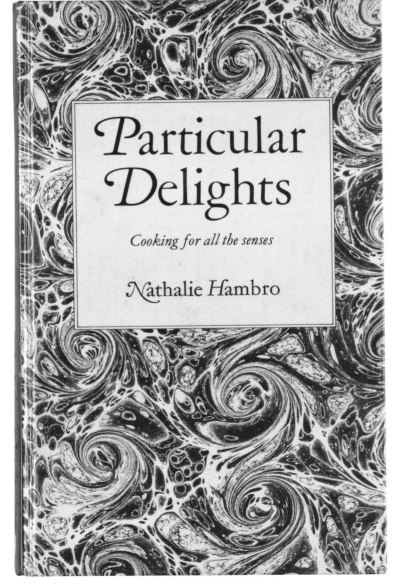

Another point which often puts people off baking their own bread is the time required for proving. As soon as they hear that a rising time of 2 or 4 hours is necessary, they sigh and claim that they haven't time to be doing this sort of thing. What they forget is that they are at liberty to go for a walk, or do the housework or see a movie. The bread doesn't care. It can look after itself without constant nursing.

The smell of baking bread is so earthy and wholesome, and the whole process so rewarding that once you have experimented you will keep on making it for your friends and family, even if you don't allow yourself to eat much of it.

Your own bread will be very much better than any from the so-called French bakeries in England. Indeed, I now find much of the bread in France tasteless or disappointing in texture, though Poilane in Paris still makes the most heavenly bread in the old-fashioned way, in wood-fired ovens. My favourites are their rye rolls and flaky apple *chaussons*.

*

Wholemeal and Sesame Bread

This recipe makes a moist, nutty bread. The oatmeal or cracked wheat gives an earthy and chewy loaf. I find that sesame seeds bring a bacon-like flavour to the bread, particularly when toasted. For a richer bread, part or all of the water may be replaced by buttermilk. This bread keeps well even though only one rising is allowed.

½ oz (15 g) fresh yeast or 2 teaspoons dried active yeast
4 tablespoons tepid water
a pinch of sugar
generous ½ pint (250 ml) warm water
2 teaspoons sea salt
1 tablespoon malt extract or molasses
¾ lb (350 g) wholemeal flour
¼ lb (125 g) strong white flour
½ lb (250 g) coarse oatmeal or cracked wheat
3 tablespoons sesame seeds

Crumble or sprinkle the yeast into the tepid water, add the pinch of sugar and stir to dissolve. Leave to bubble and become frothy (about 10 minutes). In a jug, put the warm water, stir in the salt and malt extract or molasses. Reserve.

Mix together in a bowl the two flours, oatmeal or cracked wheat and sesame seeds. Add the yeast mixture to the salted warm water and pour gradually over the dry ingredients, incorporating roughly with a wooden spoon. When the dough gets too stiff and sticky to work, turn it onto a board sprinkled with more wholemeal flour and knead for 15 minutes or until the dough is smooth and pliable. Shape into a ball, pat it all over with oil and place in a large, greased bread tin, filling it about three quarters full. Cover and set in a warm place and leave to rise until doubled in bulk (it could take up to 4 hours if left at room temperature).

Pre-heat the oven for about 10 minutes to gas 4/350°F/180°C and bake the bread for 45 minutes. The loaf should sound hollow when removed from the tin and tapped on the bottom. Leave to cool on a rack.

*

Savoury Corn Bread

This bread is a yellowish colour and the corn meal gives an unusual taste which goes well with the cheese and thyme. It can be sliced very thinly so it is suitable for toasting or sandwiches. This bread is good eaten with plenty of salted butter and black olives.

10 oz (300 g) strong white flour
6 oz (200 g) fine corn meal
1 tablespoon thyme
1 tablespoon dried yeast dissolved in 3 tablespoons tepid water
1 tablespoon brown sugar
½ pint (250 ml) warm water
2 teaspoons sea salt
3 oz (100 g) grated Cheddar cheese

them in my cookbook from memory, but found I could not remember all the details of their complicated structure: the hairy, horn-shaped stems, the green-shaded ribs blending into the twisted orange petals which end in a point. Marrow flowers can be replaced by courgette flowers, which are more widely grown now. Whichever you use, the dish should be made rapidly after picking the flowers or they wilt. I find that soda water or beer makes a lighter batter.

5 oz (150 g) plain flour
1 egg
a pinch of salt
2 tablespoons olive oil
soda water or beer
8–10 marrow flowers
granulated sugar
pepper
oil for deep frying
1 lemon cut in long wedges

Mix together the flour, egg, salt, oil and enough soda water or beer to make a light batter. Whisk well and leave to rest for 2 hours.

Cut the marrow flowers in half lengthways and remove the stalk and calyx. Dip the flowers in the batter and fry in deep oil until golden brown. Drain on absorbent paper. Sprinkle with sugar, dust with pepper. Serve as soon as possible with the lemon slices.

*

Geranium Cream

This is a velvety and luscious cream, flavoured with the scented leaves of the rose geranium. It should be served chilled to accompany any soft summer fruits, or on its own with brittle almond biscuits.

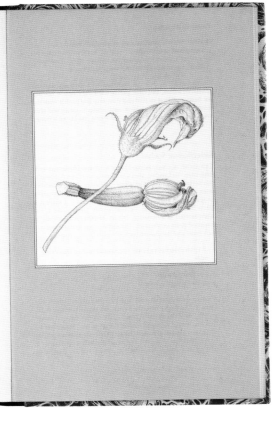

Marika Hanbury Tenison
Left Over for Tomorrow

Penguin, Harmondsworth, 1971
336 pages
180 x 110 mm (7¹/₈ x 4³/₈ in.)

Despite its somewhat dull title, this is a lifesaver of a cookery book, by a writer whose life was very far from dull. Marika Hanbury Tenison had no formal cookery training, and when she wasn't experimenting with food and writing, she would accompany her explorer husband, Robin, on his expeditions. With him she went up the Amazon to have tea with former cannibals (how did they know it was former?), and travelled around the Indonesian islands – two of the most remote places on Earth. She died of cancer aged only forty-four.

Some of the practicalities in this book come from Hanbury Tenison's Swedish mother. I particularly like the version of *pytt i panna*, a delightful Swedish way of using up cold roast beef. 'I sometimes think it's almost more delicious than the original roast beef itself', she writes. I agree. I last had it at Gothenburg airport.

Hanbury Tenison's thriftiness is relevant to any age: add onion skins to colour stock, eat cauliflower stalks like asparagus, throw chicken stuffing into soup. Imagination and initiative are more important than fresh ingredients. The recipes are rather old-fashioned, with mousses, aspic and, a particular hate of mine, tongue, but they are full of ideas. The list of what goes with what is extremely helpful.

Of course, one problem with leftovers is that they can go off, so Hanbury Tenison provides a useful guide to storing them, in either the fridge or the freezer. There's also help with equipment and the store cupboard, and with what to do with leftover wine – assuming there is any.

Opposite, bottom: The best cookery books provide more than recipes. In Hanbury Tenison's, leftovers (and we all have them) are put into categories with suggestions for their end use.

Cut meat into thin strips, dice bacon, peel and chop onion, peel and slice tomatoes (see page 18), crush garlic.

Heat oil and fry dried aubergine slices until lightly browned on both sides, drain well, and arrange on the bottom of a lightly greased baking dish. Cover aubergines with the meat strips.

Add bacon and onion to the oil and cook over a medium heat until golden brown. Add tomatoes, garlic, and parsley, and cook for 3 minutes. Season with salt and pepper, and spread the mixture over the meat and aubergine. Sprinkle over the breadcrumbs, pour over the melted butter, and cook for 20 minutes in a medium hot oven (400°F., Reg. 5) until bubbling and golden brown.

Petty i Panna   Swedish meat and potato hash

This is one of the oldest dishes I remember. It's a classic Swedish recipe, and one which my mother used to make frequently during the war. Probably I used to get bored with it then, but now I regard Petty i Panna as one of the best and most delicious ways there is of using up leftovers of roast beef. In fact the recipe is so simple and so enjoyable that I sometimes think it's almost more delicious than the original roast beef itself.

Lamb can be used in the place of beef, and if you don't fancy mixing a raw egg into your portion the eggs can be fried and arranged on top of the dish before it comes to the table.

The secret of Petty i Panna lies in cutting up all the ingredients really fine and serving it immediately.

SERVES 4.   Cooking time: 30–40 minutes.

5 potatoes	1½ oz. butter
1 lb. cooked beef or lamb	1 tablespoon olive oil
¼ lb. bacon	2 onions

1 tablespoon finely chopped parsley	salt and freshly ground black pepper
4 fresh eggs	

Peel the potatoes and cut them into really small dice. Cut the meat and bacon into small dice and finely chop the onions.

Heat the butter and oil in a large frying pan, add the potatoes, and cook for about 15 minutes until crisp and golden brown. Remove the potatoes, drain them on crumpled kitchen paper, and keep warm.

Add the onions, meat, and bacon to the fat in the pan, and cook over a moderate heat for about ten minutes, stirring frequently, until the onions and bacon are cooked through. Add the potatoes and cook for a further 5–10 minutes. Season with salt and freshly ground black pepper and mix in the finely chopped parsley.

Arrange the Petty i Panna in four piles on a warm serving dish. Make a hole in the centre of each pile and place in it a raw egg.

Serve at once.

Each person should mix the raw egg into their Petty i Panna as they receive it and season it to their liking with a few drops of Worcester and Tabasco sauce.

Scalloped Meat with Potatoes★

SERVES 4.   Cooking time: about 40 minutes.

1½ lb. cooked potatoes	½ teaspoon dry mustard
8–10 oz. cooked meat, poultry, or ham	1 tablespoon parsley, finely chopped
1 onion	salt and pepper
1½ oz. butter	¼ teaspoon paprika
¼ pint milk or thin cream	

Thinly slice potatoes. Mince meat through coarse blades of

Amount of leftover ingredient	Other main ingredients	Serves	Recipe
COOKED HAM			
2 oz.	green or red peppers, mushrooms	1	Stuffed Green or Red Peppers, page 94
2 oz. ham or bacon	cooked chicken, prawns, cod, peas, tin red pimento	4	Paella, page 141
2 oz. or more			
2–4 oz.	tin tomatoes	4	Macaroni con Pomidori, page 128
	eggs	4	Egg and Ham Cocottes, page 32
	aubergines, tin tomatoes, aubergines	4	Stuffed Aubergines, page 95
4 oz.	eggs	4	Ham Mimosa, page 127
	chicken	4	Ham and Chicken Savouries, page 134
	cooked vegetables	4	Cooked Vegetables with Ham in a Mornay Sauce, page 186
	beef or lamb, tongue, mushrooms, cooked vegetables		Mixed Meat Salad with Mayonnaise, page 167
	cooked peas, green pepper, rice	4	Ham or Chicken and Rice Salad, page 173
	eggs, mayonnaise	4	Omelette à la Paysanne, page 132

Amount of leftover ingredient	Other main ingredients	Serves	Recipe
COOKED HAM – cont.			
4 oz.	sausage meat, mushrooms	4	Mini Meat Patties, page 128
	mushrooms	4	Ham and Mushroom Custard, page 40
	eggs, cheese	4	Ham and Cheese Soufflé, page 130
4–6 oz.	green or red peppers	4	Stuffed Peppers II, page 94
	cooked potatoes	4	Autumn Ham Salad, page 174
6 tablespoons	eggs	4	Savoury Stuffed Eggs, page 31
2 thin slices	cooked asparagus spears, lettuce	4	Ham Rolls with Asparagus, page 175
6 oz.	cooked french beans, cucumber, tomatoes, black olives, anchovies	4	Mediterranean Chicken or Ham Salad, page 41
	mushrooms, bacon	4	Stuffed Bacon Rolls, page 96
	mushrooms	4	Gelda's Fancy, page 152
			Ham Filling for Savoury Pancakes, page 134
	cooked potatoes	4	Ham or Beef and Potato Salad, page 172
			Ham Omelette, page 131
8 oz.	eggs	4	
	cooked chicken	4	Chicken and Ham Velouté, page 176

Marcella Hazan

The Classic Italian Cookbook: The Art of Italian Cooking and the Italian Art of Eating

Macmillan, London, 1980 (first published 1973)
428 pages
232 x 155 mm (9⅛ x 6⅛ in.)

The original version of this book – mine is a revised and metricated edition from 1980 – was published in the United States in 1973. Hazan is actually a scientist who, on arriving in New York from Italy with her husband, Victor, started teaching Italian cooking. Scientists, it seems, make good recipe writers (see also Edouard de Pomiane, page 164), because Hazan's writing is clear, unpompous and intended for the home cook, rather than the poseur. She explains, for example, that, in Italy, antipasti are not common in home cooking, and pasta is never a main course or side dish but eaten at the start of a meal. But it is into first courses (*primi*) that Italians 'have poured most of their culinary genius and inventiveness'. Alas, she adds of others' home-made pasta, 'every treatment … has been cursory, inadequate or, even worse, misleading'.

Thus, the chapter 'I Primi' takes up 134 pages of the book (against 106 on main courses), including two on boiling pasta, despite there being no cooking process that is easier. Helpfully, Hazan tells us which pasta shape to choose for which sauce. Most recipes throughout begin with a short introduction, some of which explain how far ahead the dish can be made. Chick Pea Soup, for instance, can be prepared up to ten days in advance, while Fried Sweet Cream is best made in the morning for the evening. 'It takes patience … and part of the time you can let your mind run on other thoughts.'

The author's voice is authoritative, charming, understanding and scholarly. The book is illustrated with line drawings by George Koizumi, which are both decorative and helpful. This compendium of Italian food is the one to have, if you have only one.

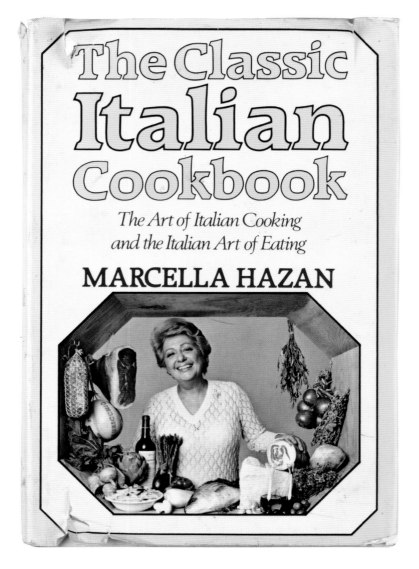

A Book for Cooks

or freeze it) into a saucepan and bring to a simmer, stirring with a wooden spoon. Add the double cream and cook for 1 minute more, stirring constantly. Check salt. Use immediately.

MENU SUGGESTIONS

In addition to *Tortellini di prezzemolo* (preceding recipe), this sauce is excellent with *Cappelletti* (page 132), *Tortelloni di biete* (page 140) and *Gnocchi verdi* (page 171). It is not disagreeable with factory-made pasta, but it is perhaps too delicate. Second courses following pasta seasoned with this sauce could be *Arrosto di vitello* (page 213), *Nodini di vitello alla salvia* (page 229), *Cotolette alla milanese* (page 228), *Arrosto di agnello pasquale col vino bianco* (page 235) and any of the chicken dishes that do not contain tomato.

Tortelloni di biete
TORTELLONI FILLED WITH SWISS CHARD

For five or six

2 large bunches [about 1 kg (2¼ lb)] Swiss chard (see note below)	1 egg yolk
Salt	60 g (2 oz) freshly grated Parmesan cheese
2½ tablespoons finely chopped onion	¼ to ½ teaspoon nutmeg
50 g (1¾ oz) prosciutto, rolled *pancetta* or green bacon	A sheet of home-made pasta dough (page 96) made with 2 eggs,
60 g (2 oz) butter	200 g (7 oz) plain flour and
200 g (7 oz) fresh ricotta	2 teaspoons milk

1 Pull the Swiss chard leaves from the stalks, discarding any bruised or discoloured leaves. If the chard is mature and the stalks are large and white, save them to make *Coste di biete alla parmigiana* (page 317). Wash the leaves in a basin in several changes of cold water until the water shows no earth deposit. Lift up the leaves and transfer them to a saucepan or stockpot without shaking them. (The water that clings to the leaves is all the water they need for cooking.) Add salt, cover the pot and cook over medium heat until tender, approximately 15 minutes, depending on the freshness of the chard.

Tortelloni are laid out on a sheet of pasta by the shallow teaspoonful. The edge of the pasta is folded over...

...and cut into squares with a fluted pastry wheel.

---

garlic, parsley, salt and pepper and mix well. Allow the prawns to steep in the marinade for at least 20 minutes at room temperature.

4 Have ready some flat, double-edged skewers. Skewer the prawns lengthways, 5 or more prawns per brochette, depending upon the size. As you skewer each prawn, curl and bend one end inwards so that the skewer goes through the prawn at three points. This is to make sure that the prawns do not slip as you turn the skewer.

In preparing spiedini di gamberoni, *put the skewer through the prawn in three places.*

5 These prawns require brisk, rapid cooking. Wait until the grill has been on for 15 minutes. Cook the prawns no more than 3 minutes on one side and 2 minutes on the other, and even less if the prawns are very small. Each side is done as soon as a crisp, golden crust forms.

6 Serve piping hot, on the skewers, with lemon wedges.

MENU SUGGESTIONS

Very tiny prawns grilled in this manner are a frequent part of Italian 'shore dinners', served together with a mixture of grilled and fried fish. The dish can be preceded by *Risotto con le vongole* (page 164), *Zuppa di vongole* (page 46), *Zuppa di cozze* (page 49) or *Trenette col pesto* (page 121). Generally no vegetable is served with it, but *Funghi trifolati* (page 325) can be a very agreeable accompaniment. Follow the prawns with *Insalata mista* (page 351).

Calamari
SQUID

It is odd how many people who will happily eat oysters and mussels dread the thought of eating another excellent mollusc, the squid. Actually, the flesh of the squid, when properly cooked, is delicate and tender, and it is no accident that fish-loving countries from Italy to Japan regard the squid and its numerous relatives as one of the sea's most delectable offerings. If you are open minded about experimenting with food, you will be well rewarded by the taste of squid.

The sac of the large Italian squid, *calamari* and *calamaroni*, exclusive of tentacles, measures from 75 to 150 or 180 mm (3½ inches to 6 or 7 inches) in length. It is available either fresh or frozen, and both are good. In Italy, freshly caught large squid is kept in the refrigerator one or two days before cooking, to relax its rigid flesh. Away from the sea it is probably already that old before it reaches the market. Use squid only when it is a pure, milky white in colour. The tastiest, sweetest squid, whether fresh or frozen, comes to the markets in early spring. Smaller squid are called *calamaretti*.

Ambrose Heath
Good Food

Faber and Faber, London, 1932
280 pages
202 x 133 mm (8 x 5¼ in.)

Very often, a cookery writer's first book is his or her best (see also Skye Gyngell, page 106), and I think this the case with Ambrose Heath's *Good Food*. Born Francis Geoffrey Miller in 1891 in Hampstead, north London, Heath wrote numerous cookery books and translated many more, including *Madame Prunier's Fish Cookery Book* (1938).

The publishers took a lot of trouble with *Good Food*, not least in having Edward Bawden as the illustrator. The book anticipated today's fashion for dividing the text into months, and Bawden created charming 'decorations' for each. May shows a small al fresco lunch; July, a country show; August, the harvest festival in church; and October, apple picking. The cover gets special treatment: 'Many light-covered Cookery Books are impracticable for use in the kitchen. The Publishers of *Good Food* desire to point out that the cover is both WATERPROOF and WASHABLE.'

Like many books of this period, although lists of ingredients are given, quantities are rare – as are cooking times. The recipes, however, are brief and simple. Each chapter starts with a useful list of seasonal ingredients; those not used in previous chapters are shown in italics. Heath has a jolly writing style: 'June for jubilation!'; July, on the other hand, is 'like one of those hostesses who overwhelm and embarrass us by the prodigality of their kindness'. October is the season not of mists but of soups, while in December, 'never has the larder seemed so infinitesimally small'. A reminder, then, of days with larders and no freezers, when grocers cut cheese from huge wheels and garlic was non-existent. Would we really want to go back?

A Book for Cooks

The following recipes are given during this month :

56

If last month it was the rivers that gave up their best for our delight, with March begins the procession of the fields. The country market reawakens, and lambs and ducklings and chickens are welcome at our repasts. Now the fishmonger waits expectantly for lenten orders, and if a few minor fish have left us, we can still contemplate with equanimity a goodly parade headed by the noble salmon. And it is as well; for Easter is still far away, Lent makes harsh demands upon many gourmands, and salt cod in its pallid winding-sheet of egg sauce has too often to be faced with as great a shudder as prompt the watery parsnips that surround it.

Salt Cod cooked with eggs, however, is a really admirable alternative. You make it by first boiling your cod (after it has been well soaked, of course)

March markets offer the denizens of the fields for our appetite's approval

Salt Cod aux Œufs

57

---

*Parsley
Eggs
Breadcrumbs
Butter
Bacon fat*

if baked with the following stuffing. Fry crisply a couple of thin rashers of streaky bacon, and chop them up finely with three onions and a good handful of parsley. Mix them with two beaten eggs and enough breadcrumbs to stiffen well. A mixture of butter and bacon fat for the baking adds distinction to your Haddock stuffed in this way.

For meats, lamb and veal will be in the greater demand. Lamb cutlets *en chaud-froid* look amazingly appetising when set round a variegated pile of vegetable salad. Cold sweetbreads can be dressed in many attractive ways, and add dignity and substance to the salads they adorn. Pâtés, for summer luncheons o: picnics, come into their own; and terrines, which are only pâtés without fawn and fragile crusts.

Cold Duckling aux Mandarines

*Duckling
Rice
Aspic jelly
Tangerines
Foie Gras*

A cold duckling is always a pleasure, but if it is prepared *aux mandarines*, it provides a double delight. Roast it in the oven and let it cool in the liquor. When cold, lay it on a bed of rice and glaze it with aspic jelly. Surround it with tangerines hollowed and filled with a *mousse* of *foie gras*, and with little heaps of chopped aspic jelly to which, in the making, have been added the juices of the duck and the tangerines.

Mousseline forcemeat is easy enough to make, and often offers a happy solution of 'what shall we eat to-day?'—the gravest problem of the summer in this changeable climate of ours. All kinds of meat, poultry and fish yield deliciously to this treatment, and there are a hundred and one ways of varying the *mousselines'* appearance and flavour. *Mousselines* of chicken coated with Mornay sauce and served on a couch of spinach, *à la florentine*, are excellent, as they also are when coated with curry sauce and bedded on rice.

156

Goslings can now be had. Most of us will eat our first roasted and stuffed with sage and onions (and do not omit a little grated nutmeg), but the German fashion of braising him with a stuffing of apples and a garnish of more apples cored and filled with red-currant jelly should not be forgotten.

And now, the triumph of the month, friend Grouse. None of us will forget the glorious Twelfth, for the noble promise it brings. But the true gourmand will look a little askance upon the air-borne firstlings on the dinner-tables of our expensive restaurants that night, preferring to wait a little till our bird is readier. September, rather, is the month in which to start eating him seriously, though perhaps August demands a grouse salad before the month is out, and we shall restrain with difficulty our impatience for cold grouse at the perfect breakfast.

In his wake come blackcock (a neglected bird), capercailzie (sometimes a little turpentiny), wild duck, the lissom leveret and the rarer woodcock: but these are also better for later eating. While the leverets are still young, a saddle cooked in the following way is supremely good. On the bottom of a dish long enough to contain it, lay the following vegetables: half a pound of minced carrots, the same of minced onions, two ounces of minced shallots, a crushed clove of garlic and a *bouquet* of thyme, parsley, bayleaf, and if possible rosemary. The saddle, which may be improved by fine larding (though, if it is very young, this is not necessary), is laid on this and set to cook. When it is nearly done, take out the vegetables and the *bouquet* and pour in a quarter of a pint of cream. Baste occasionally with this while the cooking is completed. At the last add

Roast Gosling. German fashion

*Goose
Apples
Red-currant jelly*

Roast Saddle of Leveret

*Leveret
Carrots
Onions
Shallots
Garlic
Bouquet garni
Cream
Lemon juice*

157

David Herbert

The Perfect Cookbook

Viking, Melbourne, 2003
192 pages
171 x 164 mm (6¾ x 6½ in.)

The title says it all, although it refers to the quality of the recipes rather than the book itself. To me, however, the small format, the evocative black-and-white photographs by André Martin and the typefaces – Frutiger and Garamond 3 – make for a most elegant, restrained and practical cookbook, designed by Louise Leffler. I love it. The book grew out of a series of articles for the review section of the *Weekend Australian*, and, apart from having to be perfect, the word limit for each was 150 (would that all cookery writers be so confined).

Every recipe, says Herbert, was tested and retested; it then took him a week to get the word count down. The result is that complicated or multi-ingredient recipes have been discarded, and only those that fit on a single page have been included. To combine these with black-and-white photographs was an idea of genius, especially as the pictures manage to be appetizing even in monochrome.

The dishes are arranged in alphabetical order and cover the entire range of what you might want to cook, for yourself, for your friends and for parties. Herbert's Cheese Biscuits, for example, are the best I've ever tasted, and the shortbread reaches his exacting standard of being both dry and melt-in-the-mouth. I'm not a baking cook, so when I find such recipes enjoyable and delicious it means a lot. With dishes ranging from Anzac Biscuits to Yorkshire Puddings, this is a book for tyro or unconfident cooks.

Over 120 classic recipes that work *every* time

the
perfect
cookbook

David Herbert

bread.

1 × 7 g (¼ oz) sachet (2 teaspoons)	4 cups bread flour
dry yeast	salt
1 teaspoon sugar	1 tablespoon olive oil

Dissolve the yeast and sugar in a small jug with ½ cup of tepid water. Stir well and leave for 10 minutes, or until the mixture froths.

Place the flour and a pinch of salt in a large mixing bowl. Make a well in the centre and add the yeast mixture, olive oil and 1 cup of tepid water. Mix until a firm dough forms. Add a little extra water if the dough is too dry.

Knead the dough on a lightly floured surface for 10–15 minutes, or until smooth and elastic. Place in a clean, lightly oiled bowl, cover with a cloth or plastic wrap and leave in a warm place for 1–1½ hours, or until the dough has doubled in size.

Punch down the dough with your fist to expel the air. Knead on a lightly floured surface for 2 minutes, or until smooth. Place in a large greased loaf tin.

Cover and leave for 45–60 minutes, or until the dough has doubled in size.

Preheat the oven to 200°C (400°F, Gas Mark 6).

Slash the top of the loaf a couple of times with a sharp knife. Bake for 40 minutes, or until the loaf has risen and is golden brown. Turn out the loaf, place on an oven tray and return it to the oven for 5 minutes. When cooked, the loaf should be golden and sound hollow when tapped on the bottom. Allow to cool on a wire rack.

Only use bread-making or strong flour, available from health-food shops or from the health-food section of supermarkets. Alternatively, look for bread flour at growers' markets or a local mill. Plain flour does not contain enough gluten, which gives the dough its elasticity.

Instead of making a loaf, shape the dough into whatever shapes you like and bake directly on an oven tray.

Experiment by replacing some of the white flour with wholemeal or rye flour.

20

chicken pie.

1 medium-sized chicken	2 tablespoons plain (all-purpose) flour
2 onions, quartered	1 tablespoon chopped chives or parsley
2 carrots, chopped	salt and freshly ground black pepper
1 bay leaf	1 egg, beaten
1 tablespoon olive oil	1 × 380 g (12 oz) block frozen
2 leeks, sliced	puff pastry, thawed
50 g (1¾ oz) unsalted butter	

Place the chicken, onions, carrots and bay leaf in a large saucepan. Cover with cold water and bring to the boil. Skim off any fat, reduce the heat and simmer for 1 hour.

Remove the chicken from the broth and set aside to cool. Strain the broth, discard the solids and return the strained liquid to the saucepan. Boil rapidly until it has reduced to about 2 cups. Set aside.

Remove the meat from the chicken, cut into bite-sized pieces and place in a bowl.

Heat the oil in a frying pan over medium heat. Add the leek and cook, stirring, for 4–5 minutes, or until tender. Transfer to the bowl containing the chicken meat.

Melt the butter in a small saucepan over medium heat. Stir in the flour and cook for 1 minute. Whisk in the reserved stock. Bring to the boil and continue to whisk until thickened and smooth. Stir in the chives and season well with salt and freshly ground black pepper.

Add enough of the sauce to the leek and chicken mixture to moisten it. Allow to cool.

Preheat the oven to 190°C (375°F, Gas Mark 5).

Spoon the mixture into a large pie dish or tin and insert a pie funnel (if using). Roll out the pastry to a size large enough to cover the pie. Place over the pie, pressing down on the edges to seal. Trim away any excess pastry and use to decorate the top of the pie. Brush the pastry with the beaten egg and bake for 40–45 minutes, or until the pastry is golden and has risen.

Serves 4–6

54

gingerbread biscuits.

125 g (4 oz) unsalted butter	1 teaspoon bicarbonate of soda
⅓ cup golden syrup	(sodium bicarbonate)
½ cup lightly packed brown sugar	1 tablespoon ground ginger
2 cups plain (all-purpose) flour	½ teaspoon mixed spice
½ cup self-raising (self-rising) flour	salt
	1 egg, lightly beaten

Place the butter, golden syrup and sugar in a small saucepan over low heat. Cook, stirring, until the butter has melted and the mixture is smooth. Remove from the heat and allow to cool.

Sift both flours, the bicarbonate of soda, the spices and a pinch of salt into a large mixing bowl and make a well in the centre. Pour in the melted butter mixture and the beaten egg and mix well.

Turn out onto a lightly floured surface and knead until smooth. Wrap in plastic wrap and refrigerate for 30 minutes.

Preheat the oven to 170°C (325°F, Gas Mark 3). Line two oven trays with baking paper.

Roll out the dough between two sheets of baking paper to a thickness of 5 mm (¼ in). Cut out shapes with cookie cutters and bake for 8–10 minutes, or until firm and golden brown. Allow to cool on a wire rack.

To decorate your biscuits, beat 1 egg white with an electric mixer until foamy. Gradually add 1 teaspoon of lemon juice and 1½ cups of sifted icing (confectioners') sugar, beating all the while until the mixture is thick and smooth. Tint the mixture with a couple of drops of food colouring. Attach a fine nozzle to a piping bag and pipe decorative shapes onto the biscuits.

Makes 24–30

74

Shaun Hill
How to Cook Better

Mitchell Beazley, London, 2004
240 pages
252 x 200 mm (9⁷/₈ x 7⁷/₈ in.)

Shaun Hill is the former owner of the Merchant House restaurant in Ludlow, Shropshire, which, despite Hill having to cook in a small kitchen without assistance, was named by *Restaurant* magazine in 2003 as the fourteenth best restaurant in the world. He has won numerous awards and demonstrated at such cookery schools as the Mosimann Academy in London. He is, without doubt, fully qualified to tell us how to cook better.

Although there are plenty of recipes, the chapters are all about equipment, ingredients and techniques. Chefs and home cooks work entirely differently, Hill says: chefs have all day and don't have to eat with the diners; home cooks 'aren't daft enough' to give their guests a choice. But the end result should be the same, 'a balanced and pleasurable meal'. Therefore, he explains how to plan a menu and how to get its rhythm right. On equipment, he tells us not only which knives we need but also how to sharpen them. Later, we get the master's way with mashed potato, down to which potato variety to pick, and, always a vexed subject, the perfect risotto. The text is accompanied by clear photographs showing, for instance, how to make a potato cake or chop an onion. The photographer,

Jason Lowe, and the designers, Grade Design Consultants, have alternated pretty foodie pictures with gritty black-and-white shots of knives or rice grains. We even see the maestro at the market.

This is a book that won't disappoint, for it really does explain how to cook better. The recipes are secondary to that aim.

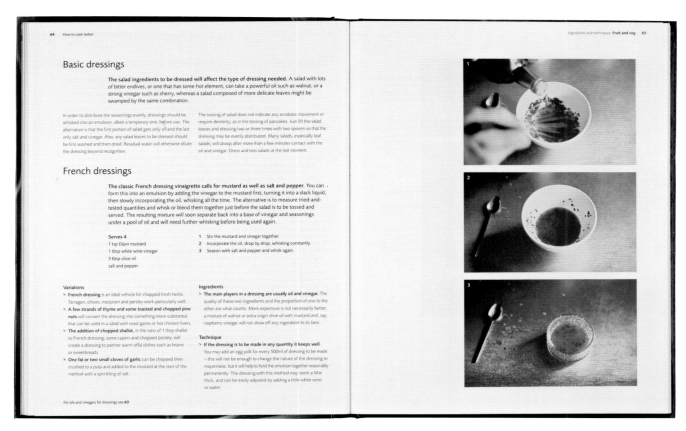

Fish

There is more variety in fish than meat. The vast range of edible species runs from oily mackerel to dry-fleshed pike, with 50 types in-between. That's before you consider the octopus and shellfish families, smoked fish such as kippers and grocery items such as preserved anchovies and sardines.

Most fish are still free range, wild creatures that have to be tracked down and caught rather than farmed like a cash crop. So your main consideration at the fishmonger's slab will be what's in peak condition.

Unsurprisingly, fish is expensive. Apart from being an ever-scarcer resource, it doesn't keep, neither improving with age like some meats nor freezing well. The resulting high cost, in comparison to some processed meat produce, has already seen out the fishmonger from most shopping centres. Prices are not purely dictated by supply and demand here, or else fish would be cheaper, but by market prices across Europe. Trawlers that have been fishing off the coast of Spain or Iceland can as easily unload at Rotterdam or Zeebrugge, if that is where their catch will fetch the best price. Similarly, quayside dealers at Brixham can tell you what is being paid for Turbot in Billingsgate in an instant, and the price of sea-bass in Milan a fraction later. Bargains are rare.

This chapter covers the details of how to buy, prepare and cook flat fish, round fish and shellfish, and explains which types of fish suit which cooking methods and what types of sauce best suit fish cooked in a variety of ways.

Green salad with Stilton quenelles and walnut dressing

This is an exercise in differing textures as well as tastes. The point of creaming a little butter into the cheese is to soften its texture so that it almost forms a counterpoint dressing to the walnut oil but without combining completely. Crisp bacon and croûtons are similarly a contrast with the leaves. A salad that is to be more than a side salad needs several points of interest to succeed and this composition can substitute for a cheese course in a formal meal as well as make a serviceable light lunch with some hot rolls.

Serves 4
50g unsalted butter
50g Stilton, crumbled
black pepper
grated nutmeg
groundnut or sunflower oil, for frying
4 rashers smoked bacon, cut into strips
white bread cut into cubes, for croûtons
mixture of mostly bitter leaves, such as
    frisée, watercress, cos lettuce, rocket
1 tbsp walnut halves

For the dressing:
1 tbsp walnut oil
1 tsp sherry vinegar

1   Use a wooden spoon to mix the soft butter and crumbled cheese together. Season to taste with pepper and nutmeg, then use two spoons dipped in hot water to mould the resulting mixture into quenelles (lozenge shapes).
2   Heat the groundnut or sunflower (definitely not walnut) oil in a pan. Crisp-fry the strips of bacon and cubes of bread separately.
3   Wash and then dry the leaves.
4   For the dressing, whisk together the walnut oil and sherry vinegar, and then toss the leaves. Serve with the walnut halves, croûtons, crisp bacon and Stilton quenelles.

Ingredients
> Use the cheese and butter when soft, or at least not straight from the fridge.

Technique
> Whisk the oil and vinegar together at the last moment before serving, as there is no emulsion to hold the dressing together.
> The cheese is salty so there will be no need to season the leaves further.

For oils and vinegars for dressings see **63**   For basic dressings see **64**

Lucas Hollweg

Good Things to Eat

Collins, London, 2011
272 pages
240 x 178 mm (9½ x 7 in.)

While this is not quite my newest book (that honour goes to *Flash Cooking*; see page 182), it is the newest by a first-time author. Until recently, Hollweg was a full-time journalist with the *Sunday Times*, writing, among other things, a weekly column on food in the paper's *Style* magazine. Then the sideline overtook the career – always the best route. 'Now, as then,' explains Hollweg, 'my starting points are always the same: what do I feel like eating and what's around at the moment? My aim is equally straightforward: to make something that tastes delicious.'

I don't know whether this debut will fill out into something more important, but the book is here because it greatly appeals to me. I suppose it's because Hollweg is not a trained cook, comes from a domestic background and just makes dishes because he enjoys being creative. His food is both simple and absolutely modern in its choice of flavours. His Tomato Tart with Basil and Goat's Cheese is hardly new but, on its ready-made puff-pastry base, makes a fine supper; Scallops with Pancetta, Spinach and Thyme is an update of an old favourite of mine. There's also French Onion Soup and Leek Vinaigrette. If I were to pick a cookery book for that desert island, this would be it.

The front cover – slate, broad beans, sloshes of olive oil – is extremely enticing, as are Tara Fisher's photographs, including one of the author himself, clearly enjoying his new career. Chef Mark Hix and food writers Rose Prince and A.A. Gill all endorse him. The book itself was designed by London-based studio Fivebargate.

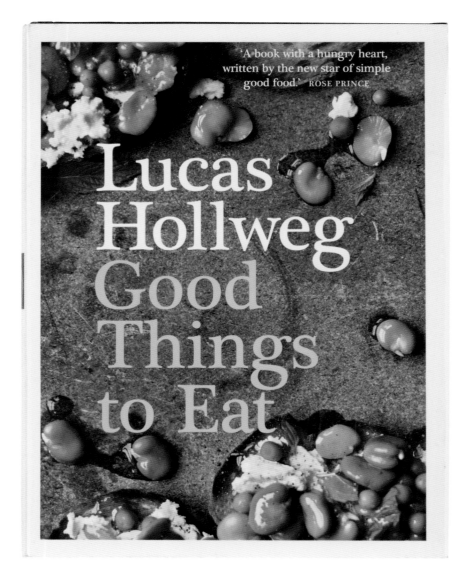

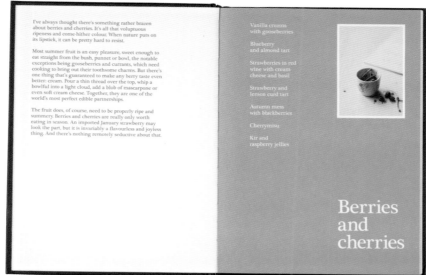

Savoy cabbage and white bean soup

This is a thick and sustaining winter bowlful that straddles the boundary between soup and stew. If you find yourself with kale or cavolo nero rather than cabbage, use them instead. You'll need to strip the leaves from the woody stems, so start with about 350g (12oz).

For 4
2 tbsp olive oil
150g (5½oz) smoked streaky bacon, roughly chopped
1 medium onion, finely chopped
2 celery sticks, finely chopped
2 medium carrots, finely chopped
4 plump garlic cloves, roughly chopped
leaves of 1 sprig of fresh rosemary, finely chopped
2 bay leaves
400g (14oz) can haricot or other white beans, drained and
  rinsed (you need about 250g/9oz drained weight)
1.5 litres (2¾ pints) chicken stock
freshly ground sea salt and black pepper
200g (7oz) Savoy cabbage leaves, roughly sliced
extra-virgin olive oil, for sprinkling
Parmesan, for grating

Heat the oil in a large saucepan and fry the bacon until just golden. Stir in the onion, celery, carrots, garlic and herbs and sweat until soft. Add the drained beans and chicken stock, stir well, then bring to the boil. Turn down the heat and simmer for 25 minutes.

Scoop out and discard the bay leaves, season the soup generously and lightly mash with a potato masher or fork, so that about half the beans are reduced to mush and half remain whole.

Add the cabbage, stir well, then return to the boil and cook for another 7–8 minutes, or until the leaves are soft. Check the seasoning, then ladle into bowls, adding a splash of olive oil and a generous grating of Parmesan before serving.

Roast potatoes, big and small

People are very particular about their roast potatoes. Some seem actually to like them soggy. For me, though, they have to be crisp on the outside with a fluffy, almost mash-like middle. This is how I do it.

Eat them as soon as possible after they leave the oven – roast potatoes don't like to be kept waiting.

For 6
2kg (4lb 8oz) medium-sized floury potatoes – preferably King Edwards or
  Maris Pipers
cooking fat: either light olive oil, sunflower, dripping or goose fat
sea salt flakes
a few whole garlic cloves, in their skins
a few sprigs of rosemary or thyme or both

Peel the potatoes and cut them in half lengthways (my preference), or into chunks about 5cm (2in) square — that's half a medium potato, maybe a third of a slightly larger one. Put them in a saucepan of salted boiling water and return to the boil. Once they're bubbling, cook for 7 minutes, then tip into a colander. Give them a good shake for a few seconds, so the outsides go fluffy, and leave them to steam-dry. The drier the outsides, the better. I often leave them for 1 hour. It won't hurt.

Preheat the oven to 200°C/400°F/Gas Mark 6. Pour enough fat into a large roasting tin to cover the bottom, then place in the oven for 10 minutes until it's thoroughly hot. Add the potatoes in a single layer, leaving a bit of space between them. Turn them in the fat, then sprinkle with sea salt flakes. You could also add a few squashed garlic cloves in their skins, plus a few sprigs of rosemary, thyme or both. Cook for 45–55 minutes, turning once, until crisp and golden. Salt and serve.

By the way
If you're cooking these with a roast in a single oven set at a lower temperature, heat the fat in a roasting tin on the hob, rather than the oven. Add the potatoes, turn them in the fat until they start to crisp and brown, then put them in the oven. If they need to crisp more at the end, you can always turn the oven up to 240°C/475°F/Gas Mark 9 for a few minutes, once you've taken out the roast to rest.

A rather nice small version
These have an almost chip-like quality that makes them as good with a steak as with a roast. You'll need fewer potatoes – probably only about 1.25kg (2lb 12oz) for 6 people. They need to be well spread out in the fat, so use two roasting tins if necessary.

Cut the potatoes into small chunks, about 2–3cm (¾–1¼in) square. There's no need to boil them first. As with the bigger potatoes, preheat the oven to 200°C/400°F/Gas Mark 6, put in a tray of fat and leave it to get hot. Toss the cubes of potato in the heated fat, adding a sprinkle of salt, plus a few whole garlic cloves and thyme and/or rosemary sprigs as you see fit. Roast for 35–40 minutes, turning halfway through, until crisp and golden brown, with soft insides. Salt well and serve.

Buttery mash

Sometimes basic mashed potatoes is all you want, but this buttery version has a particularly duvet-like comfort. A potato masher will get you only so far when it comes to getting rid of lumps. Putting the cooked potatoes through a potato ricer or old-fashioned vegetable mill (mouli) gives a better texture, and pushing them through a metal sieve is best of all. It takes only a few minutes. Either way, you need to do it while the potatoes are still warm.

For 6
1.5kg (3lb 5oz) King Edward or Maris Piper potatoes, peeled
125ml (4fl oz) whole milk
150g (5½oz) butter
salt and pepper

Cut the potatoes into even slices 1cm (½in) thick. Put them in a pan of salted boiling water, bring back to the boil, and cook for 15 minutes, or until the biggest pieces are soft and falling apart. Drain well in a colander.

Next, either mash them in the pan, put them through the finest holes of a potato ricer or vegetable mill or – my preference – rub them though a metal sieve. This honestly takes only a few minutes.

When the potatoes are mashed, put the purée back into the pan and stir over a low heat for a couple of minutes to dry out if necessary. Add the milk and stir for a couple of minutes more, then stir in the butter until the whole thing is silky and smooth. Season with plenty of salt and pepper and stir in.

Simon Hopkinson with Lindsey Bareham

Roast Chicken and Other Stories

Ebury Press, London, 1995 (first published 1994)
240 pages
214 x 155 mm (8³/₈ x 6¹/₈ in.)

Simon Hopkinson, along with co-author Lindsey Bareham (see also page 26), won numerous plaudits for this book, including both an André Simon and a Glenfiddich Food and Drink award. In 2005, writing in *Waitrose Food Illustrated* magazine, a panel of forty foodies voted it 'the most useful cookery book of all time'. Well, maybe.

What it does have is simplicity, enthusiasm, strong opinions (no tuna in *salade niçoise*) and a tendency to puncture pomposity: 'There is a tall, very silly pan called an "asparagus pan"'; just put the spears in 'viciously boiling, well-salted water'. Recipes (including that for a lovely, simple roast chicken) are interspersed with 'Fanfares', short homages to famous cooks. Elizabeth David's essays in *An Omelette and a Glass of Wine* (1984) are described as 'the finest works of food journalism ever written', Franco Taruschio's cooking 'is a joy' and George Perry-Smith was 'one of the great pioneers'. This is extremely generous in a trade that often gives no credit.

The book is divided into single-ingredient chapters arranged alphabetically, which makes for strange combinations: chocolate next to cod, for example. Each chapter contains between two and seven recipes and endearing comments alongside. Better still, each opens with a drawing by the brilliant Flo Bayley, who manages to insert wit into the pictures for brains (egg-headed chap with studious glasses) and eggs (a cracked duomo in Florence). I don't know why hake is wearing a checked scarf in the manner of Rupert Bear, but it's fun.

A Book for Cooks

CHICKEN

There is chicken, and there is chicken. The French chicken, from Bresse, is the finest in the world. It is nurtured and cosseted like no other living creature (save, perhaps, the Japanese Kobe cattle which are fed beer and given a daily massage).

The poulet de Bresse is a 'controlled' breed in France and carries its own special criteria as to production and methods of rearing. In fact, it has its own *appellation contrôlée*, as wine does. Posh bird. V. I. P. (Very Important Poulet). It has a superb flavour, due to its diet and upbringing, and also because it is properly hung, like a game bird, to allow its flavour to develop.

Naturally, there are other fine farmyard-reared birds, in Britain, as well as in France and elsewhere. And the better the bird, the better the dish cooked.

Well, up to a point.

A good cook can produce a good dish from any old scrawnbag of a chook. A poor cook will produce a poor dish – even from a Bresse chicken. I firmly believe this to be true. Take a boiling fowl, for instance; one of the toughest old birds that requires careful and controlled cooking. Poached gently for a few hours in water, with root vegetables, herbs and a little wine, this classic French bourgeois dish is a delight. *Poule au pot* (hen in a pot) is its name, and it can be eaten just as it is; you could even anglicise it with a few dumplings, if you wished, flavoured with tarragon perhaps – chicken's favourite herb.

A boiling fowl is a hen and they are often sold guts intact. Unless you are squeamish, it is interesting to discover within the cavity seven or eight partly developed eggs. These are yolks covered with a thin membrane, graded in size and

34

queuing up like an egg-production line ready for laying. Traditionally, these are removed, beaten just like a normal egg and used to enrich and thicken sauce or soup.

A dish I often make with poached chicken requires removing the bird from the stock, discarding the vegetables and herbs, and reducing the cooking liquor down to a quarter of its original. The egg yolks are then beaten with some cream, added to the liquor and cooked gently until it thickens like a custard. I like to add lots of chopped parsley. Carefully joint the bird, lay the pieces in a dish and cover with this gorgeous, richly flavoured parsley sauce. The only accompaniment necessary is some boiled potatoes.

Roasting a chicken is a joy for me; and if I am pressed to name my favourite food, then roast chicken it must be.

I would think that the nicest one I ever tasted was at Chez L'Ami Louis in Paris. The late M. Magnin used chickens from Les Landes – I think from his own farm but I am not sure – and roasted them to a divine juiciness and crispness. Today they are still as good as the first I ate 12 years ago.

At Chez L'Ami Louis, the roast chickens do have the advantage of being cooked in a wood-fired oven, their pedigree is fine and so much butter is used. The resultant chicken is cooked almost to a state of chewiness – particularly at its extremities; the parson's nose, wing tips, and undercarriage where those secret 'oysters' lie. These little nuggets are charmingly called '*les sots l'y laissent*', which, loosely translated means 'the bits that silly idiots leave behind'. The name 'oyster' presumably refers to their shape or colour, or how they slip nicely out of the natural bone structure as if they were oysters being lifted from their shells.

Anyway, the chicken at Ami Louis arrives at your table sizzling-hot in its well-worn Le Creuset, surrounded by its juices and carved there and then. The only thing served with this is a plate piled high with pommes frites of the thinnest dimensions.

Roasting and poaching (you don't *have* to use an old boiler for poaching; a good tender chicken is delicious too) are my favourite ways of cooking chicken. Grilled small joints or spatchcocked chickens (split in half and flattened) are delightful alternatives, particularly when cooked on a barbecue, having previously been marinated with herbs, garlic, olive oil, balsamic vinegar, lemon juice or what you will. If it is not outdoor weather, then it is worth investing in one of those cast-iron ribbed grills; without one it just isn't possible to achieve the searing heat that crisps and scorches the skin or flesh and gives it its distinctive taste and, of course, fabulous smell.

Incidentally, putting chicken, or anything else, save toast, under a radiant grill or salamander is *not* grilling in my book. This is fine for giving the finishing touches to a dish to be glazed or au gratin. (A frightful word that often rears its ugly head in British menuspeak is the term 'gratinated'. It is horrid and should be banned.)

Put the gelatine leaves in a bowl, cover with cold water and leave to soften. Beat together the egg yolks and caster sugar. Strain the flavoured milk into this mixture, and put back on a gentle heat stirring constantly. Cook following the instructions for Custard Sauce (see page 78), then pour into a cool bowl.

Put the softened gelatine in a small pan with 2 tbsp water and heat gently until melted. Add to the warm custard and mix thoroughly. When the custard is cold, stir in the passion fruit purée, and either place the bowl over ice or put it in the fridge.

Lightly whip the double cream with the icing sugar. When the custard has started to set, fold in the lightly whipped cream and quickly pour it into either one large soufflé dish or four individual ramekins.

There are two ways in which to do this final process: if you have put the custard in the fridge it will set to a solid lump. This then needs to be broken down into manageable liquidity either in a blender or food processor, before folding in the cream. If you use the bowl over ice method, then, from time to time, as the custard cools, draw a wooden spoon through the mixture until it has a jelly-like consistency, at which point you can fold in the cream. Either method is equally good, it just depends upon how much time you have. The end result, however, must be a thickish mixture that is still runny enough for the cream to be folded in.

ORANGE MOUSSE

This is also a bavarois (see Passion Fruit Bavarois, above), in fact, but it is made using only two leaves of gelatine, and it has a lighter texture than the passion fruit version.

The milk should be infused with the orange rind as well as the vanilla pod, and the orange juice should be added to the custard in place of the passion fruit purée. Otherwise, the method is exactly the same. These are the ingredients:

300 ml/$\frac{1}{2}$ pint milk
$\frac{1}{2}$ vanilla pod, split lengthways
grated rind of 2 oranges
2 gelatine leaves
4 egg yolks
75 g/3 oz caster sugar
juice of 3 oranges
300 ml/$\frac{1}{2}$ pint double cream
1 tbsp icing sugar

EGGS

The versatility of eggs is a constant source of amazement, and it upsets me sometimes when they are just taken for granted. The number of dishes that can be made from eggs, plus their many supporting acts, is, quite simply, magical. Without eggs, where would be our mayonnaises, hollandaises, béarnaises, custards, cakes, omelettes, or Yorkshire puddings? How would we make lovely clear soups, meringues and jellies, without egg whites? And breakfasts, Sunday suppers, and picnics would never be the same again.

This section could easily be the longest if I allowed myself to run wild, so it should be said that these five recipes are tried and tested favourites that I would never tire of eating.

81

Madhur Jaffrey

Madhur Jaffrey's Indian Cookery

BBC, London, 1991 (first published 1982)
200 pages
228 x 154 mm (9 x 6 in.)

A combination of an attractive and intelligent actress for an author, the BBC television series *Indian Cookery* and an urge on the part of the British public to learn about Indian cuisine meant that this book had sold more than 500,000 copies by 1991 (the date of my paperback edition). It had been reprinted eighteen times.

Madhur Jaffrey manages to demystify Indian cooking. The dishes generally have frighteningly long lists of ingredients, but, as in the case of a chicken dish with sixteen ingredients, you often find that many of them are spices and seasonings, which makes it far less scary. The author has also taken the trouble to explain these spices and flavourings and how to treat them. For example, 'When a recipe calls for cardamom seeds, you can … take the seeds out of the pods (a somewhat tedious task, best done while watching television)', which makes it much easier. Next, she suggests how to construct a menu and what equipment is needed. All this without either talking down to her readers or obscuring a simple action with jargon. No wonder this book sold so well.

The front cover features a cheery photograph of the author (who starred in *Shakespeare Wallah*, 1965) clutching a bag of unthreatening Indian foods, from bananas to okra. The text – set in Ehrhardt – is divided into columns, with the ingredients in one and the method in another. Recipes are frequently simple, such as potatoes with sesame seeds or spicy scrambled eggs, which will tempt the beginner. The photographs, however, are lifeless.

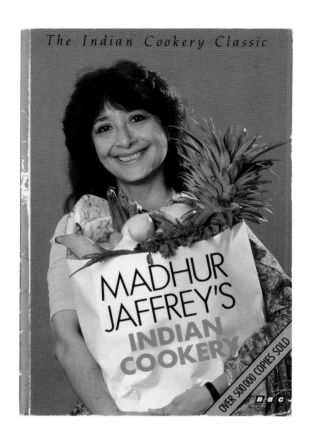

third of the liquid left. Stir several times during this cooking period.

Put in the browned onions and the *garam masala*. Stir gently to mix and turn heat to low. Cook gently, uncovered, for another 10 minutes. Stir a few times during this period, taking care not to break the turnips.

Spoon off the oil that floats to the top and serve hot.

'Royal' lamb or beef with a creamy almond sauce
Shahi korma

There are many Indian dishes that were inspired, a few centuries ago, by dishes from other countries. *Shahi korma* – lamb cubes smothered in a rich almond and cream sauce – owes its ancestry to Persian food.

It could be served with rice (perhaps 'Spiced basmati rice', page 148) or a bread (*naan*, *chapati*, or *paratha*) and a vegetable such as 'Cauliflower with potatoes', (page 109). It would be good to have some kind of tomato or onion relish on the side. When I want a quick, but elegant, meal, I have been known to serve *shahi korma* with plain rice and a crisp green salad.

In my recipe here, I have cooked *shahi korma* the traditional way, that is on top of the cooker. If you like, you could do the final long cooking in the oven. This is particularly useful if you are making a large meal and need the top of the cooker for other dishes. Just preheat the oven to gas mark 4, 350 °F (180 °C) and, once you have combined the meat, salt, cream and water and brought it to a boil, you can cover the pot and put it in the oven instead. The cooking times and other general directions remain the same.

Serves 4–6:
8 cloves garlic, peeled
A 1 inch (2.5cm) cube of fresh ginger, peeled and coarsely chopped
2 oz (50g) blanched, slivered almonds
6 tablespoons plus 4–8 fl oz (100–225ml) water
7 tablespoons vegetable oil
2 lb (900g) boned lamb from the shoulder or leg or stewing beef (chuck), cut into 1 inch (2.5cm) cubes
10 whole cardamom pods
6 whole cloves
A 1 inch (2.5cm) stick of cinnamon
7 oz (200g) onions, peeled and finely chopped
1 teaspoon ground coriander seeds
2 teaspoons ground cumin seeds
¼ teaspoon cayenne pepper
1½ teaspoons salt
½ pint (275ml) single cream
¼ teaspoon garam masala (page 18)

Put the garlic, ginger, almonds, and 6 tablespoons of the water into the container of an electric blender. Blend until you have a paste.

Heat the oil in a wide, heavy, preferably non-stick pot over a medium-high flame. When hot, put in just enough meat pieces so they lie, uncrowded, in a single layer. Brown the meat pieces on all sides, then remove them with a slotted spoon and put them in a bowl. Brown all the meat this way.

Put the cardamom, cloves, and cinnamon into the hot oil. Within seconds the cloves will expand. Now put in the onions. Stir and fry the onions until they turn a brownish colour. Turn the heat down to medium. Put in the paste from the blender as well as the coriander, cumin, and cayenne. Stir and fry this mixture for 3–4 minutes or until it too has browned somewhat. Now put in the meat cubes as well as any liquid that might have accumulated in the meat bowl, the salt, the cream, and 4 fl oz (100ml) water. If you are cooking beef, add another 4 fl oz (100ml) water. Bring to a boil. Cover, turn heat to low and simmer lamb for 1 hour and beef for 2 hours or until the meat is tender. Stir frequently during this cooking period. Skim off any fat that floats to the top. Sprinkle in the *garam masala* and mix.

N.B. The whole spices in this dish are not meant to be eaten.

Whole leg of lamb in a spicy yoghurt sauce
Raan masaledar

If you are having guests for dinner, this might be the perfect dish to serve. It is quite impressive – a whole leg dressed with a rich sauce, served garnished with almonds and sultanas. I often serve it with 'Sweet yellow rice' (page 157) and a green vegetable.

Tandoori-style chicken
Tandoori murghi

I have, I think, found a way to make tandoori-style chicken without a tandoor! The tandoor, as I am sure you all know by now, is a vat-shaped clay oven, heated with charcoal or wood. The heat inside builds up to such an extent that small whole chickens, skewered and thrust into it, cook in about 10 minutes. This fierce heat seals the juices of the bird and keeps it moist while an earlier marinating process ensures that the chicken is tender and well flavoured. The result is quite spectacular.

To approximate a tandoor, I use an ordinary oven, pre-heated to its maximum temperature. Then, instead of cooking a whole bird, I use serving-sized pieces – legs that are cut into two and breasts that are quartered. The cooking time is not 10 minutes because home ovens do not get as hot as tandoors. Still, breasts cook in about 15–20 minutes and legs in 20–25 minutes.

Tandoori chicken may, of course, be served just the way it comes out of the oven with a few wedges of lemon, or it can, without much effort, be transformed into *Makkhani murghi* (see next recipe) by smothering it with a rich butter-cream-tomato sauce. Both dishes are excellent for dinner parties as most of the work can be done a day ahead of time. The chicken is marinated the night before so all you have to do on the day of the party is to cook it in the oven for a brief 20–25 minutes just before you sit down to eat. If you wish to make the sauce, all the ingredients for it except the butter may be combined in a bowl the day before and refrigerated. After that, the sauce cooks in less than five minutes and involves only one step – heating it. Both these chicken dishes may be served with rice or *naan* and a green bean or cauliflower dish.

OPPOSITE PAGE:
Spiced basmati rice, *Masaledar basmati* (page 148)
Aubergine cooked in the pickling style, *Baigan achari* (page 100)
Kashmiri red lamb stew, *Kashmiri rogan josh* (page 53)

OVERLEAF:
Cod steaks in a spicy tomato sauce, *Timatar wali macchi* (page 95)
Rice with peas, *Tahiri* (page 149)
Gujerati-style cabbage with carrots, *Sambhara* (page 106)

Madhur Jaffrey

Lady Jekyll, DBE

Kitchen Essays: With Recipes and Their Occasions

Nelson, London, 1922
264 pages
184 x 131 mm (7¼ x 5⅛ in.)

Lady Jekyll, created a dame in 1918 for her good works during the First World War, was the first *Times* cook, writing essays on entertaining and food in the early 1920s. These were collected into a small, charming, buckram-bound book, without any illustrations but with lots of wit. Lady Jekyll came from an artistic family – her Liberal MP father was a patron of the Pre-Raphaelites – and her first dinner party included such guests as poet Robert Browning, art critic John Ruskin and Pre-Raphaelite artist Edward Burne-Jones, which, to us, might seem overwhelming.

But Agnes Jekyll, judging by the chapter 'Food for Artists and Speakers', would not have been at a loss: 'they cannot give out their best soon after a substantial meal', she notes, while, in the case of parliamentary elections, 'a little care in the selection and preparation of suitable foods may even turn the tide of fortune'. It's nice to think that her Mousse of Egg and Sardine in small, white-china ramekin cases might actually have got the Liberals into Parliament. She's in favour of meatless meals – 'newly-laid eggs scrambled so deliciously with young asparagus' – even if her suggested menu for 'Their First Dinner-Party' includes a 3.6-kilogram (8-lb) saddle of lamb and 2.7 kilograms (6 lb) of turnips.

This is a charming period piece, worth reading for its gentle humour and such chapters as 'In the Cook's Absence', 'Luncheon for a Motor Excursion in Winter' and 'Food for the Punctual and the Unpunctual'. The punctual get a nice grilled chicken, while the unpunctual must make do with warmed-up leftovers flavoured with 'Papprika'. Serves them right.

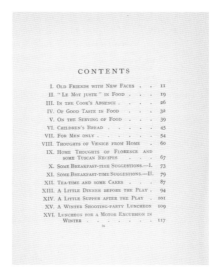

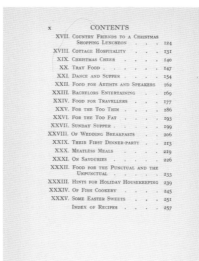

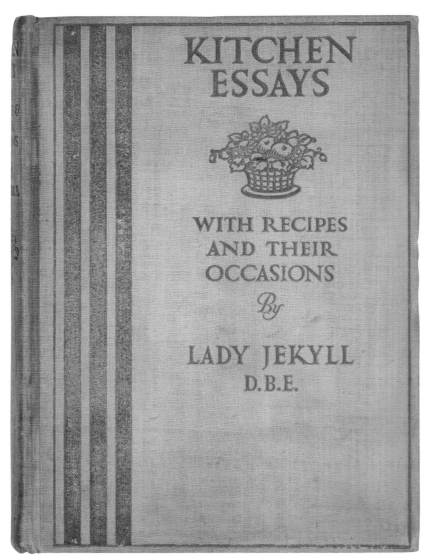

KITCHEN ESSAYS

WITH RECIPES AND THEIR OCCASIONS

By

LADY JEKYLL
D.B.E.

supper only, but *many* suppers, because we are uncertain of the hour he will sup in."

He is a bold man who would call on his cook for such devotion and elasticity in these days !

In unjust contrast this passage from Hawkesworth's Life of Dr. Swift shows what can befall a punctual and deserving master : " The dean had a kitchen wench for his cook, a woman of a large size, robust constitution and coarse features, her face very much seamed with the smallpox and furrowed by age ; this woman he always distinguished by the name ' Sweetheart.' It happened one day that ' Sweetheart ' greatly over-roasted the only joint he had for dinner ; upon which he sent for her, and with great coolness and gravity : ' Sweetheart,' says he, ' take this down into the kitchen and do it less.' She replied that was impossible. ' Pray, then,' said he, ' if you had roasted it too little, could you have done it more ? ' ' Yes,' she said, easily could she have done that. ' Why,

then, Sweetheart,' replied the dean, ' let me advise you, if you must commit a fault, commit a fault that can be mended.' "

The punctual and the unpunctual are always with us, so it is a wise cook who knows her own master, and in preparing dinner she may like to make choice of these few suggestions according to the measure of her hope or her experience.

For the Punctual. *Poulet Grillé Saint Jean.*

Bone a nice chicken, or, if a novice, let it be boned at the purveyor for future imitation. Prepare a farce from veal or the best parts of a rabbit in the usual way, with $\frac{1}{2}$ teacupful cream, 1 whole egg, and seasoning added to the pounded meat. Fill the inside of the boned bird, which will be spread out flat, with the farce, and cook under the gas or electric griller. Serve it, preferably, on a silver-plated grill above a meat dish, or on a long fireproof dish, cut right across in thick 1 inch slices, with perfectly-made bread-sauce, gravy, and a garnish of watercress, or a cold Tartar sauce if preferred.

Soufflé de Prunes à la Russe.

Boil $\frac{1}{2}$ lb. French plums till soft, rub through a hair sieve, keep the purée soft and moist ; whisk into it by degrees whilst hot 6 whites of eggs. Fill the mixture into a low plated dish and bake for 10 minutes in a sharp oven. Send up with some vanilla iced cream served separately, or some small blobs of stiffly-whipped cream dropped on the top of the soufflé as it goes in.

For the Unpunctual, try a savoury dish of *Papprika*, thus :—

Skin 4 large onions, cut up, and stew them a bright golden colour with 6 oz. fresh butter. Rub this through a fine sieve with $\frac{1}{2}$ pint sour cream, a saltspoonful of salt, $\frac{1}{2}$ teaspoonful Papprika pepper (procurable at all Stores), and add your previously jointed and cooked chicken, or slices of cooked meat, game, or rabbit ; let this heat thoroughly and slowly ; serve in a casserole with plain boiled rice, slightly flavoured with Papprika, and a green vegetable.

Iced Chicken Soufflé with Curried Livers.

Pound the breast of a boiled chicken, adding $\frac{1}{2}$ pint béchamel sauce, and pass it through a hair sieve. Whip $\frac{1}{2}$ pint cream ; add it to the chicken. Take a white fireproof soufflé dish, stand a small jar in the centre, filling the soufflé dish around with the chicken cream. Set it in the ice cave for some 2 hours. Remove jar and fill in the space with 6 or 8 curried chicken livers, trimmed, and put in a stewpan with a walnut of butter, and seasoning. Cook these for some 10 minutes ; add 1 teaspoonful each of curry powder, curry paste, and 1 tablespoonful desiccated cocoanut (previously steeped and stirred in hot milk and most of the nut part eliminated) and a little chopped shallot. Let the livers cook in this for another 10 minutes to absorb most of the moisture before letting them get cold and adding to the chicken soufflé. With this serve cold curried rice and brown bread-and-butter sandwiches with a little chutney in them.

For a long-suffering sweet, try this *Apricot Purée.*

Stew 1 lb. best evaporated apricots

Sybil Kapoor

Taste: A New Way to Cook

Mitchell Beazley, London, 2003
208 pages
252 x 200 mm (9⅞ x 7⅞ in.)

Although the science of taste and flavour is not exactly new, Sybil Kapoor's book considers it in depth and with a clarity of explanation that seems to defeat many scientists. There are, she says, five tastes: sour, salt, bitter, sweet and umami, a recent discovery (think soy sauce or chicken stock). These are detected by taste receptor cells in the mouth. Flavour, on the other hand, is detected by the nose, in aromas wafted through the air. 'Every culinary ingredient has myriad flavours and usually several tastes.' Tomatoes are unusual in combining all five tastes, which may explain their popularity.

It is by knowing an ingredient's constituent tastes, and by playing to them, that great dishes are created. A simple example would be adding bitter almond, sugar and cream to a peach, thereby drawing out its essence. Each taste receives its own chapter (with the exception of umami, about which not enough is known), and is further defined alongside relevant recipes. Salt, Kapoor says, might include bacon, seaweed and Parmesan; sweet runs to parsnips, scallops and bananas. But, overall, the author is trying to get us to think for ourselves by suggesting how to emphasize what is already there.

The photographs, by David Loftus, involve sexy close-ups of rhubarb stalks, soy sauce bubbles and sticky brown sugar. This is a pioneering work for the dedicated but unscientific cook who needs to understand more about why food tastes good.

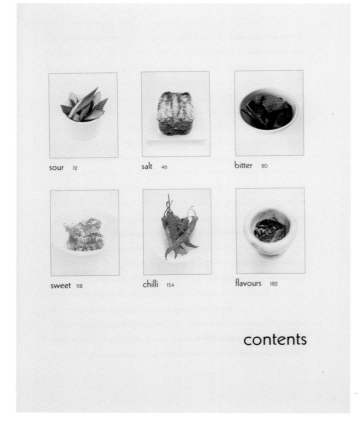

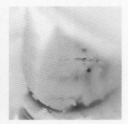

honey

The reason honey seems sweeter than sugar (sucrose) is that it is made from fructose and dextrose (glucose), and fructose tastes sweeter than sucrose although it has the same calorific value. Curiously, highly flavoured, aromatic flower honey, such as lavender or heather, tastes less sweet.

Another facet of honey is that it quickly caramelizes when subjected to heat, making it admirably suited to marinades and glazes. Duck, lamb, pork and chicken all benefit from this caramelized bitter-sweetness, as do roasted or grilled fruits such as figs or peaches. Its sticky nature also lends it to vinaigrettes. However, although honey's distinctive taste works well with other strong tastes, such as vinegar, umami soy sauce and bitter sweet nut oils, care should be taken when adding it to delicately flavoured puddings as its taste can overpower them.

sugar

The irresistible sweetness of sugar has led man astray as surely as the apple in the Garden of Eden. Today, sugar cane and sugar beet are the world's two main sources of sugar (sucrose). The former also produces unrefined brown sugars which taste less sweet and increasingly bitter (in a nice minerally way); the darker and less refined they are. The darkest is molasses sugar, followed by dark muscovado, pale muscovado, demerara, and golden, unrefined caster, granulated and icing sugar.

Although the predilection for sweet-tasting food is universal, sugar's culinary use varies greatly from culture to culture, depending on how and when it was incorporated into its cooking. In Thailand, for example, sweet spiced fish is normal in a balanced savoury meal, while in India a spicy rich meal is finished with an intensely sweet, small pudding.

bananas

The sheer pleasure of eating a freshly picked banana in the tropics is hard to match. As palm leaves rustle in the sultry air, their sweet, soft flesh fills the mouth with subtle aromas. These delicate notes are lost when bananas are shipped, half-ripe, across the world. Green bananas are usually called plantain. They contain little sugar and a lot of starch, and are normally cooked in savoury dishes. Ripe bananas, however, are the opposite, with 20% sugar and 2% starch, and are best in sweet dishes, cooked or raw.

I will only be dealing with ripe dessert bananas (*Musa hybrids*). Their sweetness can be enhanced by a little sourness, for example from tamarind, soured cream, lime juice or rum. Salt, and bitter foods such as chocolate or Angostura bitters, imbue bananas with a satisfying complexity, while sweet ingredients such as coconut milk complement them.

dates

A soft date melts in the mouth like a piece of fudge. The fruit of the date palm (*Phoenix dactylifera*), the date is regarded as a staple food in the Middle East, where cooks can choose from a delectable array of red, brown and yellow varieties, each with their own subtle flavour and texture. Over 2000 varieties are cultivated in the Arabian peninsula alone. Dried dates contain up to 80% of sugar. In the West, only a few varieties of semi-dried dates are sold, normally Medjool, Deglet Noor, Hadrawi and Hayani.

The date's very sweetness makes it difficult to cook unless it is diluted by other tastes. Middle Eastern cooks excel at transforming dates into sweetmeats flavoured with nuts, butter and orange-flower water. The Moroccans have a penchant for cooking them in aromatic lamb tagines and in the West they are added to sticky puddings and cakes.

---

soups

The art of cooking lies in understanding the tastes and how to combine them to enhance a dish. It is, however, equally important to fit the dish to the mood of the occasion. This, again, can be achieved by taste, as different combinations fulfil different needs. Soup, for example, is usually eaten to stimulate the appetite and refresh the palate, although when consumed as a main course it should also satisfy. Consequently, salt and umami are critical tastes when making soup, as the latter, in particular, ensures that it is both stimulating and satisfying.

In reality, most cooks already use both tastes. The intense sweet-salty taste of a good home-made stock is actually that of umami. So is the taste of the Japanese stock dashi, which is made from kelp and dried bonito flakes. Umami adds an appetizing note to the dish and

enhances the savoury-sweet taste of the other ingredients. Thus the vegetables and pasta in a minestrone made with chicken stock will taste sweeter and more delectable. Add Parmesan and the umami effect will be increased further. However, since umami can reduce sourness or bitterness, it is sometimes necessary to reinforce that aspect of a recipe to make it taste more stimulating and interesting. Crème fraîche, for example, is added to the sorrel and lettuce soup on p.23 to re-emphasize the sorrel's acidity.

Salt has a gentler effect. If used in moderation, it will amplify the other tastes by enhancing any intrinsic sweetness, sourness and bitterness in a recipe. Beware, however, of using it excessively as too much salt has the opposite effect of dulling all the tastes before ultimately making a dish unpalatable.

butternut squash and parmesan soup

A clever way to stimulate the taste buds and add a salty-umami depth to a recipe is to add Parmesan. Here, Parmesan rind is simmered with chicken stock and naturally sweet sautéed onions and butternut squash. The stock and Parmesan give the soup a delicate savoury-sweet taste, while the sweetness of the vegetables is reduced a little by crème fraîche. The chilli adds a sensory kick. The result is a sweet-savoury soup that makes a satisfying light main course, since it contains no bitterness and little sourness.

serves 6

2 onions, roughly chopped
1 clove of garlic, roughly chopped
½ teaspoon chilli flakes or to taste (optional)
3 tablespoons olive oil
2 medium butternut squash
1 litre (1¾ pints) chicken stock
1 bay leaf
3 sprigs of fresh parsley
70g (2½oz) piece of Parmesan cheese rind
115ml (4fl oz) crème fraîche
salt and freshly ground black pepper
roughly shaved Parmesan cheese to serve

1 Gently fry the onions, garlic and chilli flakes in the olive oil in a large saucepan for about 10 minutes, or until soft and golden. Meanwhile, cut off the tough skin of the butternut squash. Scrape out and discard the seeds, then roughly dice the flesh and stir it into the sautéed onions. Cover and continue to cook, stirring occasionally, until the squash begins to soften.

2 Add the stock, herbs and Parmesan rind and simmer gently for 45 minutes, or until the squash is meltingly soft. Discard the herbs and Parmesan rind, scraping any gooey cheese into the soup. Liquidize the soup, add the crème fraîche, and season to taste. Serve piping hot scattered with Parmesan cheese shavings.

Nigella Lawson

How to be a Domestic Goddess: Baking and the Art of Comfort Cooking

Chatto & Windus, London, 2000
384 pages
245 x 182 mm (9⅝ x 7⅛ in.)

This is the second of Nigella Lawson's many books, and one written when she was still fairly unknown. According to the blurb, the book 'is not about being a goddess, but about feeling like one'. It is dedicated to her first husband, the late John Diamond: 'For John, goddess-maker'.

The reason I chose this book is because it was groundbreaking in its day. We can credit the author with the fashionable rise of baking in Britain, with the independent cook making a business of cupcakes, and with the craze for colourful macaroons. Speaking at the Hay Festival in 2011, Lawson said her book was 'an important feminist tract in its own right, and I'm not being entirely ironic'. Baking was a woman's craft, thus less applauded. 'There's something intrinsically misogynistic about decrying a tradition because it has always been female.' The columnist Jemima Lewis, writing in the *Sunday Telegraph* (5 June 2011), added: 'Historically speaking, she has a point. The British have an unrivalled tradition of cakes and puddings – thanks to generations of forgotten women.' You need only look at handwritten recipe books by these 'forgotten women' to see that 90 per cent of the dishes were baked.

At the start of her stellar career, Lawson went out of her way to bring back baking and give the forgotten women their own voice at last. So, as a feminist manual as well as a cookery book, it is worth collecting. I love its gilded endpapers of glam cooks in pinnies. Petrina Tinslay's photographs do the cakes, tarts and pies full justice.

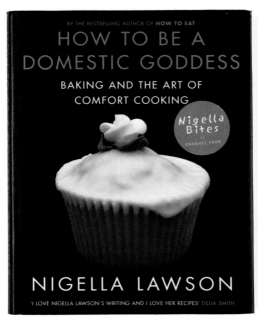

DOUBLE APPLE PIE

I don't want to nominate favourites, but even so, I have to say this is a pie I am ecstatic about – perhaps because it's so far removed from what I've spent my life cooking.

The notion of putting Cheddar in the pastry of an apple pie is not a new one but I was pleased all the same to see how well it worked. I've used a Springform tin (learning a lesson from the pizza rustica, above), which makes this a good, hefty, sliceable pie.

The double-apple element – Coxes to hold their shape, Bramleys to make for an appley-velvet background – does entail quite a bit of work, but it isn't difficult work, just moderately time-consuming. Anyone who's hanging about the house claiming to want to help should be handed a vegetable peeler and an apple corer without delay.

for the pastry:	for the filling:
50g cold unsalted butter, diced	**750g Bramley apples** (about 3 large), peeled and cored
50g Trex or other vegetable shortening	**1kg Cox apples** (about 10), peeled, cored and cut into eighths
250g self-raising flour	**80g unsalted butter**
50g finely grated Cheddar	pinch of ground cloves
1 large egg	good grating of nutmeg
iced water to bind	**2 large eggs**, beaten
pinch of salt	**100g caster sugar**
22cm Springform tin	

Make the pastry in a food processor as normal: pulse the butter and Trex into the flour until it looks like crumbs. Leaving the mixture in the bowl, put the grating blade in and process the cheese into the crumb mixture. Replace the normal blade, and add the egg, iced water and salt to bind. Turn the pastry out and press it into two discs, one slightly smaller than the other. Wrap each in clingfilm and put them in the fridge to rest for at least 20 minutes.

Preheat the oven to 200°C/gas mark 6, putting in a baking sheet. Slice the Bramleys into small chunks and fry in half the butter until they become soft and begin to lose their shape. Add the cloves and nutmeg. Tip the apple mush into the food processor, and purée, pulsing so as not to make it too like baby food. Add about three-quarters of the beaten egg and all of the sugar and pulse again to mix. Fry the Coxes in the other half of the butter and cover them to help them cook a little. Cook for about 10 minutes: they should be tender but still holding their shape.

Roll out the larger disc of pastry and line the tin with it, letting it hang over the sides. Pour in the puréed mixture, and then push the Cox pieces into the purée to coat them. Roll out the smaller disc of pastry to form the top. Lay over the pie, and curl the

---

BUTTER CUT-OUT BISCUITS

It's not hard to make biscuits that hold their shape well while cooking; it's not hard to make biscuits that taste good and have a melting, buttery texture: what's hard is to find a biscuit that does all of these things together. This one, by way of a wonderful American book, *The Family Baker*, does: so any time you want to play supermummy in the kitchen, here is where you start.

Like all doughs, it freezes well, so it makes sense – in a smug, domestic kind of a way – to wrap half of this in clingfilm and stash it in the deep freeze until next needed. It's hard to specify exactly how much icing you'll need, but you might end up using more than specified below if you're using a lot of different colours. I always cut out the newly acquired age of the child on his or her birthday. My children couldn't contemplate a birthday party without them.

175g soft unsalted butter	**1 teaspoon baking powder**
200g caster sugar	**1 teaspoon salt**
2 large eggs	**300g icing sugar**, sieved, and food colouring
1 teaspoon vanilla extract	biscuit cutters
400g plain flour, preferably Italian 00, plus more if needed	**2 baking sheets**, greased or lined

Preheat the oven to 180°C/gas mark 4.

Cream the butter and sugar together until pale and moving towards moussiness, then beat in the eggs and vanilla. In another bowl, combine the flour, baking powder and salt. Add the dry ingredients to the butter and eggs, and mix gently but surely. If you think the finished mixture is too sticky to be rolled out, add more flour, but do so sparingly as too much will make the dough tough. Halve the dough, form into fat discs, wrap each half in clingfilm and rest in the fridge for at least 1 hour. Sprinkle a suitable surface with flour, place a disc of dough on it (not taking out the other half until you've finished with the first) and sprinkle a little more flour on top of that. Then roll it out to a thickness of about ½ cm. Cut into shapes, dipping the cutter into flour as you go, and place the biscuits a little apart on the baking sheets.

Bake for 8–12 minutes, by which time they will be lightly golden around the edges. Cool on a rack and continue with the rest of the dough. When they're all fully cooled, you can get on with the icing. Put a couple of tablespoons of just-not-boiling water into a large bowl, add the sieved icing sugar and mix together, adding more water as you need to form a thick paste. Colour as desired: let the artistic spirit within you speak, remembering with gratitude that children have very bad taste.

Makes 50–60.

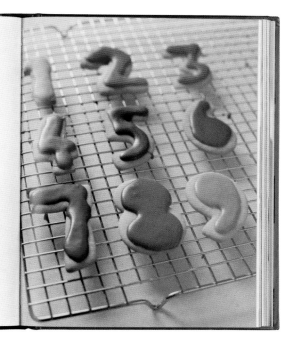

Mrs C.F. Leyel and Miss Olga Hartley

The Gentle Art of Cookery: With 750 Recipes

Chatto & Windus, London, 1925
460 pages
188 x 125 mm (7³/₈ x 4⁷/₈ in.)

Along with garden historian and gardener Eleanour Sinclair Rohde (page 172), Hilda Leyel helped to revive the use of herbs in post-war Britain. I remember in the 1960s searching for advice on growing and using herbs before finding Leyel's shop on Baker Street in London, Culpeper House, named after the famous herbalist Nicholas Culpeper. She also founded the Society of Herbalists in 1927, two years after her most famous book was published.

Mrs C.F. Leyel, as she was known (she married a theatrical manager and later divorced), could be writing today. She lists the ways in which *The Gentle Art* differs from other cookery books: a whole chapter on cold Sunday suppers; a chapter of flower recipes; an 'Arabian Nights' chapter, including *imam bayaldi*, moussaka and sesame cakes. One for children is bound to succeed since it consists mostly of such treats as chocolate fudge, gingerbread and meringues. But the 'ostrich egg', a dozen separated eggs in a pig's bladder? 'Serve the enormous ostrich egg in a Béchamel sauce'. The little things would run screaming. And, proving that olive oil didn't just come from a chemist's in pre-war Britain, she suggests Lucca or Provençal, the latter being 'more suitable to the English palate'.

'This is not intended to be an elementary handbook on cookery', Leyel says sternly, 'but has been written for those who appreciate the fact that good cooking is one of the attainable amenities of life if extravagance is eliminated'. Olga Hartley, a suffragist, was her assistant in its writing.

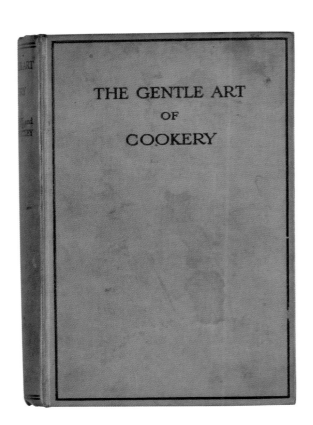

BRANDY SNAPS

❡ A quarter of a pound of treacle, one ounce of flour, one ounce of butter, half a teaspoonful of ginger, a quarter of a teaspoonful of allspice.

Mix the flour and spices in a basin. Melt the butter and treacle over the fire and pour it on to the flour and mix it thoroughly. Grease a baking sheet, and on to it put teaspoonfuls of the mixture far apart. Bake it slowly. They will spread out and become thin.

After taking the sheet from the oven, let it stand for a minute, then loosen the cakes with a knife, turn them over, and curl them round a greased stick, when they will harden at once.

CHOCOLATE FUDGE

❡ One pound of best granulated sugar, four penny bars of chocolate, half a teacupful of milk, a piece of butter the size of a walnut.

Put the sugar in a double saucepan and mix it with the milk to form a thick paste. Grate the chocolate into it, and add the butter. Put it on a slow fire and do not let it come to the boil till the sugar and the chocolate are melted. Then let it boil for five minutes, stirring it hard all the time. Take it off the fire, beat it till it is thick, and pour it on to buttered soup plates or dishes.

Cut it into squares before it gets cold.

OMELETTES IN SAUCERS

Children can make omelettes for themselves very simply. This is the recipe :

388

❡ Well butter a saucer. Beat up an egg in a cup, season it with salt, add a little chopped parsley. Pour the beaten egg into the saucer and put the saucer in the oven for a minute or two till the egg is set.

This makes quite a nice little omelette, and the child can put into it a little puffed rice or other harmless ingredient—it will amuse the child and won't hurt the omelette.

MERINGUES

❡ Six fresh eggs, three-quarters of a pound of icing sugar.

Separate the whites of six fresh eggs very carefully from the yolks. Whisk them to a very stiff froth and gradually whip in three-quarters of a pound of icing sugar.

Line an oven tray with thick white paper and lay the mixture in tablespoonfuls on the paper. They should keep the shape of the spoon. Sift more sugar over them and put them in a gentle oven. Bake them till they are a pale brown, then gently remove them from the paper, and when quite cold scoop out some of the inside and fill them with vanilla-flavoured whipped cream.

The whole success of meringue making depends upon the oven being just right, and they must be looked at from time to time.

GINGERBREAD

The joy of the old-fashioned gingerbread, sold at every English fair was, of course, the

389

the petals into the liquid. Repeat this procedure until the liquid has gained considerable flavour from the petals.

To every gallon of liquor put three pounds of loaf sugar and mix it well. Now place it in a cask, and put in a piece of toast covered with yeast to ferment it. Allow it to stand for thirty days. Wine and spices may be added to it.

A similar process may be used for making wine from the following flowers :

Carnations, Wallflowers, Violets, Primroses, and any other heavily scented flowers.

Mr. Marcel Boulestin's Recipe in his book
"Simple French Cooking"

OMELETTE AUX FLEURS DE SALSIFIS

❡ This omelette is not easy to make, not because it is difficult to do it well, but because it is not easy to get the necessary flowers.

Salsifis flowers are not usually sold in shops ; in fact they are only to be found in the vegetable garden in the late spring. The best salsifis for this purpose is the one imported from Spain, which has black roots and yellow flowers.

Nip them literally in the bud, and wash them well in several waters to get rid of the kind of milk which oozes from them when you break them. Then dry them in a cloth for a few minutes, after which cook them in butter till they are brown, with salt and pepper. Mix them with

408

the beaten eggs, and make your omelette in the ordinary way. Do not be surprised to see the buds open in the hot butter. It affects them more quickly than the sun. Some show a few already yellow petals ; it is a pretty sight ; also the taste is delicious.

VIOLET TEA

❡ Pour half a pint of boiling water on to one teaspoonful of dried violets ; leave it for five minutes. Strain it, and sweeten it with honey.

This is very soothing to people suffering from bronchitis.

MARMALADE OF VIOLETS

❡ Half a pound of violet flowers, one and a half pounds of sugar, half a cup of water.

Take half a pound of violet flowers picked from their stalks and crush them in a mortar.

Boil the sugar and water to a syrup, and when boiling add the flowers. Allow it to come five or six times to the boil on a very slow fire. Stir it with a wooden spoon, and pour it while hot into little pots.

VIOLET NOSEGAYS

❡ Take fresh violets ; tie them in bunches of ten or twelve flowers with cotton.

Boil some sugar until it pearls or bubbles. Try a little in a spoon and blow hard upon it. The bubbles should leave the spoon and float in the air like soap bubbles. Then let the sugar

409

Alastair Little and Richard Whittington

Keep it Simple: A Fresh Look at Classic Cooking

Conran Octopus, London, 1993
192 pages
253 x 200 mm (10 x 7⅞ in.)

Charming, modest, self-taught (but with a Cambridge degree in social anthropology and archaeology), Alastair Little is not a typical chef. He was, however, called the 'Godfather of British Cooking' for the food in his minimalist, eponymous former restaurant. *Keep it Simple* is not a typical chef's book. For a start, he and his co-author, Richard Whittington, tested the recipes in a domestic kitchen (I was once fortunate enough to be given lunch by him in his own small kitchen, cooked with effortless ease). His dishes are simple, but not necessarily quick or easy. Here, 'simple' means letting the ingredients shout for themselves.

The book is divided into seasons, and the recipes into sections on, among other things, *mise en place*, utensils needed and how to serve the whole. Most dishes are Mediterranean-based (Little has run a cookery school in Italy): Sole Florentine, Orvieto Chicken, Confit Sarladaise. And I note that his *salade niçoise* includes both boiled new potatoes and cooked French beans. I do the same, but see Jacques Médecin's views about this (page 144).

Little's expertise as a chef is evident in the sections on what to have in the store cupboard and fridge, how to check for freshness and what equipment you will need. Architect Brian Ma Siy's beautiful drawings, of the kitchens and techniques, are at once clear, individual and dashing. The luscious photographs are by David Gill. As you would expect from Conran Octopus, the design, based around a sans serif typeface, is elegant and effortless.

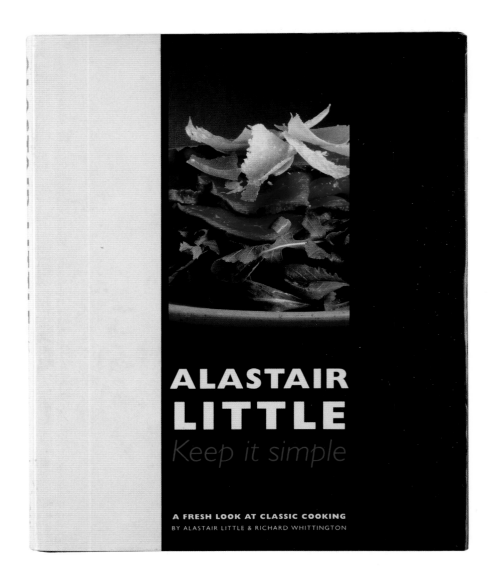

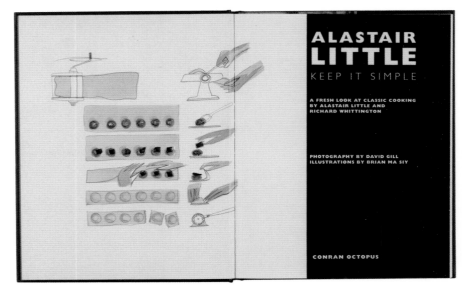

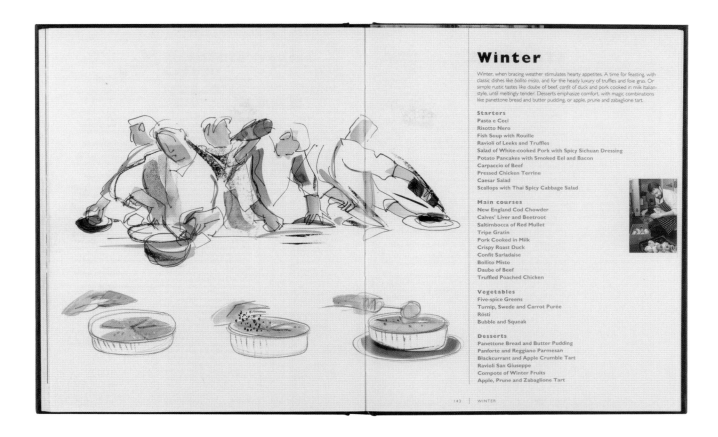

Winter

Winter, when bracing weather stimulates hearty appetites. A time for feasting, with classic dishes like bollito misto, and for the heady luxury of truffles and foie gras. Or simple rustic tastes like daube of beef, confit of duck and pork cooked in milk Italian-style, until meltingly tender. Desserts emphasize comfort, with magic combinations like panettone bread and butter pudding, or apple, prune and zabaglione tart.

Starters
Pasta e Ceci
Risotto Nero
Fish Soup with Rouille
Ravioli of Leeks and Truffles
Salad of White-cooked Pork with Spicy Sichuan Dressing
Potato Pancakes with Smoked Eel and Bacon
Carpaccio of Beef
Pressed Chicken Terrine
Caesar Salad
Scallops with Thai Spicy Cabbage Salad

Main courses
New England Cod Chowder
Calves' Liver and Beetroot
Saltimbocca of Red Mullet
Tripe Gratin
Pork Cooked in Milk
Crispy Roast Duck
Confit Sarladaise
Bollito Misto
Daube of Beef
Truffled Poached Chicken

Vegetables
Five-spice Greens
Turnip, Swede and Carrot Purée
Rösti
Bubble and Squeak

Desserts
Panettone Bread and Butter Pudding
Panforte and Reggiano Parmesan
Blackcurrant and Apple Crumble Tart
Ravioli San Giuseppe
Compote of Winter Fruits
Apple, Prune and Zabaglione Tart

Calves' Liver with Melted Onions and Sage

Veal liver is one of the most subtle and expensive offals you can buy and that subtlety is all-important for this sauté. Seared calves' liver, still pink and juicy in the middle, is vastly superior to any other animal's liver. Lambs' liver, for example, just will not do.

Calves' liver comes almost exclusively from box-reared animals, and you have to decide for yourself whether or not this is a moral issue. It is worth seeking out an organic butcher and finding out whether there is any alternative and kinder method of veal production, but most of what is available comes from Holland where darkened, boxed living conditions are standard. Even so, obtaining calves' liver is not easy outside London.

The first time you cook this dish, I suggest you do so for two rather than four people – in which case halve the quantities. There will seem to be a lot of onions when you first start out, but they cook down to a fraction of their original bulk as the water evaporates from them.

Ingredients
450g / 1lb calves' liver, cut into 4 thin slices
4tbsp flour
1tbsp sunflower oil
55g / 2oz butter
4 large sage leaves
5tbsp dry white wine, or 2tbsp balsamic or sherry vinegar
2tbsp Chicken Stock (see page 19)
salt and pepper

FOR THE MELTED ONIONS:
8 large onions
85g / 3oz butter
bay leaf
2tbsp white wine vinegar
1tbsp caster sugar

Utensils
heavy casserole dish with lid
sauté pan large enough to hold all the liver (or 2 sauté pans)
metal spatula

Mise en Place
At least 2 hours ahead, prepare the Melted Onions: slice the onions into thin rings. Melt 55g / 2oz of the butter in the casserole over a low heat. Stir in the onions and bay leaf. It is important not to allow the butter to brown – you are making a white compote, not caramelized onions, which are a different dish altogether.

Put on the lid and cook, covered, over a very low heat for 30 minutes, by which time the onions will have started to collapse. Remove the lid and stir thoroughly. Cover again and continue to cook for a further 1 hour.

Remove the bay leaf and add the vinegar and sugar. Season with salt and pepper. Stir and turn up the heat to medium. Cook to evaporate the liquid, stirring while you do so. Stop cooking before the onions take on colour. Keep warm for immediate use, or store in a closed container in the fridge for up to 1 week.

Prepare the liver: carefully remove any tubes or threads from the liver. Put the flour on a plate and season well. Coat the pieces of liver in the seasoned flour and shake off any excess.

Cooking
Heat the sauté pan over a medium heat. Put a tablespoon of sunflower oil in the pan with a knob of butter and gently lay the slices of liver in this. Cook for 2 minutes, then turn. Scatter over the sage leaves and cook for 60 seconds more.

Serving
Arrange beds of the warm onion compote on 4 warmed plates, place the cooked liver slices on top of them and keep warm.

Turn up the heat under the pan and deglaze it with the wine or vinegar, scraping and stirring. Add 2 tablespoons of chicken stock and bubble before swirling in a knob of butter to finish the sauce. Pour over the liver and serve immediately.

The Calves' Liver with Melted Onions and Sage is served here with Hasselback Potatoes, see page 132.

Elisabeth Luard

European Peasant Cookery

Grub Street, London, 2004 (first published
1986)
544 pages
244 x 173 mm (9⅝ x 6¾ in.)

Modern cookery has been a journey from French haute cuisine to the everyday food of ordinary people. Peasant food. All the fashionable language used around good food, such as seasonality, local ingredients, simplicity, revealing the ingredients' flavours rather than hiding them – this is peasant food. From the 1950s onwards, home cooks have been striving to eat like Italian or Spanish farmers. Even French farmers.

While plenty of writers caught on to this, they directed their interest to a single country or even region. Elisabeth Luard, by contrast, takes the entire area of Europe for her magisterial book (akin in size and style to *James Beard's American Cookery* – see page 30 – but even more wide-ranging). This is rural cooking, she argues. Urban food is bourgeois, and haute cuisine derives from Rome and the medieval banquet.

Luard ascribes the book's genesis to a period in the late 1960s when she was living in a remote Andalusian valley. The Iron Curtain was still in place, and the people of the region 'were … locked in what some might call a medieval way of life'. She raised her children there, with her writer husband, Nicholas, and later lived for a year in the Languedoc region of France. Inevitably, many of the recipes are Mediterranean, but plenty, such as gravlax and Jansson's Temptation, come from Scandinavia. She touches on the Hungarians' love of grilled meat (inherited from their nomadic Magyar ancestors), although peasant cooking generally was a form of Arte Povera, rarely using prime cuts of meat. This is a whopping book of considerable scholarship but without pretension: no illustrations, no designer frills. Like peasant food, it's good, solid stuff.

A Book for Cooks

POULTRY AND BARNYARD

CHICKEN

Even the poorest European peasant household could usually support a few barnyard fowl – good egg-layers often provided the wife's only cash crop. Farmyard hens were primarily kept for eggs rather than meat and although a few young cockerels were fattened up for high days and holidays, peasant recipes concentrate on ways of dealing with tough elderly birds past their egg-laying prime: plenty of soups, stews and slow cooking.

The slaughter of poultry was invariably women's work, as I discovered during my days in Andalusia when Maria Magdalena, the wife of our local baker in the little village of Pelayo, refused to sell me, as a regular customer, a bird for the pot unless I learned to kill it myself. Maria kept hens and sold eggs as a sideline, but sometimes at Christmas she would act as agent for the farmers who lived in the hills behind, and they would walk their turkeys and geese down to the little bakery beside the main road for her to sell on their behalf. The unwary purchaser, perhaps a motorist on the way down to the town below, was likely to find his Christmas dinner fully feathered and squawking on the seat beside him unless he specified otherwise in advance.

While Maria Magdalena consented to act as chief executioner, she would make her customer secure the bird's legs, and then, with one swift sure movement, double over the chicken's head and sever the spine at the base of the skull. She preferred to pluck dry, rather than dipping the bird in a bucket to dampen the feathers first. Sitting out on the back stoop in the sun and working from head to tail, it never took her more than three minutes a bird. Heads, feet, gizzards and necks all went for the stew pot. In a mature egg-layer, any of the little golden unlaid eggs she found inside would go to enrich the *puchero*. Nothing was ever wasted.

COCK-A-LEEKIE
(Scotland)

Kissing cousin to the ancient English dishes of malachi and gallimaufry, much like the Welsh cawl and the French pot-au-feu, cock-a-leekie – maybe because it's so good and so simple – has survived in more or less original form. Spoon food for hungry field workers, it can be made with a good strong bone stock rather than the more luxurious fowl – traditionally, the loser in a cockfight, since the bird's sinewy drumsticks fortify the broth. In these daintier times, a boiling fowl will do.

Quantity: Serves 6
Time: Preparation: 10 minutes
    Cooking: About 2½ hours

1 large boiling fowl (at least 2kg/4 lb)
3.5 litres/6 pints spring water
1 level tablespoon sea salt
1 teaspoon crushed peppercorns
At least 2kg/4 lb leeks

Utensils: A roomy stew pot and draining spoon

Wipe over the chicken and put in the stew pot. Cover with water, bring to the boil, and turn down the heat to a gentle simmer. Skim off the grey foam which rises, then season with salt and crushed peppercorns and leave to cook for 2½ hours.

Rinse the leeks, trim off the tips of the leaves (leaving most of the green) and chop into short lengths. Add half the leeks to the pot after the first half hour. After 2 hours, add the rest. The soup must be very thick with leeks – by the end; the first addition should have boiled down until they've become almost liquid themselves. Some cooks further thicken the broth with a handful of oatmeal.

To serve, joint the chicken – just pull it gently apart with a fork – and ladle directly from the pot, chicken and leek together. Or, for a more substantial dish, cook sliced potatoes in the broth, and serve the soup first, with the chicken and potatoes afterwards.

Suggestions:

• The inclusion of prunes or raisins in the soup is a matter of furious debate among cock-a-leekie experts. If you wish, add a handful of either to the broth after the first hour of cooking. The diplomatic M. Talleyrand, experiencing the dish on a visit to the Scottish capital, suggested that the prunes be cooked in the broth but removed before service. This, he suggests, would colour and sweeten the soup without interfering with the delicate flavour of the leek, a member of the onion tribe and naturally sweet.

• Some traditional recipes advocate the inclusion of a drop of treacle – an addition which serves the same purpose as the prunes. Others, under the French influence perhaps, stir in a handful of shredded greens.

• The soup is sometimes thickened with a handful of fine-ground oatmeal.

---

after washing. Take out a piece of confit and melt it gently in a pan. Remove and reserve the confit and keep it warm. Fry the cooked, drained cabbage in the melted fat till it gilds a little, sprinkle with caraway and salt, return the confit to the pan and braise all together, loosely lidded for 20 minutes.

POTTED GOOSE LIVER
Confit de foie gras (France)

Selecting your foie gras raw for potting is much easier if it has already been removed from the original owner. If the liver is still in the bird, as is not unusual in French country markets in goose-fattening areas, feel the tautness of the skin and the swell of the curve. A plump skin, pearly with fat, is a fair indication the liver will be equally plump and pearly. If the liver is laid out for inspection, you're looking for firmness and paleness – ivory is the colour to look for – only lightly tinged with pink and without dark veining. The fattened-liver tradition can be traced back to the days of the Pharaohs in Egypt: the wild geese which gorged themselves on the sweet grasses of the Nile flood-plain found themselves unable to take flight. In France, Toulouse, Périgueux and Strasbourg are the main centres of production. Austria, Hungary and former Czechoslovakia also produce fattened livers, though they never seem to achieve the creamy perfection of the hand-reared Toulouse goose.

Quantity: Serves 6-8
Time: Start a day ahead
    Preparation: 10 minutes
    Cooking: 1-1½ hours

1 fresh foie gras (1-2kg/2-4 lb)
1-2 tablespoons rough salt
1 tablespoon marc or white brandy (optional)

Utensils: Conserving jars with screw or snap-top lids and a large saucepan or deep roasting tin

If the foie gras is still in the bird, detach it with care, looking out for the dark green gall bladder which must not be allowed to spill its bitter juices on the liver. Check for and remove it with a small sharp knife any dark blood vessels or veins. Place the liver on a clean plate and sprinkle with salt; place another clean plate on top and weight it down with a few tins. You may also, if you like, sprinkle a tablespoon of marc or white brandy over the foie. (Madame Escrieux, whose instructions these are, preferred to drink the brandy as she contemplated the pleasure to come.) Leave overnight.

Next day, drain off the juices, dust off excess salt and pat dry. Sterilise the conserving jars – wash thoroughly and pop in a low oven for 20 minutes to dry. Cram the liver, divided as appropriate, into the conserving jars, seal down and place the jars in a pan of water which comes right up the sides. Boil steadily for 1 hour if each jar contains 500g/1 lb foie, for 1½ hours if the foie is 1kg/2 lb. Or stand the jars in a baking tray with boiling water and bake at 350°F/

180°C/Gas 4 for 10 minutes longer than you need for the top heat.

The jars will keep perfectly, unopened and in a cool larder, for several months – if you can withstand the temptation. The French enjoy their foie gras with a glass of the finest sweet wine the neighbourhood can produce – Montbazillac, Sauternes, those who live near Chateau Yquem are doubly blessed.

BRAISED GOOSE GIBLETS
Alicot de gesiers (France)

Yet another use for another part of the mighty goose – even the bones make a wonderful stock for a lentil soup. In fact, there's barely a part of the creature which cannot be made into something delicious. For an alicot, you will need the giblets (all but the foie gras, of course) from 2-3 fine fat geese on market day – delicacies often sold separately from the liver and the carcass. If fattened geese are not a speciality of your area, the dish can be made with the giblets of an ordinary roasting goose or duck. However, you will miss the pale sweet goose fat which Roman gourmets, who prized it more highly than butter, considered an aphrodisiac. Their ladies, more sensibly, used it as a cosmetic – as a body cream and to beautify their complexions.

Quantity: Serves 6-8
Time: Preparation: 30 minutes
    Cooking: 2 hours

1kg/2 lb goose or duck giblets (heart, gizzard, neck, wingtips, livers if available)
500g/1 lb onions
4 garlic cloves
2 tablespoons goose-dripping or pure white pork lard
250g/8 oz salt pork (petit salé) or unsmoked streaky bacon, diced
3 large carrots
500g/1 lb tomatoes (tinned is fine)
300ml/½ pint stock or white wine and water
½ teaspoon crushed peppercorns
small bunch bay leaf, rosemary, thyme, parsley

Utensils: A heavy casserole with a lid

Pick over, trim, wipe and slice the giblets as necessary. Skin and chop the onion and garlic. Melt the dripping in the casserole, add the onion and garlic and leave to fry gently while you dice the pork fat or bacon. Push the onions to one side and add the giblets and the diced pork or bacon.

Preheat the oven to 300°F/150°C/Gas 2.

Leave all sizzling gently while you scrape and slice the carrots. Peel and chop the tomatoes – to loosen the skins ready for peeling, cover with boiling water. Tomato skins never seem to break down however long you cook them, and end up, even after a couple of hour's stewing, marooned

Richard Mabey

Food for Free:
A Guide to the Edible
Wild Plants of Britain

Fontana, London, 1975 (first published 1972)
192 pages
196 x 127 mm (7¾ x 5 in.)

Foraging for food has become chic, with restaurants everywhere dropping elder flowers, ceps and samphire into their dishes. Richard Mabey's comprehensive book from the 1970s was what started the trend (he later went on to write the magisterial *Flora Britannica* and *Fauna Britannica*, well worth reading but not about food).

My one rule in choosing these cookery books has been that they must include recipes, however vague, as well as descriptions, and Mabey's book squeezes in by its rooty whiskers. So, there's advice on eating horse mushrooms (stew them in milk and serve with a white sauce and

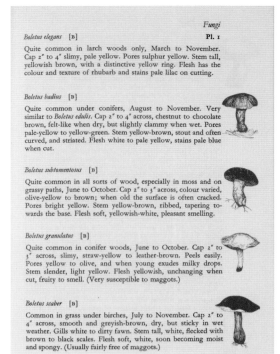

hot redcurrants), while sorrel gets a proper soup recipe. Scallops, he says, should be fried for 40 minutes (absolutely not true; five will suffice).

Each item is classed as A, B or C: A is common, good to eat and treated in full; B, rather too much like A but treated in less detail; and C, mainly historical, not recommended or rare. Curiously, wild garlic is a C, whereas today's trend is to use it as much as possible when it's in season, for everything from soup to covering cheese. So fashions change.

Mabey's book is full of folklore and folk names: alexanders is 'hellroot' in Dorset but 'megweed' in Sussex; wood sorrel is also known as 'bread-and-cheese' and 'fox's meat'; the shaggy cap mushroom is 'lawyer's wig' to some. A final list of poisonous foods definitely not for free includes death cap, panther cap and fool's parsley. As one who was poisoned (although not fatally) by Cornish wild funghi, I advise everyone to read this book carefully before foraging.

The problem with fashionable food foraging is that you might mistake a deadly water hemlock for a tasty sweet cicely. Mabey provides careful illustrations to help you avoid such an event.

common limpet, *Patella vulgata*, is common enough on rocky shores, and can grow up to 2½" across. But it is normally somewhat smaller than this, and consequently a fair number – and a fair degree of scrambling – are needed to gather enough for a meal.

Do not pick them from piers or jetties, but from out-of-town rocks that are covered daily by the tide. They can be prised from the rocks with a knife or dislodged with a hefty kick. Soak them in the usual way and then boil like cockles until the meat floats free of the shell. Be warned, though: limpets can be very tough, and they may need considerable further simmering or baking. In the Isle of Man they fry them at Easter.

Mussels *Mytilus edulis* [c]

Mussels are amongst our commonest and most delectable shellfish. But they are also responsible for most cases of shellfish poisoning. This has been happening with such frequency recently that I felt that a C rating would have to be given to indicate the need for special caution.

It is not difficult to see why mussels are becoming increasingly infected. They pump at least ten gallons of water through their bodies every day. Given the condition of some of our coastal waters this is enough to enable a single fish to concentrate a substantial amount of contaminant over a period of months. There have also been plagues of a highly toxic plankton – the notorious 'red tides' – along many European coasts during recent breeding seasons. Mussels strain out these poisonous plants during their normal feeding, and concentrate the toxin in their livers to levels that can be dangerous for both birds and man. (Incidentally, the North American Indians, always wise and resourceful with wild foods, knew all about the dangers of these tiny plants. They would prohibit the taking of mussels until the 'red tide' had passed, and even set guards along the beaches.)

But if you follow the tips given on p. 22 you are very unlikely to eat a bad mussel. Gather them from clean stony shores at low tide outside the summer months, let them stand through at

26

least two changes of fresh tap water and carefully check that each one is still alive before cooking.

As a change from moules marinières, try baking them in their shells in hot ash, and popping in a mixture of butter, garlic and parsley as the shells open.

Scallop or Clams *Pecten maximus* [c]

Scallops are the huge, classic shells that came to be the oil company's symbol. You find them occasionally on the lower shore – that strip of sand that is only uncovered during very low tides.

Like clams (p. 25) scallops need a substantial amount of cooking. After washing and scalding, cut away the white and orange fish, dust with flour or breadcrumbs and fry for about forty minutes. They have a superbly fleshy, almost poultry-like flavour.

Oyster *Ostrea edulis* [c]

Oysters have not always been the expensive delicacy that they are now. For centuries they were one of the great staples of working-class diet. In the fifteenth century 4d would buy eight gallons. As late as the mid-nineteenth, Dickens could make Sam Weller say:

'... poverty and oysters always seem to go together ... the poorer a place is, the greater call there seems to be for oysters ... here's a oyster stall to every half-dozen houses. The street's lined with 'em. Blessed if I don't think that ven a man's wery poor, he rushes out of his lodgings, and eats oysters in reg'lar desperation.'

But in the latter half of the nineteenth century prices suddenly rocketed, and there is little doubt that the cause was the irresponsible over-harvesting of the beds to meet the demands of expanding townships.

Today you will be lucky to find many wild oysters. The ones that still remain round our coasts are mostly under cultivation in private beds. So if you should chance upon one, clinging to a rock in some estuary or creek, best leave it where it is. But if eat it you must, there is only one way: raw, with lemon and paprika pepper.

27

Although fennel seeds are still mentioned in the British Pharmaceutical Codex as a remedy for 'winde' (no doubt the reason they are chewed after Indian meals) a more reliable range of uses today is as flavouring for fish dishes. Fennel is especially good with oily fish, though the tradition of using it in this way probably derives from nothing more than the plant's preference for coastal areas. The dried stalks form the basis of the famous Provençal red mullet dish, *rouget flambé au fenouil*. The finely chopped green leaves are also good to add to liver, potato salad, parsnips, and even, Len Deighton recommends, apple pie.

A dish that can really charm out and make use of the cool fragrance of fennel is okrochka, an exotic cold soup from Greece. It is a perfect dish on a warm evening, and utilises some of the other summer herbs you may gather in this section.

Mix two cartons of yoghurt (plain or apple) with roughly the same quantity of milk in a sizeable bowl. Add one cup of diced fresh cucumber, ⅓ cup of chopped pickled cucumber or gherkin, ⅓ cup of diced cooked chicken, and a handful of finely chopped fennel leaves. Add any other summer herbs that you have available – mint, parsley, and chives are particularly good – but they must be fresh, and not in such quantities that they mask the fennel. Season with salt and freshly ground pepper and put in the fridge for at least two hours.

Before serving, add two roughly chopped hard-boiled eggs to the soup, and sprinkle the surface with a little more black pepper and fresh herbs.

The taste is extraordinary, the different flavour and textures of the ingredients being preserved quite intact and independent by the yoghourt.

PLATE 5 Green Vegetables: Stems

128

PLATE 5

Lady Maclean's Diplomatic Dishes

Collins, London, 1975
256 pages
253 x 200 mm (10 x 7 7/8 in.)

Although in the tradition of cookery books written by aristocratic ladies and their friends, this is more fun. Lady Maclean, daughter of the 16th Lord Lovat, was the wife of Sir Fitzroy Maclean, inspiration (it is said) for James Bond. Sir Fitzroy served in the British Embassy in Moscow during the Stalinist years.

Unlike earlier aristocratic efforts (see Dorothy Allhusen, page 20), Veronica Maclean's book consists of the hand- or typewritten recipes sent by friends together with, where applicable, their addresses and crests. Matilda, Duchess of Argyll offers Spanish Almond Soup below a ducal coronet and an address in Paris; H.E. Lady Wilson sends Russian Sorrel Soup from the British Embassy in Moscow. H.E. Mrs David Bruce supplies Œufs Benedictine from Washington, D.C., and Mrs Ian Fleming, writing from Jamaica, Œfs (*sic*) James Bond. Other famous folk include Winston Churchill (Paté de Foie Gras en Brioche), Madame Pol-Roger (Veal Kidneys with Dill), Lady Diana Cooper (Soupe Verte) and Mrs Averell Harriman (Caramel Ice). There are princesses, counts, duchesses and ladies galore; ambassadors and their wives provide dishes from the then Yugoslavia, Monaco, Turkey, Spain, Morocco, Sweden and Brazil (ensuring that the book's title is justified). There's even a recipe from Tibetan lama Yeshe Tsultim, 'in co-operation with Lady Egremont'.

The reproductions of the original letters do away with the need for illustrations, although the endpapers showing grand ambassadorial banquets are terrific.
My copy includes a stapled-in errata by Lady Maclean ('For 1 teaspoon nutmeg read ½ teaspoon nutmeg'). And what fun to serve Cold Chicken Rothschild (from Baronne Cécile de Rothschild, 29 Faubourg St Honoré, Paris).

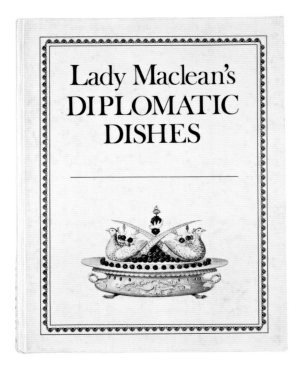

A Book for Cooks

BRITISH EMBASSY,
ISTANBUL.

IÇ PILAV

Iç Pilav means pilav with things inside it – ('icincle' = inside in Turkish,) and it is an excellent and versatile dish.

Put the rice for the pilav on a large flat dish and pour boiling water on to it. When this is cold strain it and wash it under a cold tap. Drain well.

Melt 2½ tbs of butter in a big pan and gently cook a chopped onion, to which you add a tablespoon of pine kernels, frying them together till golden. Now add the strained rice and turn over in the butter for about 5 minutes.

Then add:

1½ tbs of currants
1½ tbs of skinned and chopped tomatoes
1½ tbs spring onions or chives, chopped fine

Season with pepper, salt, a little sugar, dill, rosemary (2 leaves). Finally add 1½ cups of chicken stock or white stock. Stir together briefly and bring quickly to the boil for 5 minutes, without a lid. Now cover the pan and cook very slowly for 6-8 minutes till the stock is all absorbed and the rice is cooked to your liking. Chopped fried liver can be added if it is to go with lamb – chicken livers with chicken – chopped parsley too should be stirred in. Possibly the chives (or spring onions) are better added now if they are very tender – it depends on their size. Cover with a napkin and the lid and a weight and leave on the side of the Aga or cooker for half an hour or so. Stir before serving and dust with cinnamon. A little allspice is a change that can be made. It very much depends on what it is to accompany. The important part with all pilavs is the 'rest' at the end, which is very helpful to a hostess who wants to go and change.

Mrs. G.M. Warr

-54-

BEAUFORT CASTLE.
BEAULY.
INVERNESS-SHIRE.

JOAN'S RISOTTO OR BEAUFORT BROWN RICE

4 tbs good dripping or oil	salt and pepper
6 rashers of bacon	1¼ cups of rice
1 medium onion, minced	1½ tbs the dry Vermouth
1 clove garlic, minced	1 tsp browning
¼ lb button mushrooms	2 tbs Worcestershire sauce
1-¼ lb chicken livers, halved	2-3 cups boiling chicken stock or consommé
a walnut of butter, a little flour	⅓ cup grated Parmesan

Melt dripping or oil in a heavy pan or casserole. Put in the chopped bacon rashers, the minced onion and garlic and the sliced mushrooms. Cook gently until onions and mushrooms are soft, but do not burn. Cut the chicken livers in half, dust them with flour and sauté them in butter in a separate pan for 3-4 minutes only. Add them to the onion and mushroom mixture, scraping in the juices. Now add the dry rice and cook together for a few minutes. Stir in a tablespoon and a half of Vermouth, the Worcester sauce and enough browning to darken, simmer and then pour in the hot stock or consommé, 2-3 cups to begin with. (The liquid should cover the rice by the width of two fingers). Stir all together and put in a hot oven (375-425 F or Gas 5-6) for at least 20 minutes.* Look at it occasionally and stir a few times with a fork, tasting to see when it is ready. Add a little more stock when necessary, but this quantity should absorb all the liquid, and cook to an "al dente" point without going mushy or sticking. Remove from the oven, correct seasoning and turn on to a hot serving dish. Have a bowl of grated parmesan cheese ready and hand separately.

* The time depends on the kind of rice used.

Lady Lovat and Mrs. Joan Birnie

-55-

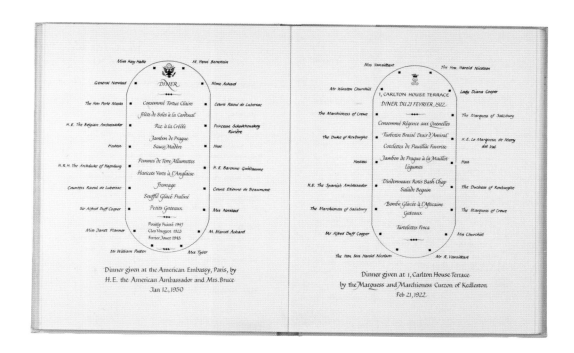

Dinner given at the American Embassy, Paris, by
H.E. the American Ambassador and Mrs. Bruce
Jan 12, 1950

Dinner given at 1, Carlton House Terrace
by the Marquess and Marchioness Curzon of Kedleston
Feb 21, 1922

Above: Seating arrangements,
so dear to the Victorians,
survived for generations in
embassies, where a diplomatic
incident could explode with
the bombe surprise. Hence the
need for complex table plans.

Lady Maclean

143

Jacques Médecin

Cuisine Niçoise: Recipes from a Mediterranean Kitchen

Translated and edited by Peter Graham
Penguin, Harmondsworth, 1983 (first
published 1972)
240 pages
197 x 128 mm (7¾ x 5 in.)

Jacques Médecin's father and grandfather
were both mayors of Nice. Jacques became
mayor in 1966. A year later he was its
representative in the National Assembly, and
then, in 1976, secretary of state for tourism
under Jacques Chirac. He died in exile in
Uruguay in 1998, having served time for
plundering the city's finances. His obituary
in *The Independent* called him its 'dictator'.
When he was not plundering and ravishing
(he was saved from bigamy on a
technicality), he was cooking.

This, therefore, is the authentic look at
the food of Nice, which became part of
France only in 1860. Before that, it belonged
to the Kingdom of Sardinia, now part of
modern-day Italy. Consequently, the food
is completely distinct, neither French nor
Italian, as evidenced in the book by the fact
that the name of each recipe is given in
three languages: Niçard (the local dialect),
French and English. Its best-known dish is
salade niçoise, and Médecin provides the
'true' version, saying, 'all over the world,
I have had the most unpleasant experience
of being served up leftovers masquerading
as *salade niçoise*'. His version, La Salada
Nissarda, uses tomatoes, hard-boiled eggs,
anchovies/tuna, cucumber, green peppers,
spring onions, broad beans/artichokes,
garlic, black olives, basil and dressing.
'Never, never, I beg you, include boiled
potato or any other boiled vegetable.'
Oh dear: mea culpa.

The recipes, inspired by Provençal and
Italian food, are easily followed and full
of old friends. There are lots of tomatoes,
fish dishes and pastas. Extraordinarily,
pissaladière is here copied from Elizabeth
David. Whatever Médecin's past, you can
forgive the old rogue for his excellent book.

---

140   *Cuisine Niçoise*

3. Ease the leaves of the cabbage open, and put the sliced carrots and
onion in the middle with a sprinkling of thyme, salt, and pepper. Cover
the casserole and put in a low oven for 20 minutes.
4. Remove the casserole from the oven, ease the leaves of the cabbage
open again and drop in the rice. If the cabbage looks likely to dry up, add
a little boiling water. Cover and bake for another 45 minutes.
5. Just before serving, lay the slices of ham over the top of the cabbage
and cover. When they have had time to heat up, serve.

155 LU CAOULÉ BELGA

Les Choux de Bruxelles

Brussels Sprouts   *For 6*

2 lb/1 kg Brussels sprouts	2 cloves garlic, peeled
6 tbs olive oil	salt, pepper

1. Trim and wash the sprouts. Put them in salted boiling water and
simmer for 15 minutes (boiling damages the compactness of the leaves).
2. Plunge in cold water and drain. Heat the olive oil in a frying pan until
it is just beginning to smoke, then add the sprouts. Fry gently until
cooked.
3. Chop the garlic finely and sprinkle over the sprouts. Add salt and
pepper to taste.
● Brussels sprouts can also be served as a purée: simply purée them
after the final stage and decorate with fried *croûtons*.

156 LI COUGOURDÉTA EN SALADA

Les Courgettes en Salade

Courgette Salad   *For 6*

12 very small courgettes	1 tbs vinegar or ½ tbs lemon juice
4 tbs olive oil	salt, pepper

1. Wash the courgettes and blanch in salted boiling water for 20
minutes. Drain.
2. Make a salad dressing with the other ingredients, pour it over the
courgettes when they are lukewarm, and serve.

Vegetables   141

157 LI COUGOURDÉTA FARCIT

Les Courgettes Farcies

Stuffed Courgettes   *For 12*

12 small courgettes (round, if	5 leaves basil
possible – see page 11)	4 oz/100 g grated Parmesan
1 large onion	2 eggs
2 oz/50 g rice	salt, pepper
1 clove garlic, peeled	breadcrumbs
2 oz/50 g *petit salé* (see page 15)	1 tbs olive oil

1. Wash the courgettes and blanch them in unsalted water for 15
minutes along with the onion, peeled and quartered.
2. Cook the rice in plenty of water for 20 minutes, then drain.
3. Cut the courgettes in half and place them, cut-side up, on a table.
Scoop out the flesh of each half-courgette with a small spoon, taking care
not to pierce the skin.
4. Chop the courgette flesh, the onion, garlic, *petit salé*, and basil.
5. Mix well in a large bowl with the Parmesan, rice and beaten eggs. Add
salt and pepper to taste.
6. Fill the courgettes with this mixture, sprinkle with a few breadcrumbs, and arrange in a previously oiled gratin dish. Cook in a medium
oven for 45 minutes.

158 LI FLOU DÉ COUGOURDÉTA FARCIT

Les Fleurs de Courgettes Farcies

Stuffed Courgette Flowers   *For 6*

18 courgette flowers	2 eggs
2 small courgettes	2 oz/50 g grated Parmesan
1 onion, peeled	salt, pepper
1 oz/25 g rice	1 tbs olive oil
1 oz/25 g *petit salé* (see facing page 15)	1 clove garlic, peeled

1. Remove the pistil from each courgette flower.
2. Blanch the courgettes and the onion for 15 minutes, then drain.
3. Boil the rice for 20 minutes, then drain.
4. Chop the onion, mash the courgettes with a fork, cut 6 courgette
flowers into strips, chop the *petit salé*, and beat the eggs. Put in a large

---

1. Put into a large mixing bowl the sugar, flour, rum, raisins (previously soaked in the orange-blossom water), the pine-nuts, lemon rind, aniseed, finely chopped citron peel, melted butter, and 5 tablespoons warmed olive oil. Mix well until a smooth paste is obtained, then add the baking powder and bread dough.
2. Mix thoroughly with a wooden spoon, but do not knead. Turn on to an oiled baking sheet and mould the mixture into a thick disc that is slightly higher in the middle.
3. Cover with a damp cloth and leave to rise at kitchen temperature for 8 hours.
4. Make incisions in the disc as indicated in Figure 1 and fold over the flaps towards the centre, carefully interleaving them as shown in Figure 2.
5. Put into a hot oven for 15 minutes, then turn the heat down to medium and bake for 1 hour. If, in the course of baking, the bread seems to be turning too brown, open the oven door for a minute or two. Then continue to bake as before.

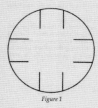 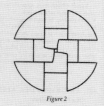

Figure 1   *Figure 2*

232   LI GANSA
Les Ganses
Ganses

Mardi Gras in Nice, when the city's well-known *Carnaval* takes place, would be unthinkable without this delicious Niçois version of dough-nuts. When carefully made – and I insist on the word carefully – *ganses*

not only make a light sweet course, but also go well with morning coffee or tea.

There exist several ways of making *ganses*. Here are two of them, one compact and almost biscuit-like, the other featherlight.

First version

9oz/250g flour	1 pinch salt
3oz/75g sugar	oil for deep-frying
2 egg yolks	icing sugar
4 tbs orange-blossom water	

1. Make a well in the flour, put in the sugar, egg yolks, orange-blossom water, salt, and a few drops of cold water, and mix well until a smooth dough is obtained.
2. Let it rest for 1 hour in a cool place.
3. Break the dough into walnut-sized pieces, and roll them out until very thin (1½ mm thick).
4. With a pastry cutter, cut the dough into strips measuring ¾ inch/2 cm wide and 6 to 8 inches/15 to 20 cm long. Tie the strips into loose knots, or make a slit in the middle along most of their length.
5. Drop the *ganses* into very hot oil and fry until golden, turning over once during cooking. Drain and toss immediately in icing sugar.

Second version

9oz/250g flour	4oz/120g butter
½ tsp baking powder	2 tbs milk
3 tbs sugar	oil for deep-frying
1 pinch salt	icing sugar
2 eggs	

1. Make a well in the flour, put in the baking powder, sugar, salt, eggs, and softened butter, and mix well. Add enough milk (about 2 table-spoons) to make a smooth, light dough.
2. Let it rest for 30 minutes.
3. Roll out the dough until very thin (1½ mm thick), and cut out the *ganses* as described in the first version.
4. Drop the *ganses* into very hot oil and fry until golden, turning over once during cooking. Drain and toss immediately in icing sugar.

261   LU ABRICO A MITAN
Les Abricots en Moitiés
Halved Apricots

apricots
sugar

1. Use unbruised, slightly unripe apricots. Slit them open and remove the stones.
2. Pack the apricots into jars and cover with sugar syrup (1 lb 2 oz/500 g of sugar per 1¾ pints/1 litre of water).
3. Seal and sterilize for 30 minutes.
● Extra flavour can be obtained by breaking open the stones and adding the halved kernels to the apricots before sterilizing.

262   LI CÉRIEÏA
Les Cerises
Cherries

cherries
sugar

1. Remove the cherry stalks, and wash the fruit carefully.
2. Pack the cherries into jars and cover with sugar syrup (1 lb 2 oz/500 g of sugar per 1¾ pints/1 litre of water).
3. Seal and sterilize for 20 minutes.

263   LI CÉRIEÏA A LA BRANDA
Les Cerises à la Branda
Cherries in Grappa*

2 lb/1 kg cherries	9oz/250g sugar
4 cloves	2¼ pints/1¼ litres *grappa*
1 stick cinnamon	

1. Shorten the cherry stalks, and wash the fruit carefully. Put in a large bowl with the spices.

*See A Note on Drinks, page 226.

2. Melt the sugar in a little water over a low heat. Remove from heat, add the *grappa*, and leave to cool.
3. Add to the cherries in the bowl. Distribute the contents of the bowl evenly between the number of jars you wish to fill (the cherries should come up to within 1 inch/3 cm of the top, and be covered with liquid).
4. Seal the jars, leave in sunlight for a few days, and store.

264   LA COUMPOSTA DÉ MAÏOUSSA
La Compote de Fraises
Strawberry Compote

2 lb/1 kg strawberries
1½ lb/700 g sugar

1. Hull the strawberries and wash if necessary. Drain and put in a bowl with the sugar. Shake until well covered with sugar.
2. Transfer strawberries and sugar delicately to jars. Seal and sterilize for 20 minutes.

265   LU PESSEGUÉ A MITAN
Les Pêches en Moitiés
Halved Peaches

yellow peaches
sugar

1. Peel the peaches, which should be unblemished and slightly unripe, cut in half, and remove the stones.
2. Pack the peach halves into jars, cut side down, and cover with sugar syrup (1 lb 2 oz/500 g of sugar per 1¾ pints/1 litre of water).
3. Seal and sterilize for 30 minutes.
● Whole peaches can also be preserved in this way, using a syrup made of 2¼ lb/1 kg sugar per 1¾ pints/1 litre of water. But it is not a very practical system, as only a very few peaches can fit into each jar.

Patricia Michelson

The Cheese Room

Michael Joseph, London, 2001
224 pages
215 x 152 mm (8½ x 6 in.)

'I am only surprised that Patricia stopped talking about cheese … for long enough to write this passionate book', says Nicholas Lander of the *Financial Times*. And he's right: the book is passionate, almost an autobiography. One section is subtitled 'When Beaufort Met Patricia'. She was skiing, and on her way back to her chalet stopped to buy a piece of Beaufort to nibble: 'The taste was so satisfying that I expect it was then I decided my life had to change.'

It did: two London cheese shops, two books about cheese (this is the first) and international recognition is what Beaufort did for Patricia. And, it must be said, what Patricia did for Beaufort is just as heroic. Not only does she produce the most delicious cheeses, properly cared for, but also her passion for them has aroused passions in others (I hate the clichéd use of 'passion', when it just means a slight liking for, but here it is fully merited).

As well as guidance on maintaining and maturing your cheeses (Michelson treats them like pets), there are chapters on such topics as cheeses for all seasons and how to make your own, interspersed with travelling tales from Cork, Manhattan and beyond. There are also plenty of recipes, many of which have international appeal and are quick and perfect for small cooking spaces. Along with Croque Style Curnonsky and Fondue Savoyarde, she even loves Dairylea with Heinz spaghetti, and cheese on toast using thick-cut white bread, the best Cheddar – and Marmite.

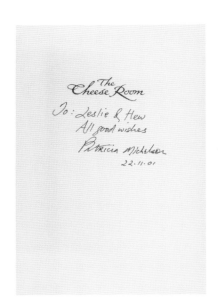

My copy of *The Cheese Room* was a Christmas present, thoughtfully signed by the author. It makes both the book and the author more companionable.

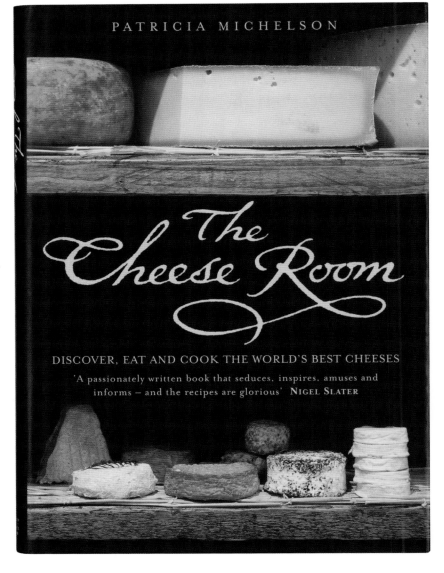

A Book for Cooks

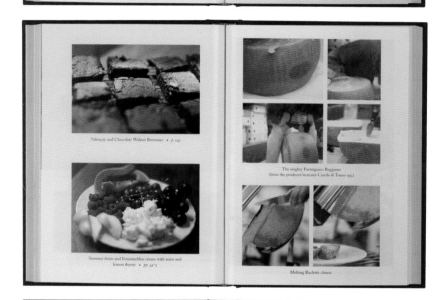

Lyndsay and Patrick Mikanowski

Potato

Grub Street, London, 2005
192 pages
309 x 238 mm (12¹/₈ x 9³/₈ in.)

If you think of the potato as 'the humble
spud', then this book is dedicated to
disabusing you of that notion. From the front
cover, featuring a potato totem made out of
crimson, golden-yellow and imperial-purple
specimens balanced one on top of the other,
Potato makes one of the most disregarded
vegetables into something glorious.

The two authors – she a trained
sociologist, he an art director – treat the
history of the potato before challenging
top chefs to produce their favourite potato
dishes. Thus, we learn that the potato, found
wild in the Andes and cultivated there for
thousands of years, was central to the Inca
civilization. When the Spaniards discovered
it in the sixteenth century, it was secretly
transported to Europe, only to lead, by the
mid-nineteenth century, to starvation in
Ireland when the crop failed. Then, as
now, it was a staple food. There is a useful
section on varieties, suggesting which to boil,
which to mash, which to roast and which to
chip. Red Duke of York first appeared in
1842, and British Queen in 1894.

In their contributions, the chefs – mostly
French, for this was originally a French
publication – specify their chosen varieties.
Bintje is used for Cheesy Potato Purée,
while the extraordinary Vitelotte is made into
DayGlo-purple crisps. Thomas Keller of the
French Laundry in Yountville, California,
uses the Ratte variety to make a delightful
Spring Vegetable Salad. There's even a
Peruvian chef, who teams Amarilla potatoes
with tuna.

This book must be the ultimate table
candy. It is huge, colourful and quite
beautiful. The photographs, by Grant Symon,
present the chefs in monochrome and the
potatoes in glorious colour.

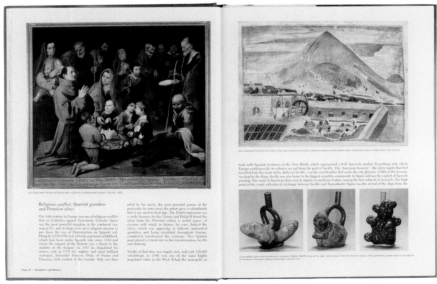

How to plant

Provided the plants are healthy and the soil well-structured, well-drained and kept cool and moist under the mulch, all you have to do is plant. Avoid heavy soils: potatoes like sandy, well-drained soil. Good use of mulch year after year is an excellent way of making the soil less heavy. The best moment is the spring, but wait for the soil to warm up, when the grass begins to grow. Potatoes are sensitive to frost and you should keep an eye on the weather forecast and protect young plants from the slightest chill. In the warmest climates you can plant up to four weeks ahead, further north and east you should wait as long as possible. The best place is one that gets as much light as possible. Potatoes like open space with no shadows from trees or high walls. If you are planting potatoes in a plot for the first time, get rid of the weeds and till the surface, burying any clods and little plants still in them. Then spread your mulch.

Once you have entirely covered the plot with mulch and are ready to plant, leave plenty of space around each potato: a square metre or 100cm between each plant and between rows if you are planting a lot of plants. You will find this space useful to work in for mulching and banking up, and if the plants are not touching, there is less chance

which is harmful to all the life going on in the compost. Drinking water is precious: men drink it, not plants. You should never see the surface of the earth, which should always be covered in mulch at least 5cm thick although 10cm is better.

Mulch provides an ideal home for predators, but it is also inhabited by predators' predators. A silent and relentless battle goes on, a barely visible orgy where the bigger ones eat the smaller and the smallest parasites eat the big ones until they are all dead and everything decomposes. This is called balanced ecology and is a self-supporting system. Spiders, tiny wasps, beetles and their voracious larvae, fungus that preys on insects and fungus that preys on other fungus represent a whole crucial life. A few toads and hedgehogs are always welcome and will sort out your slugs and snails. Don't use slug pellets: hedgehogs, birds and other small mammals will die as a result and you will be killing off other garden helpers needlessly. And make way for moles. In short, you should let everything live. A plant under attack is an unbalanced plant, which means that you have made a wrong decision either about your plant or about its site. No digging: you can exercise your muscles and relations with your neighbours by fetching constant supplies of vegetable waste.

When planting, you can measure the distance between plants with your foot.

Flowers from the cultivar Maris Piper

Freshly lifted new potato with delicate skin.

Charlotte Potatoes in a Salt Crust

Alain Passard [Paris, France]

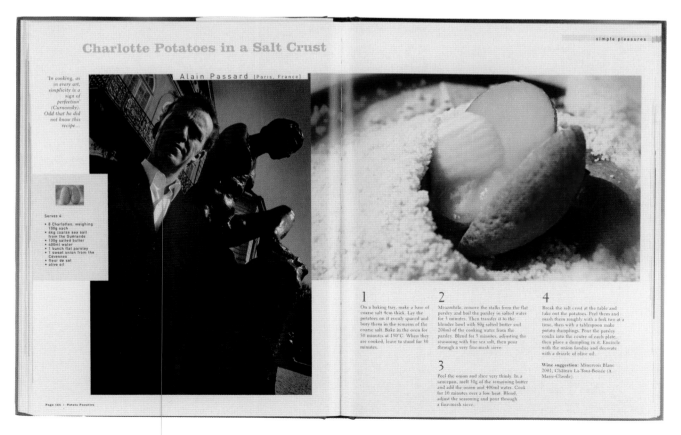

'In cooking, as in every art, simplicity is a sign of perfection' (Curnonsky). Odd that he did not know this recipe...

Serves 4

- 8 Charlottes, weighing 100g each
- 4kg coarse sea salt from the Guérande
- 130g salted butter
- 400ml water
- 1 bunch flat parsley
- 1 sweet onion from the Cévennes
- fleur de sel
- olive oil

1
On a baking tray, make a base of coarse salt 4cm thick. Lay the potatoes on it evenly spaced and bury them in the remains of the coarse salt. Bake in the oven for 50 minutes at 150°C. When they are cooked, leave to stand for 30 minutes.

2
Meanwhile, remove the stalks from the flat parsley and boil the parsley in salted water for 3 minutes. Then transfer it to the blender bowl with 80g salted butter and 200ml of the cooking water from the parsley. Blend for 5 minutes, adjusting the seasoning with fine sea salt, then pour through a very fine-mesh sieve.

3
Peel the onion and slice very thinly. In a saucepan, melt 50g of the remaining butter and add the onion and 400ml water. Cook for 10 minutes over a low heat. Blend, adjust the seasoning and pour through a fine-mesh sieve.

4
Break the salt crust at the table and take out the potatoes. Peel them and mash them roughly with a fork two at a time, then with a tablespoon make potato dumplings. Pour the parsley coulis into the centre of each plate, then place a dumpling in it. Encircle with the onion fondue and decorate with a drizzle of olive oil.

Wine suggestion: Minervois Blanc 2001, Château La-Tour-Boisée (A. Marie-Claude).

Lyndsay and Patrick Mikanowski   **149**

Orlando Murrin

A Table in the Tarn: Living, Eating and Cooking in South-West France

HarperCollins, London, 2008
256 pages
226 x 160 mm (8⅞ x 6¼ in.)

In the early 2000s, Orlando Murrin – former editor of *Good Food* magazine and creator of *Olive*, its sister BBC publication – moved to south-west France with his partner, Peter Steggall. There they bought Le Manoir de Raynaudes and set it up as a gastronomic hotel. This is the story of how it was achieved, with added recipes.

I love this book, not least for Jonathan Buckley's atmospheric photographs, which make me long to visit (sadly, Murrin and Steggall have moved on). I love the ambience of the *manoir*, its cool rooms, its lighting, Murrin at his grand piano. I love the cheerful staff and local farmers (with their less-than-cheerful dogs), the trays of ripe quinces and the baskets of tomatoes. If anyone needs help on how to create a superb restaurant with rooms, then this is the book. There's advice on equipment (I bought an alligator chopper on Murrin's say-so) and Bulthaup kitchens. The editor of *Homes and Antiques* helped with the decor (it shows). The lush garden is complete with daturas and herbs, while a picture of Murrin shows him harvesting micro-salads in the greenhouse.

And then, the recipes. They are sort-of traditional south-west France: Agen prunes with saddle of lamb, roast duck with olives, millionaire mendiants, walnut rolls, plus the odd Thai lemongrass soup thrown in. All delicious. There's even a list of Murrin's favourite cookery books (many of which are included here).

Although it is extremely pretty, this is no coffee-table book. It's neat, unglossy, superbly practical and irresistible.

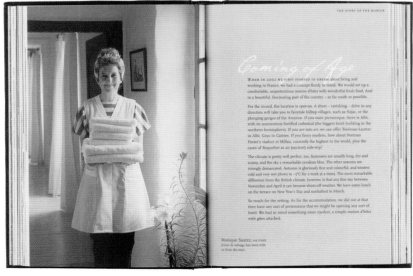

When we were creating the Manoir, I asked my friend Robert Carrier, then living reclusively in Provence, for advice. He gave me many inspiring suggestions for dishes, including this superb, featherlight Roquefort tart.

Robert's Roquefort and chive tart

Serves 6 or 8 as a starter

150g plain flour: replace 1–2 tbsp with semolina or cornmeal for crunch

salt, pepper, pinch of cayenne

85g unsalted butter

FOR THE FILLING

good handful of chives and parsley, roughly chopped (save a pinch of chives for garnishing)

200g mascarpone

100g Roquefort

1 tbsp unsalted butter, softened

3 eggs

300ml double cream or crème fraîche

You will need a 23cm tart tin, about 3.5cm deep

Make the pastry by processing the dry ingredients, adding the butter then just enough water – 2–3 tbsp – so the pastry just begins to form a ball. If possible chill for an hour, then roll out thinly and line the tin. Again if convenient, chill or briefly freeze the pastry case. Scrumple up a big sheet of baking paper then unscrumple it and lay it over the pastry. Cover with baking beans and bake at 190°C (170°C fan) for 20 minutes, till firm. Remove paper and beans and continue baking for 5 minutes till the base is dry but not cracked.

Make the filling by whizzing herbs, mascarpone, Roquefort and butter in the processor till smooth. Add the eggs, process well, then the cream and seasoning: pepper and a pinch of cayenne (no salt). Pour into the hot pastry case and immediately put in the oven, still at 190°C (170°C) for 25 minutes, till golden, slightly puffed and just set in the centre. Serve at room temperature.

RAYNAUDES SECRET — Savoury tarts: three important tips. Don't throw away excess pastry after rolling out – scraps can be useful to patch cracks that appear towards the end of blind baking. Make sure the blind-baked pastry case is piping hot when you pour in the filling so that if the filling does find a hole it is instantly sealed. And if you appear to have too much filling, discard rather than overfill.

French pigeons are young, juicy, fresh and bred for the table – like American squab. In the south-west, every house worthy of the name has a *pigeonnier*, either built in (as at the Manoir) or detached.

Breast of pigeon with Armagnac jus

Serves 6

3 plump young pigeons, cleaned

FOR THE JUS

a little duck or goose fat, or vegetable oil

1 medium onion, carrot and stick of celery, roughly chopped

1 bay leaf

splash of Armagnac

25g chilled butter (optional)

TO COOK

a little duck or goose fat, or olive oil, or clarified butter

Using a small sharp knife, cut the breasts off the pigeons, keeping the skin on (just as you would remove a chicken breast, but on a smaller scale). Flatten with the palm of your hand, season well all over and refrigerate covered until ready to serve.

Discard any liver and entrails in the carcases (I find they make the sauce taste too strong) and cut the remainder (skin and bones) up as best you can using a heavy knife or poultry shears – aim for pieces no bigger than about 5cm. Use to make pigeon stock as on page 150, defat, then reduce to a jus.

To cook the pigeon, heat the duck fat or oil till smoking and put in the pigeon breasts skin side down. Cook for 2 minutes (if they are burning turn down the heat), then the other side for 2 minutes longer. Check the doneness with a knife – they should be medium rare, with a hint of blood. Rest in a low oven, or tented with foil, for 5–10 minutes before slicing into 2 or 3 and serving with the jus, on a crisp straw potato cake (see overleaf).

MAKE IT LOOK GREAT

Like duck breasts, pigeon can bleed rather unattractively on to the plate in the short period before being conveyed to the table. If this worries you, the solution invented by Andonis, chef-proprietor of nearby hotel *Le Cuq-en-Terrasses*, is to mask it in a ruby-coloured sauce – perhaps by stirring redcurrant jelly, or fresh myrtles, into the pigeon jus above.

Orlando Murrin   151

Jill Norman

The New Penguin Cookery Book

Michael Joseph, London, 2001
576 pages
244 x 187 mm (9⅝ x 7⅜ in.)

An extract from my own review of this book (for *Country Life*) appears on the paperback version: 'If you buy only one cookery book, make it this one. Jill Norman fills the book with modern recipes to excite today's demanding cook. She cooks Thai, she kneads bread, she guts octopus, she freezes granita. Not a gimmick in sight, not a word wasted.' A decade later, I stand by this.

Norman is famous for editing Elizabeth David (page 66), which can't have been easy, and for being David's literary trustee. She is also a trustee of the Jane Grigson Trust (Grigson, page 102, having been encouraged by David). Perhaps even more importantly, Norman was the editor who, in the 1960s and 1970s, put together the *Penguin Cookery Library*, which made that publisher pre-eminent on kitchen shelves.

Later, she went solo, publishing such individualists as Nathalie Hambro (page 110).

This book followed the then fifty-year-old original *Penguin Cookery Book* (1952), Norman hinting that it had become old-fashioned. 'I learned to cook from books … . The means I developed for judging the merits of a submitted typescript was to try the recipes that looked most interesting and those that looked most unlikely.' Her family ate, 'mostly uncomplaining, through weeks of Indian, Chinese, Mexican, Hungarian, Spanish, Middle Eastern and Caribbean food', which may not be the recipe for a happy family but is certainly good for a cookery writer. The book, set in Minion, is neat and orderly, with elegant sepia headlines and ingredient lists. It's a pleasure to handle.

Opposite: A book this comprehensive doesn't have space for photographs. But Suzanne Olding's illustrations, combined with the use of sepia and black type, make it a pleasure to use.

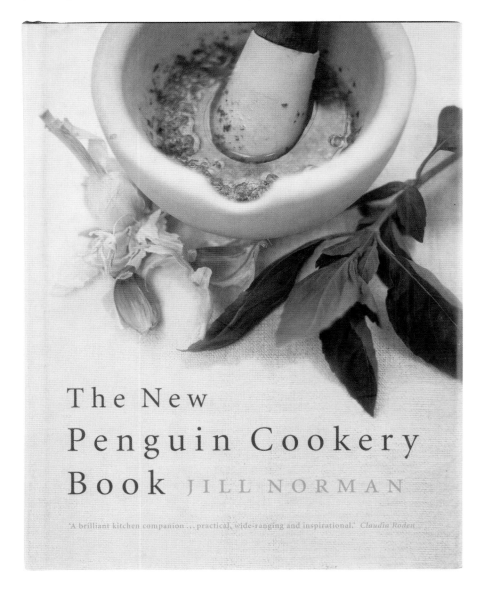

The New
Penguin Cookery
Book JILL NORMAN

'A brilliant kitchen companion … practical, wide-ranging and inspirational.' *Claudia Roden*

A Book for Cooks

Variation
· Serve the okra cool with a vinaigrette dressing.

Spiced sautéed okra

For 4	small piece ginger, chopped finely	1 garlic clove, peeled and chopped finely
400g okra		
3–4 tbs sunflower oil	½ tsp ground cumin	salt
1 onion, peeled, cut in half and sliced thinly	½ tsp ground coriander	2–3 tbs water
	¼ tsp ground pepper	1 tbs lime or lemon juice

Slice the okra into thin rounds. Heat a heavy pan and when it feels hot to your
hand held over it, add the oil. Put in the onion, reduce the heat somewhat and
sauté for 3 minutes, until the onion starts to colour. Add the spices, garlic and salt.
Put in the okra, toss it in the spices, then sprinkle over 2–3 tbs water. Cook, stirring
from time to time, until the okra is tender but still crisp, about 6–8 minutes.
Sprinkle over the lime or lemon juice and serve.

Onions

Chopped onions are a staple flavouring ingredient at the heart of so many dishes that
it is easy to forget how delicious they can be in their own right. See notes on choosing
(p. 91), storing (p. 91), preparation (p. 94) and all the cooking methods (pp. 95–100).

Onions do not brown well in a microwave, but if cooked with butter in an
uncovered dish, sliced onions will caramelize: cook 500g onions with 60g butter for
30 minutes. Microwaving is also a useful way of cooking small whole onions without
fat. Arrange them in one layer in a dish. Cook 250g onions with 100–125ml liquid in
a covered dish for 8 minutes; for 500g use 250ml liquid and cook for 15 minutes.

Baby onions, their roots trimmed first, can also be blanched in a microwave before
further cooking; this is also an easy way to avoid the fiddly business of peeling small
raw onions. Put unpeeled onions in a dish, add 1 tbs water for 250g, cover and cook
for 1 minute. For 500g, add 2 tbs water, cover and cook for 2 minutes. Slip off the
skins when they are cool enough to handle.

Baked onions

This dish is capable of many variations, the recipe below using halved onions and
taking nearly an hour to cook. It can also be made with small whole onions, which
will cook in about half the time, or with sliced onions, tossed first in the oil and
vinegar and spread in a dish with herbs scattered between them. These will take
about 40 minutes to cook.

A couple of bay leaves can be added or used to replace the herbs given below. A
wine or cider vinegar is fine, but gives less depth of flavour than sherry or balsamic
vinegar.

For 4	1 tbs brown sugar	3 tbs olive oil
4 large onions, peeled	salt and freshly ground pepper	6 tbs water
1 tbs chopped rosemary or thyme or 8 fresh sage leaves	3 tbs sherry vinegar or balsamic vinegar	

Heat the oven to 200°C, 400°F, gas 6. Cut the onions in half, across, and put them
cut side down in an ovenproof dish just big enough to hold them side by side.
Sprinkle over the herbs and sugar and season with salt and pepper. Spoon over the
vinegar, oil and water and bake, covered, for 20 minutes, then uncovered for a
further 30–40 minutes. Baste the onions frequently. Add a little more water if the
juices are reducing too quickly.

Roasted onions

A simple way of cooking onions in the oven is to roast them in their skins. They
take a long time in a low oven, but can be cooked at the same time as a casserole.
The onions are juicy and caramelize slightly in their skins.

For 4	salt and freshly ground pepper	chopped parsley or mint
4 large or 8 medium onions, unpeeled	olive oil or butter	

Heat the oven to 170°C, 325°F, gas 3. Put the whole onions in a baking tin and cook
them, uncovered, for 2–2½ hours. Serve as they are (taking the skins off at the
table) with salt and pepper, olive oil or butter and a small bowl of chopped herbs.

Ramen noodles with vegetables

Ramen are the Japanese equivalent of Chinese egg noodles (which can be used as a
substitute). The vegetables can be varied according to what is in season.

For 4	2 small leeks, quartered lengthways and cut into short lengths	4 oyster mushrooms, sliced thinly
300g dried ramen noodles		200g baby spinach
1 litre vegetable stock (p. 4)	2 courgettes, cut in thin strips	3 spring onions, sliced finely diagonally
	250g mange-tout, trimmed	

Cook the noodles in plenty of boiling water until tender, drain and rinse in cold
water. Heat the stock and simmer the vegetables until softened: start with the leeks,
courgettes and mange-tout, add the mushrooms after 3–4 minutes and the spinach
2–3 minutes later. They will then need only 1 minute more. Scoop out the
vegetables, bring the stock back to the boil and add the noodles. Let them heat
through for 1 minute, then put the noodles into 4 deep warmed bowls, ladle over
the broth, arrange the vegetables on top and scatter over the spring onion.

Variation
· Instead of cooking the vegetables in stock, stir-fry them in 2 tbs oil, adding them
to the wok or pan in the order given, and finish with 1 tbs light soy sauce. Serve as
in the main recipe.

Fish and seafood

There are more than sixty varieties of fish available in the UK. Sea bass,
halibut, red and grey mullet, monkfish and turbot are usually available at
good fish counters alongside the familiar cod, haddock, sole and plaice.
Fish from warm waters – pomfret, swordfish, parrot fish, snappers and
breams – are increasingly common. Although small native brown shrimps are now hard to
find, except as potted shrimps, the variety of seafood has widened with the arrival in our
shops of spiny Mediterranean lobsters, tiger prawns from Thailand
and huge shrimps from the west coast of Africa. The best suppliers
identify the source – region, country or ocean – of their fish, although
distance is not always a criterion in determining what is freshest.

Jamie Oliver
The Naked Chef

Michael Joseph, London, 1999
256 pages
245 x 187 mm (9⅝ x 7⅜ in.)

The book's blurb describes Oliver as 'Britain's most talented, exciting and unpretentious young chef'; his biography adds that 'He is twenty-three and this is his first book.' Here we are, then, more than a decade later, and Jamie is now a world brand, still exciting and, even if the unpretentiousness has a slightly forced feel to it, still possessed of some of that genuine cheeky charm he arrived with in 1999. He has also become a major campaigner for good-quality food, especially in schools.

The title has nothing to do with Jamie starkers, but refers instead to unadorned cooking. Here was a restaurant chef who had learned his trade at London's Neal Street Restaurant and River Café trying to adapt his skills to a kitchen in a basement flat. With such a pedigree, his first book was necessarily Italian-based, and it's true that Italian food is both simple and adaptable to small spaces. The secret, according to his college lecturer, is 'all about knowing your commodities'. Strange to think about tomatoes, pasta and garlic as commodities, but that's lecturers for you.

So the photographs by Jean Cazals (and, no doubt, the original BBC television series) focus on this young lad pottering about and poking around in markets. Other photographs are simply beautiful and near abstract, such as that of yellow, crimson and pistachio-coloured swatches of pasta hanging on the back of a chair. The book was intended to inspire the beginner, and it does just that. It was also a groundbreaker in that it was deliberately aimed at such young men as Jamie himself. Looking back at it now, I'd say it hit a bullseye.

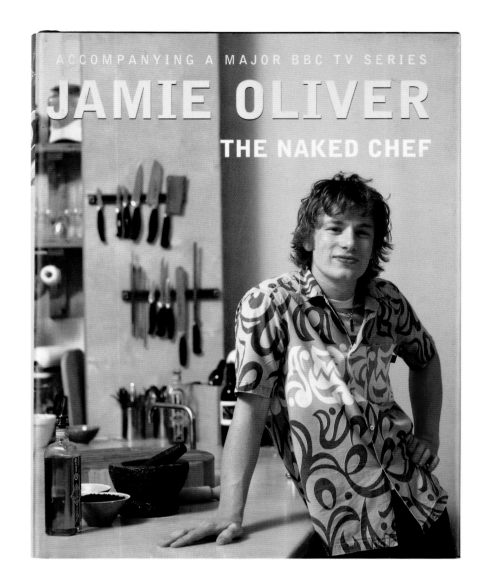

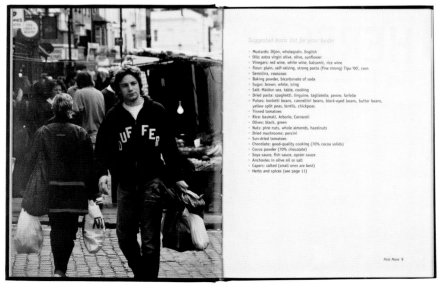

Baked Red Mullet with Oregano, Lemon and Black Olive Mash

Red mullet are very plentiful in our waters and are easily obtainable, so there is no excuse for them not being fresh. You can cook them whole, or ask your fishmonger to scale, fillet and pinbone them. I also like to use this recipe for sea bass, sea bream and John Dory. It's simple, fresh and has a delicate flavour.

Serves 4

4 fillets of red mullet
½ clove of garlic
salt and freshly ground black pepper
1 handful of fresh oregano, picked
2 tablespoons olive oil
juice of ½ lemon
black olive mash (see page 141)

Score the skin side of the fillets across at an angle, so that the marinade can penetrate the fish. In a pestle and mortar smash up the garlic, then add a teaspoon of salt and the oregano. Pound this up to a pulp (or very finely chop) and stir in the olive oil and the juice of ½ a lemon. Smear this all over the fillets. This amount should just cover all the fillets (you don't want them swimming in the marinade!). Lay the fillets on a clean baking tray, skin side up. Place at the top of a hot oven (highest temperature) and roast for about 7 minutes (cooking at the top of the oven helps to make the skin nice and crispy). Take care not to overcook the fish.

Serve the mullet beside the black olive mash, with a simple green salad.

Ravioli of Borage, Stinging Nettles, Marjoram and Fresh Ricotta

This is delicious and you should try it. When young borage and stinging nettle leaves are picked (with a pair of Marigolds – mmm, very nice), washed and plunged into boiling salted water, they lose all their sting – they feel like spinach but hold most of their shape and texture. Chopped and slowly fried with a little butter, marjoram and garlic stinging nettles are absolutely excellent.

Serves 4–6

2 good handfuls of young stinging nettle leaves
2 good handfuls of young borage leaves
2 tablespoons olive oil
1 knob of butter
1 clove of garlic, chopped
1 handful of fresh marjoram, picked
salt and freshly ground black pepper
freshly grated nutmeg to taste
400g/14oz ricotta cheese
100g/3–4oz Parmesan cheese
455g/1lb basic pasta recipe (see page 47)
extra butter and Parmesan to serve

After carefully picking your stinging nettles and borage leaves, wash them well in water and then plunge them into boiling salted water for 30 seconds. This will wilt the leaves and will take away the sting (don't be tempted to cook them for too long). Drain them in a colander and remove any excess water by squeezing them in a tea-towel. Roughly chop and put into a semi-warm, thick-bottomed pan with the olive oil, butter, garlic and marjoram. Cook gently, seasoning as you go, and adding the nutmeg to taste. After a couple of minutes it should be tasting very flavoursome. Remove from the heat and allow to cool.

Once the nettles and borage have cooled, fork in your ricotta, add the final seasoning and Parmesan to taste and toss gently. Fill the ravioli (see page 65) and cook in boiling salted water for 3–4 minutes, until tender. Serve 3 or 4 ravioli per person, with some knobs of butter over the top and some grated Parmesan. I like to pick the purple borage flowers, fry them until crisp in clarified butter (see page 227), and scatter them over the pasta before serving.

Richard Olney

The French Menu Cookbook

Collins, London, 2010 (first published 1970)
446 pages
233 x 150 mm (9 1/8 x 5 7/8 in.)

I include this book because in August 2010 it came top of the *Observer Food Monthly*'s 50 Best Cookbooks poll. Simon Hopkinson (page 124), another 'Best Cookbook' author, is even quoted on the jacket as saying it is his 'most cherished cookery book'. All this totally escapes me, which proves how very personal these choices are. Where Hopkinson finds 'glorious prose', I find Olney annoyingly wordy.

In his introduction Olney writes, 'No recipes are given which involve products unavailable in America' (the book first appeared in 1970 in the United States). But what about one of his 'Four Simple Summer Luncheons à la Provençale', which demands lambs' feet and stomachs? Olney could find only one butcher in New York who 'claimed to be able to get the feet', while 'In Iowa … lambs' tripes are out of the question.' And does this dish, which takes up three pages, really qualify as a simple summer luncheon? I think not.

In his introduction to this new edition (a replica of the original), Paul Bertolli reckons that the book was perfect for his work as the chef at Chez Panisse because it gives complete menus, some of which are achievable by the home cook. It's also fair to say that Olney was a scholar and a purist, and that his dishes are historically accurate. The design is elegant, with only a few drawings – by Gösta Viertel – to illustrate the chapter on kitchen layout and equipment. Otherwise, only a soft pink in the headings, captions and frames around the menus breaks up the monochrome type. Worth having on your shelves, however, as one of the world's most lauded cookery books.

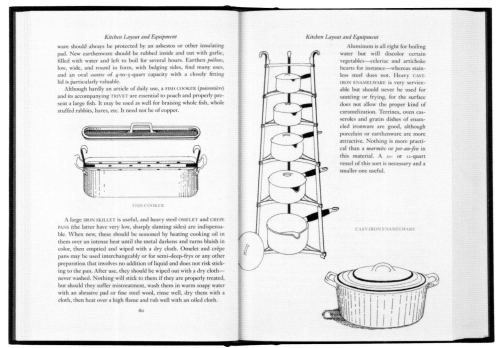

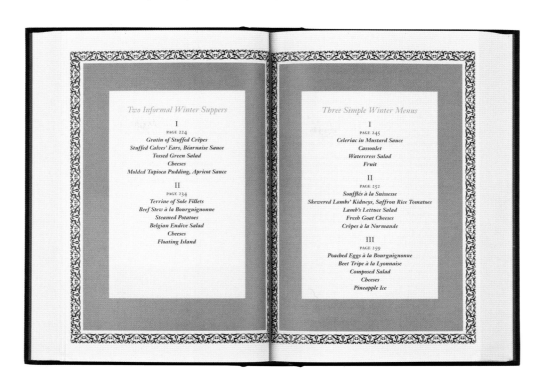

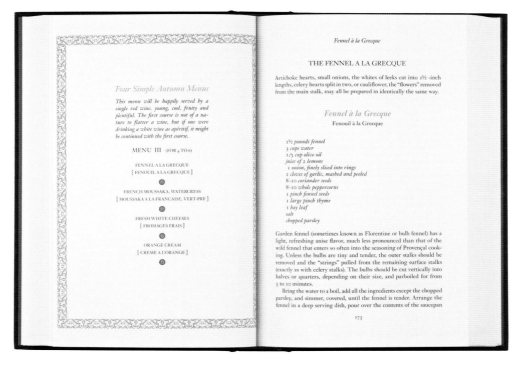

Four Simple Autumn Menus

This menu will be happily served by a single red wine, young, cool, fruity and plentiful. The first course is not of a nature to flatter a wine, but if one were drinking a white wine as apéritif, it might be continued with the first course.

MENU III   (FOR 4 TO 6)

FENNEL A LA GRECQUE
{ FENOUIL A LA GRECQUE }

FRENCH MOUSSAKA, WATERCRESS
{ MOUSSAKA A LA FRANCAISE, VERT-PRE }

FRESH WHITE CHEESES
{ FROMAGES FRAIS }

ORANGE CREAM
{ CRÈME A L'ORANGE }

Fennel à la Grecque

THE FENNEL A LA GRECQUE

Artichoke hearts, small onions, the whites of leeks cut into 1½ -inch lengths, celery hearts split in two, or cauliflower, the "flowers" removed from the main stalk, may all be prepared in identically the same way.

Fennel à la Grecque
Fenouil à la Grecque

1½ pounds fennel
3 cups water
1/3 cup olive oil
juice of 2 lemons
  1 onion, finely sliced into rings
2 cloves of garlic, mashed and peeled
8-10 coriander seeds
8-10 whole peppercorns
1 pinch fennel seeds
1 large pinch thyme
1 bay leaf
salt
chopped parsley

Garden fennel (sometimes known as Florentine or bulb fennel) has a light, refreshing anise flavor, much less pronounced than that of the wild fennel that enters so often into the seasoning of Provençal cooking. Unless the bulbs are tiny and tender, the outer stalks should be removed and the "strings" pulled from the remaining surface stalks (exactly as with celery stalks). The bulbs should be cut vertically into halves or quarters, depending on their size, and parboiled for from 5 to 10 minutes.

Bring the water to a boil, add all the ingredients except the chopped parsley, and simmer, covered, until the fennel is tender. Arrange the fennel in a deep serving dish, pour over the contents of the saucepan

173

Yotam Ottolenghi and Sami Tamimi

Ottolenghi: The Cookbook

Ebury Press, London, 2008
304 pages
283 x 193 mm (10⅞ x 7¼ in.)

One of the book's two authors, Yotam Ottolenghi, is an Israeli whose first word as a child was 'soup'. He studied philosophy and became a journalist before realizing that food was his future. Like Ottolenghi, Sami Tamimi was born in Jerusalem, but to Palestinian parents. The two men met in London in 1999 and, since then, have opened several combined restaurants and shops there.

I love this book (and have given it to friends) because it helps you understand how to display what you make. The shops' windows are filled with delicacies laid out on well-used wooden boards; wide, colourful dishes are contrasted against plain white walls. The designer, Alex Meitlis, convinced the owners that 'a white space with white shiny surfaces is what's going to make your concoctions stand out'. As a result, the beetroot salad, saffron rice, brownies and nut-dusted meringues look extremely appetizing.

Ottolenghi and Tamimi's food philosophy is 'we make the best of what we have and don't interfere with it too much. We keep food as natural as possible, deliberately avoiding complicated cooking methods.' What is exotic, however, are the ingredients: tahini, sumac and za'atar (a spice mix) all feature in Middle Eastern cuisine, as do orange-blossom and rose water; sweet potatoes, feta cheese and pink peppercorns are other popular ingredients. Nigel Slater (page 188) praises the food as 'modern, smart and thoughtful', and I totally agree. My favourite recipes – so far – are French beans and mangetout with hazelnut and orange; tuna with papaya salsa; fried scallops with saffron potatoes, asparagus and samphire; and the delightful pistachio-covered shortbread.

Authors' books should have a consistent style from one to the next. *Ottolenghi*'s distinctive look is the work of photographer Richard Learoyd and designers BLOK and objectif.

'This is simply wonderful cooking … modern, smart and thoughtful. I love it.'
Nigel Slater

You can prepare both the tuna and the salsa a day in advance and keep them chilled. The salsa will actually improve as its flavours intensify. It will keep for up to 5 days in the fridge. Slice the tuna just before serving it. It is extremely important that the fruit for the salsa is ripe and sweet. Pakistani mangoes, available from May to August, are unrivalled for their sweet flesh and perfumed aroma.

To get more flavour out of the pistachios, you could roast them in the oven at 170°C/Gas Mark 3 for about 8 minutes. If it is the visual effect that you're after, leave them untoasted, as they lose some of their vibrant green colour when baked.

... and yes, we do know that cooked fish should not, under any circumstances, go on a blue chopping board (kitchen hygiene rules). Still, this board had so much history carved into it that Richard, the photographer, insisted on using it for this shot. The poor old board went straight into the bin, taking with it a chunk of history.

Seared tuna with pistachio crust and papaya salsa

1 Start with the salsa. Peel the cucumber, halve it lengthways, then scoop out and discard the seeds. Cut it into 1cm dice and put it in a bowl. Add all the rest of the salsa ingredients, stir well and season with salt and pepper. Taste and adjust the seasoning, then chill. It is advisable to allow it to rest for at least an hour for all the flavours to combine.
2 Now for the tuna. Preheat the oven to 250°C/Gas Mark 10, or as high as it will go. Chop the pistachios, preferably in a food processor, until you get fine crumbs. Scatter them on a baking tray and mix with the lemon zest, then set aside.
3 Take the tuna loin and use a sharp knife to divide it along its length into 2 or 3 cylindrical pieces. They should be 6–7cm thick and show the layers of the loin at their ends. Brush the tuna with the olive oil and season with salt and pepper. Place a griddle pan or a heavy cast iron pan over a high heat and leave for a few minutes to heat up. Place the tuna pieces in the pan and sear lightly for 3–4 minutes in total, turning them around as you go. Remove from the pan and leave to cool down a little.
4 Now brush the tuna generously with the mustard and then roll it in the chopped pistachio mixture, using your fingers to cover any bare patches. Place the tuna in a baking tray, transfer to the oven and roast for 5–6 minutes. Check carefully (stick a knife in; it should come out cold), as it might not take that long. What you want is a slightly raw centre with a 1–2cm ring of cooked meat around it. Remove and allow to cool down completely.
5 To serve, cut the tuna into slices 2cm thick. Serve with the salsa on the side or poured on top.

serves 6

150g shelled pistachio nuts
grated zest of 1 lemon
1kg tuna loin
2 tbsp olive oil
5 tbsp Dijon mustard
coarse sea salt and black pepper

Papaya salsa
1 mini cucumber
1 large, ripe papaya, peeled, seeded and cut into 1cm cubes
1 large, ripe mango, peeled, stoned and cut into 1cm cubes
2 red chillies, seeded and finely chopped
10g fresh ginger, peeled and grated
1 small red onion, finely chopped
grated zest and juice of 2 limes
2 tbsp lemon juice
2 tbsp Thai fish sauce
4 tbsp olive oil
2 tbsp caster sugar

Roasted beef fillet (↗ page 110)

Roast pork belly (↗ page 114)

Yotam Ottolenghi and Sami Tamimi   **159**

John Pawson and Annie Bell

Living and Eating

Ebury Press, London, 2001
304 pages
245 x 188 mm (9⅝ x 7⅜ in.)

It was a brilliant idea to bring together the minimalist architect John Pawson and chef Annie Bell. The result is exactly what the title suggests. Indeed, the emphasis is less on food than on living. Pawson gives his strong views on worktops and sinks, cookers, storage and lighting in the kitchen. He is pro dishwashers but not keen on waste disposers ('lack of grace'). His crockery of choice is white Wedgwood Queensware, his favoured cutlery (hooray), silver Georgian three-pronged forks. Antique silver, 'the most beautiful of all cutlery', is not even wildly expensive compared to modern steel.

As you would expect, the book has been carefully and minimally designed by Pawson, with William Hall, using a sans serif typeface in either black or grey. There is lots of white space. The photographs, by Christoph Kicherer, are as much about the kitchen and its equipment as about the food. The two authors appear in the kitchen – Pawson in white, Bell in black – and there are shots of picnics and parties. The pictures are spare and elegant; even some of the food manages to look restrained.

The recipes start with family meals and then broaden out. 'Hence the seven different recipes for roasting a chicken and almost as many for cooking spaghetti and noodles.' The authors decry 'the dinner party charade', suggesting that what we give guests should be roughly similar to what we eat on our own. In this, as in its design and advice, this is a thoroughly modern book, a recipe for the twenty-first century.

Guinea Fowl roasted with Rosemary and Garlic

The flavour of a guinea fowl is something like a chicken aspiring to be a pheasant. As such it is that much stronger in personality, and enjoys the company of those two old roués rosemary and garlic. Try serving this with Spiced Sweet Potatoes (see page 170).

Serves 3

1 head of garlic, broken into cloves
1.2 kg oven-ready guinea fowl
50 g unsalted butter, softened
5 rosemary sprigs, 5–7cm long
Juice of 1 lemon
Sea salt, black pepper

Preheat the oven to 200°C, fan oven 190°C, gas 6. Peel 2 garlic cloves and cut into long thin slivers. Make a number of incisions in the guinea fowl breasts and legs and insert the garlic slivers. Smear the butter over the bird. Tuck a sprig of rosemary in between each leg and breast. Put the remaining garlic cloves into the cavity, along with 2 rosemary sprigs.

Place the guinea fowl in a roasting dish. Pull the leaves off the remaining rosemary sprig and scatter over the bird. Pour over the lemon juice and season with salt and pepper. Roast for 45 minutes, basting halfway through. By the end the skin should be golden and crispy. Cover the guinea fowl loosely with foil and leave to rest in the roasting dish for 15 minutes.

Remove the bird to a plate, tipping any juices back into the dish. Reheat the juices while you carve. Serve the guinea fowl on warm plates. Strain the pan juices, give them a stir and spoon over the meat to serve.

Chicken, Spinach and Lemon Pie

A chicken pie with a golden glazed lid of pastry is one of the finer sights of the domestic hearth, and this one tastes as good as it looks.

Serves 4

1 head of garlic
10 free-range chicken thighs
Sea salt, black pepper
1 tablespoon extra virgin olive oil
3 heaped tablespoons flour
150 ml white wine
4 thyme sprigs
1 lemon
15 g unsalted butter
250 g young spinach leaves
125 ml double cream
500 g puff pastry
1 organic egg yolk, mixed with 1 tablespoon milk, to glaze

Slice the top and bottom off the head of garlic using a sharp knife and separate the cloves, then slit the skins and slip them off the cloves. Season the chicken thighs with salt and pepper. Heat the olive oil in a large saucepan or sauté pan, add half the chicken thighs and fry, turning, until coloured on all sides. Transfer to a plate with a slotted spoon. Fry the remaining chicken thighs in the pan, adding the garlic cloves towards the end, so they soften without colouring.

Return all the chicken to the pan, sprinkle with the flour and turn the chicken to coat it. Stir in the wine, which will thicken as it blends with the flour, and let this seethe for a minute. Pour in 225ml water and stir until the sauce is smooth. Add the thyme, 2 long strips of finely pared lemon zest, and some seasoning. Bring to a simmer, cover and cook over a low heat for 30 minutes, stirring once.

While the chicken is cooking, melt the butter in a frying pan, add the spinach and toss until it wilts, then drain in a sieve, squeezing out as much water as possible using the back of a spoon.

Transfer the cooked chicken thighs to a bowl. Once they are cool enough to handle, discard the skin and remove the chicken from the bone, then cut into shreds. Discard the thyme sprigs and lemon zest from the sauce. Stir in the cream, add a generous squeeze of lemon juice and adjust the seasoning. Stir the spinach and chicken into the sauce and leave to cool to room temperature.

Preheat the oven to 220°C, fan oven 200°C, gas 7. Roll out two thirds of the pastry thinly on a lightly floured surface and use to line a deep 1.7 litre pie dish. Spoon in the chicken and spinach filling. Roll out the remaining pastry, brush the pastry rim with eggwash and position the lid. Trim the pastry lid, leaving a good 1cm for shrinkage, reserving the trimmings. Press the edges together with a fork, and trim them again to tidy if you like.

Brush the top of the pie with eggwash. Cut out some leaves from the pastry trimmings, mark veins using the tip of a sharp knife, then position the leaves on top of the pie and brush with eggwash. Bake in the oven for 45–50 minutes until the pastry is crisp and golden. Serve straightaway.

Purées and Sauces

Aioli

This voluptuous golden emulsion is a profound expression of garlic, and much has been written of its desired quality. The rosy heads that come from Provence with their fat pearly cloves are perfect. You can use as few as two, or a whole head plus, but a happy medium of around six cloves is about right—still no shrinking violet.

Our dedication to good food stops short of making aioli with a pestle and mortar, however appealing that might be if someone else were cooking. There is a compromise—invest any physical energy in crushing the garlic cloves to a paste with a sprinkling of salt, and then whisk the mayonnaise by hand. It's that much easier than the pestle and mortar route and can still boast more authenticity than a whirring blade.

As for the oil, it is virtually impossible to produce a light mayonnaise that relies entirely on extra virgin olive oil. A powerful Tuscan oil would be a disaster. Provencal olive oil is altogether gentler and you can just about get away with using 100% of this oil if it is the right time of year—some months after the harvest when it will have mellowed. Sicilian oils too are gentle—Ravida oil will have mellowed sufficiently by the summer. But playing safe, half extra virgin and half groundnut oil is a better bet. Try to make the aioli a couple of hours ahead to allow time for the flavours to develop.

Serves 6–8

Sea salt
6 cloves garlic, peeled and chopped
2 large organic egg yolks
350 ml groundnut oil
225 ml extra virgin olive oil
2 teaspoons lemon juice
1 teaspoon pastis, such as Pernod

Sprinkle a little salt over the garlic, then crush and chop it to a paste using the flat edge of a knife. Alternatively use a garlic press, adding a little salt to the resulting pulp. Whisk the egg yolks and garlic together in a large bowl. Very gradually whisk in the groundnut oil, just a few drops at a time to begin with and then, once the mayonnaise has taken, in a more generous stream. Then whisk in some of the olive oil in a steady stream. As the mayonnaise becomes too thick to whisk, add some of the lemon juice followed by the Pastis, and then keep whisking in the oil. Taste it and add a little more lemon juice if necessary. Store it covered in the fridge and bring back to room temperature before eating.

Rescue remedy
If the aioli does the unmentionable and splits, whisk another egg yolk in a clean bowl and gradually whisk in the curdled mayonnaise. To reduce the risk, include a teaspoon of Dijon mustard in with the egg yolk at the beginning.

John Pawson and Annie Bell

Sir Hugh Plat

Delightes for Ladies: To Adorne Their Persons, Tables, Closets and Distillatories with Beauties, Banquets, Perfumes and Waters

Crosby Lockwood & Son, London, 1948
(reprint; first published 1602)
200 pages
216 x 137 mm (8½ x 5⅜ in.)

Sir Hugh Plat was an Elizabethan, born around 1552 and dying in 1608, a few years after the queen. He was more an inventor and alchemist than a cookery writer, having been knighted by James I for his inventions, which included mixing sea coal and clay to make fuel. Plat was a Londoner (his father was a brewer with property in St Pancras), christened and buried at – appropriately enough – St James Garlickhythe, a City church.

The long introduction to my edition is tedious in the extreme, but when you get to Sir Hugh (the pages have been reset from facsimiles of the edition of 1609, but using Fell type, which appeared some sixty-five years after the book was first published), the pace quickens. Despite the differences in the language, the terms and the use of 'f' instead of 's', the recipes are usable. 'Gelly of Strawberries, Mulberries, Rafpifberries, or any fuch tender fruite' is perfectly clear, as is 'Marmelade of Lemmons or Orenges'. 'Clouted creame' (clotted cream) says, 'Take your milke beeing new milked; and prefentlie fet it vpon the fire from morning untill the euening, but let it not feeth: and this is called my Ladie Youngs clowted creame.' Simple.

Like many early cookery books, it covers more than food: hair dyeing, removing freckles, cleaning one's teeth. 'A delicate ftoue to fweat in' was a Tudor Turkish bath.

DELIGHTES
FOR LADIES, TO
adorne their Perfons,
Tables, Clofets, and
Diftillatories:
With
BEAVTIES, BANQVETS,
Perfumes & Waters.

Reade, Practice, & Cenfure.

AT LONDON,
Printed by HVMFREY
LOWNES.
1609.

A slightly enlarged facsimile of the title-page to the edition of 1609. The press of Humfrey Lownes at the 'Star' on Bread Street Hill flourished in the early years of the seventeenth century. He published among other notable works a folio edition of The Faerie Queen, *Drayton's* Poly-olbion, *and the musical works of William Byrd.*

To all true Louers of Art,
and knowledge.

SOmetimes I write the formes of burning balles,
Supplying wáts that were by woodfals wrought,
Sometimes of tubs defended fo by arte,
As fire in vaine hath their deftruction fought:
Sometimes I write of lafting Beuerage,
Great Neptune and his pilgrims to content:
Sometimes of food, fweet, frefh, and durable,
To maintaine life, when all things els were fpent:
Sometimes I write of fundrie forts of foile,
Which neither Ceres nor her handmaides knew.
I write to all, but fcarfly one beleeues,
Saue Diue and Denfhire, who haue found thē true.
When heauens did mourne in cloudie mantles clad,
And threatned famine to the fonnes of men:
When fobbing earth denied her kindly fruit
To painfull ploughmen and his hindes: euen then
I write relieuing remedies of dearth,
That Art might helpe where Nature made a faile.
But all in vaine, thefe new borne babes of Arte,
In their vntimely birth ftraight-way do quaile.
Of thefe and fuch like other newfound skils,
With painefull pen I whilome wrote at large,
Expecting ftill my countries good therein,
And not refpecting labour, time or charge:
But now my pen and paper are perfum'd,
I fcorne to write with copprefle or with gall,
Barbarian canes are now become my quils,
Rofewater is the inke I write withall:
B 2

A Book for Cooks

---

19 *Aliter & optime.*

TAke halfe a pound of white diftilled vinegar, two new laide Eggs with their fhelles, two fpoonfulls of the flowers of brimftone, let thefe macerate in the vinegar by the fpace of three daies: then take out the Egges, and pricke them full of holes with a needle, but not too deepe, leaft any of the yolke fhould happen alfo to iffue, let that liquor alfo mixe with the vineger, then ftraine all through a fine cloath, and tie vp the brimftone in the cloth like a little ball, dip this bal in the ftrained liquor, when you vfe it, and pat it on the place three or foure times euerie day, and this will cure any red face in twelue or fourteen daies. Some doe alfo commende the fame for an approued remedie againft the morphew; the brimftone ball muft be kept in fome clofe thing from the ayre.

20 *How to take away any pimple from the face.*

BRimftone ground with the oile of Turpentine, and applied to any pimple one houre, maketh the flefh to rife fpungeous: which being annointed with the thick oyle of butter that arifeth in the morning from new milke fodden a little ouer night, will heale and fcale away in a few daies, leauing a faire fkinne behinde. This is a good fkinning falue.

21 *To helpe any Morphew, funneburning, itch, or red face.*

STeepe two fliced Lemmons being large and faire in a pinte of Conduit water, leaue then foure or fiue daies in infufion couering the water, then ftraine the water, and diffolue therein the quantitie of a hafell nut of fublimate (fome holde a dramme a good proportion to a pint of water) finely powdered: let the patient wet a cloth therein, and rub the place where the griefe is, euerie morning and euen-

ing a little, till the hew doe pleafe her: you may make the fame ftronger or weaker according to good difcretion.

22 *For the Morphew.*

TAKE a pinte of diftilled Vinegar, laie therein two new laid egges whole with their fhelles, three yellow Docke rootes picked and fliced, two fpoonefuls of the flowers of brimftone, and fo let all reft three daies, and then vfe this liquor with a cloth, rubbing the place three or foure times euery day, and in three or foure daies it commonly helpeth: put fome bran in your cloth before you moiften your cloth therein, binding it vp in form of a little ball. This of Maifter *Rich* of Lee, who helped himfelfe and a gallant Ladie there-with in a fewe dayes.

23 *To take away the freckles in the face.*

VVASH your face in the wane of the moone with a fpunge, morninge and euening with the dif-tilled water of Elder Leaues, letting the fame drie into the fkinne. Your water muft be diftilled in *Maie*. This is of a Trauailer, who hath cured himfelfe therby.

24 *To cure any extreame bruife vpon a fore fall, on the face, or any other member of the body.*

PRefently after the fall make a great fire, and applie hote cloathes one after another without intermiffion, the patient ftanding neere the fire for one houre and a halfe, or till the fwelling bee cleane abated. This I knewe proued with good fucceffe in a maid that fell downe a paire of ftaires, whereby all her face was extremely disfigured. Some holde opinion that the fame may bee perfourmed with clothes wet in hote water and wroonge out againe before application. Then to take away the chaungeable colours, which doe accuftomablie followe all bruifes, fhred

Edouard de Pomiane

Cooking in 10 Minutes; or, The Adaptation to the Rhythm of Our Time

Translated by Peggie Benton
Faber and Faber, London, 1967
(first published 1930)
144 pages
183 x 122 mm (7¼ x 4¾ in.)

If you think this is an unlikely title for a book by a French cookery writer, you'd be correct. Edouard de Pomiane was Polish, born in Paris in 1875 to a Polish-émigré couple who had fled to France in 1863, changing their name from Pozerski in the process. Before writing his first cookery book, Pomiane was a scientist at the Institut Pasteur, and although his recipes are marvels of brevity (as is the cooking involved), it is his sense of humour that makes them memorable.

Take, for example, Spinach: 'You can buy spinach in tins. Open it. Drain it in a colander. Do not use an iron pan to warm it or the spinach will turn black.' Or Lobster with Mayonnaise: 'Buy half a cooked lobster. Serve it with mayonnaise.' The dedication is to Mrs X, 'asking for ten minutes of her kind attention'.

The inspiration for the book was Pomiane's scorn for the intricacies of French cuisine after an earlier work of his, *Cooking in Six Lessons* (1930), had been rubbished by French reviewers: 'I was criticised for teaching the art of cooking in six lessons when everyone knows it takes ten years.'

Elizabeth David was an ardent admirer of Pomiane, calling his writing 'courageous, courteous, adult' (*An Omelette and a Glass of Wine*; 1984). Julian Barnes said his food was 'regional, bourgeois, undoctrinaire' (*The Pedant in the Kitchen*; 2003). To that I would add that the recipes deliberately de-mystify cooking. 'Modern life spoils so much that is pleasant', writes Pomiane. 'Let us see that it does not make us spoil our steak or our omelette.' My edition has illustrations after Toulouse-Lautrec, a perfect choice.

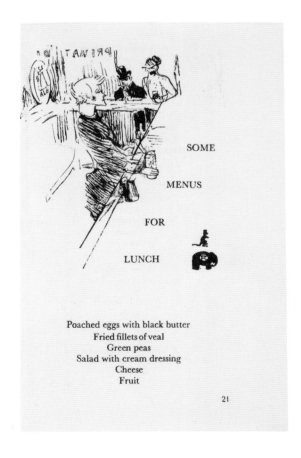

A Book for Cooks

In ten minutes you have just time to boil a small fish. You have plenty of time to cook it in a frying pan, and still more time to fry it in fat.

You see that your only difficulty will be in making a choice when you decide to replace meat by fish for your main course.

WHITING

Boil some salted water in a saucepan. Add a spoonful of vinegar, a bay leaf and some spices— pepper, mace, curry, etc.

Take the fish which has been cleaned by the fishmonger and carefully washed by you, and plunge it into the saucepan. Let it boil ten minutes. During this time melt some butter and squeeze in a few drops of lemon juice.

Lift the fish out of the water carefully so as not to damage it.

Put it on a dish, sprinkling with melted butter and breadcrumbs.

SKATE WITH BLACK BUTTER

Boil a pound of skate for ten minutes in salted, vinegared water.

68

In the meantime melt two ounces of butter in a frying pan. Add some chopped parsley. The parsley browns—the butter too. It turns the colour of mahogany. Lift the pan from the fire. After a few minutes add a teaspoonful of vinegar. (It does not splutter too much as the butter has already cooled a little. Otherwise the hot butter would spurt out of the pan on coming into contact with the vinegar.) Lift the skate out of the water. Drain it. Put it on a dish. Pour the black butter over it. Pepper a little. Salt to your taste. Serve.

69

---

side. Put them on to a hot dish. Pour two table-spoonfuls of Madeira into the pan. Let it boil. Pour it on to the steak.

TOURNEDOS DAUPHINOISE

Prepare half a pound of mushrooms à la crème in a frying pan.

In a second frying pan prepare two tournedos with Madeira.

Pour the mushrooms into a deep dish with the *tournedos* on top. Pour over them the Madeira sauce from the pan.

TOURNEDOS ROSSINI

Prepare some *tournedos* with Madeira. Add some truffle peelings to the sauce.

Put the *tournedos* on to a very hot dish. Put a slice of truffled foie gras trimmed to the size of the meat on each *tournedos*. Pour the Madeira and truffle sauce over them.

This is a dish for special occasions.

A GOOD BEEFSTEAK

Sometimes one must be satisfied with a simple beefsteak.

Buy ten ounces of rump steak. Make some butter smoking hot in a frying pan. Cook the steak three minutes on each side; salt, parsley and fried potatoes.

102

RUSSIAN BITOCKS

Buy half a pound of minced beef. Mix this with a quarter of its volume of stale breadcrumbs w h i c h have been soaked and squeezed free of surplus water. K n e a d them together. Salt, pepper. Add a yolk of egg and stir it in. Make four rissoles. Fry them in butter, four minutes on each side. Dissolve the glace in the pan with a little wine and very little cognac. Pour this sauce over the *bitocks*. Serve with noodles which have been cooked in boiling water and tossed in fresh butter.

VEAL

There will, of course, never be any question of joints of veal roasted slowly in the oven or cunning-ly concocted stews. We shall be confined to escalopes and cutlets. But these two will give us abundant satisfaction, as you will see.

103

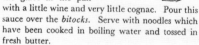

Sarah Raven

Sarah Raven's Garden Cookbook

Bloomsbury, London, 2007
464 pages
245 x 185 mm (9⅝ x 7¼ in.)

Sarah Raven is multi-talented, but her interests are gardening and food. This book, her first on food, explores them in the context of her family home, Perch Hill in East Sussex. In line with modern thinking, she encourages local, seasonal food and a reduction in meat-eating. She contrasts the miserable greengrocers of Britain twenty years ago ('floppy lettuce and cabbage') with today's farmers' markets, such exotics as figs and Florence fennel, and food picked the night before. 'You will see that these are good times for fruit and veg.'

As a gardener, Raven knows what she's talking about: 'I have poured enormous amounts of myself and my life into this book. I think of it as a compendium of everything I've loved in the garden and the kitchen over the last fifteen or twenty years.' If you love her style, the colourful flowers, the relaxed but sociable meals, the pleasures of growing your own food, then this is the book for you.

As well as recipes, there is advice on which varieties of lettuce, tomato or potato to choose, for Raven conducts extensive growing and tasting trials. She explains that lettuce will perk up if soaked in water for a few hours, and that tomatoes should not be kept in the fridge. The recipes are not exceptional but draw together dishes that she loves.

The photographs, by Jonathan Buckley, are perfection: the garden, outdoor meals, onions drying on wires, nasturtium flowers in a salad. This is a book, designed by Karl Shanahan of SMITH, that is irresistible.

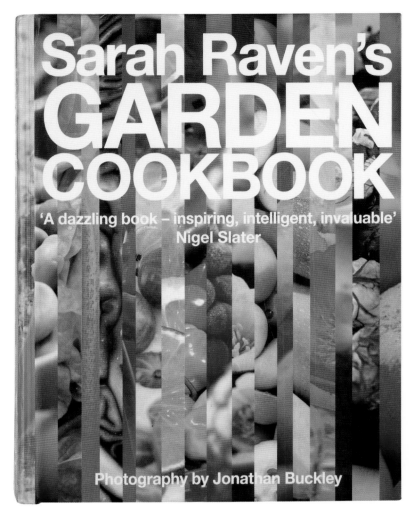

Rösti potatoes

Rösti potatoes might be fattening, but no more so than chips, and they have infinitely more flavour.

For 6 large rösti:
3 or 4 potatoes (Desiree is ideal)
2 tablespoons chopped onion
Handful of chopped flat-leaf
**   parsley**
1 tablespoon flour
Salt and black pepper
2 tablespoons vegetable oil
50g butter

Preheat a medium (180°C/gas mark 4) oven.

Grate the potatoes on a coarse grating disc and twist them in a tea towel to squeeze out the moisture. Once the potatoes are dryish, put them into a bowl with the onion, parsley and flour, and season them well with salt and pepper.

Heat the oil and butter in a heavy-based pan and spread the potato mixture over the pan. Push it down hard with the back of a spoon. Cook until the bottom is brown and crisp – it will then hold together better – and turn to cook the underside until golden brown.

Allow to cool and cut into either wedges or rounds. Reheat them in the preheated oven for a few minutes to make them really crunchy.

Nutmeg mashed potato

I first had this with my brother-in-law, Andrew Wallace, and now almost always add nutmeg to my mash. If you want to try something different, add 3 bay leaves to the potato cooking water and another couple of bay leaves when you heat the milk.

Many chefs are keen on using baked potatoes, scooped out, for mash, claiming this method gives better flavour and creamier texture. I've done a taste and texture comparison between the baking and boiling techniques, and I don't think it makes any difference.

For 4:
6 large potatoes (Maris Piper
**   makes great mash)**
Salt and black pepper
150g butter
150ml milk (or cream)
Freshly grated nutmeg, to taste

Cut the potatoes in half (not into small chunks, as this makes them watery) and boil in salted water for about 15 minutes until they're soft, but not overcooked.

Drain and mash thoroughly with butter, salt, pepper and some milk or cream with grated nutmeg.

You can keep this warm in the oven, covered in little knobs of butter and some foil, for up to an hour, or dot with butter and brown.

Rosemary saddleback potatoes

These are delicious and quicker to cook than roast potatoes, and you really get the taste of rosemary. While they are raw the potatoes are sliced, but not quite to the bottom, so that they fan out slightly when they're cooked. The flavours of the herbs and oil – it's worth using extra virgin olive oil – soak right into the potatoes. If you can find them, Edzell Blue potatoes make the showiest-looking saddlebacks. Pesto is a good alternative to rosemary, and try them with garlic and anchovies pounded in a mortar with black pepper.

For 8:
750g potatoes
6 tablespoons extra virgin olive oil
Leaves from 5 sprigs of rosemary
Salt and black pepper

Preheat the oven to 190°C/gas mark 5. Peel the potatoes, or keep the skins on if you prefer. Cut them in slices just under 1cm thick, stopping just before the bottom of the potato.

Put them on to an oiled baking tray and scatter over the rosemary, pushing the herbs right down into the slices. Douse with olive oil and season with salt and pepper.

Put them in the oven and roast for about 1 hour until they're golden brown.

Quinces and medlars

The quince is a handsome yellow-green fruit, like an irregular, furry-skinned pear with a fragrant, fruity-rose smell that reminds me of Turkish delight. If you can bear not to eat them all straight away, put a bowl of quinces somewhere warm – near a fireplace or radiator – and they'll look good and scent the room for several weeks. They are currently fashionable with chefs, so let's hope they become more widely available, as they are a very delicious fruit. At the moment they can be difficult to find.

Quinces are good eaten in savoury dishes as well as puddings. They're invaluable added to almost any stew – just include a few peeled pieces as an odd but pleasant surprise. And there's the Spanish classic *membrillo* – quince paste – eaten with manchego cheese (see page 380). I also love quinces as jelly: make this just as you would Medlar jelly (see page 381). Spread it on toast, or mix up a couple of tablespoons with Greek yoghurt or crème fraiche to eat with fresh fruit. It's lovely with pineapple and blueberries.

Medlars aren't as good to eat as quinces, but they make a lovely fragrant jelly. This is delicious eaten on toast for breakfast and is perfect with pork and gentle-tasting spring lamb. Medlars have odd-looking fruits, like a cross between a russet apple and a rose hip, traditionally eaten on the high tables of Cambridge and Oxford colleges, where they were said to be a great delicacy. You can only eat them uncooked once soft, or 'bletted', but I think that at this stage they're like a rotten pear and revolting!

Quinces and medlars both make good trees for a smaller garden, with large single pink (quince) or white (medlar) flowers in late spring. If you have room, plant your own. Medlars have wonderful autumn colour and an interesting bark and shape that look good even in the winter. In late autumn they're covered in fruit.

Claudia Roden
A Book of Middle Eastern Food

Penguin, Harmondsworth, 1970
(first published 1968)
488 pages
180 x 110 mm (7 1/8 x 4 3/8 in.)

Claudia Roden wrote her classic book in 1968, when interest in Middle Eastern food was subdued, to say the least. She was brought up in Cairo and got to know the foods of the various communities there: Jewish, Armenian, Coptic and, of course, Arab. After the Suez Crisis of 1956, when foreigners were expelled from Egypt, her family settled in London, which must have been quite a culture shock. In her introduction, she explains that the book 'is the joint creation of numerous Middle Easterners who, like me, are in exile … . It is the fruit of nostalgic longing for … a food that was the constant joy of life in a world so different from the Western one.'

Thus, we learn how couscous can vary in texture, from light in the Moroccan city of Fez to heavy in Tunisia; how the French influence in Algeria has led to the inclusion of beans, peas and carrots in the dish; and how to cope with a couscousier. But Roden isn't Jane Grigson (page 102): her recipes are scholarly but, somehow, lack passion and enjoyment for the food. Curious, as this is a lament for things past.

The dishes come from all over the region – Syria, Iran, Greece, Turkey, Algeria and Morocco, among others – and vary in date, from 1226 (al-Baghdadi's vinegar dressing) to modern Israeli (avocado purée). Now that most large towns (and online shops) can provide the once recherché ingredients, this book deserves a good, long look.

More than forty years old, Roden's classic looks less dated than many because the publishers used illustrations, by Joanna Tyldesley, in the text, rather than photographs.

448   MIDDLE EASTERN FOOD

Rose-Petal Jam

An exquisitely delicate jam which I have not been able to prepare successfully with the roses from my own garden. The petals remained tough under the tooth, whereas they should offer only a slight resistance.

I have, however, recently been told that certain varieties of rose exist such as the 'wild eglantine' which would be suitable for jam-making. I am therefore giving the recipe for those who are fortunate enough to have a rose which will make a good jam.

1 lb. fresh rose petals, preferably red   1 lb. sugar
Juice of 2 or more lemons   2–3 tablespoons rose water [optional]

Pick fresh, mature, red petals. Make sure they have not been sprayed with insecticide. Cut off their white ends. Wash and drain them. Leave them whole if you like, or mince them finely with some of the lemon juice.

Simmer the petals in 1 pint water until tender. It may take only a few minutes or much longer, according to the variety of rose used. Add the sugar and lemon juice, and cook until the syrup thickens – usually about 10 minutes. Add a little rose water if the petals do not have a strong perfume of their own.

Sherbets and Drinks · Sharbat

The Egyptians have various kinds of sherbets or sweet drinks. The most common kind is merely sugar and water, but very sweet; lemonade is another; a third kind, the most esteemed, is prepared from a hard conserve of violets, made by pounding violet-flowers and then boiling them with sugar. This violet-sherbet is of a green colour. A fourth kind is prepared from mulberries; a fifth from sorrel. There is also a kind of sherbet sold in the streets which is made with raisins, as its name implies; another kind, which is a strong infusion of liquorice-root, and called by the name of that root; a third kind, which is prepared from the fruit of the locust tree, and called in like manner by the name of the fruit.*

I HAVE long been haunted by the cries and songs of the street vendors in Cairo in my childhood. Most often, it was drinks that they were selling, to quench the thirst of passers-by or, as

* Lane, *Manners and Customs of the Modern Egyptians.*

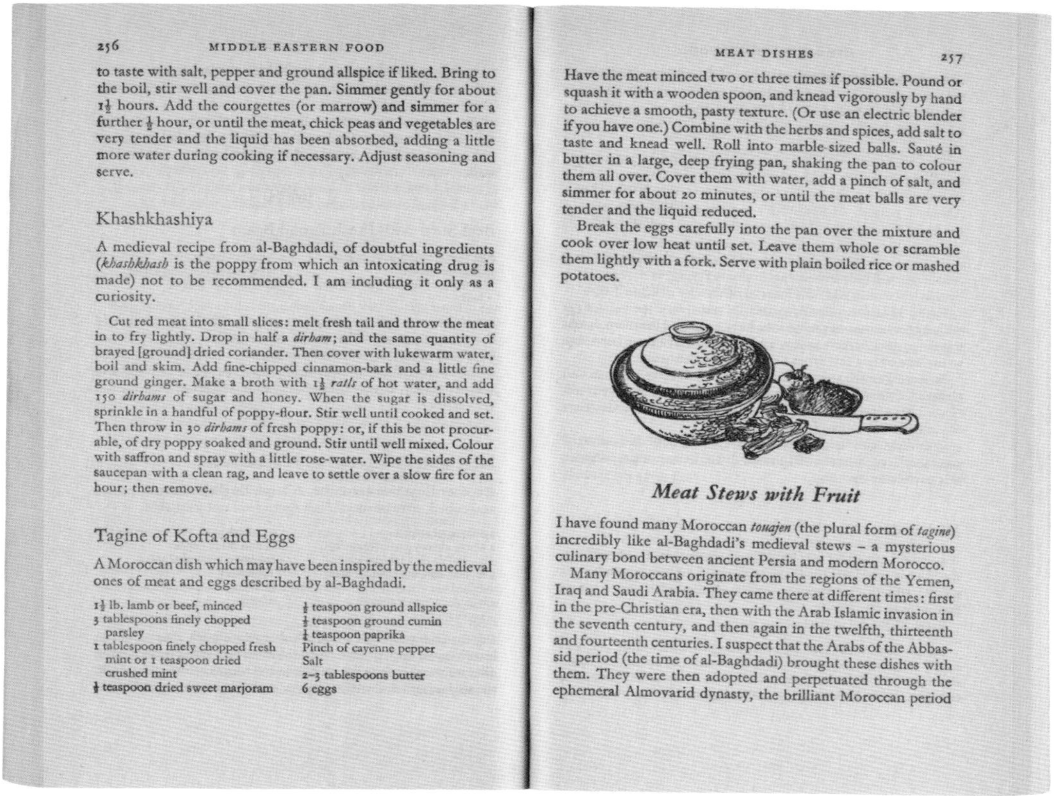

to taste with salt, pepper and ground allspice if liked. Bring to the boil, stir well and cover the pan. Simmer gently for about 1½ hours. Add the courgettes (or marrow) and simmer for a further ½ hour, or until the meat, chick peas and vegetables are very tender and the liquid has been absorbed, adding a little more water during cooking if necessary. Adjust seasoning and serve.

Khashkhashiya

A medieval recipe from al-Baghdadi, of doubtful ingredients (*khashkhash* is the poppy from which an intoxicating drug is made) not to be recommended. I am including it only as a curiosity.

Cut red meat into small slices: melt fresh tail and throw the meat in to fry lightly. Drop in half a *dirham*; and the same quantity of brayed [ground] dried coriander. Then cover with lukewarm water, boil and skim. Add fine-chipped cinnamon-bark and a little fine ground ginger. Make a broth with 1½ *ratls* of hot water, and add 150 *dirhams* of sugar and honey. When the sugar is dissolved, sprinkle in a handful of poppy-flour. Stir well until cooked and set. Then throw in 30 *dirhams* of fresh poppy: or, if this be not procurable, of dry poppy soaked and ground. Stir until well mixed. Colour with saffron and spray with a little rose-water. Wipe the sides of the saucepan with a clean rag, and leave to settle over a slow fire for an hour; then remove.

Tagine of Kofta and Eggs

A Moroccan dish which may have been inspired by the medieval ones of meat and eggs described by al-Baghdadi.

1½ lb. lamb or beef, minced
3 tablespoons finely chopped parsley
1 tablespoon finely chopped fresh mint or 1 teaspoon dried crushed mint
½ teaspoon dried sweet marjoram
½ teaspoon ground allspice
½ teaspoon ground cumin
¼ teaspoon paprika
Pinch of cayenne pepper
Salt
2–3 tablespoons butter
6 eggs

Have the meat minced two or three times if possible. Pound or squash it with a wooden spoon, and knead vigorously by hand to achieve a smooth, pasty texture. (Or use an electric blender if you have one.) Combine with the herbs and spices, add salt to taste and knead well. Roll into marble-sized balls. Sauté in butter in a large, deep frying pan, shaking the pan to colour them all over. Cover them with water, add a pinch of salt, and simmer for about 20 minutes, or until the meat balls are very tender and the liquid reduced.

Break the eggs carefully into the pan over the mixture and cook over low heat until set. Leave them whole or scramble them lightly with a fork. Serve with plain boiled rice or mashed potatoes.

Meat Stews with Fruit

I have found many Moroccan *touajen* (the plural form of *tagine*) incredibly like al-Baghdadi's medieval stews – a mysterious culinary bond between ancient Persia and modern Morocco.

Many Moroccans originate from the regions of the Yemen, Iraq and Saudi Arabia. They came there at different times: first in the pre-Christian era, then with the Arab Islamic invasion in the seventh century, and then again in the twelfth, thirteenth and fourteenth centuries. I suspect that the Arabs of the Abbassid period (the time of al-Baghdadi) brought these dishes with them. They were then adopted and perpetuated through the ephemeral Almovarid dynasty, the brilliant Moroccan period

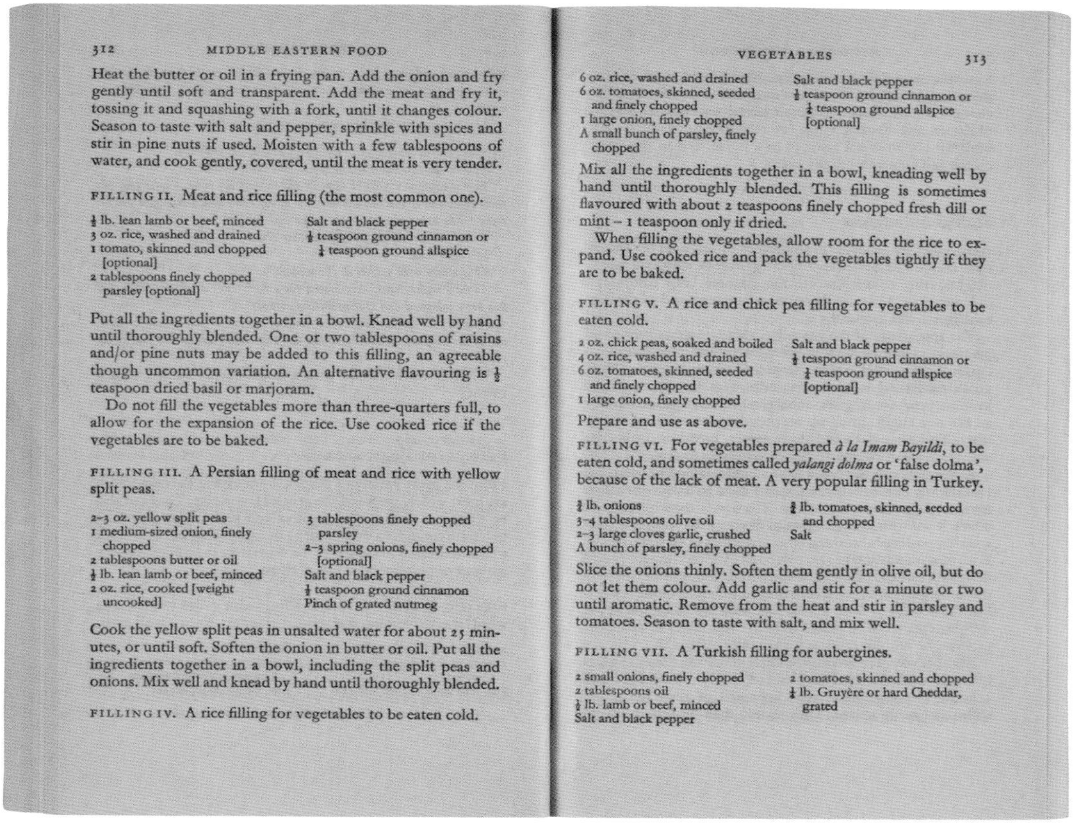

Heat the butter or oil in a frying pan. Add the onion and fry gently until soft and transparent. Add the meat and fry it, tossing it and squashing with a fork, until it changes colour. Season to taste with salt and pepper, sprinkle with spices and stir in pine nuts if used. Moisten with a few tablespoons of water, and cook gently, covered, until the meat is very tender.

FILLING II. Meat and rice filling (the most common one).

½ lb. lean lamb or beef, minced
3 oz. rice, washed and drained
1 tomato, skinned and chopped [optional]
2 tablespoons finely chopped parsley [optional]
Salt and black pepper
½ teaspoon ground cinnamon or ¼ teaspoon ground allspice

Put all the ingredients together in a bowl. Knead well by hand until thoroughly blended. One or two tablespoons of raisins and/or pine nuts may be added to this filling, an agreeable though uncommon variation. An alternative flavouring is ½ teaspoon dried basil or marjoram.

Do not fill the vegetables more than three-quarters full, to allow for the expansion of the rice. Use cooked rice if the vegetables are to be baked.

FILLING III. A Persian filling of meat and rice with yellow split peas.

2–3 oz. yellow split peas
1 medium-sized onion, finely chopped
2 tablespoons butter or oil
½ lb. lean lamb or beef, minced
2 oz. rice, cooked [weight uncooked]
3 tablespoons finely chopped parsley
2–3 spring onions, finely chopped [optional]
Salt and black pepper
½ teaspoon ground cinnamon
Pinch of grated nutmeg

Cook the yellow split peas in unsalted water for about 25 minutes, or until soft. Soften the onion in butter or oil. Put all the ingredients together in a bowl, including the split peas and onions. Mix well and knead by hand until thoroughly blended.

FILLING IV. A rice filling for vegetables to be eaten cold.

6 oz. rice, washed and drained
6 oz. tomatoes, skinned, seeded and finely chopped
1 large onion, finely chopped
A small bunch of parsley, finely chopped
Salt and black pepper
½ teaspoon ground cinnamon or ¼ teaspoon ground allspice [optional]

Mix all the ingredients together in a bowl, kneading well by hand until thoroughly blended. This filling is sometimes flavoured with about 2 teaspoons finely chopped fresh dill or mint – 1 teaspoon only if dried.

When filling the vegetables, allow room for the rice to expand. Use cooked rice and pack the vegetables tightly if they are to be baked.

FILLING V. A rice and chick pea filling for vegetables to be eaten cold.

2 oz. chick peas, soaked and boiled
4 oz. rice, washed and drained
6 oz. tomatoes, skinned, seeded and finely chopped
1 large onion, finely chopped
Salt and black pepper
½ teaspoon ground cinnamon or ¼ teaspoon ground allspice [optional]

Prepare and use as above.

FILLING VI. For vegetables prepared *à la Imam Bayildi*, to be eaten cold, and sometimes called *yalangi dolma* or 'false dolma', because of the lack of meat. A very popular filling in Turkey.

¾ lb. onions
3–4 tablespoons olive oil
2–3 large cloves garlic, crushed
A bunch of parsley, finely chopped
¾ lb. tomatoes, skinned, seeded and chopped
Salt

Slice the onions thinly. Soften them gently in olive oil, but do not let them colour. Add garlic and stir for a minute or two until aromatic. Remove from the heat and stir in parsley and tomatoes. Season to taste with salt, and mix well.

FILLING VII. A Turkish filling for aubergines.

2 small onions, finely chopped
2 tablespoons oil
½ lb. lamb or beef, minced
Salt and black pepper
2 tomatoes, skinned and chopped
¼ lb. Gruyère or hard Cheddar, grated

Judy Rodgers

The Zuni Café Cookbook

W.W. Norton, New York, 2002
552 pages
252 x 202 mm (9⁷/₈ x 8 in.)

American chef Judy Rodgers has an impeccable pedigree: Chez Panisse in Berkeley, California, and the three-Michelin-star La Maison Troisgros in Roanne, France. Named after a Native American tribe, San Francisco's Zuni Café originally served Mexican food; however, under Rodgers, who joined in 1987, the food became more Mediterranean.

This book does not pretend to be anything other than a restaurant cookery book. Zuni's entire repertory is here, including two dishes for which it is famous: Zuni Caesar salad, and Zuni roast chicken with bread salad. The latter, which the cafe cooks in a brick oven, is workable in an ordinary oven; the secret is the chicken's small size and 24-hour salting, which leaves it succulent. The recipe for the Caesar salad, which outsells every other dish by three to one, needs to be followed carefully. No cheap cheese instead of Parmesan, sourdough (a San Francisco speciality) for the croutons, and salt- rather than oil-packed anchovies.

By a neat coincidence, Elizabeth David (page 66) was an early visitor to Zuni, in its Mexican days. Rodgers says, 'she smelled something delicious and followed her nose to find Billy [West, the first owner] grilling chicken in the alley behind the restaurant.' She came back every time she was in San Francisco.

As well as containing the complete Zuni menu, the book is full of advice on ingredients and methods. Set in Foundry Old Style, it is easy to read and follow. The tempting photographs, by Gentl and Hyers, are clumped together, with the page of the relevant recipe given in the caption.

Here are two more fruit conserves I keep on hand to serve with cheese. {For suggested pairings, see pages 449 to 454.}

DRUNKEN RAISINS

Place raisins in a narrow container and add enough brandy, grappa, or Port to barely cover, then top off with a little water. Cover, shake, and set in a warm spot. Taste in about an hour and sweeten with sugar or honey to taste. Cover, shake again, and leave at room temperature for a few days, then refrigerate.

You can serve these raisins as soon as a day after making them, but they only improve as they become swollen with syrup. In any case, leave uncovered for an hour or so before using. Once refrigerated, they keep for ages, eventually becoming very suave and mellow.

DRIED FIGS *in* RED WINE

This condiment is easy to put together and keeps for months. Make it at least a few days before you plan to serve it, to allow time for the figs to swell and the flavors to mellow. Dried figs vary in dryness; the ones I use are chewy-moist – like the paste in a Fig Newton. They are fairly tender to begin with and absorb most of the scant wine syrup after a few days. If your figs are really dry, rinse them quickly under water before combining with the wine.

FOR ABOUT 1 PINT:

1-1/2 cups red wine {you can use a light, medium, or full-bodied red here}
2 bay leaves
A wide, 1-inch-long strip of orange zest, removed with a vegetable peeler

8 ounces dried Black Mission figs {about 20 large or 36 small figs}
About 1 teaspoon honey

Place the wine in a small saucepan with the bay leaves and simmer to reduce to a scant 1/2 cup. While the wine is reducing, cut the figs in half and place in a 2- to 4-cup storage vessel with a tightly fitting lid. Drop the orange zest in with the figs.

Add the honey to the warm reduced wine, stir, and pour over the figs. It won't seem like enough liquid. Cover and shake. Leave to swell for a few days, shaking or stirring a few times to redistribute the scant wine syrup, then refrigerate. Serve at room temperature.

SAUCES *&* RELISHES

SPICY SQUID STEW *with* RED WINE *&* ROASTED PEPPERS

HERE IS A DISH TO CHALLENGE THE DOGMA THAT THE BEST COOKING LETS ingredients and flavors sing clearly in the finished dish {or only nudges them into harmony}. In this recipe, you radically change the character, flavor, look, and texture of every ingredient – and the murky, complicated result is delicious. We make many variations on this recipe, adding diced fennel or leeks to the vegetable mix, or finishing the stew with a spoonful of cooked lentils, charred cherry tomatoes, or coarsely chopped blanched chard leaves.

Squid stew makes a great first or main course, followed by a roasted bird or grilled lamb chops with salad on the side. A few spoonfuls of leftover stew make a great crostini topping.

Wine: Quivira Dry Creek Cuvée, 1999

FOR 4 TO 6 SERVINGS:

2-1/4 pounds whole squid
About 6 tablespoons mild-tasting olive oil
Salt
1 cup plus 2 tablespoons red wine
3/4 cup chopped drained canned tomatoes or 1-1/2 cups chopped peeled ripe tomatoes
3/4 cup diced carrots {3 ounces}
3/4 cup diced celery {3 ounces}
3/4 cup diced yellow onions {3 ounces}
1 or 2 small dried chiles

3 garlic cloves, coarsely chopped, plus 1 clove, peeled, to rub the toasts
2-1/2 teaspoons tomato paste
A branch of fresh basil
A few wide strips of orange zest {removed with a vegetable peeler}
2/3 cup peeled roasted red or green bell pepper {about 8 ounces raw pepper, 1 medium}, cut into large dice, with its juice {see page 303}
4 to 6 thick slices of chewy, peasant-style bread

Begin to clean the squid by pulling out the tentacles as you grasp the body with the other hand. Look in the soft matter attached to the tentacles for the silver ink sac – it looks like a drop of mercury. Carefully transfer it to a small cup. Trim away the soft matter, cutting between the eyes and the "neck" of the tentacles. Squeeze the neck; a hard pea-sized "beak" should pop it out. Discard it. Set the tentacles aside. To clean the bodies, starting at the closed tip of each, use your finger or the dull edge of a knife to gradually press and flatten the body, forcing

out the insides. {Imagine you are flattening a toothpaste tube.} Cut the bodies into 1/3-inch rings. Rinse and drain the bodies and tentacles. You should have about 1-1/2 pounds cleaned squid.

Warm a tablespoon or two of olive oil in a 10-inch skillet over medium heat. Test with a piece of squid; when the oil sizzles on contact, add about half of the squid and cook briskly for about 45 seconds, stirring or tossing to cook evenly. Season lightly with salt, then tip the barely cooked meat into a 4-quart saucepan. Add another tablespoon or two of oil to the skillet and cook the rest of the squid.

Pour the red wine into the skillet to deglaze the squid juices, and stir and scrape as the liquid reduces by one-third. Add the tomatoes. If using canned tomatoes, simply heat through; if using fresh tomatoes, simmer to reduce by about half. Pour the mixture over the squid. It should be about half submerged in liquid.

Add the remaining 2 to 4 tablespoons olive oil, the carrots, celery, onions, chilis, chopped garlic, and tomato paste. Pick the leaves off the branch of basil and set them aside. Drop the stems into the stew. Twist and drop the strips of orange zest into the pan. Place the ink sacs in a fine strainer, hold over the stew, and bathe with a few spoonfuls of the red wine and juices, pressing to extract the ink. Stir it into the darkening stew. Cover and simmer gently for about 20 minutes. The squid and vegetables will now be nearly submerged in liquid. The squid will be shrunken and may be disturbingly hard.

Taste for salt and add the roasted peppers and their juice. Simmer uncovered until the squid becomes just tender. How long this takes varies enormously, depending on the squid, the pan, and the burner; allow 10 to 30 minutes. Check again for salt, and spiciness – if the stew is too mild for your taste, fish out the chili pods, crush them with a little of the liquid in a small dish, and add a little, or all, of this super-spicy dose to the pot. Otherwise, remove the chilis and the basil stems and cool the stew completely. Cooling and then reheating the stew makes the squid more tender.

To serve, reheat gently, adding the reserved basil leaves as the stew comes to a simmer. Taste. The finished stew should be rich and slightly thick. Offer toasted or grilled bread rubbed with the garlic.

Eleanour Sinclair Rohde
A Garden of Herbs

Herbert Jenkins, London, 1926 (revised
edition; first published 1920)
320 pages
212 x 135 mm (8³/₈ x 5³/₈ in.)

When I first had a garden, in Yorkshire
in 1968, I was desperate to plant herbs.
It's hard to believe today, but, back then,
it was almost impossible either to research
English herbs or to buy them. My interest
was encouraged by two indomitable English
ladies: Hilda Leyel (page 134) and Eleanour
Sinclair Rohde.

Mrs Rohde's book is a compendium
of herbal recipes and remedies taken
from a variety of texts from the fifteenth
century onwards, starting with Mayster
Jon Gardener's *The Feate of Gardening*
(1440) and including excerpts from
The Accomplished Lady's Delight (1719)
by Mrs Mary Eales, confectioner to Queen
Anne; and *The Modern Cook* (1733) by
Vincent La Chapelle, chief cook to the
Prince of Orange. Although Rohde's text
is old-fashioned and hard to follow, you
will learn how to make vinegar (from the
seventeenth-century diarist and writer
John Evelyn), cinnamon toast and sloe
gin, the last two hardly altered today.
There is also advice on herbs as medicine,
including a cure for sore feet from 1588:
'Take Plantaine and stampe it well, and
anoynt your feete with the juice thereof
and the greefe will swage'. I am not entirely
sure, however, about wormwood brandy
or a salad of thistle leaves, even though,
according to Evelyn, 'the late Morocco
Ambassador and his retinue were very
partial' to the latter. Thyme can be used
'to enable one to see the Fairies'.

The book has plenty of black-and-
white illustrations from early books, mostly
from the sixteenth century, which don't
really help.

A Fifteenth Century Garden

60   A GARDEN OF HERBS

and to a good handful or two so done put a quart of
Cream and boil it up gently with them. Put in a blade
of Mace, season with fine sugar and Orange-Flower
water. Strain it and draw it up with the Yolks of two
or three Eggs, and clip off the tops of a handful of the
Flowers and draw up with it and dish as you please.—
From *The Receipt Book of Joseph Cooper*, Cook to
Charles I, 1654.

ANOTHER WAY.—Take two ounces of Syrup of
Cowslips and boil up in your Cream and season it as
before. Thicken it with the Yolks of three or four
Eggs, and put in two ounces of candy'd Cowslips
when you draw it up. Dish it in Basons and Glasses,
and strew over some candy'd cowslips.—*Ibid.*

TO KEEP COWSLIPS FOR SALATES.—Take a quart of
White Wine Vinegar, and halfe a quarter of a pound
of fine beaten Sugar, and mix them together, then take
your Cowslips, pull them out of the podds, and cut
off the green Knobs at the lower end, put them into
the pot or glasse wherein you mind to keep them, and
well shaking the Vinegar and Sugar together in the
glasse wherein they were before, powre it upon the
Cowslips, and so stirring them morning and evening
to make them settle for three weeks, keep them for
your use.—*A Book of Fruits and Flowers*, 1653.

TO CONSERVE COWSLIPS.—Gather your flowers in
the midst of the day when all the dew is off, then cut
off all the white, leaving none but the yellow blossome
so picked and cut, before they wither, weigh out ten

Distilling in a Herb Garden

them to clear, strong Broth ; let them boil Tender with a Handful of Green Pease. Let your garnishing be Cucumbers and Lettuce. Use no thickening in this Soop. So serve it.—*The Receipt Book of Patrick Lamb*, Master Cook to Charles II, James II, William and Mary, and Queen Anne, 1716.

To make Carrot Soup.—Boil your carrots, cleanse them, beat them in a mortar or wooden tray, put them into a pipkin with Butter, white Wine, Salt, Cinnamon, Sugar, shred Dates, boil'd currants. Stew these well together. Dish them on Sippets, garnish with hard Eggs in Halves or Quarters and scrape in Sugar.—From *The Receipt Book of John Nott*, Cook to the Duke of Bolton, 1723.

To make Meagre Broth for Soop with Herbs.—Set on a Kettle of Water and put in two or three crusts of Bread and all sorts of Good Herbs, season it with Salt put in Butter and a bunch of Sweet herbs, boil it for an hour and a half, then strain it through a Sieve or Napkin. This will serve to make Lettuce Soop, Artichoke Soop, Asparagus Soop, Succory Soop, and Soop de Santé with Herbs.—*Ibid.*

To make Potage the French Way.—Take hard lettuce, sorrel and chervil of each a like Quantity or any other Herbs you like as much as half a peck will hold pressed down, pick, wash and drain them. Put them in a Pot with fresh butter, then add water, Salt, some whole cloves and a crust of Bread and

when it is boild take out the crust of bread and put in the yolks of a couple of eggs well beaten and stir together over the fire. Lay in a Dish some slices of Bread. Pour it in, serve it up.—*Ibid.*

Pottage without the sight of Herbs.—Mince several sorts of sweet herbs very fine—Spinage, Parsley, Marigold flowers, Succory, Strawberry and Violet Leaves. Pound them with oatmeal in a Mortar. Boil your oatmeal and herbs in broth and serve.—*Ibid.*

To make a Pottage for one or two Persons.—Take four Handfuls of Pot-herbs, pick'd, wash'd, and cut small, two or three Onions cut small likewise, three or four Leeks, Half an Ounce of fresh Butter or Bacon, four Spoonfuls either of fine Flour, pounded Rice, Oatmeal, or peel'd Barley, a Dram of Salt, and a little Pepper ; boil the whole in three Quarts of Water, which must be reduced to a Pint and a Half, and kept for use. You may make, at the same time, Pottage enough for three or four days.—*The Modern Cook*, by Vincent la Chapelle, Chief Cook to the Prince of Orange, 1744.

A moistening and cooling Broth with Herbs.—Take some Leaves of Sorrel, Beet, Lettuce, Purslane, and Chervil, two large handfuls of each, pick, wash and cut them all small, let them boil with a Crust of Bread and two Drams of fresh Butter in two Pints of Water, which when half boiled away is to be taken off and strained through a Sieve.—*Ibid.*

berries, wild tansy, three pintes of new Milke. Still all these together and wash your face therein.—*The Good Housewife's Handmaid*, 1585.

Strawberry and Almond Tansy.—Take four quarts of new milk and half a pound of the sweet almond flour, two ounces of lemon juice and half a pint of strawberry juice. Put to these two pounds of fine sugar and a quart of Canary. Stir them together and beat them till they froth, and become of a pleasant colour.—*Ibid.*

Strawberry Leaf Tea.—On two large handfuls of the young leaves pour a quart of boiling water.

Strawberry and Woodruff Tea.—On equal quantities of young strawberry leaves and woodruff pour one quart of boiling water.

A Cordial Water of Sir Walter Raleigh.—Take a gallon of Strawberries, and put them into a pinte of *aqua vitæ*, let them stand so four or five days, strain them gently out, and sweeten the water as you please, with fine Sugar, or else with perfume.

Strawberry Water.—To a quart of water you must have a pound of strawberries which squeeze in the same water, then put in four or five ounces of sugar with some lemon juice ; if the lemons are large and juicy one lemon is enough to two quarts of water. All being well mixed put it through a straining bag, put

it in a cool place and give it to drink.—From *The Receipt Book of Vincent la Chapelle*, Chief Cook to the Prince of Orange, 1744.

TANSY

" I have heard that if maids will take wild Tansy and lay it to soake in Buttermilk for the space of nine days and wash their faces therewith, it will make them look very faire."—*The Virtuose Boke of Distyllacion*, by Master Jherom Brunswyke, 1527.

Our garden tansy was originally the wild tansy, but all the old herbalists say that the latter has far more virtue both in its leaves and flowers. The name tansy is derived from Athanasia (immortality), and the plant is dedicated to St. Athanasius. A tansy was a favourite dish in the eighteenth century, and was as inseparable from a bill of fare for Easter as roast goose at Michaelmas, or a gooseberry tart at Whitsun. Before mint became recognised as the proper accompaniment to roast lamb, tansy was used in the same way. Tansy puddings and tansy cakes were commonly eaten during spring, and tansy tea was a recognised cure for colds and rheumatism.

Tansy Tea.—Dry bunches of tansy (leaves and flowers) in the summer. On one ounce of the dried tansy pour a pint of boiling water.

How to make a Tansy in Lent.—Take all maner of hearbes and the spawn of a Pike or of any other fish

A Garden of Herbs

ELEANOUR SINCLAIR ROHDE

Irma S. Rombauer and Marion Rombauer Becker

Joy of Cooking

Bobbs-Merrill, Indianapolis and New York,
1975 (sixth edition; first published 1931)
928 pages
234 x 164 mm (9¼ x 6½ in.)

In common with America's other famous cookery book, Fannie Farmer's *Boston Cooking-School Cook Book* (1896; page 88), *Joy*, as it is known, was born of tragedy. Struggling both emotionally and financially following her husband's suicide, Irma S. Rombauer, its author, used some of the money that had been left to her to finance the private printing of the book in 1931. Five years later, it was picked up by a commercial publishing house.

As Marion Rombauer Becker, Irma's daughter, writes in her acknowledgements, *Joy* was a family affair. Her mother gathered the recipes, often from friends (many of whom, like Irma, were ethnic Germans), while Marion did the testing. In turn, her sons – cordon bleu-trained Ethan, and Mark, interested in natural foods – 'have reinforced *Joy* in many ways'. The printing history in my copy alone says it all: by 1980, the sixth edition had been reprinted twenty-one times.

Joy is surprisingly cosmopolitan. The items in a list of suggested antipasti are not just Italian; there are also rollmops, pickled beets with caviar, and ceviche. Foods – caviar, for example, and such 'seaside tidbits' as Atlantic jackknife clams and California mussels – are explained with simple line drawings. We learn how to keep lobsters alive and make salt-water taffy. I now know what kosher salt is (large-grain sea salt); this ingredient, used in American recipes, had long confused me.

Illustrations are limited to the clear line drawings, by Ginnie Hofmann and Ikki Matsumoto. The text is in a small, sans serif typeface but very readable. The endpapers repeat 'Joy' endlessly in ultramarine. Somehow, despite *Joy*'s encyclopaedic qualities, it is also a friendly book. I can see exactly why it swept through American kitchens.

A Book for Cooks

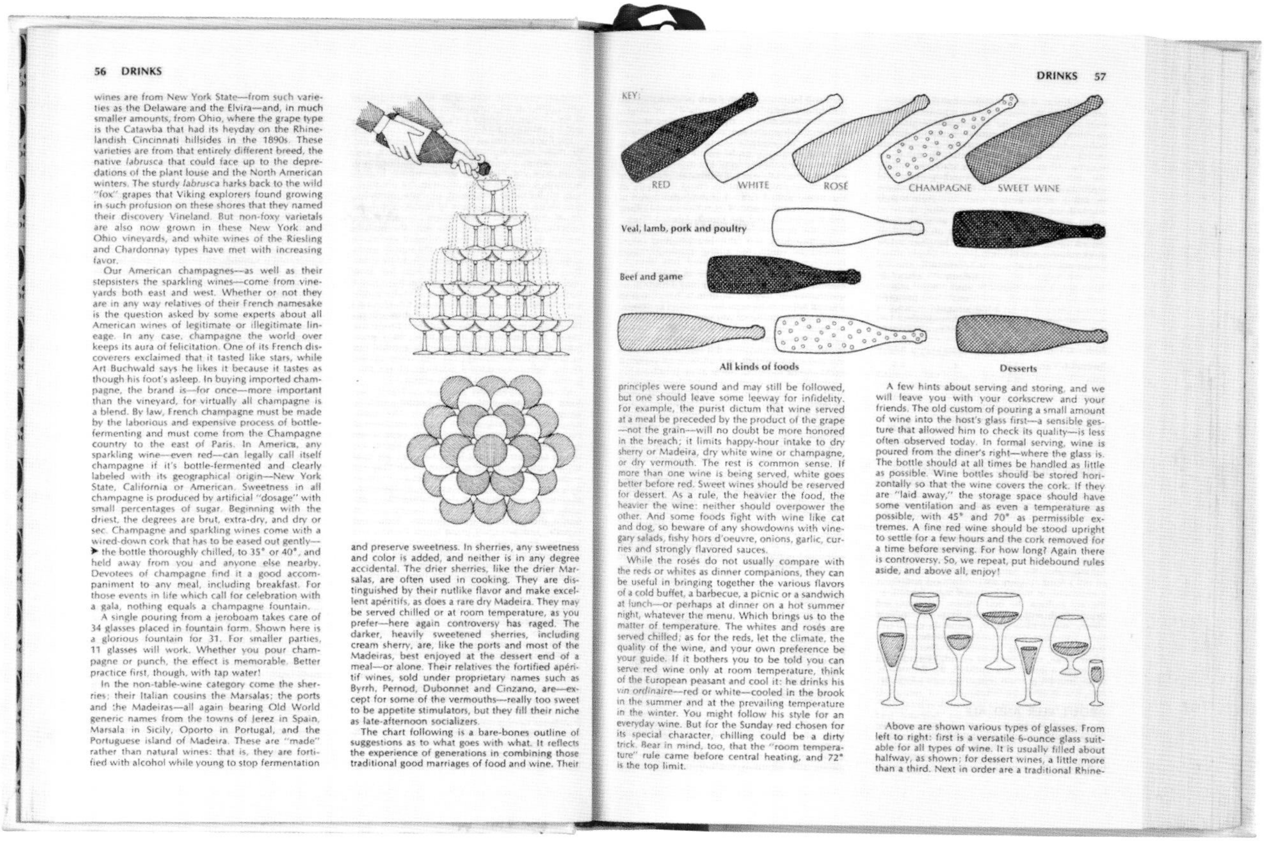

56 DRINKS

wines are from New York State—from such varieties as the Delaware and the Elvira—and, in much smaller amounts, from Ohio, where the grape type is the Catawba that had its heyday on the Rhinelandish Cincinnati hillsides in the 1890s. These varieties are from that entirely different breed, the native *labrusca* that could face up to the depredations of the plant louse and the North American winters. The sturdy *labrusca* harks back to the wild "fox" grapes that Viking explorers found growing in such profusion on these shores that they named their discovery Vineland. But non-foxy varietals are also now grown in these New York and Ohio vineyards, and white wines of the Riesling and Chardonnay types have met with increasing favor.

Our American champagnes—as well as their stepsisters the sparkling wines—come from vineyards both east and west. Whether or not they are in any way relatives of their French namesake is the question asked by some experts about all American wines of legitimate or illegitimate lineage. In any case, champagne the world over keeps its aura of felicitation. One of its French discoverers exclaimed that it tasted like stars, while Art Buchwald says he likes it because it tastes as though his foot's asleep. In buying imported champagne, the brand is—for once—more important than the vineyard, for virtually all champagne is a blend. By law, French champagne must be made by the laborious and expensive process of bottle-fermenting and must come from the Champagne country to the east of Paris. In America, any sparkling wine—even red—can legally call itself champagne if it's bottle-fermented and clearly labeled with its geographical origin—New York State, California or American. Sweetness in all champagne is produced by artificial "dosage" with small percentages of sugar. Beginning with the driest, the degrees are brut, extra-dry, and dry or sec. Champagne and sparkling wines come with a wired-down cork that has to be eased out gently—➤ the bottle thoroughly chilled, to 35° or 40°, and held away from you and anyone else nearby. Devotees of champagne find it a good accompaniment to any meal, including breakfast. For those events in life which call for celebration with a gala, nothing equals a champagne fountain.

A single pouring from a jeroboam takes care of 34 glasses placed in fountain form. Shown here is a glorious fountain for 31. For smaller parties, 11 glasses will work. Whether you pour champagne or punch, the effect is memorable. Better practice first, though, with tap water!

In the non-table-wine category come the sherries; their Italian cousins the Marsalas; the ports and the Madeiras—all again bearing Old World generic names from the towns of Jerez in Spain, Marsala in Sicily, Oporto in Portugal, and the Portuguese island of Madeira. These are "made" rather than natural wines: that is, they are fortified with alcohol while young to stop fermentation and preserve sweetness. In sherries, any sweetness and color is added, and neither is in any degree accidental. The drier sherries, like the drier Marsalas, are often used in cooking. They are distinguished by their nutlike flavor and make excellent apéritifs, as does a rare dry Madeira. They may be served chilled or at room temperature, as you prefer—here again controversy has raged. The darker, heavily sweetened sherries, including cream sherry, are, like the ports and most of the Madeiras, best enjoyed at the dessert end of a meal—or alone. Their relatives the fortified apéritif wines, sold under proprietary names such as Byrrh, Pernod, Dubonnet and Cinzano, are—except for some of the vermouths—really too sweet to be appetite stimulators, but they fill their niche as late-afternoon socializers.

The chart following is a bare-bones outline of suggestions as to what goes with what. It reflects the experience of generations in combining those traditional good marriages of food and wine. Their

DRINKS 57

KEY: RED WHITE ROSÉ CHAMPAGNE SWEET WINE

Veal, lamb, pork and poultry

Beef and game

All kinds of foods

Desserts

principles were sound and may still be followed, but one should leave some leeway for infidelity. For example, the purist dictum that wine served at a meal be preceded by the product of the grape —not the grain—will no doubt be more honored in the breach; it limits happy-hour intake to dry sherry or Madeira, dry white wine or champagne, or dry vermouth. The rest is common sense. If more than one wine is being served, white goes better before red. Sweet wines should be reserved for dessert. As a rule, the heavier the food, the heavier the wine: neither should overpower the other. And some foods fight with wine like cat and dog, so beware of any showdowns with vinegary salads, fishy hors d'oeuvre, onions, garlic, curries and strongly flavored sauces.

While the rosés do not usually compare with the reds or whites as dinner companions, they can be useful in bringing together the various flavors of a cold buffet, a barbecue, a picnic or a sandwich at lunch—or perhaps at dinner on a hot summer night, whatever the menu. Which brings us to the matter of temperature. The whites and rosés are served chilled; as for the reds, let the climate, the quality of the wine, and your own preference be your guide. If it bothers you to be told you can serve red wine only at room temperature, think of the European peasant and cool it: he drinks his *vin ordinaire*—red or white—cooled in the brook in the summer and at the prevailing temperature in the winter. You might follow his style for an everyday wine. But for the Sunday red chosen for its special character, chilling could be a dirty trick. Bear in mind, too, that the "room temperature" rule came before central heating, and 72° is the top limit.

A few hints about serving and storing, and we will leave you with your corkscrew and your friends. The old custom of pouring a small amount of wine into the host's glass first—a sensible gesture that allowed him to check its quality—is less often observed today. In formal serving, wine is poured from the diner's right—where the glass is. The bottle should at all times be handled as little as possible. Wine bottles should be stored horizontally so that the wine covers the cork. If they are "laid away," the storage space should have some ventilation and as even a temperature as possible, with 45° and 70° as permissible extremes. A fine red wine should be stood upright to settle for a few hours and the cork removed for a time before serving. For how long? Again there is controversy. So, we repeat, put hidebound rules aside, and above all, enjoy!

Above are shown various types of glasses. From left to right: first is a versatile 6-ounce glass suitable for all types of wine. It is usually filled about halfway, as shown; for dessert wines, a little more than a third. Next in order are a traditional Rhine-

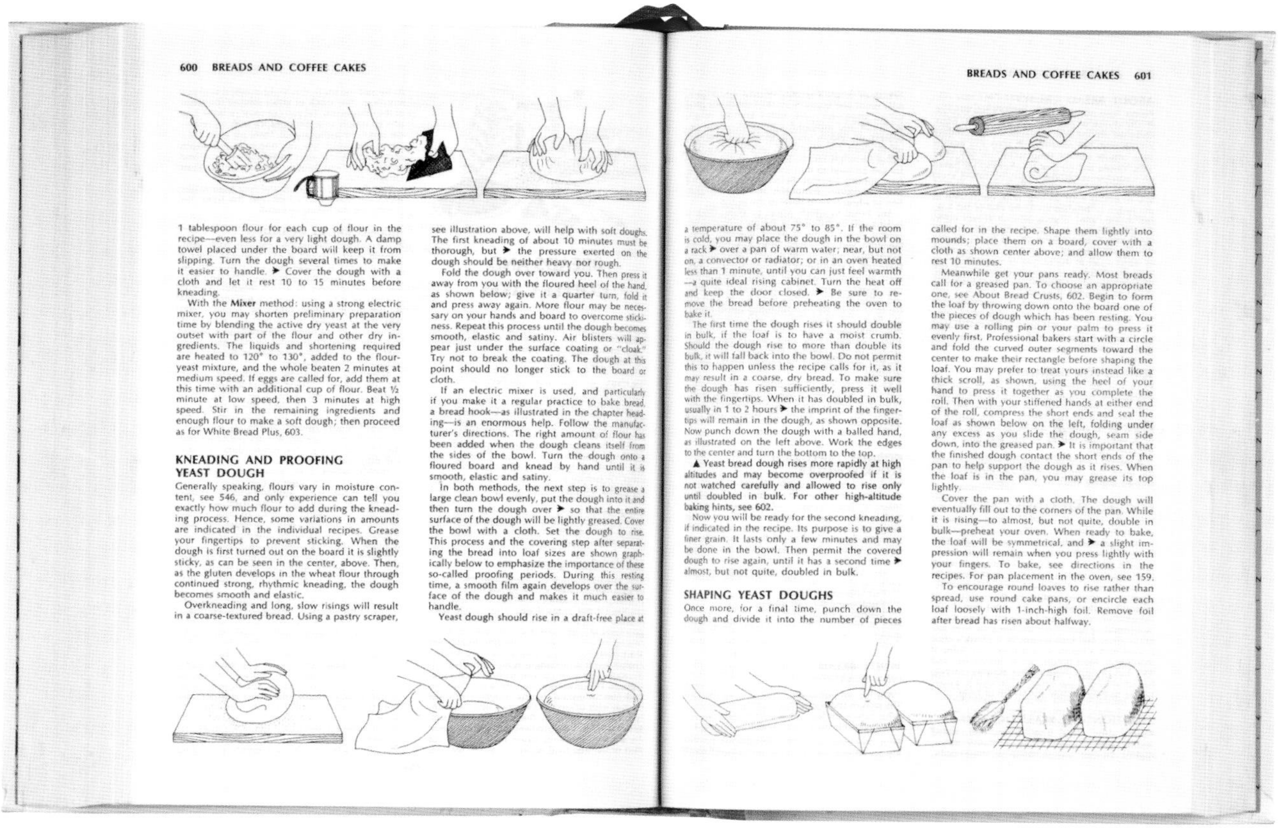

600 BREADS AND COFFEE CAKES

1 tablespoon flour for each cup of flour in the recipe—even less for a very light dough. A damp towel placed under the board will keep it from slipping. Turn the dough several times to make it easier to handle. ➤ Cover the dough with a cloth and let it rest 10 to 15 minutes before kneading.

With the **Mixer** method: using a strong electric mixer, you may shorten preliminary preparation time by blending the active dry yeast at the very outset with part of the flour and other dry ingredients. The liquids and shortening required are heated to 120° to 130°, added to the flour-yeast mixture, and the whole beaten 2 minutes at medium speed. If eggs are called for, add them at this time with an additional cup of flour. Beat ½ minute at low speed, then 3 minutes at high speed. Stir in the remaining ingredients and enough flour to make a soft dough; then proceed as for White Bread Plus, 603.

KNEADING AND PROOFING YEAST DOUGH

Generally speaking, flours vary in moisture content, see 546, and only experience can tell you exactly how much flour to add during the kneading process. Hence, some variations in amounts are indicated in the individual recipes. Grease your fingertips to prevent sticking. When the dough is first turned out on the board it is slightly sticky, as can be seen in the center, above. Then, as the gluten develops in the wheat flour through continued strong, rhythmic kneading, the dough becomes smooth and elastic.

Overkneading and long, slow risings will result in a coarse-textured bread. Using a pastry scraper, see illustration above, will help with soft doughs. The first kneading of about 10 minutes must be thorough, but ➤ the pressure exerted on the dough should be neither heavy nor rough.

Fold the dough over toward you. Then press it away from you with the floured heel of the hand, as shown below; give it a quarter turn, fold it and press away again. More flour may be necessary on your hands and board to overcome stickiness. Repeat this process until the dough becomes smooth, elastic and satiny. Air blisters will appear just under the surface coating or "cloak." Try not to break the coating. The dough at this point should no longer stick to the board or cloth.

If an electric mixer is used, and particularly if you make it a regular practice to bake bread, a bread hook—as illustrated in the chapter heading—is an enormous help. Follow the manufacturer's directions. The right amount of flour has been added when the dough cleans itself from the sides of the bowl. Turn the dough onto a floured board and knead by hand until it is smooth, elastic and satiny.

In both methods, the next step is to grease a large clean bowl evenly, put the dough into it and then turn the dough over ➤ so that the entire surface of the dough will be lightly greased. Cover the bowl with a cloth. Set the dough to rise. This process and the covering step after separating the bread into loaf sizes are shown graphically below to emphasize the importance of these so-called proofing periods. During this resting time, a smooth film again develops over the surface of the dough and makes it much easier to handle.

Yeast dough should rise in a draft-free place at

BREADS AND COFFEE CAKES 601

a temperature of about 75° to 85°. If the room is cold, you may place the dough in the bowl on a rack ➤ over a pan of warm water; near, but not on, a convector or radiator; or in an oven heated less than 1 minute, until you can just feel warmth —a quite ideal rising cabinet. Turn the heat off and keep the door closed. ➤ Be sure to remove the bread before preheating the oven to bake it.

The first time the dough rises it should double in bulk, if the loaf is to have a moist crumb. Should the dough rise to more than double its bulk, it will fall back into the bowl. Do not permit this to happen unless the recipe calls for it, as it may result in a coarse, dry bread. To make sure the dough has risen sufficiently, press it well with the fingertips. When it has doubled in bulk, usually in 1 to 2 hours ➤ the imprint of the fingertips will remain in the dough, as shown opposite. Now punch down the dough with a balled hand, as illustrated on the left above. Work the edges to the center and turn the bottom to the top.

▲ **Yeast bread dough rises more rapidly at high altitudes and may become overproofed if it is not watched carefully and allowed to rise only until doubled in bulk. For other high-altitude baking hints, see 602.**

Now you will be ready for the second kneading, if indicated in the recipe. Its purpose is to give a finer grain. It lasts only a few minutes and may be done in the bowl. Then permit the covered dough to rise again, until it has a second time ➤ almost, but not quite, doubled in bulk.

SHAPING YEAST DOUGHS

Once more, for a final time, punch down the dough and divide it into the number of pieces called for in the recipe. Shape them lightly into mounds; place them on a board, cover with a cloth as shown center above; and allow them to rest 10 minutes.

Meanwhile get your pans ready. Most breads call for a greased pan. To choose an appropriate one, see About Bread Crusts, 602. Begin to form the loaf by throwing down onto the board one of the pieces of dough which has been resting. You may use a rolling pin or your palm to press it evenly first. Professional bakers start with a circle and fold the curved outer segments toward the center to make their rectangle before shaping the loaf. You may prefer to treat yours instead like a thick scroll, as shown, using the heel of your hand to press it together as you complete the roll. Then with your stiffened hands at either end of the roll, compress the short ends and seal the loaf as shown below on the left, folding under any excess as you slide the dough, seam side down, into the greased pan. ➤ It is important that the finished dough contact the short ends of the pan to help support the dough as it rises. When the loaf is in the pan, you may grease its top lightly.

Cover the pan with a cloth. The dough will eventually fill out to the corners of the pan. While it is rising—to almost, but not quite, double in bulk—preheat your oven. When ready to bake, the loaf will be symmetrical, and ➤ a slight impression will remain when you press lightly with your fingers. To bake, see directions in the recipes. For pan placement in the oven, see 159.

To encourage round loaves to rise rather than spread, use round cake pans, or encircle each loaf loosely with 1-inch-high foil. Remove foil after bread has risen about halfway.

Janet Ross and Michael Waterfield

Leaves from Our Tuscan Kitchen; or, How to Cook Vegetables

Penguin, Harmondsworth, 1977
(revised edition; first published 1899)
208 pages
198 x 128 mm (7¾ x 5 in.)

If you were to pick up this little masterpiece with no knowledge of its history, you would imagine that it had been written within the past few years. A book of traditional Tuscan vegetable cookery, it is arranged so that each vegetable has a section to itself (Jane Grigson did something very similar in 1978; see page 102).

In 1860 Janet Ross, née Duff Gordon, married Henry Ross (who had helped archaeologist Sir Austen Henry Layard excavate the ancient city of Nineveh, now in modern-day Iraq), and they went to live in a trecento villa just outside Florence. There, she carefully recorded the vegetable dishes created by her cooks, notably Giuseppe Volpe, who worked for her for thirty years. The resultant book was published in 1899 and is, without fussing about it, easily adaptable for vegetarians.

Tuscan cookery doesn't do fashion or fusion, it just carries on in its sublime old way. So, more than a century since Ross compiled her book, Tuscans are still eating Asparagi alla Parmigiana, Pomodori al Forno and Fagioli alla Fiorentina. I know, because I had a house in Tuscany, too, and, like Ross, was overwhelmed by the quality, freshness and variety of the vegetables found in small markets, and by the bravura simplicity of the Tuscan way of cooking them.

My edition of the book has been slightly updated to recognize such advances as deep freezes and polythene bags. Suitably, this work was done by Michael Waterfield, Ross's great-great-nephew and owner of the Wife of Bath restaurant in Kent. Even those who dislike Brussels sprouts, cabbage and broccoli will find new, inventive ways of making them palatable.

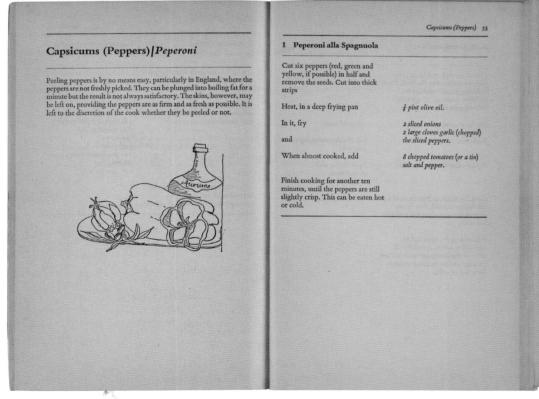

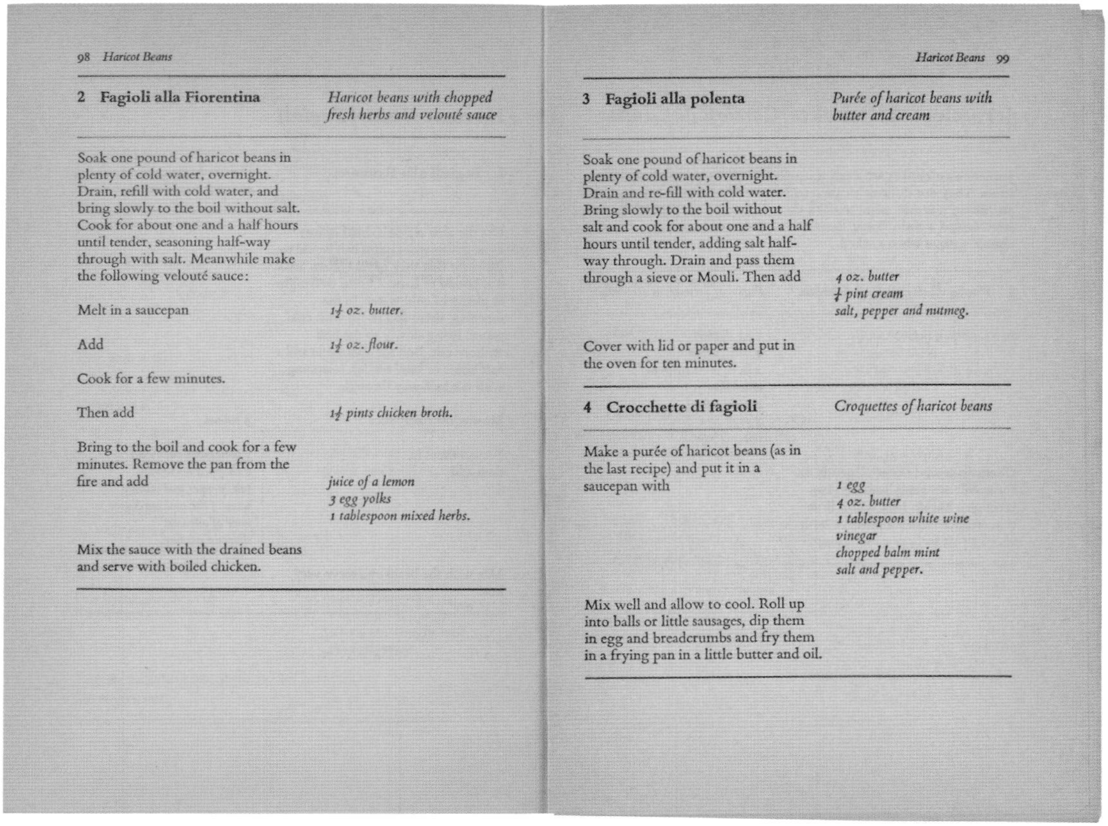

2 Fagioli alla Fiorentina   *Haricot beans with chopped fresh herbs and velouté sauce*

Soak one pound of haricot beans in plenty of cold water, overnight. Drain, refill with cold water, and bring slowly to the boil without salt. Cook for about one and a half hours until tender, seasoning half-way through with salt. Meanwhile make the following velouté sauce:

Melt in a saucepan	*1¼ oz. butter.*
Add	*1¼ oz. flour.*

Cook for a few minutes.

Then add	*1¼ pints chicken broth.*

Bring to the boil and cook for a few minutes. Remove the pan from the fire and add

*juice of a lemon
3 egg yolks
1 tablespoon mixed herbs.*

Mix the sauce with the drained beans and serve with boiled chicken.

3 Fagioli alla polenta   *Purée of haricot beans with butter and cream*

Soak one pound of haricot beans in plenty of cold water, overnight. Drain and re-fill with cold water. Bring slowly to the boil without salt and cook for about one and a half hours until tender, adding salt half-way through. Drain and pass them through a sieve or Mouli. Then add

*4 oz. butter
¼ pint cream
salt, pepper and nutmeg.*

Cover with lid or paper and put in the oven for ten minutes.

4 Crocchette di fagioli   *Croquettes of haricot beans*

Make a purée of haricot beans (as in the last recipe) and put it in a saucepan with

*1 egg
4 oz. butter
1 tablespoon white wine vinegar
chopped balm mint
salt and pepper.*

Mix well and allow to cool. Roll up into balls or little sausages, dip them in egg and breadcrumbs and fry them in a frying pan in a little butter and oil.

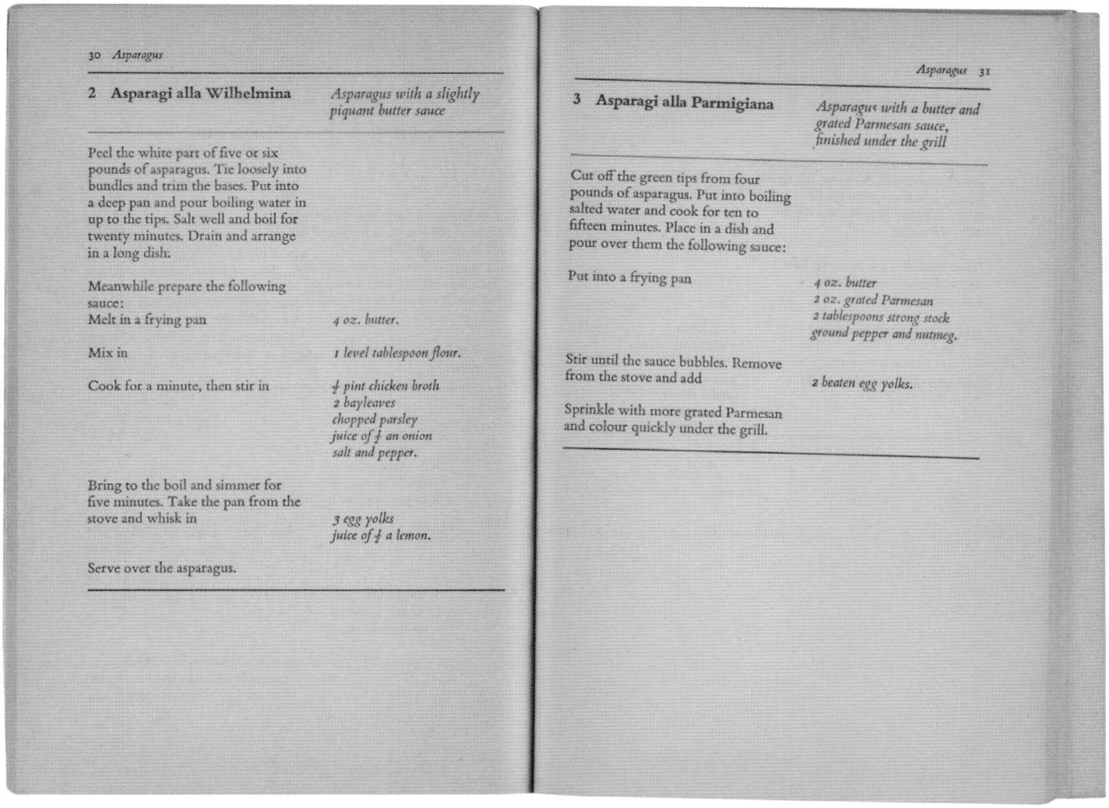

2 Asparagi alla Wilhelmina   *Asparagus with a slightly piquant butter sauce*

Peel the white part of five or six pounds of asparagus. Tie loosely into bundles and trim the bases. Put into a deep pan and pour boiling water in up to the tips. Salt well and boil for twenty minutes. Drain and arrange in a long dish.

Meanwhile prepare the following sauce:

Melt in a frying pan	*4 oz. butter.*
Mix in	*1 level tablespoon flour.*
Cook for a minute, then stir in	*¼ pint chicken broth*

*2 bayleaves
chopped parsley
juice of ¼ an onion
salt and pepper.*

Bring to the boil and simmer for five minutes. Take the pan from the stove and whisk in

*3 egg yolks
juice of ¼ a lemon.*

Serve over the asparagus.

3 Asparagi alla Parmigiana   *Asparagus with a butter and grated Parmesan sauce, finished under the grill*

Cut off the green tips from four pounds of asparagus. Put into boiling salted water and cook for ten to fifteen minutes. Place in a dish and pour over them the following sauce:

Put into a frying pan

*4 oz. butter
2 oz. grated Parmesan
2 tablespoons strong stock
ground pepper and nutmeg.*

Stir until the sauce bubbles. Remove from the stove and add

2 beaten egg yolks.

Sprinkle with more grated Parmesan and colour quickly under the grill.

Jeremy Round

The Independent Cook

Pan, London, 2001 (first published 1988)
592 pages
196 x 129 mm (7¾ x 5⅛ in.)

Jeremy Round was hired as cookery writer for the new *Independent* newspaper in 1986, aged only twenty-nine. In 1989 he was awarded the Glenfiddich Restaurant Writer of the Year Award. That same year he died. In an article published in *The Independent* on the tenth anniversary of his death, Hilly Janes, who had hired him, wrote, 'I always knew he'd be irreplaceable. He was.' This was his only book, one that Clarissa Dickson Wright refuses to lend to anyone, it is so valuable to her.

By all accounts, Round was delightful: funny, knowledgeable, modest. Josceline Dimbleby (page 78), contributing to the same *Independent* article as Janes, recalls him eating stuffed baby octopus in Portugal, 'ink pouring down his chin. Rather like a madly happy Dracula.'

It is now almost a cliché to shop seasonally. This was far from the case when the book first came out in 1988. Round says in his defence, 'Strawberries are now offered for ten months of the year … . But, for flavour, nothing comes close to the English outdoor grown strawberries that can only be found for perhaps ten weeks.'

Round takes seasonal cooking to its logical conclusion. Each monthly chapter begins with shopping lists for seasonal products, from vegetables to cheese, with the best in bold type. These are followed by suitable recipes, nearly half of which are for vegetarians. At the start of the book there is a list of recommended equipment and store-cupboard necessities; at the end, the best months for particular foods are explained by code – a star for best British, a transparent star for best imported, and a small dot for available (although not particularly recommended). Round also explains, briefly, how to cook the foods. Dickson Wright is correct to hold on to her copy.

PAN COOKS

'A wonderful book . . . jam-packed with good sense, it is fun and I can't wait to get my teeth into the recipes.'
Phillipa Davenport, *Financial Times*

Jeremy Round
The Independent Cook

A FOOD WRITING CLASSIC: EVERYTHING ALWAYS WORKS AND EVERYTHING IS ALWAYS DELICIOUS

A Book for Cooks

This soup, a thick greenish mush, is both cooler and inflamer – best eaten in very small portions on hot, humid days by the pool. Behind the cocktail-belt, pan-American touches of canned tomato juice and gin, is a base of onion, celery and green pepper, which Louisiana-born chef Beany Macgregor calls the 'holy trinity' of Creole and Cajun cooking. They give a distinctive, slightly bitter, metallic tone to all the area's most famous dishes, from gumbo to jambalaya. The recipe is an adaptation of a Bloody Mary Soup concocted by Ed Keeling, executive chef of the New Orleans Hyatt Regency.

250ml canned tomato juice
60g celery – chopped
90g onion – peeled and chopped
60g sweet green pepper – de-seeded and chopped
4 heaped tablespoons chopped parsley
50ml gin
salt and freshly ground black pepper

Liquidize. Chill.

Dishes of sautéed peppers and tomatoes scrambled together with eggs are common to many parts of southern Europe and the Mediterranean. The French-Basque version, pipérade, includes onion, but I prefer this Turkish menemen, which doesn't.

A popular quick meal at any time of the day, it is most commonly prepared in a double-handled metal skillet, to order, in small restaurants and pastry shops all over the country. The best peppers to use are long and pale with thin, moderately hot-tasting flesh (they are called *sivri biber* if you should happen to live near a Turkish store). Alternatives in this country are milder green chillies or a mixture of ordinary sweet green pepper and hot green chillies to your own pain threshold. Don't even think of making this if you only have canned tomatoes.

30g butter
2 large, heavy, firm, sweet, very red ripe tomatoes
– skinned, seeded and cut into strips
120g finely sliced sweet green pepper (see above)
salt
4 very fresh, free-range eggs – beaten

Heat butter in a small frying pan. Add tomatoes and pepper and cook for 5–6 minutes over a medium flame, until the

good scraper, but the most delectable in flavour – the potato equivalent of the truffle – is the pink fir apple: expensive, grown in relatively small quantities but now widely distributed through the supermarkets.

As for other salad vegetables, supplies of excellent outdoor-grown celery should now continue right through until December. British growers seem to have turned to Chinese leaves in a big way, leading to low prices (although I can take or leave this vapid vegetable). Look for ripe, sweet marmande, or beef, tomatoes.

Shopping list

Aubergines, avocados, **beetroot** (new-season), Belgian chicory, broad beans, **broccoli** (calabrese), **cabbages** (**summer varieties** such as Primo, with Sugarloaf following), carrots, **cauliflowers**, celery, chilli peppers, **Chinese leaves**, courgettes, cucumbers, fennel, **garlic**, globe artichokes, green beans (**French and runner**), greens, herbs (especially **basil**, chives, dill, **fennel, marjoram, mint,** parsley, rosemary, **sage,** tarragon, **thyme**), **kohlrabi** (new-season), leeks (new-season), lettuce and **many varieties of salad leaf,** mange-tout, **marrows** and **squashes,** mooli, mushrooms (cultivated), **okra, onions** (including **pickling**), **parsnips** (new-season), peas, **peppers** (capsicums), potatoes (second earlies including **pink fir apple**), **radishes,** spinach, spring onions, swedes (new-season), **sweetcorn, tomatoes** (including **large beef** or **marmande, plum** and **cherry** varieties), turnips (new season), watercress.

Some stores are now making a big thing of baby vegetable varieties – for example leeks, courgettes and kohlrabi. The tiny yellow courgettes are especially pretty. If you like your sweetcorn to live up to its name, look for the Supersweet variety. Also look for pak choi, rocket and chanterelles.

FRUIT

A brief respite in the strawberry and raspberry season will be followed by the autumn second-cropping at the end of this month. Look out especially for Scottish raspberries. Connoisseurs are supposed to be able to tell from which side of the country they come by flavour and appearance alone; something to do with the Gulf Stream, I expect.

Peaches, nectarines and melons are at their peak this month. A friend serves them in a salad just sprinkled with Amaretto, the almond flavoured liqueur, or fresh fruit juice with a few drops of ratafia essence, which brings out the sweetness beautifully. Yellow honeydew melons are particularly good at the beginning of August. Watermelons will get larger through the month until they are sold by the slice as well as whole.

The summer abundance is augmented by the appearance of English plums, which I think are jolly good in summer puddings, although most people don't agree with me. Most varieties have a very short season – here one week, gone the next – so it is worth keeping a close eye on the market as the month progresses. Early Laxton, Rivers' Early Prolific, Czar and Opal

Michel Roux
Eggs

Quadrille, London, 2005
304 pages
210 x 160 mm (8¼ x 6¼ in.)

Unlike the subjects of many single-ingredient cookery books (tomatoes, potatoes, onions), eggs allow the cook to make both sweet and savoury dishes. Eggs, indeed, must be the most adaptable of foods available (only milk comes anywhere near), and Michel Roux, a much-awarded chef, including three Michelin stars at the Waterside Inn at Bray, Berkshire, deals with them perfectly.

For a start, Roux doesn't limit himself to just hens' eggs. We have here everything from tiny quails' eggs (15–20 grams/½–¾ oz) to gigantic ostriches' eggs (500–600 grams/1 lb 2 oz – 1 lb 4 oz), along with a caveat that wild birds' eggs are strictly protected. (I once talked to a scientist who, decades ago, had sampled lots of wild birds' eggs. Wrens', he said, were the most disgusting, but, at least, small.) We learn how to tell the freshness of an egg: place it in water. If it sinks, it's good; if it floats, throw it away. We also discover that the author likes free-range, organic eggs. Me too.

Before moving on to more complicated recipes, Roux takes us through boiled, poached, scrambled and fried eggs; omelettes and batters; sauces, from mayonnaise to mornay; and pastries. We get hints on making soufflés, crème brûlée and lemon curd.

In fact, this is the most useful book on egg cookery you can imagine, much of it vegetarian. The publishers have not been able to resist eggy-coloured endpapers and type, but the photography, by Martin Brigdale, is both appetizing and helpful.

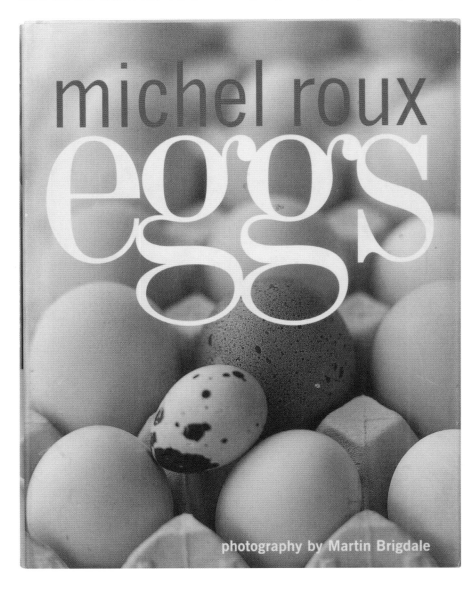

A Book for Cooks

soft-boiled eggs with vanilla caramel & brioche

serves 4

4 medium eggs
1 vanilla pod, split lengthways
4 slices of brioche loaf
for the caramel sauce
100g caster sugar
1 tsp lemon juice

A day in advance, put the raw eggs in an airtight container with the split vanilla pod, and refrigerate for 24 hours. The flavour of the vanilla will permeate the egg shells.

To make the caramel, put the sugar in a heavy-based, deep saucepan and dissolve over a gentle heat, stirring continuously. As soon as it turns to a light caramel colour, turn off the heat and pour in 100ml boiling water and the lemon juice. Take care as the caramel is liable to splutter and spit. Stir the caramel with a small whisk and cook over medium heat for 2–3 minutes, until it has a syrupy consistency. With the tip of a knife, scrape in a few seeds from the vanilla pod. Pour into a small jug and keep at room temperature.

Toast the brioche slices, remove the crusts and cut into soldiers; keep warm.

Soft-boil the eggs (see page 18) the way you like them, and put them into egg cups. Eat with a teaspoon, letting everyone drizzle some caramel over their egg and dip their brioche soldiers into the soft yolks.

'For anyone with a sweet tooth, this is breakfast heaven. Be prepared to cook extra eggs as they are addictive! Add a pinch of salt to the caramel for an interesting salty-sweet flavour.'

scrambled eggs

Scrambling is the finest way to cook eggs in my opinion. My brother, Albert, uses the classic method of cooking them slowly in a bain-marie, but I prefer the quicker, more modern approach of scrambling eggs in a pan over a low heat on a heat diffuser. Perfect for breakfast, lunch or a weekend brunch, they always look inviting, whether you present them on a plate, on toast or in warm pitta bread. For a taste of Mexico, I mix them with snipped herbs, chopped tomatoes and diced red onions, and serve them cold in tacos. When truffles are in season, simply macerate a few raw truffle peelings or trimmings in the eggs for several hours, then scramble them to make the most perfect dish imaginable. The recipes in this chapter take account of the seasons and they are some of my favourite egg dishes. I encourage you to try them all ...

poached eggs

45

Half-fill a wide saucepan, about 10cm deep, with unsalted water. Add 3 tbsp white wine vinegar and bring to to the boil.

Break an egg into a ramekin or small bowl and tip it gently into the pan, at the point where the water is bubbling.

Repeat with the other eggs, but do not poach more than 4 eggs at a time. Poach for about 1½ minutes.

Poached eggs are usually eaten as soon as they are ready, but they can be cooked ahead and kept in cold water in the fridge for up to 2 days. To reheat, immerse the poached eggs in a bowl of boiling water for 30 seconds only.

Using a slotted spoon or small skimmer, lift out the first egg and press the outside edge lightly to check it it is properly cooked.

As soon as the egg is cooked to your liking, remove it with the skimmer or slotted spoon. Either serve immediately, or transfer to a bowl of iced water and leave for about 10 minutes.

Trim the edges with a small knife to make a neat shape. This will also cut off the excess white that inevitably spreads during cooking. The poached egg is now ready.

Laura Santtini

Flash Cooking: Fit Fast Flavours for Busy People

Quadrille, London, 2011
176 pages
248 x 185 mm (9¾ x 7¼ in.)

Not only is this the newest cookery book here, but also it pioneers a new technique, which the publisher calls 'the everyday cooking of the future'. Basically, Santtini has invented a series of marinades, rubs, salts and pastes ('flavour bombs', as she calls them) that immediately enhance the taste of less complex foods, such as chicken, veal and salmon. The theory behind 'flash cooking' is difficult to describe, but the technique itself, once tried, is hard to ignore. Santtini has even invented an umami paste and powder for sale in the shops (umami being a newish, fifth taste, savoury in kind; see page 130); ingredients include tomato, anchovy, porcini mushrooms and Parmesan. The resulting product, she claims, can take its place alongside such common recipe additions as Worcestershire and soy sauce.

Take, for example, tuna steak marinaded in umami paste and fried in olive oil and garlic. Mirin and soy are added to the frying fish; then, more mirin and soy, plus a dab of butter, make up a sauce to be poured over the fish. Lime wedges and furikake (a dry Japanese condiment) are the only accompaniments. This takes just a few minutes to cook but has incredible flavour.

Santtini is half Italian, a quarter Persian, a bit of Sephardic Jew, plus some Irish and English, so mixing cultures comes naturally. I think that, as the range of readily available ingredients becomes more international in scope, this is the way forward for cooking. I find Santtini's missionary position on healthy eating, her philosophical asides and her jaunty style irritating, but nothing detracts from the gold in this alchemical book.

The concept behind *Flash Cooking* may be revolutionary, but the design, by Untitled, and the photography, by Adam Laycock, are conventional.

Quick Taste #5 Umami Paste Tuna Teriyaki

- 2 tuna steaks
- 2 tsp Taste #5 Umami Paste
- 3 tbsp olive oil
- freshly ground black pepper
- 3 garlic cloves, thinly sliced
- about 5 tbsp mirin (Japanese rice wine)
- about 2 tbsp soy sauce
- knob of butter

to serve
- furikake or sesame seeds
- lime wedges

The ratio of mirin to soy sauce should be around 2:1, even when splashing. This recipe is also delicious using beef or venison steaks, as well as Portobello mushroom steaks. The umami paste can be replaced with sun-dried tomato paste.

1 Rub 1 or 2 teaspoons of Taste #5 Umami Paste into each steak (depending on size but enough for it really to flavour the fish). Drizzle with olive oil on both sides, and add a good grinding of pepper. If time permits, leave to marinate for 20 minutes and for the steaks to come to room temperature.
2 Heat a non-stick frying pan with a little oil in it and, when hot, add the garlic slices. Cook the steaks on both sides to your taste (I like to sear the outside and leave the inside slightly blue).
3 Just before your steaks are cooked to taste, splash with a good glug of mirin and a splash of soy sauce (observing the 2:1 rule as per the note above). Remove the steaks from the pan and leave to rest on a warmed plate.
4 Lower the heat under the pan and deglaze it with another splash each of mirin and soy sauce, and another smaller squeeze of Taste #5 Umami Paste. Add a knob of butter, stir and pour this delicious glossy sauce over each steak.
5 Serve topped with furikake or sesame seeds and with some lime wedges on the side.

Flash Fish 33

Flash Glazed Cauliflower Cheese Steaks

- 1 large cauliflower
- 1 tbsp harissa paste (rose or ordinary)
- 1 tbsp olive oil, plus more for frying
- sea salt and freshly ground black pepper
- 75g feta cheese, crumbled

These vegetable steaks are wonderful served with Pomegranate Vinaigrette (page 23) and plenty of chopped fresh mint. The harissa glaze can be replaced with any Flash Glaze (page 13); omit the feta and serve with a Flash Finishing Yogurt (page 21) instead.
For a short cut, season the cauliflower steaks with any of the Flash Seasonings (page 12) and fry in a little olive oil. Sprinkle with a Flash Finishing Salt (page 19) and serve with any of the Finishing Yogurts (page 21) and a scattering of chopped fresh herbs.

1 Preheat the oven to 180°C (fan160°C)/350°F/gas mark 4.
2 Using a sharp knife, cut 2 thick slices of cauliflower, starting from the top centre of the head and cutting right down through the stalk. (Use what's left over for soup.)
3 Mix the harissa paste with the oil and brush this over the cauliflower steaks on both sides. Season with a little salt and pepper.
4 Fry the steaks in a lightly oiled pan until golden on both sides. Remove from the pan and place on a baking tray.
5 Brush the tops of the steaks with the remaining glaze and bake in the oven for about 10 minutes.
6 Top with cheese and return to the oven until the cauliflower is tender and the cheese has taken on some colour and is beginning to melt.

114 Flash Recipes

Laura Santtini

Niki Segnit

The Flavour Thesaurus: Pairings, Recipes and Ideas for the Creative Cook

Bloomsbury, London, 2010
400 pages
215 x 134 mm (8½ x 5¼ in.)

This book deservedly won both a Jeremy Round Award for Best First Book and an André Simon Award for the best food book. It is divided into sixteen 'flavour themes', such as 'Roasted', 'Earthy', 'Marine' and 'Bramble & Hedge', which are then subdivided into foodstuffs; 'Bramble & Hedge', for instance, consists of sections on rosemary, sage, juniper, thyme, mint, blackcurrant and blackberry. Specific flavour matches are then listed under each foodstuff; rosemary, for example, teams with chocolate, lemon, mushroom, pork and watermelon.

As I have rosemary growing in the garden and dark chocolate in the larder, I go for the recipe Little Pots of Chocolate and Rosemary Cream. My dessert dilemma is instantly solved.

But Segnit does far more than this. She discusses the science of flavours, she drops in history (Anne of Cleves wore rosemary in her hair when marrying Henry VIII) and, best of all, there are masses of suggestions from all round the world, written with humour and charm. 'Dill is complex, demanding and opinionated. Think Velma in *Scooby-Doo* (basil is Daphne).' Then the dill section travels to Laos, Finland and China by way of Sweden (dill and shellfish) and Poland (dill and potato).

The endpapers feature the contents of the *Thesaurus* in the form of a multicoloured pie chart, each segment representing a different chapter: 'Citrussy' is lime-coloured; 'Mustardy', of course, is mustardy. These diagrams, as well as the book's overall design, were the work of Peter Dawson of Grade Design. They are the only illustrations, but the complex index is a marvel, and the bibliography runs to five pages. A must for any collection.

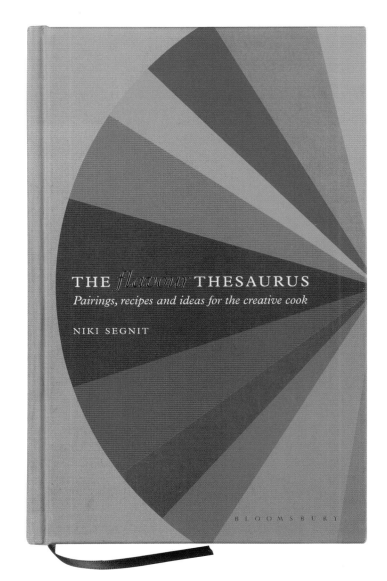

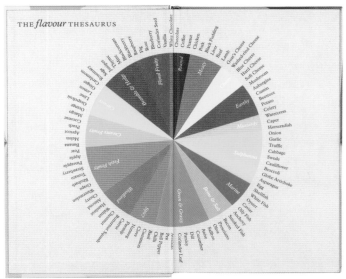

A Book for Cooks

SULPHUROUS

Onion

Garlic

Truffle

Cabbage

Swede

Cauliflower

Broccoli

Globe Artichoke

Asparagus

Egg

Onion

The hardest workers in the food business. Across the species that comprise the *Allium* genus, onion contributes a range of distinct flavours, from the light, herbal freshness of chive to the delicate, perfumed flavour of shallots, the tear-jerking boisterousness of the bulb onion, and the more vegetal, green-tinged earthiness of leeks and spring onions. Raw, onions lend a sharp, crisp edge to dips and salads; roasted or braised, they become sweet and succulent; fried until black-edged, they add a bittersweet dimension to a hotdog.

Onion & Anchovy: On a rainy day in Venice with friends, we went hunting for lunch in the backstreets of Dorsoduro. We chose a café with a short menu and no English spoken. Dorsoduro is a little less touristy than San Marco, the other side of the Grand Canal, and the proprietor and his wife seemed delighted to entertain some *inglesi* in their restaurant, as if the very idea of foreign visitors to Venice was a novelty. We wanted to try the local dish of bigoli pasta with anchovies and onions. A platter so enormous a gondolier might have punted it on to our table arrived, along with several pitchers of Soave. Bigoli is like wholewheat spaghetti but thicker, with a nutty, rugged character. It makes an ideal carrier for the sweet and salty mixture of onions and anchovies. You can make this with wholewheat spaghetti if you can't get the real thing. For two people, soften 3 thinly sliced large onions in 2–3 tbsp olive oil over a medium heat for about 20 minutes, without letting them colour. Once they've had about 10 minutes, add 4 or 5 chopped anchovies. Mix them in, break them up a bit and season, bearing in mind how salty the anchovy is to begin with. Cook the pasta until it is *al dente*. Drain it, reserving about a tablespoon of water, and return both to the pan. Place back on the heat and stir in the sauce. For an extra touch of sweetness, add a tablespoon of currants to the onion mix. You could try some of anchovy's other matches in this too: a little rosemary, perhaps, some blanched chopped broccoli or a sprinkling of capers.

Onion & Bacon: *See Bacon & Onion, page 169*
Onion & Beef: *See Beef & Onion, page 46*

Onion & Beetroot: Beetroot's sweetness is offset to great effect by raw onion. When cooked, onion takes on a sweetness of its own, which can be balanced out by vinegar in this beetroot and onion chutney to serve with homemade sausage rolls or in cheese sandwiches. Simmer 700g diced onions with 450g peeled, cored and diced eating apples in 300ml red wine vinegar until tender – this takes about 20 minutes. Add 700g diced cooked beetroot, another 250ml vinegar, 400g sugar, 1 tsp salt and 2 tsp ground ginger. Boil for a further 30 minutes. Spoon into sterilised jam jars while still hot and seal. Makes about 5 standard (450g) jars' worth.

107

---

notes of asparagus. Cook a handful of slivered almonds in a knob of butter over a low heat for 6–7 minutes, until golden. Remove from the heat, add 1 tsp lemon juice and ½ tsp salt, and pour over your cooked spears.

Almond & Banana: *See Banana & Almond, page 277*

Almond & Blackberry: There's no such thing as a free crumble. The price you pay for the astonishing late-summer abundance of inkily delicious blackberries is to walk away with pulls in your jumper and stains on your skirt. Almond's sweetness calms some of blackberry's wild spiciness in this blackberry and almond crumble. Butter a deep 21cm dish and fill with blackberries to a depth of 3–4cm. Sprinkle with 2 tbsp sugar. In another bowl, rub 175g plain flour and 75g butter together until they have a breadcrumb-like consistency. Stir in 75g golden caster sugar and 50g roughly chopped, toasted flaked almonds. Sprinkle this on top of the blackberries and bake at 200°C/Gas Mark 6 for about 30 minutes.

Almond & Blackcurrant: *See Blackcurrant & Almond, page 332*

Almond & Blueberry: Fine in your muesli, but you wouldn't want to meet them at a party, would you? Almond is pale, characterless and shy unless toasted. Blueberry is usually just plain insipid. The Spartan, Ivanhoe and Chandler cultivars of blueberry are worth looking out for, but beware the faint-praise-worthy Duke, described variously as mild and moderately flavoured. Things improve considerably if you add some almond extract or, even better, Amaretto, to whipping cream and whisk until the cream holds its shape. Fold in a handful of blueberries and some toasted almond slivers, holding back a few of the almonds to sprinkle over the top.

Almond & Butternut Squash: *See Butternut Squash & Almond, page 229*
Almond & Cardamom: *See Cardamom & Almond, page 313*
Almond & Cauliflower: *See Cauliflower & Almond, page 122*
Almond & Cherry: *See Cherry & Almond, page 247*

Almond & Chicken: In Spain, the Moorish influence is easily discernible in almond-thickened recipes such as *gallina en pepitoria*, a favourite dish at fiestas. Fry 1.5kg chicken joints in olive oil until golden, then set aside. Soften a finely chopped large onion in a little oil with 2 crushed garlic cloves and a bay leaf. Put the chicken back into the pot and pour over 150ml fino sherry and just enough chicken stock or water to cover. Bring to the boil, put a lid on and leave to simmer while you make the *picada* in Hazelnut & Garlic (page 240), except use 30 almonds and no hazelnuts and add a pinch of saffron, a few pinches of ground cloves and 1 tbsp parsley. When you have a paste, add it to the chicken mixture and continue to simmer until the chicken is completely cooked (45–60 minutes from beginning to simmer). Just before serving, you may need to

242

---

remove the chicken and keep it warm while you boil the sauce to reduce and thicken it. Many recipes suggest adding a couple of finely chopped boiled egg yolks at the end for the same reason. Serve with boiled rice.

Almond & Chilli: *See Chilli & Almond, page 207*
Almond & Chocolate: *See Chocolate & Almond, page 13*

Almond & Cinnamon: These work well together in cakes, pastries and biscuits. They also meet in one of the strata of Morocco's legendary *bastilla* pie. Spiced poached pigeon meat, very lightly scrambled eggs and a mixture of ground almonds, ground cinnamon and sugar are layered between super-fine leaves of *warqa* pastry. Be warned, *bastilla* is fiddly and time-consuming to make. It's faster to fly to Fez and back than attempt it at home – meaning, of course, it's utterly exquisite. As is *keneffa*, the lesser-known sweet version that's often served at weddings. This intersperses the same delicate *warqa* pastry with cinnamon and almonds. My anglicised take on this treat is to make puff pastry horns and fill them with a cinnamon- and almond-flavoured *crème pâtissière*.

Almond & Coconut: When vanilla extract is called for in coconut cakes, biscuits and puddings, try substituting almond extract for half of it. You'll get the same flavour-bolstering, rounded quality but with a nuttier, more sympathetic edge.

Almond & Coffee: *See Coffee & Almond, page 19*
Almond & Fig: *See Fig & Almond, page 339*
Almond & Garlic: *See Garlic & Almond, page 111*

Almond & Ginger: Gingerbread and marzipan on cold night air is the smell of a Christmas market. Add the warm notes of cinnamon, clove and lemon basking in simmering red wine, with chestnuts and bratwursts scorching over coals, and you can enjoy your own miniature *Weihnachtsmarkt* in the comfort of your own home. It's traditional to cut the gingerbread into the shape of buildings and people, the marzipan into animals. In 1993, Roland Mesnier, the Clintons' pastry chef, made a gingerbread White House and no fewer than 21 marzipan likenesses of Socks the cat.

Almond & Grape: *See Grape & Almond, page 251*
Almond & Hard Cheese: *See Hard Cheese & Almond, page 65*
Almond & Hazelnut: *See Hazelnut & Almond, page 238*
Almond & Lamb: *See Lamb & Almond, page 49*

Almond & Lemon: Ground almond soothes lemon's sharpness in cakes and tarts. In Kew, southwest London, deep little tarts called maids of honour are baked and sold at The Original Maids of Honour Shop. They're said to

243

Dan Silverman and JoAnn Cianciulli

Lever House: The Lever House Cookbook

Clarkson Potter, New York, 2006
240 pages
249 x 250 mm (9¾ x 9⅞ in.)

This book is an unusual combination: architecture and food. Lever House opened in New York in 1952 and, according to architectural critic Lewis Mumford, the public reacted as though it were the eighth wonder of the world. It was the city's first curtain-wall skyscraper, built in the International style, and the large number of visitors almost brought the lifts to a standstill. It was designed by Gordon Bunshaft of the then obscure firm of Skidmore, Owings & Merrill. The first eighteen pages of the book are all about the building.

Today, as photographs of the restaurant show, the design has an eerily dated feel: lots of blonde wood and aeroplane styling (which was, of course, very smart in 1952, when only 3 per cent of Americans had travelled by plane). Wisely, the restaurant's owners have not messed about with the interior, and the signature hexagon shapes, used on its ceilings and windows, appear throughout.

Dan Silverman, the much-lauded executive chef, uses many cheffy tricks (notably in the presentation of the food), but, essentially, his dishes are not that complex: Grilled Black Sea Bass with Cilantro-Mint Sauce and Sautéed Spinach, for example, or Haricots Verts with Pork Butter. Lever House has a famous 'cookie' plate on its menu, and recipes for four varieties are included here.

This book is gastro porn par excellence, with close-ups of ingredients, steaks and lobsters curiously mixed with black-and-white shots of architecture. The first double-page spread shows a blueprint of the restaurant. I wish I could tell you more, but the publishers treat captions as a scarce commodity.

It is now normal for restaurant-based cookbooks to use photos of the kitchen, the staff, the dining rooms and the waiters. *Lever House*, designed by Level, concentrates on the iconic building of its title.

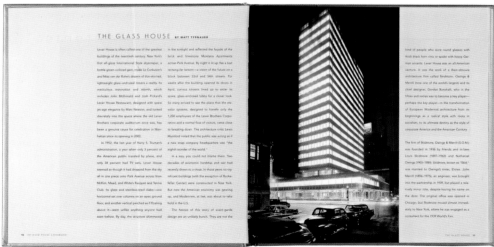

Vegetables play an important role on the menu at Lever House. They are an integral part of how we do what we do and how we do it so well. I have worked hard to cultivate relationships with an ever-widening group of farmers and purveyors to supply us with the highest-quality fruits and vegetables available.

The Union Square Greenmarket, being a stone's throw from the restaurant, has also been a great source of inspiration. It is always exciting to see the first local strawberries, corn, or squash blossoms at farmers' stands—and challenging to try to think of great ways to showcase these products. Sometimes, the best thing we can do is quite simple, such as haricots verts with shallots and butter (page 169). And then sometimes it can be fun (and quite tasty!) to do something a bit more elaborate, like our potato gratin (page 175). Whatever sides you ultimately decide to make, be sure that the ingredients are fresh, and that you give their cooking and seasoning the attention that is their due.

RISOTTO WITH LOBSTER, SWEET CORN, AND GARDEN PEAS SERVES 4

When local white and bicolor corn become available in New York, this is one way for us to showcase it. Succulent lobster meat, freshly shucked peas, and lots of sweet corn combine to make a really wonderful summer risotto. If you can't find savory and don't want to use thyme, you could substitute fresh basil. Traditionally, risottos containing seafood do not include cheese, but feel free to add a little freshly grated Parmigiano if you like.

1 tablespoon sea salt
1 live lobster (1½ pounds)
5 tablespoons unsalted butter
3 large shallots, minced
1 cup Arborio rice
Generous pinch of kosher salt and freshly ground black pepper
½ cup dry white wine, such as Sauvignon Blanc
2 ears sweet white corn, shucked, kernels cut from the cob (about 1 cup)
1 cup sweet peas, frozen or fresh (if using fresh peas, blanch for 2 minutes in salted boiling water; if using frozen, run under cool water for 2 minutes to thaw)
1 teaspoon chopped fresh savory or thyme leaves
Juice of ½ lemon, if desired

Fill a large stockpot three-quarters of the way with water and add the sea salt; bring to a rapid boil over medium-high heat. Carefully ease the lobster into the pot, and cook for 8 minutes, until the shell is bright red. Using tongs, carefully remove the lobster to a side platter.

Working with rubber gloves, use a sort of sideways twist to break the legs, claws, and tails off of the bodies. Using a big knife, split the tails in half lengthwise. Gently wash away any visible veins or roe with cold water. On a work surface, rest the tails on their sides and, using the palm of your hand, press down on them to break off the outer shells; cut the tail

meat into bite-size pieces. With the back of a knife, crack the claws and wiggle the meat out from the shell. Place the knuckles on the work surface, whack them open, remove the shell, and carefully pick out the meat with your fingers. You should have at least 1 cup of meat.

Heat the stock in a saucepan over medium-low flame; keep warm at a simmer, but don't let it boil.

Place a large sauté pan over high heat and add 3 tablespoons of butter. When the butter is melted, add the shallots and cook them for 3 minutes, until translucent, stirring often. Add the rice, and stir for a minute or two, until the grains are opaque and slightly toasted; season with salt and pepper.

Deglaze with the wine and cook until almost evaporated. Pour in 1 cup of the warm stock, stir until the rice has absorbed all the liquid, and then add another cup. Keep stirring while adding the stock 1 cup at a time, allowing the rice to drink it in before adding more, until the rice has been cooking for about 12 minutes.

Fold in the corn and cook for 1 minute to incorporate. Add the peas and savory, cook another minute or two, until the rice is almost tender. Taste the rice frequently at this point, keeping in mind that it will continue to cook even after you turn off the flame—it should not be dry or mushy.

Fold in the lobster, adjust the seasoning, give a squeeze of lemon juice if you like, and finish the risotto with the remaining 2 tablespoons of butter. Serve immediately in warm bowls.

Nigel Slater

Appetite

Fourth Estate, London, 2000
448 pages
245 x 188 mm (9⅝ x 7⅜ in.)

I had real difficulty deciding which of Slater's books to choose. But this one best demonstrates his philosophy: food and cooking are fun. 'I want to tell you about the pleasure, the sheer unbridled joy, of cooking without a recipe', he starts. Slater believes that following recipes is just slavishly obeying others' rules. Despite this, his book is actually full of recipes, but ones that act as steps to further experiment.

Slater lists a survival guide: you do not have to cook every day; you can live on home-made soup and toast. And, once you drop the idea that cooking is a duty, unwillingly borne, you get his point. He explains that careful seasoning makes food taste better, and describes how to match tastes, the kit you need and how to work the seasons. The first recipe, A Really Good and Very Easy White Loaf, doesn't appear until page 158. This is followed by two tomato sauces. I tried just one; it is brilliant. Next on my list is A Simple, Useful Sauce for Every Day. Slater doesn't insist that pasta must be home-made, and concedes that a sausage sandwich 'is quite as delicious as a Thai chicken curry that uses eighteen ingredients' (but a Thai curry with nineteen ingredients is listed, too). In fact, he removes the guilt and replaces it with delight.

The book, designed by Vivid Design, is beautiful – as you might expect – and Jonathan Lovekin's photographs are as tasty as the recipes. The typeface is sans serif, while the dedication is to Slater's dogs, which probably eat better than most of us. And why not?

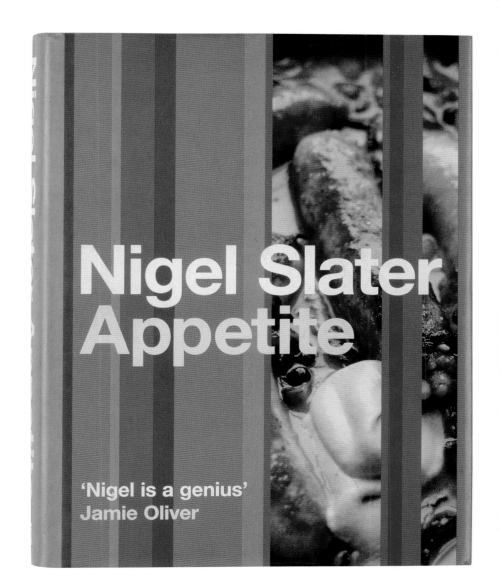

Whiz the curry paste ingredients in a food processor till you have a vivid, spicily fragrant slush.

Peel and roughly chop the pumpkin or squash. Cut the aubergines lengthwise into quarters and then into fat chunks (small round ones can simply be quartered). Fry them in the oil – a deep frying pan will suffice – until both pumpkin and aubergine are softening, then add the mushrooms. The heat should be quite high, as the vegetables need to brown here and there. Spoon' in about four tablespoons of the paste (more can be added later but it is too early to taste yet) and let it fry and sizzle. Stir so it doesn't stick.

Pour in the coconut milk and stock, scatter in the green peppercorns and leave to simmer until the vegetables are fully tender. Taste the curry, adding a little more paste if you think it needs it, in which case you will have to cook it for a few minutes longer. Either way it should be ready within ten minutes. Scatter the herbs over. You will need some rice here, either fragrant Thai rice or unauthentic but nevertheless delicious basmati.

and more

♦ **a green chicken curry.** Swap the vegetables for 750g boned chicken pieces and fry them off instead of the vegetables. This is unauthentic (Thai cooks just slide the raw chicken into the curry sauce) but I find frying it gives a better flavour.

♦ **a green prawn curry.** Use 500g large prawns instead of the aubergines and squash. No need to fry them off, just throw them in the curry sauce after you have added the coconut milk.

♦ **a fish curry.** Check out the Indian one on page 305, but you might like to make a Thai version from the blueprint above. Try adding approximately 750g mixed prepared fish (can I suggest monkfish, briefly cooked-open mussels, and prawns?) just after you have added the coconut milk. The fish will need just ten minutes to cook.

♦ **a mushroom and spinach curry.** Drop the aubergine and squash from the ingredients above and increase the quantity of mushrooms to 650g. Chestnut, button and oyster mushrooms are good – add the more fragile ones last, in this case the oyster mushrooms. Cut up any that seem very big before you fry them. When the coconut milk comes to the boil, slide in some spinach leaves – a fat handful per person – that you have quickly cooked and squeezed dry.

---

grilled chicken for a summer barbecue

I will not pretend to be a fan of the barbecue but, perversely, I do love eating out of doors. Of course, food eaten in the open air cannot make even so much as a nod towards sophistication. It must be punchy, loud and spicy. What I call Food With Balls. In reality you may find that all you need is a slightly heavier hand than usual with the salt, which seems to have a magical effect on anything cooked over the embers of a fire. Chilli, garlic, ginger and mint are my favourite barbecue flavourings. I may be alone in this, but to me they just seem to feel right with anything that has a slightly charred skin, such as chicken or lamb that has caught on the bars of the grill.

Makes enough for 4 skewers

yogurt – a large teacup
mint leaves – a loose handful
red and green chillies – 1 or 2 of each, depending on their heat
ground turmeric – a teaspoon
garam masala – a mild one, about a teaspoonful
ginger – a thumb-sized piece
a lime
chicken – 500g boned white and brown meat

Scoop the yogurt into a mixing bowl. Chop the mint leaves and chillies and add them to the yogurt with the turmeric and garam masala. Peel the ginger and grate it coarsely, then fold it into the yogurt with the grated zest of the lime and a few grinds of pepper. Keep the lime for squeezing over the finished chicken.

Cut the chicken into large chunks. They should be small enough to thread comfortably on to a skewer but large enough to remain juicy. In other words, about the size of a chicken liver. Dunk the chicken pieces into the spiced yogurt and set aside for at least an hour. If you can leave them for twice as long, then so much the better. No longer though; leave them overnight and they will get wet and woolly. Thread the chicken on to metal or wooden skewers. If you are using wooden ones it is best to soak them first so they do not burn. Get your griddle pan or barbecue warm (I will not go into the intricacies of barbecuing here, you probably know more about it than I do, anyway).

Constance Spry and Rosemary Hume

The Constance Spry Cookery Book

J.M. Dent, London, 1956
1246 pages
234 x 153 mm (9¼ x 6 in.)

Constance Spry was to twentieth-century cooks what Mrs Beeton was to those of the nineteenth. If her huge tome is some 500 pages shorter than Beeton's (page 32), it's because it doesn't include first aid or veterinary tips. Rather, advice given sticks to kitchen design, store cupboards and gadgets, alongside hundreds of recipes.

Spry was a born teacher: in Ireland in the early 1900s she lectured on first aid; then, as a headmistress in London's East End, she taught teenage factory workers flower arranging, eventually becoming society's favourite flower arranger. After the Second World War, she opened a cookery school with Rosemary Hume at Winkfield Place near Windsor, Berkshire (where she died in 1960, having fallen down the stairs. Her last words were, apparently, 'Someone else can arrange this'). Behind the bossy façade was a somewhat rackety character who, according to writer Diana Souhami, had a lesbian affair with the painter Gluck (Hannah Gluckstein). Spry's most famous dish, Coronation Chicken, created for foreign delegates at the coronation of Elizabeth II in 1953 (see opposite, bottom), was actually the work of her co-author, who, you note, barely features in the credits.

Griping apart, this is an extremely useful compendium, ranging from the optimum size for chips (about the width and length of a man's little finger) to sucking-pig. The dishes are not as old-fashioned as you might imagine, and there are lots of suggestions on accompaniments (and which other cookery books to own). The book has been so popular that there are plenty of early editions to be had for a modest sum. But certainly it should be in any comprehensive collection.

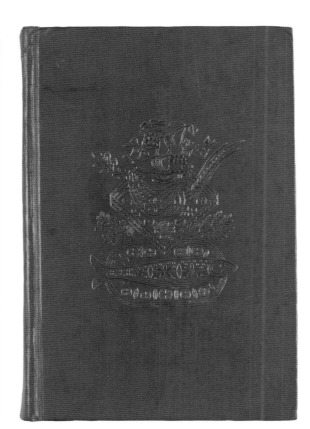

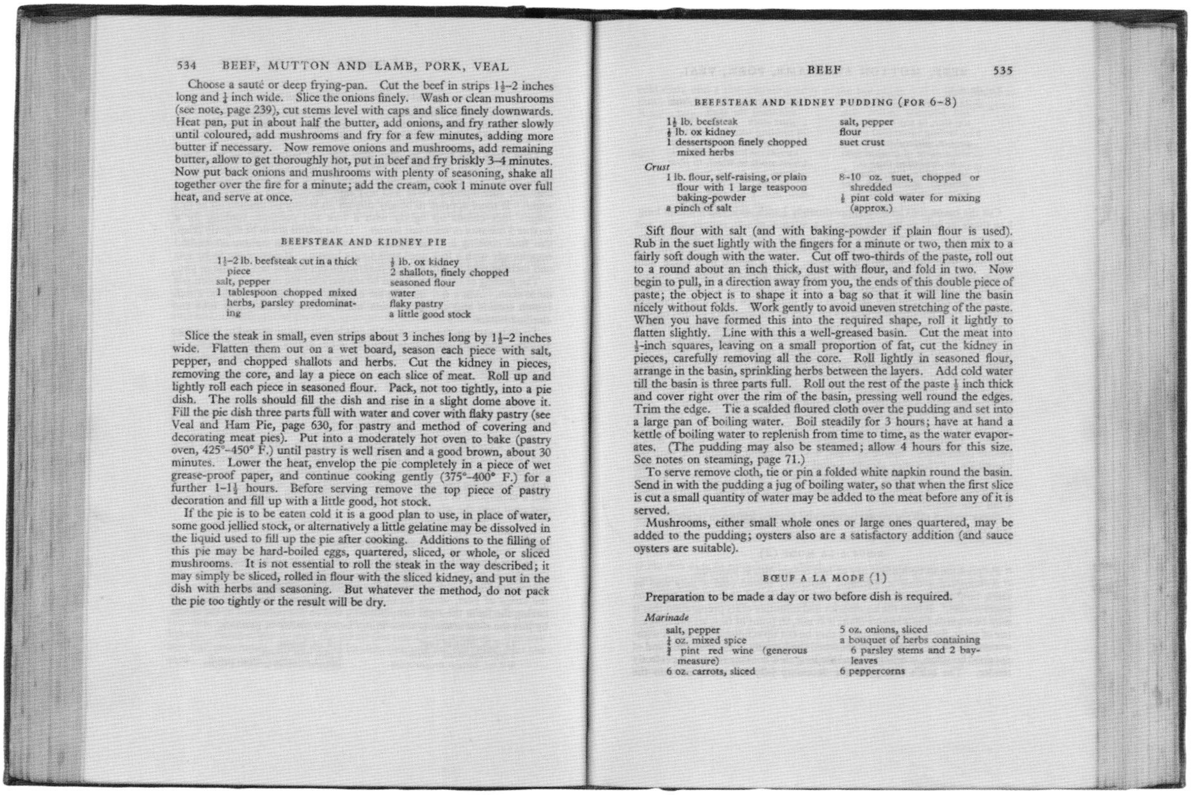

534 BEEF, MUTTON AND LAMB, PORK, VEAL

Choose a sauté or deep frying-pan. Cut the beef in strips 1½–2 inches long and ¼ inch wide. Slice the onions finely. Wash or clean mushrooms (see note, page 239), cut stems level with caps and slice finely downwards. Heat pan, put in about half the butter, add onions, and fry rather slowly until coloured, add mushrooms and fry for a few minutes, adding more butter if necessary. Now remove onions and mushrooms, add remaining butter, allow to get thoroughly hot, put in beef and fry briskly 3–4 minutes. Now put back onions and mushrooms with plenty of seasoning, shake all together over the fire for a minute; add the cream, cook 1 minute over full heat, and serve at once.

BEEFSTEAK AND KIDNEY PIE

1½–2 lb. beefsteak cut in a thick piece
salt, pepper
1 tablespoon chopped mixed herbs, parsley predominating
½ lb. ox kidney
2 shallots, finely chopped
seasoned flour
water
flaky pastry
a little good stock

Slice the steak in small, even strips about 3 inches long by 1½–2 inches wide. Flatten them out on a wet board, season each piece with salt, pepper, and chopped shallots and herbs. Cut the kidney in pieces, removing the core, and lay a piece on each slice of meat. Roll up and lightly roll each piece in seasoned flour. Pack, not too tightly, into a pie dish. The rolls should fill the dish and rise in a slight dome above it. Fill the pie dish three parts full with water and cover with flaky pastry (see Veal and Ham Pie, page 630, for pastry and method of covering and decorating meat pies). Put into a moderately hot oven to bake (pastry oven, 425°–450° F.) until pastry is well risen and a good brown, about 30 minutes. Lower the heat, envelop the pie completely in a piece of wet grease-proof paper, and continue cooking gently (375°–400° F.) for a further 1–1½ hours. Before serving remove the top piece of pastry decoration and fill up with a little good, hot stock.

If the pie is to be eaten cold it is a good plan to use, in place of water, some good jellied stock, or alternatively a little gelatine may be dissolved in the liquid used to fill up the pie after cooking. Additions to the filling of this pie may be hard-boiled eggs, quartered, sliced, or whole, or sliced mushrooms. It is not essential to roll the steak in the way described; it may simply be sliced, rolled in flour with the sliced kidney, and put in the dish with herbs and seasoning. But whatever the method, do not pack the pie too tightly or the result will be dry.

BEEF 535

BEEFSTEAK AND KIDNEY PUDDING (FOR 6–8)

1½ lb. beefsteak
½ lb. ox kidney
1 dessertspoon finely chopped mixed herbs
salt, pepper
flour
suet crust

Crust
1 lb. flour, self-raising, or plain flour with 1 large teaspoon baking-powder
a pinch of salt
8–10 oz. suet, chopped or shredded
½ pint cold water for mixing (approx.)

Sift flour with salt (and with baking-powder if plain flour is used). Rub in the suet lightly with the fingers for a minute or two, then mix to a fairly soft dough with the water. Cut off two-thirds of the paste, roll out to a round about an inch thick, dust with flour, and fold in two. Now begin to pull, in a direction away from you, the ends of this double piece of paste; the object is to shape it into a bag so that it will line the basin nicely without folds. Work gently to avoid uneven stretching of the paste. When you have formed this into the required shape, roll it lightly to flatten slightly. Line with this a well-greased basin. Cut the meat into ½-inch squares, leaving on a small proportion of fat, cut the kidney in pieces, carefully removing all the core. Roll lightly in seasoned flour, arrange in the basin, sprinkling herbs between the layers. Add cold water till the basin is three parts full. Roll out the rest of the paste ½ inch thick and cover right over the rim of the basin, pressing well round the edges. Trim the edge. Tie a scalded floured cloth over the pudding and set into a large pan of boiling water. Boil steadily for 3 hours; have at hand a kettle of boiling water to replenish from time to time, as the water evaporates. (The pudding may also be steamed; allow 4 hours for this size. See notes on steaming, page 71.)

To serve remove cloth, tie or pin a folded white napkin round the basin. Send in with the pudding a jug of boiling water, so that when the first slice is cut a small quantity of water may be added to the meat before any of it is served.

Mushrooms, either small whole ones or large ones quartered, may be added to the pudding; oysters also are a satisfactory addition (and sauce oysters are suitable).

BŒUF A LA MODE (1)

Preparation to be made a day or two before dish is required.

Marinade
salt, pepper
¼ oz. mixed spice
¾ pint red wine (generous measure)
6 oz. carrots, sliced
5 oz. onions, sliced
a bouquet of herbs containing 6 parsley stems and 2 bay-leaves
6 peppercorns

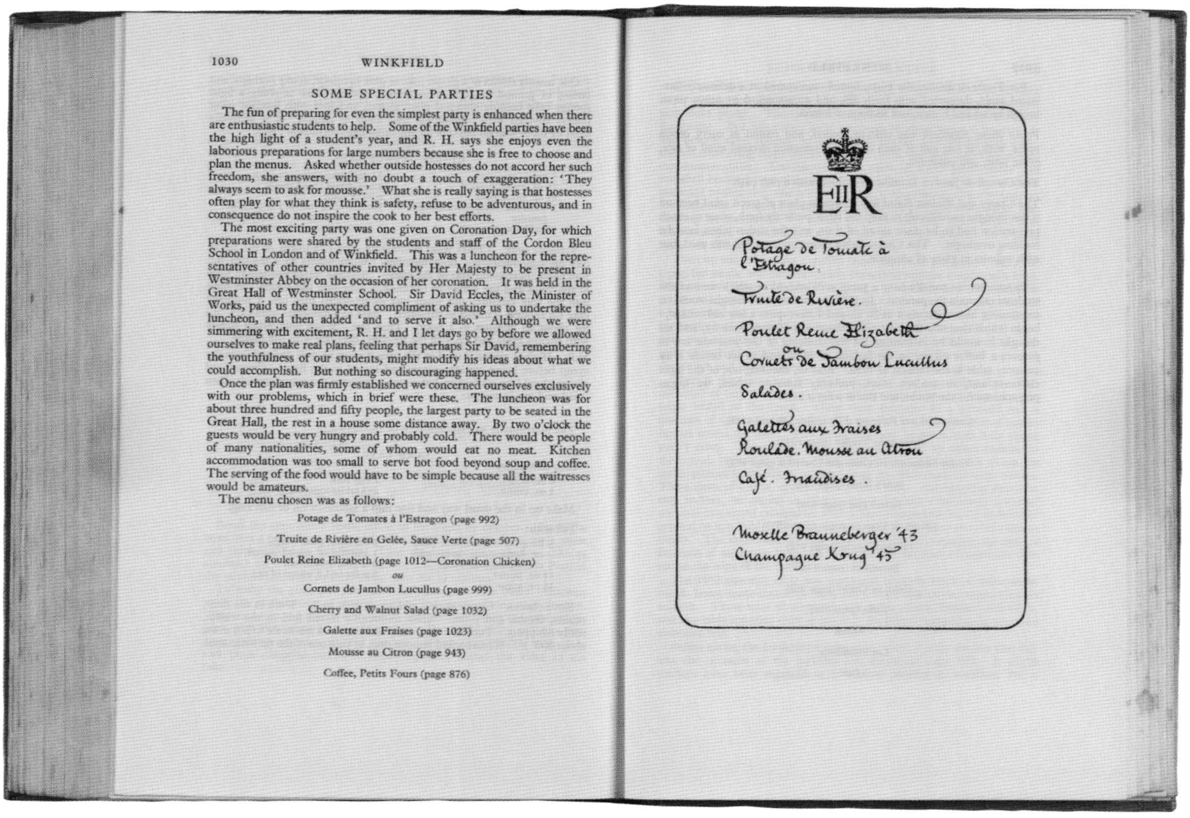

1030 WINKFIELD

SOME SPECIAL PARTIES

The fun of preparing for even the simplest party is enhanced when there are enthusiastic students to help. Some of the Winkfield parties have been the high light of a student's year, and R. H. says she enjoys even the laborious preparations for large numbers because she is free to choose and plan the menus. Asked whether outside hostesses do not accord her such freedom, she answers, with no doubt a touch of exaggeration: 'They always seem to ask for mousse.' What she is really saying is that hostesses often play for what they think is safety, refuse to be adventurous, and in consequence do not inspire the cook to her best efforts.

The most exciting party was one given on Coronation Day, for which preparations were shared by the students and staff of the Cordon Bleu School in London and of Winkfield. This was a luncheon for the representatives of other countries invited by Her Majesty to be present in Westminster Abbey on the occasion of her coronation. It was held in the Great Hall of Westminster School. Sir David Eccles, the Minister of Works, paid us the unexpected compliment of asking us to undertake the luncheon, and then added 'and to serve it also.' Although we were simmering with excitement, R. H. and I let days go by before we allowed ourselves to make real plans, feeling that perhaps Sir David, remembering the youthfulness of our students, might modify his ideas about what we could accomplish. But nothing so discouraging happened.

Once the plan was firmly established we concerned ourselves exclusively with our problems, which in brief were these. The luncheon was for about three hundred and fifty people, the largest party to be seated in the Great Hall, the rest in a house some distance away. By two o'clock the guests would be very hungry and probably cold. There would be people of many nationalities, some of whom would eat no meat. Kitchen accommodation was too small to serve hot food beyond soup and coffee. The serving of the food would have to be simple because all the waitresses would be amateurs.

The menu chosen was as follows:

Potage de Tomates à l'Estragon (page 992)

Truite de Rivière en Gelée, Sauce Verte (page 507)

Poulet Reine Elizabeth (page 1012—Coronation Chicken)

ou

Cornets de Jambon Lucullus (page 999)

Cherry and Walnut Salad (page 1032)

Galette aux Fraises (page 1023)

Mousse au Citron (page 943)

Coffee, Petits Fours (page 876)

Jeanne Strang

Goose Fat and Garlic: Country Recipes from South-West France

Kyle Cathie, London, 2003 (revised edition; first published 1991)
352 pages
234 x 156 mm (9¼ x 6⅛ in.)

The cuisine of south-west France, so carefully described in this book, is both specific and delicious. I can't have too much of it – and I certainly own at least four cookery books describing it lovingly. This one is the best, probably because Jeanne Strang lived in the region for forty years, eating, cooking and researching the food over the decades. Before that, she helped Raymond Postgate with the first *Good Food Guide*, launched in 1951.

Goose Fat and Garlic is more than a recipe book: it also describes the way of life in the region, which stretches from the Limousin in the north to the Pyrennes in the south, and where, as the title implies, the cooking medium of choice is goose fat rather than olive oil.

Strang reports that, deciding on goose for Christmas lunch one year, she was given a hissing, flapping bird. Then, because Christmas in France is a quiet, somnolent day, all the electricity was turned off for repairs. Crayfish also come live, from Strang's own stream, and there are the ethical questions surrounding foie gras (I was given some in Périgord, and it was delicious – but I won't buy it). Then Strang explodes the idea that Agen prunes come from Agen (Villeneuve-sur-Lot, actually) or Bayonne ham from Bayonne (Orthez). She tells us how to cure a ham – you need a cool, dry cellar – and offers four recipes for daube (braised beef stew). And, should you wish to make walnut tart in the style of Madame Sylvestre from Bouzic, this is where to look.

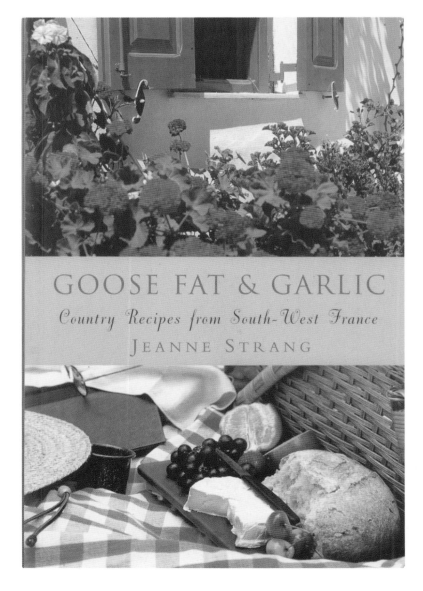

A Book for Cooks

in mid-summer. These bulbs or *têtes* are left on their stalks for three months to dry in the warm air out of direct sunlight so it is no uncommon sight to see rows of the huge bunches hanging to dry under the eaves of a barn or on a covered balcony. They are then brought to market in October. By careful purchase or clever planting, everyone has a store of garlic throughout the year. Garlic likes to grow in a moist but sandy soil with plenty of sun to plump out the cloves.

In the Garonne valley around Toulouse there are huge areas of garlic production. Grenade-sur-Garonne claims to produce the best garlic in the South-West but it is also grown extensively over towards Albi in the Tarn. A rival area, around Saint Clar towards the Gers, specializes in *l'ail blond de Lomagne*. This, together with another white-headed variety (it is the colour of the outer skins of the cloves which earn them their names) called *l'ail rond de Limousin*, appears first, to be followed by *le violet* with its large, purple-veined heads which keep quite well. But these are out-classed by *l'ail rose de Lautrec*. This is the most expensive variety as it is the long-keeper and so is always in great demand. There are special garlic fairs from July onwards but at local markets the garlic stalls also appear, laden with neatly-bound bunches. Garlic is sold by weight and the tresses usually weigh half a kilo or one kilo. How many heads make up one kilo depends on the variety and their freshness. There are on average eight *gousses* (cloves) per *tête* (head), though there are variations in size of the cloves, with the *violets* and *blancs* slightly larger than the *rose*. Recipes in this book refer to a clove of these local varieties – which are roughly the size of a butter bean. All of them are larger than those imported from the New World and which appear out of season in English and French shops and are much stronger.

The green 'germ' which may start to sprout inside a clove in winter can be indigestible and for that reason, some cooks remove it before chopping. By the way, we have never seen a garlic crusher in a peasant kitchen: chopping or gently crushing with the blade of a knife are the methods recommended locally.

LE CASSOULET

SEVEN GREEK CITIES claimed to be the birthplace of Homer. As many towns in the South-West of France claim the distinction of having invented the *cassoulet*. Definitive proof would be a prize dearly to be won, for the *cassoulet* is to many the emblem of the region, like roast beef to the British or *sauerkraut* to the Germans. Essentially, it is a bean stew, perfumed with garlic and goose or pork fat and enriched by a variety of fresh or preserved meats which vary according to district. But some magic chemistry manages to fuse the aromas and textures to produce a creamy amalgam of flavours, topped with a crispy crust which sets off to perfection the gently bubbling richness beneath. It is a gloriously original and distinctive dish: no other cuisine has produced anything quite like it. It is so different from any other *plat* that it is difficult to know which section to put it in – hence this one all to itself.

Connoisseurs of the *cassoulet* are justified in claiming that the beans are just as important as the meats. Anyone, they say, can prepare a *confit* of duck or goose, or make sausages in the Toulouse style or provide from his own farm or buy at the local butcher any other meat that is required. But the beans are something quite different. As many towns and villages claim to produce the finest beans as to have invented the dish itself. Tarbes, Lavelanet, Luchon, Pamiers, Cazères; the list is endless and each has its supporters. The bean is elevated almost to poetic status with fancy claims to the derivation of its patois name *mounjetto* – '*un petit moine*' perhaps. More likely that the word is derived from the

---

many other unidentifiable pieces of pig, all described as *fritons*. These cheaper cuts are best crisped up in the frying pan and served with lentils or beans.

But there remain some parts which do not preserve well by this method, so these are eaten fresh. In any case, having devised so many ways of looking after future needs, the farmer is entitled to the treat of some fresh pork – especially at the beginning of Lent – and what better when the weather is still cold than a comforting stew of pig's trotters with *flageolets*.

Pig's feet are eaten all over France. Breadcrumbed and deep-fried, they are called *Ste-Ménéhould* up in the North-East. Otherwise they are good on a bed of mashed potato with a vinaigrette, or stuffed with a savoury meat mixture. Cooks in the South-West remain faithful to the following dish. Two days are needed for it in English kitchens because fresh *flageolets* are unobtainable in England. If you can get fresh ones in France and are cooking this dish there, you can telescope operations into one day.

LES PIEDS DE PORC AUX FLAGEOLETS
Pig's trotters with flageolet beans

Serves 2

2 pig's trotters, cleaned and scraped	bay leaf
2 onions	125 ml (4 fl oz) dry white wine
2 carrots	125 ml (4 fl oz) red wine vinegar
1 stick celery	salt, pepper
3 large cloves garlic	125 g (4 oz) dried *flageolets*

1st day: put the trotters in a casserole with a close-fitting lid. Add one of the onions, a carrot, the celery, one garlic clove, all chopped, plus the bay leaf, wine and half the vinegar. Season. Add water to cover, bring it slowly to the boil and barely simmer for 4 hours. Remove the trotters and keep in a cool place overnight, together with the strained stock in which they were cooked. Put the *flageolets* to soak.
2nd day: Sweat the other onion, carrot and 2 cloves of garlic, all chopped, in the fat which has congealed on top of the stock. Put in the trotters, the beans and the rest of the vinegar. Add seasoning and cover with the stock. Bring to the boil and simmer, covered, for about 1 hour by which time the beans should have absorbed most of the liquor and thickened it, though it may be necessary to top up with a little more if it is all absorbed before the beans are cooked.

Another way of presenting pig's trotters in a thoroughly country style comes from the upper valley of the Lot where they add some lean beef to a stew which might otherwise have been just too rich. The flaming of the trotters helps to reduce the fattiness too.

LA POUTEILLE
Stew of pig's trotters with beef

Serves 6

4 pig's trotters, split down the middle	1 small glass *eau-de-vie* or brandy
1 tablespoon goose or pork fat	salt and pepper to taste
8 shallots or 1 large onion, thinly sliced	60 g (2 oz) flour
	1 bottle red wine
700 g (1½ lb) lean stewing beef, cut into 5 cm (2-inch) cubes	bouquet garni
	700 g (1½ lb) potatoes, peeled and cubed

Ask your butcher to split the trotters for you. Clean and dry them. Melt the fat in a heavy frying pan and gently brown the trotters all over without letting the fat get too hot. Meanwhile warm a flameproof casserole and preheat your oven to 150°C, 300°F, Gas Mark 2.

Transfer the trotters to the warmed casserole and keep them hot. In the remaining fat in the frying pan, sweat the shallots or onion, then add the beef pieces to seal them. Then transfer the onion and beef to the casserole and put this over a medium heat on the top of the stove while you *flamber* the contents. Warm the *eau-de-vie* in a soup ladle, set it alight and pour quickly over the meat in the casserole. When the flames have died down, season well and sprinkle in the flour. Add the wine gradually, mixing it with the flour, and bring the sauce back to the boil. Add the bouquet garni, cover the pot and transfer it back to the oven, leaving it to cook for 2 hours. Check from time to time that it is not simmering too fast.

After this time, add the potatoes. See that the pot comes back to the simmer, if necessary heating it on the top of the stove. Continue to cook for another half hour or so, until the potatoes are ready. Check the seasoning and serve on to hot plates.

---·---

Moving up off the ground a little, one arrives at the *jambonneau*, literally 'baby ham' which is a polite title for the shin or hock. The hind ones are more tender and contain less bone. After a light salting, they are often

David Tanis

Heart of the Artichoke and Other Kitchen Journeys

Artisan, New York, 2010
352 pages
250 x 190 mm (9⅞ x 7½ in.)

David Tanis is one of the chefs at Alice Waters's Chez Panisse in California (see page 200), a culinary stable as prolific as London's River Café – perhaps because both have women bosses. Uniquely, however, he spends six months in charge of Chez Panisse's kitchen and the rest of the year in Paris, writing and cooking for private dinner parties in a tiny kitchen. He is both professional chef and amateur party-giver: an ideal combination.

Unlike many cookery books, this one gets personal. The first section includes Tanis's 'private rituals'. These range from peeling apples to travelling with harissa, chillies, limes, sea salt, cheese and a penknife. An idea worth copying. He comments on the minutiae of making pesto (pick the basil leaves from the stalks and leave in the cool overnight) and the flavour of smoke. His menus, says Waters, 'are incomparable. They all share a certain quality of harmonious simplicity uniquely his'. So it's fitting that the book is arranged by season, by menu. For example, under 'Cooking American' in the autumn section, we have Shrimp 'Cocktail' in a Glass, Peppery Chicken Wings, Fried Green Tomatoes, Spicy Cabbage Slaw, Scalloped Corn and Molasses Pecan Squares, recipes that make the heart beat more strongly.

In common with so many American cookery books, this one is beautiful. The cover is a tasty aubergine colour, the endpapers a citrus lime. The photographs, by Christopher Hirsheimer, are, like the recipes, both simple and seductive, occasionally bursting into double-page spreads. The designer, Jan Derevjanik, has rightly seen no need for any other flourishes.

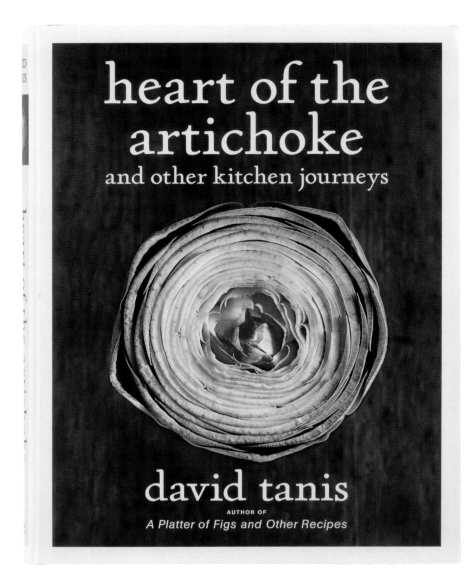

Kitchen Rituals

Ordinary, private moments in the kitchen should be celebrated and savored. The smell of freshly brewed coffee and toasting bread is always heady. Peeling carrots and onions for a simple stew can be meditative. Boiling pasta while chopping garlic hits a primordial nerve. Washing lettuces in cool water is refreshing and relaxing. Are you cooking a fine humble meal for yourself? An omelette to share with a friend? Mixing up a batch of sausage? Making a small pot of jam?

Every cook has his rituals. Here are some of mine.

11.

Mexican Breakfast

The Mexican dish chilaquiles is a quick, satisfying breakfast made from leftover tortillas. Every cook makes chilaquiles differently. Sometimes it's lightly fried strips of day-old tortilla, mixed with a spicy tomato salsa and served as an accompaniment to fried eggs. Other versions are long simmered and quite saucy, and some add meat, usually chicken. My go-to variation is more like a cross between a stir-fry and scrambled eggs.

BREAKFAST FOR ONE: Cut 4 day-old corn tortillas into strips. Heat a cast-iron skillet, add a little vegetable oil or lard, add the tortilla strips and a little salt, and stir to coat them. The tortilla strips will wilt, then crisp, which is what you want. Throw in a big handful of chopped cilantro, scallions, and chopped jalapeños and stir them around. Add a spoonful of red or green salsa if you like. Now add 2 beaten eggs seasoned with salt and pepper. Mix and stir the eggs with the tortillas until the eggs are set. Finish the chilaquiles with a little crumbled queso fresco.

Ann and Franco Taruschio

Leaves from the Walnut Tree: Recipes of a Lifetime

Pavilion, London, 1995 (first published 1993)
256 pages
232 x 152 mm (9¹/₈ x 6 in.)

When it opened in the early 1960s, the Walnut Tree, a pub in the village of Llanddewi Skirrid on the Welsh borders, was as near a miracle as is possible in the restaurant trade. It was the favourite British restaurant of Elizabeth David (page 66); writer Jan Morris, in her introduction to *Leaves from the Walnut Tree*, describes it as young in spirit and unpretentious. Its husband-and-wife owners – he Italian, she English – used the best Welsh food. Their cooking, as this book demonstrates, knew no boundaries.

The Taruschios bought a pub because restaurants were expensive and a new one would have had licensing problems. Ann, in her introduction, draws a charming picture of mine host Franco with the locals: neither could understand the other, and garlic smells from the kitchen caused mutterings. Cannelloni and lasagne in the 1960s 'were treated with suspicion'.

There are plenty of Italian recipes here, alongside such Welsh dishes as laver bread and Lady Llanover's salt duck (Lady Llanover wrote a cookery book in 1867 and converted many of the local pubs into temperance inns; the dish itself was worked out with Elizabeth David). Then Thai food appears, a result of the influence of the Taruschios' adopted Thai daughter, Pavinee – even though she was brought up by Irish nuns. So, on consecutive pages you find Belgian Leek Soup, Thai Fisherman's Soup and Melanzane in Carrozza.

The recipes are beautifully clear, with ingredients listed in a sidebar, and there's help with sources, too. The book's subtitle is the key, says fellow restaurateur Shaun Hill (page 120). There's thirty years' experience in this small book.

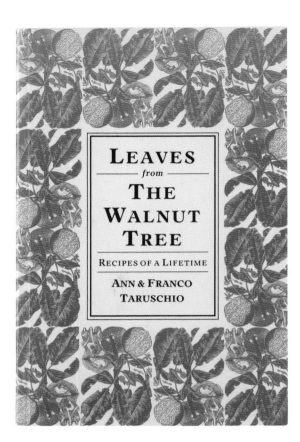

Sarah van Niekerk's evocative wood engravings (opposite, bottom) really lift this rather serious book, making it a pleasure to open. The design is by Peter Luff.

LADY LLANOVER'S SALT DUCK

For this dish use only the breast of duck left on the bone. Weigh the duck breasts and for every 2.8kg/6lb of duck meat and carcass rub in 225g/8oz of coarse sea salt. The duck should be placed in a deep container, breast-side down. Keep in a cool place. After 1½ days turn the breasts over. After 3 days rinse off the salt, place the duck breasts in a deep oven dish and stand it in a baking tray. Cover the duck with cold water and also put water in the baking tray. Place the tray in the centre of an oven set at 160°C/300°F/gas 2 and cook uncovered for 1½ hours. Remove the duck breasts from the liquid and leave to cool. Serve the duck breast thinly sliced with gooseberry pickle, crab apple and rowanberry jelly (both on page 64) and pickled damsons (opposite).

August Hall, Lady Llanover, wife of Benjamin Hall, later Baron Llanover of Big Ben fame, lived at Llanover Court near Abergavenny.

She was a very influential figure in Welsh cultural life during the 19th century. She promoted the Welsh language, literature, costume and also the Eisteddfod. One of the deeds she is very much remembered for round here is that she closed all the pubs in Llanover!

(62)

Lady Llanover published her cookery book The First Principles of Good Cookery in 1867. In 1991 a facsimile was published. Bobby Freeman wrote the introduction to the book, explaining its significance in the history of cooking and the background of Lady Llanover's life. Bobby asked us to arrange a menu culled from the book for its launch. The first course we devised, with the help of Elizabeth David, was Lady Llanover's salt duck.

PICKLED DAMSONS

Wash and prick the damsons with a silver fork. Make a syrup from the sugar and vinegar. Put the damsons in the syrup and bring the syrup back to the boil. Remove the damsons quickly at this point, with a perforated spoon, and lay them on flat trays to quickly cool. Add the spices to the syrup and boil for a further 5–10 minutes or until the syrup thickens again. Put the fruit carefully into sterilized glass jars, strain the syrup over the fruit while it is still hot. Cover while still hot. Keeping time? Until next crop. Good served with Lady Llanover's salt duck.

4 litres/7pt damsons

1.8kg/4lb preserving sugar

450ml/¾pt red wine vinegar

1 10cm/4in stick cinnamon

6 cloves

(63)

LAMB WITH POLENTA AND ARTICHOKES
AGNELLO CON POLENTA E CARCIOFO

SERVES 4

2 best ends of lamb (about 6 chops each)

olive oil

2 eggs, beaten for egg wash

Herb and breadcrumb coating

115g/4os fresh breadcrumbs

1 teaspoon each of fresh thyme, parsley, chives, and oregano, finely chopped

salt and freshly ground black pepper

Sauce

600ml/1pt rich lamb stock flavoured with rosemary (page 130, omitting the tomato purée)

Reduce the stock by two-thirds, and keep warm.

Trim the lamb, removing all the fat, and clean the bones to the eye of the meat. Seal the lamb in a little olive oil.

To prepare the coating, mix the breadcrumbs, herbs and salt and pepper together. Brush the outer surface of the lamb with the beaten egg and then cover with the breadcrumb mixture, pressing well to bind the crumbs.

Place the lamb in a roasting tray and cook in an oven set at 190°C/375°F/gas 5 for about 7 minutes or until the meat is pink. Remove the meat from the oven and leave it to rest for 4 minutes.

Carve the meat into chops, pour the strained sauce on plates and place 3 chops on each plate. Serve with grilled *polenta alla marchigiana* (page 103) and fried artichokes (page 218).

WELSH LAMB WITH GARLIC SAUCE

SERVES 6

6 best end of Welsh lamb (each strip with 4–5 chops)

olive oil

2 eggs, beaten for egg wash

Herb and breadcrumb coating

115g/4os fresh breadcrumbs

1 teaspoon each of chopped fresh chervil, tarragon, thyme, parsley, chives and basil

salt and freshly ground black pepper

Garlic sauce

3 heads of garlic (do not remove skins)

300ml/1pt white wine

300ml/1pt water

300ml/1pt lamb stock

salt and freshly ground black pepper

30 cloves garlic, peeled

olive oil

sprigs of thyme or mint

Trim the lamb, removing all the fat, and clean the bones up to the eye of the meat.

Prepare the garlic for the garnish. Bring the 30 peeled cloves of garlic to the boil in just enough water to cover them. Strain. Repeat this process 3 times, then leave to cool.

Deep-fry the garlic cloves in olive oil until golden and crisp on the outside, still soft on the inside. Drain and leave on kitchen paper.

Now make the sauce. Leaving the skins on the garlic, gently bring the heads to the boil in the mixture of white wine, water and lamb stock. Cook until tender. Pass the garlic mixture through a sieve, pressing well, then liquidize. Adjust the seasoning and consistency. It should be a pouring consistency. You may need to add more water. Keep warm.

Seal the lamb in oil.

To prepare the coating. Mix together the breadcrumbs, herbs and seasoning. Brush the outer surface of the lamb with the beaten egg, then cover with the breadcrumb mixture, pressing well to bind the crumbs. Place the lamb in a roasting tray

VEGETABLES

*V*egetables to the Italians mean not only a contorno—a side dish—to go with the main meal but also a dish on their own, to be served as an antipasto, or even as a main course, if they have been prepared with a meat stuffing. In the past this was very common as it made a small amount of meat go further. Vegetables are stuffed, grilled, fried, baked, but rarely plain boiled. If a vegetable such as spinach or cicoria (chicory) is boiled it is then tossed in oil and garlic. Wild vegetables are very much used in the Marche as are wild salad leaves and herbs.

*G*reengrocers and market stalls are piled high with locally grown vegetables, still damp from being freshly picked. Stall holders and shopkeepers will prepare vegetables for soups like minestrone, or zuppa di verdura (vegetable soup); they will also pod peas and shell beans if requested.

*T*wo Italian farmers, Peppe and Pasquale, who farm locally, supply us with good organic vegetables and various salad leaves for most of the year. Franco grows his own herbs and also some of the vegetables we use, such as cardoons, celery, artichokes and many others.

Shizuo Tsuji

Japanese Cooking:
A Simple Art

Kodansha, Tokyo and New York, 1980
520 pages
256 x 181 mm (10$\frac{1}{8}$ x 7$\frac{1}{8}$ in.)

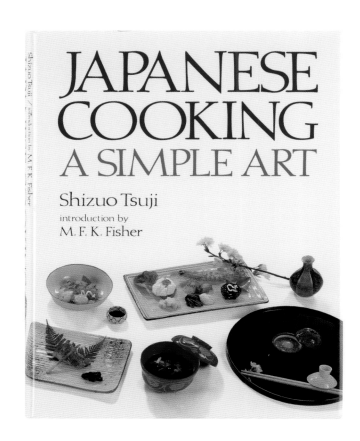

Judging by this book, Japanese cooking is a far from simple art. In 520 pages there are 510 sketches, which make it clear that we're in for such games as holding a slice of onion together with a toothpick and fanning rice with a delicate oriental fan as you toss it. Other illustrations show how to cut carrot plum blossoms and turnip chrysanthemums. A rare photograph shows a low Japanese table laid with irises arranged in bamboo rafts and 'a *sashimi* of the choicest sea bream … concealed in hollowed sections of bamboo stalk'. Gold dust has been thinly applied to sheaths of dried bamboo. Simple?

In her introduction, M.F.K. Fisher (page 92) suggests a different reason for this book: 'Books like this one are written – stubbornly, proudly – by people like Shizuo Tsuji who cannot tolerate letting their national taste falter and die.'

What this book does, then, is teach us about the infinite care and patience the Japanese put into not only the taste of their food but also the look and significance of it. The Japanese are probably the most beauty-conscious nation in the world, and if that means making fried bean curd look like old-fashioned purses, I don't see why not. Further reasons to treasure such masters as Tsuji, who died in 1993, are that he ran the largest school for chefs in Japan, and was the owner of one of the world's most extensive collections of Bach recordings. American food writer Craig Claiborne (page 48) thought this book well worth collecting, and so do I.

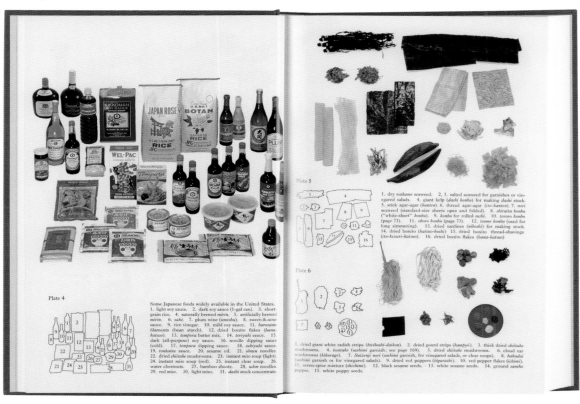

Plate 4

Some Japanese foods widely available in the United States. 1. light soy sauce. 2. dark soy sauce (1-gal can). 3. short-grain rice. 4. naturally brewed *mirin*. 6. *sahé*. 7. plum wine (*umeshu*). 5. artificially brewed sauce. 8. rice vinegar. 10. mild soy sauce. 11. *harusame* filaments (bean starch). 12. dried bonito flakes (*hana-katsuo*). 13. *tempura* batter mix. 14. *teriyaki* sauce. 15. dark (all-purpose) soy sauce. 16. noodle dipping sauce (cold). 17. *tempura* dipping sauce. 18. *sukiyaki* sauce. 19. *tonkatsu* sauce. 20. sesame oil. 21. *sōmen* noodles. 22. dried *shiitake* mushrooms. 23. instant *miso* soup (light). 24. instant *miso* soup (red). 25. instant clear soup. 26. water chestnuts. 27. bamboo shoots. 28. *udon* noodles. 29. red *miso*. 30. light *miso*. 31. *dashi* stock concentrate.

Plate 5

1. dry *wakame* seaweed. 2, 3. salted seaweed for garnishes or vinegared salads. 4. giant kelp (*dashi konbu*) for making *dashi* stock. 5. stick agar-agar (*kanten*). 6. thread agar-agar (*ito-kanten*). 7. *nori* seaweed (standard-size sheets open and folded). 8. *shiraita konbu* ("white-sheet" *konbu*). 9. *konbu* for rolled *sushi*. 10. *toroto konbu* (page 73). 11. *oboro konbu* (page 73). 12. *tsume konbu* (used for long simmering). 13. dried sardines (*niboshi*) for making stock. 14. dried bonito (*katsuo-bushi*) 15. dried bonito thread-shavings (*ito-kezuri-katsuo*). 16. dried bonito flakes (*hana-katsuo*)

Plate 6

1. dried giant white radish strips (*hiraboshi-daikon*). 2. dried gourd strips (*kanpyō*). 3. thick dried *shiitake* mushrooms. 4. *matake* (*sashimi* garnish; see page 169). 5. dried *shiitake* mushrooms. 6. cloud ear mushrooms (*kikurage*). 7. *Suizenji nori* (*sashimi* garnish, for vinegared salads, or clear soups). 8. *hahadai* (*sashimi* garnish or for vinegared salads). 9. dried red peppers (*togarashi*). 10. red pepper flakes (*ichimi*). 11. seven-spice mixture (*shichimi*). 12. black sesame seeds. 13. white sesame seeds. 14. ground *sanshō* pepper. 15. white poppy seeds.

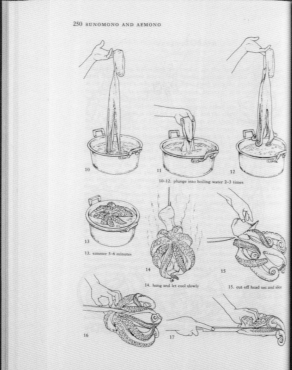

10–12. plunge into boiling water 2–3 times

13. simmer 5–6 minutes

14. hang and let cool slowly   15. cut off head sac and slice

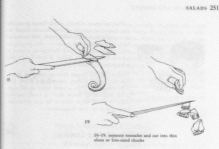

16–19. separate tentacles and cut into thin slices or bite-sized chunks

VARIATION: You may also use cold, thinly sliced steamed abalone, or cold, flaked, poached white-fleshed fish.

Chrysanthemum Turnip
(Kikka Kabu) 菊花かぶ (color plate 11)

This do-ahead dish is practically effortless, but the easy decorative cutting technique transforms turnips into blossoms. Serve this "chrysanthemum" vegetable as a tangy appetizer or garnish for any grilled food.

4 servings

6 medium or small turnips
1 tsp salt in 1 quart (1 L) water
2-inch (5-cm) square giant kelp (konbu)
1 cup SWEET VINEGAR (see page 242)
½ tsp finely chopped, seeded red pepper

To prepare: Trim and peel the turnips and cut off tops level. Rest a turnip on its flat top on a cutting board between two bamboo skewers. Cross-score as deeply and as finely as possible. The skewer guards will keep the knife from cutting all the way through. Cut each turnip into 4 to 6 pieces.
    Put cut turnips in salt water in which the kelp (konbu) has been left to soak. Let soak 20 minutes, then remove and squeeze out excess water by hand, one by one.

---

soybeans. Simmer, covered, with a drop-lid (otoshi-buta) or circle of baking paper with a vent (see page 220) for 30 minutes, or until tender. Stir occasionally. Simmering liquid should be almost entirely reduced by the end of the cooking time.

To serve: Serve—hot or cold—3 or 4 heaping Tbsps in small dishes.
    Combines well with YELLOWTAIL TERIYAKI (page 200) and SAVORY CUP CUSTARD (page 214).

Burdock or Carrot Kinpira
(Kinpira Gobō or Ninjin) きんぴら牛蒡又はにんじん

A popular vegetable dish. The concentrated flavors of soy and saké give this dish a piquancy suggestive of Kinpira, a strong and dashing mythical hero of old Japan. Carrot may be effectively substituted for burdock.

6 servings

1 medium burdock root, scrubbed with a brush, or 3 medium carrots
few Tbsps vegetable oil

for simmering
2 Tbsps saké
2 Tbsps dark soy sauce
1 scant Tbsp sugar
¼ tsp red pepper flakes (ichimi) or seven-spice mixture (shichimi)

To prepare and cook: Cut burdock in shavings as if sharpening a pencil (the sasagaki cutting technique, see page 142). Keep cut burdock in water to avoid discoloration. (Scrape carrots and cut into 2-inch [5-cm] julienne strips.)
    Coat the bottom of a frying pan with a few Tbsps oil, heat, and add vegetable. Stir-fry over high heat till vegetable begins to soften (about 3 minutes). Add the saké to the pan, stir in the soy sauce and sugar, and continue stir-frying over medium heat till the liquid has been almost completely reduced. Stir occasionally to keep the vegetable from sticking to the pan. Flavor to taste with red pepper flakes or seven-spice mixture.

To serve: Serve hot or at room temperature. Either serve family style in a large dish or in small individual dishes during the rice course. This dish also is a fine companion for saké. Keeps one week, refrigerated in a sealed container.
    Combines well with CHICKEN-'N-EGG ON RICE (page 283) and MISO SOUP (page 156).

VARIATIONS: Konnyaku (devil's tongue jelly)—rub cake with salt, lightly pound, wash, and cut into thin 1-inch squares.
    Lotus root (renkon)—scrape surface, cut into thin rounds, then quarter the rounds. Till ready to use, keep cut lotus root in water with a drop of vinegar to whiten it.
    Minced meat—for a different effect, you may also use ground meat (pork, beef, chicken) together with the vegetable. Use ¼ pound (115 g) and fry with the vegetable.

Potatoes Simmered in Miso
(Jaga-imo Miso-ni) じゃがいも味噌煮

Jaga-imo, the common Japanese name for the Irish potato, is short for Jagatara-imo, "Jakarta potato." Introduced from Java by the early Dutch traders, they are also sometimes called barei-sho, "horse-bell potato" from the resemblance of little round new potatoes to the small ball-shaped bells on Japanese pack-horse bridles.

4 servings

5 medium potatoes
2 cups dashi
6 Tbsps white (or 4 Tbsps red) miso
4 pods okra, washed and trimmed (or 12 pods snow peas; tender green peas; or French-cut green beans may also be used)

To prepare: Peel potatoes and cut into quarters (into sixths, if large Idaho potatoes). Parboil in slightly salted water till tender but not flaky, then drain well.
    In ½ cup of the dashi, soften the miso and strain through a sieve.

To cook and serve: Into a medium-sized pot put the remaining 1½ cups dashi and the parboiled potatoes. Heat over medium heat till simmering.
    Add the strained, softened miso. Mix. Cover with a drop-lid (otoshi-buta) or circle of baking paper with a vent (see page 220) and simmer or gently boil for 20 minutes.
    Parboil okra in lightly salted water for 2 or 3 minutes, rinse in cold water, then cut into ¼-inch (¾-cm) rounds. (Parboil substitutes in lightly salted water until almost tender, then rinse in cold water.)
    To serve, use a slotted spoon to transfer portions (5 potato pieces per serving) to deep individual dishes, then top with a few Tbsps of the hot miso liquid. Garnish with okra rounds (or substitute) and serve immediately.
    Combines well with SAKÉ-SIMMERED MACKEREL (page 225) and SALT-PICKLED CHINESE CABBAGE (page 322).

Alice Waters
Chez Panisse Café Cookbook

HarperCollins, New York, 1999
288 pages
253 x 176 mm (10 x 6⅞ in.)

I bought this book second-hand and already signed. Authors, faced with piles of books and aching hands, often develop a rushed signature. Waters is no exception.

Alice Waters, founder and owner of Chez Panisse in Berkeley, California, has written numerous cookery books, but I have chosen this one, her seventh, as it is one of the most beautiful I have ever seen. This is because it eschews gastro-porn photographs in favour of real works of art: block prints by David Lance Goines, a Berkeley-based printer and designer who had been friends with Waters for more than thirty years (and had eaten at the restaurant since day one) when he collaborated on this book. From the courgette-covered endpapers to the chapter openers ('Fish and Shellfish' is my favourite), the book is a joy.

So is Waters, a crusader who (as she wrote when Chez Panisse opened in 1971) intended her food to 'create a community of friends, lovers and relatives that spans generations and is in tune with the seasons, the land and human appetites'. Thus, the present craze for local ingredients, seasonal food and farmers' markets was pioneered by her. When I visited the restaurant, I had Terra Firma Farm tomatoes with hand-made mozzarella. 'One of the first things a customer sees on coming up the stairs to the cafe', Waters writes, 'is an eye-catching basket of vegetables. Every day a designated chef decides what produce looks the most beautiful … like a beautiful seventeenth-century Spanish tabletop still-life painting.'

Most of the dishes, such as Roast Pork Loin with Rosemary and Fennel, or Dandelion Salad with Vinaigrette, are Mediterranean – Waters was inspired by Elizabeth David (page 66) – but with a Californian sun-filled sense of ease. Waters's Chez Panisse Foundation teaches 'the interwoven pleasures of growing, cooking and sharing food'. She is a heroine.

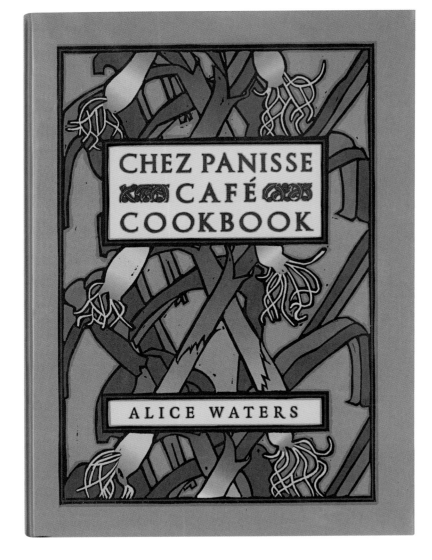

A Book for Cooks

HOME-CURED PANCETTA

Pancetta is the delicious salt-cured pork belly used in so many Italian dishes. Pancetta adds flavor to any number of things—warm asparagus salad, baked sea scallops, grilled quail, and many other dishes, including pasta. Some Italian pancetta is smoked, but we generally prefer the simpler salt-cured version. Commercially produced domestic pancetta varies in quality. Some Italian butcher shops still make their own, flavored with pepper, allspice, and bay. We've had good success making our own pancetta over the last several years, and the method works well at home. Ask your butcher for the thickest belly available, evenly streaked with lean and fat. The powdered dextrose counteracts the saltiness. It is used instead of table sugar because it tastes less sweet. Note that this procedure takes nearly two months.

2 ounces coarse, additive-free salt
1 ounce powdered dextrose
1 teaspoon curing salt (for cooked meats)
2½ pounds fresh pork belly

Mix together the salt, dextrose, and curing salt, and rub the mixture into the meat until all sides are well coated. It is important to use all of the salt mixture. Place the seasoned pork belly in a shallow glass pan just large enough to contain the meat. Cover the meat with a piece of parchment paper, place a weight on top, and refrigerate for 24 hours, during which time a brine will form.

After 24 hours, check the level of the brine. If it has not covered the pancetta, make an additional brine with 1⅓ ounces salt, ¾ ounce dextrose, and ¾ teaspoon curing salt dissolved in 2 cups water, and pour it over the pancetta to cover completely. Refrigerate, covered, for 15 days.

Remove the pancetta from the brine; rinse quickly under cold water and blot dry with paper towels. Lay the pancetta on a rack and refrigerate uncovered for 10 to 12 days, turning it once a day, until the surface is completely dry. Wrap the pancetta loosely in parchment paper or cheesecloth, to allow air circulation, and continue to refrigerate for another 45 days. The pancetta is now ready to use and may be sliced as needed.

LAMB

CHERRY CLAFOUTIS

By mid-April, there will be cherries from Lagier Ranches in the Central Valley: big baskets of cherries still covered with dew to put out on the tables in the Café and to use for cherry tarts, cherry ice cream, and cherry clafoutis. The traditional French clafoutis is a dish of unpitted sour cherries baked in a batter. The pits infuse the dessert with an almond flavor. In this version, with sweeter, pitted cherries, the addition of almond extract enhances the flavor and makes it taste more like the French original.

Serves 4.

1 pound sweet cherries (preferably Bings), washed and pitted
2 teaspoons fresh lemon juice
¼ teaspoon grated lemon zest
A pinch ground cinnamon
½ cup sugar
2 eggs, separated
3 tablespoons sugar
2 tablespoons flour
1 teaspoon vanilla extract
¼ teaspoon almond extract
½ cup cream
A pinch salt
Powdered sugar

Preheat the oven to 350°F. Lightly butter a baking pan large enough to hold the cherries loosely in a single layer. Prepare the cherries and arrange them in the pan. Sprinkle with the lemon juice, zest, cinnamon, and sugar. Bake until the fruit is tender, about 15 minutes, stirring once or twice.

Raise the oven temperature to 375°F. Butter another gratin dish large enough to hold the cherries in a single layer, or use four individual gratin dishes. Drain the cooked cherries, reserving their juice in a small saucepan. Arrange the cherries in the bottom of the baking dish. Beat together the egg yolks and sugar until well blended. Beat in the flour, vanilla, almond extract, and cream.

Beat the egg whites with a pinch of salt until they form soft peaks. Stir a little of the whites into the batter, and then carefully fold in the rest. Pour the batter over the fruit in the baking dish, letting a little fruit show through the top.

Bake in the upper third of the oven for about 20 minutes, until the batter has puffed and browned. While the clafoutis is baking, reduce the fruit juices to a thin syrup. When the clafoutis is done, dust it with powdered sugar and serve warm with a drizzle of the syrup.

Alice Waters

Patricia Wells

Patricia Wells at Home in Provence: Recipes Inspired by Her Farmhouse in France

Scribner, New York, 1996
352 pages
253 x 203 mm (10 x 8 in.)

An American living in France, Patricia Wells is hugely respected in her adopted homeland, having been made a Chevalier de l'Ordre des Arts et des Lettres for her cookery writing in the country. She is also the only foreigner to have worked as the restaurant critic for *L'Express* magazine – an equal honour, I guess. Of her handful of cookery books, including a collaboration with French chef Joël Robuchon, this is the one I like best, because it is so personal.

'Home' is Chanteduc, an eighteenth-century farmhouse, a place that transformed the lives of Wells and her family: 'It symbolized all the essential elements of happiness we sought.' The recipes, which come from the region, are '*whole* foods, meaning I prefer to roast a fish whole'. Lamb isn't boned, chicken remains intact. Dishes include Petite Friture, Winemaker's Duck, Monsieur Henny's Eggplant Gratin and Chanteduc Clafoutis, made with the farmhouse's own cherries. And look out for Scrubbed Toast: 'So what's the big deal … ? Try it and you'll see.'

What makes this book particularly sumptuous is the choice of Robert Fréson for the photographs. Far from being a food photographer, he's a renowned

photojournalist. Many of the pictures are portraits of Chanteduc plus fishmongers, vegetable stallholders (one of whom is seen kissing Wells), street musicians, beekeepers, cheesemongers and Wells herself working in the kitchen. Close-ups of market stalls at Vaison-la-Romaine, showing bread, cheese, olive servers, seven kinds of tapenade and piles of artichokes, make me long to be there. Oh, yes: the food photos are pretty good too.

A Book for Cooks

8

POULTRY & GAME

PLUMP CHICKENS AND TURKEYS FROM THE Bresse region, local pigeon and quail, fresh and wild rabbit, and moist mallard duck raised by our very own winemaker make up the family poultry larder from season to season. Give me a whole chicken and I'll turn it into a feast, gently coaxing handfuls of herbs beneath the skin, tucking it into the bread oven to roast to a crispy, golden tenderness. Rabbits have long been part of the history and lore of our farmhouse, so naturally they find their way to the table, with a Provençal version (Chanteduc Rabbit with Garlic & Preserved Lemons) as well as one from Italy's Piedmont (Pina's Braised Rabbit.) My butcher, Roland Henny, adds his expertise, supplying us with his version of Rabbit Bouillabaisse, while a trip to Switzerland and lunch at grand chef Fredy Girardet's inspired me to create a new family favorite, Duck with Lime & Honey.

FACING PHOTOGRAPH: *A corner of the Chanteduc kitchen, with an assortment of wooden kegs for homemade vinegars.*

Noncooks think it's silly to invest two hours' work in two minutes' enjoyment; but if cooking is evanescent, well, so is the ballet.
JULIA CHILD

SUMMER PISTOU

Our wedding anniversary falls at the end of summer, the time our good friends Rita and Yale Kramer make their annual visit. They usually insist on preparing an anniversary feast, and, inevitably, Yale proudly spends the day chopping and peeling, shelling and simmering, making a memorable version of pistou, a summery vegetable soup. This also happens to be one of my favorite dishes to prepare and serve throughout the season. It's an ideal way to get children who won't eat vegetables to devour them, and after many wasp-troubled meals outdoors, I've learned that wasps don't come near the soup! So hurrah again for pistou.

There are as many recipes for pistou as there are cooks who prepare it, and I am particular about what should go into mine. I insist upon an abundance of carrots for color, a mix of fresh white beans as well as cranberry beans, leeks for a touch of elegance, lots of whole garlic, and plenty of green beans. I like the pasta to be as diminutive as possible so it doesn't overwhelm. My recipe differs from more traditional versions in that rather than tossing all the vegetables into the mix at one time, I sweat some of the vegetables first in oil for better color and depth of flavor. Finally, I love mixing the traditional Gruyère with the untraditional Parmesan, adding yet another layer of flavor to one of summer's greatest dishes. Note that while the soup starts out a brilliant green, the color fades as the vegetables cook. This is why a touch of tomato and carrot are nice, and why a verdant hit of garlic and basil pistou not only thickens the soup but boosts the flavor and color as well.

THE BEANS
3 tablespoons extra-virgin olive oil
3 plump, fresh garlic cloves, peeled and minced
1 pound (500 g) fresh small white (navy) beans in the pod, shelled, or 8 ounces (250 g) dried small white beans (see Note)
1 pound (500 g) fresh cranberry beans in the pod, shelled, or 8 ounces dried cranberry beans (see Note)
Bouquet garni: several fresh bay leaves and several sprigs of summer savory and thyme, tied securely with household twine
Sea salt and freshly ground black pepper to taste

(continued on next page)

Patricia Wells

Florence White

Good English Food, Local and Regional: Famous Food and Drink of Yesterday and Today Recorded with Recipes

Jonathan Cape, London, 1952
288 pages
198 x 133 mm (7¾ x 5¼ in.)

Florence White was the founder, in 1928, of the English Folk Cookery Association, which today sounds laughable. Folk cookery? What could that be? Drearily impossible medieval spitted peacocks? Gruel? Vast barons of beef? Well, the book has that tendency, with a whole chapter on cooking small wild birds, in which thrushes, blackbirds, sparrows, starlings and moorhens are executed and eaten. Sparrows can be treated like wheatears, in a Dutch oven, or cooked in a pie like blackbirds. Starlings, says Lieutenant Colonel Cameron (a copy of his book from 1917, *Wild Foods of Great Britain*, 'should be in every house'), 'make good eating' as long as their heads are cut off immediately after being shot.

Most of the recipes are from older sources. Sir Walter Scott's *Ivanhoe* (1819) is quoted on spitting birds; the Reform Club in London is remembered as serving laver with roast mutton '*circa* 1850'; and Lady Eleanor Byng, writing in the early 1930s, recalls being taught how to find truffles 'by an old under-gardener'. Young ladies as truffle dogs. Even Pope Leo XIII is brought into play (although I wonder how he qualifies as English) with his Favourite Beverage. Lemon, tea and Marsala 'can be strongly recommended for modern cocktail parties', says the author. An erratum slip at the front points out that in the recipe for Sandringham Christmas Cake 'veal' should read 'peel'.

So yes, a laugh and a period piece, but in *Culinary Pleasures* (2005), a look at cookery books in Britain, Nicola Humble says that Florence White's books encouraged later serious research into the history of British food, collecting dishes that might otherwise have been lost.

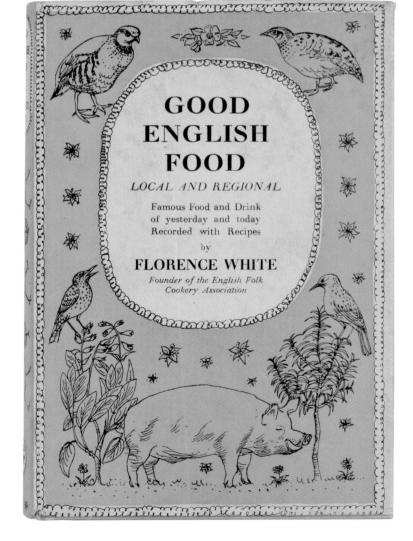

Above and right: Before the advent of glistening foodie photographs, publishers were at a bit of loss when it came to covers. This design, with its huge birds and small pig, is naive enough to be charming.

Ashdown Pickles

Given by Lady Margaret Campbell

INGREDIENTS: 1 lb. of apples; 1 lb. of cucumbers; ½ lb. onions.

METHOD

The apples trimmed, the cucumbers peeled and seeds taken out. These apples, cucumbers and onions chopped very fine. When chopped and mixed, spread on a dish and sprinkle over it ¼ lb. of salt. Let it remain on the dish 24 hours, taking care to stir it now and then with a wooden spoon. After 24 hours put it into a colander and press it down with a weight over it to extract all the water. Put it into a jar, cover with common vinegar, ½ oz. of black pepper ground, one spoonful of cayenne, 4 oz. of salt. When all is mixed together well, bottle it, and put it in a jar, a little vinegar to cover the pickle.

[N.B. — These pickles are fit to eat a week after being made, but when kept they are better.]

To Pickle Broom Buds

Given by Mr. W. L. Carter

Take your buds before they be yellow on the top, make a brine of vinegar and salt, which you must do only by shaking it together till the salt be melted, then put in your buds and keep stirred till they be sunk within the vinegar; be sure to keep close covered.

46

The following four recipes were kindly given to me in 1929 by Mr. P. E. Martineau of Bath from his grandmother's MS. cookery book.

The Family Indian Pickle

INGREDIENTS: gallon of vinegar boiled and cold: 4 oz. curry powder; 4 oz. flour of mustard; 3 oz. ginger bruised; 2 oz. turmeric; ½ lb. shallots; 2 oz. garlic (slightly baked); ¼ lb. salt; 2 drachms (= 55 grains) cayenne pepper.

METHOD

In February mix in a large unglazed jar with bladder at top well covered. Set this on trivet by fireside for 3 days, shaking it well thrice a day.

Then in summer put in the vegetables having previously parboiled them separately in brine *strong enough to bear an egg*, this is *de rigueur*. Drain them, spread out in the sun or before the fire for 2 days before putting into the pickle.

Salad Dressing

To Keep

INGREDIENTS: 2 teaspoonfuls of dry mustard; 2 teaspoonfuls of salt; 1 teaspoonful of anchovy; 1 teaspoonful of Worcester Sauce; 1 teaspoonful of brown sugar; 6 teaspoonfuls of Tarragon vinegar; 6 teaspoonfuls of Chili vinegar; 8 teaspoonfuls of common vinegar.

47

Ordinary Pickle for Brawn

Equal parts of vinegar and water, with 2 oz. of salt, the same of sugar, and 3 or 4 cloves. Take it out of the Pickle, dry it and send it in cold for lunch or breakfast.

Oxford Brawn Sauce

Blend smoothly with a teaspoonful of oil, 2 teaspoonfuls of moist sugar and one of mustard; when smooth, add a little vinegar, and by degrees mix 2 tablespoonfuls of vinegar and as much oil, quite smooth. In some cases a preponderance of oil is required, in some of vinegar. It may be proportioned to taste, but must always be mixed with great care.

Potted Pork as a Breakfast Dish

This is a Cotswold dish, the recipe for which has kindly been sent us by Mrs. Morris of Broadway, Worcester.

The oddments of meat from newly killed pork pig were chopped up and put into stone jars with lids, flavoured with a little mace, cloves, pepper and salt.

The jars were then set in the oven and left to cook for several hours, then taken out and left to cool. The meat would set in a jelly like the meat in pork pies. Stored in a cool, dry place the contents would keep for two or three weeks if necessary.

166

PART FOUR

HEN HOUSE AND DAIRY

The country houses and farmsteads of England were never more wealthy, populous and happy than during the mid-Victorian age, — the age of Trollope's novels and John Leech's pictures.
G. M. Trevelyan
History of England

1. HEN HOUSE

As a girl I used to stay with Chancellor and Mrs. Edmonds and their family of several boys and girls in The Close at Exeter, consequently in May, 1933, when trekking through Devon in search of food and cookery lore for *The Queen* newspaper, I was delighted to visit Godfrey Edmonds' poultry farm, Bowcombe, near Kingsbridge. Godfrey studied at Reading, and one of his specialities is churkeys.

CHURKEYS. ONE DAY OLD CHICKS

In these he does a flourishing business in one-day chicks, being the only poultry farmer in England who specializes in this extraordinary bird.

You might think 'Churkeys' are a hybrid fowl, or a cross between a turkey and a chicken, because they have the bare long neck of a turkey and the body and legs of a barndoor fowl; but Mr. Edmonds says they are not. He says they are an Australian bird — the

167

Katharine Whitehorn

Cooking in a Bedsitter

Virago, London, 2008 (first published 1961)
224 pages
196 x 125 mm (7¾ x 4⅞ in.)

I did have a first edition of this book but I used it so much it fell apart into greasy sections. I bought this one for old times' sake. As the publishers say, it has been in print for more than forty years, and they have had the sense to keep the original Kenneth Mahood cartoon on the cover. In 1961 people dressed for dinner even in a bedsitter.

Whitehorn explains the book's creation: 'Towards the end of the fifties a man called Tony Facer … realized that all cookery books, even the ones for beginners, assumed that the cook had a kitchen. But he … lived in one room and had only a single gas-ring.' Whitehorn had been sacked from *Woman's Own* and, just married, lived in an attic flat.

'I was no great shakes as a cook – a fact I concealed from the publisher.' But, on the other hand, her audience was likely to be just as hopeless.

After listing the hazards of bedsit cookery, such as no water supply and no storage space, the book jumps straight in with a recipe for toast. When burnt it should be scraped, but remember to '*bang* the toast hard'. Later we get Mushroom Beef ('not quick but dead easy'): braising steak, a tin of mushroom soup and frozen peas.

What this book can do is teach people to feed themselves. It should be required reading for students and young couples. Once you've mastered Hot Dogs, you may be ready for Croque Monsieur.

CONTENTS

Cook cobs in boiling salted water 15 mins. Drain. Spread butter over the cobs, and eat in your fingers, tearing off the kernels with your teeth. Paper napkins are a help for those who find they get the butter in their ears.

20 mins.

CARROT RAGOUT

2 carrots	1 rasher of bacon
1 potato	herbs, salt, pepper
1 small onion	1 teaspoon fat

Peel and slice carrots, potato, and onion. Fry onion gently in saucepan for a few minutes, add potato, carrots and chopped rasher and turn in fat for a minute or two. Add small cup water, herbs, salt, pepper. Simmer gently 40 mins. Keep an eye on it to see it does not burn.

1 hr.

SPAGHETTI, MACARONI, RICE, RAVIOLI, PIZZA

SPAGHETTI

There are innumerable different sauces for spaghetti or if you are feeling really poor and hungry you can simply eat it with butter and grated cheese, or even just with butter. A few possibilities are given below; but the great thing is to experiment for yourself. However you cook the sauce, you cook the spaghetti itself like this:

25 long strands of spaghetti at least	a panful of boiling water salt

Into a panful of boiling salted water lower your spaghetti by holding the ends in one hand while the other ends soften in the water. You will gradually be able to wind the whole lot into the pan. Boil until it is just tender—10–15 mins. Don't go on till it is all soggy.

Other forms of Italian pasta are cooked in exactly the same way, but take a longer or shorter time depending on what they are made with. They should all have some 'bite' left when you take them out of the water.

STANDARD SAUCE

1 onion	salt, pepper;
1 rasher of bacon	garlic (optional)
2 or 3 tomatoes	tomato paste (optional)
grated Parmesan cheese	

First cook the spaghetti and drain it. Then fry onion and bacon until bacon is crisp and onion soft—just under 10 mins. Add tomatoes, the flavourings, and a little of the cheese. Add the spaghetti to heat up; move out on to plate and sprinkle with more cheese.

½ hr., including spaghetti cooking.

SPAGHETTI BOLOGNESE

1 onion	¼ teaspoon French mustard
¼ lb. minced beef	grated Parmesan cheese
tomato paste	oil for frying
salt, pepper, herbs	

Cook spaghetti. Drain. Fry the onion, and when it is soft add a squeeze of tomato paste, the seasonings and a tablespoon of water. Stir. Put in mince, and break it up

---

CHAPTER X

Two Rings

*

A good many bedsitters are equipped with a sort of double gas-ring, which offers rather more scope to the cook than a single ring. A really expert cook can do almost anything with two burners except bake; but for most of us the chief advantage is that the time of cooking can be cut down by cooking vegetables and main dishes simultaneously. Most of the recipes already given that require potatoes or rice cooked beforehand can be speeded up by cooking the starchy food alongside the rest of it—spaghetti, for instance, or sausages and mash, or saucepan fish pie. With others, you can boil the potatoes separately instead of frying them alongside the meat, or you can pad out a rather less filling dish by adding potatoes to it. Remember that there's nothing to stop you boiling two vegetables together—potatoes and carrots, rice and onion.

The recipes that follow are no more than a few suggestions for you to work on. For really inexperienced two-ring cooks, it is worth while blowing two shillings on an admirable Ministry of Food pamphlet called *The ABC of Cookery*, which

assumes you know nothing *at all* and practically starts by drawing a picture of an egg and saying 'This is an Egg'.

One of the chief advantages of two-ring cooking is that it enables you to use a method of cooking rice which is absolutely foolproof in all circumstances.

RICE

First put on a kettle, with a little water in it. Then put a spoonful of fat into your heaviest saucepan. When it is hot, turn some measured rice in it for just a minute or two, until it is transparent; then add exactly twice as much very hot water as you had rice. Add salt, pepper, a bay leaf if you have or like it. Clamp the lid on, with a cloth between the lid and pan. Put on lowest possible gas, for exactly half an hour.

At the end it will be dry and fluffy and ready to eat. It can stand for up to ten minutes without getting cold.

The advantage of this method is that, having got the rice on, you don't give it another thought until you want to eat it, thus leaving your mind and hands free to make whatever else you are eating.

MAIN DISHES WHICH NEED A SEPARATE VEGETABLE

DEVILLED DRUMSTICKS
(two helpings)

1 small packet drumsticks	1 chicken soup cube
1 dessertspoon	¼ teaspoon mustard
Worcester sauce	salt, pepper
1 dessertspoon flour	1 teaspoon butter

Paula Wolfert
Moroccan Cuisine

Grub Street, London, 1998 (first published 1973)
288 pages
232 x 154 mm (9¹/₈ x 6 in.)

This American writer is in the tradition of such scholar cooks as Elizabeth David (page 66) and Alan Davidson (page 68). Wolfert wants to write about authenticity rather than adapting a nation's food to different cultures. Like David, she immersed herself in her chosen country, Morocco, living there in the 1960s: 'Morocco is the only place I know where there is nothing that I do not love ... . For me it is one of the world's great cuisines.' The book isn't comprehensive, but includes the food she likes best.

In order for a country to produce a world-class cuisine, says Wolfert, it needs fine ingredients, a variety of cultural influences, a history (including foreign occupation) and, surprisingly, 'a refined palace life'. Morocco has all four. So does Britain, of course, but I'm sure it doesn't appear in lists of the world's best cuisines.

One of Morocco's great dishes is couscous, and here we have twenty-two different recipes, from such cities as Fez, Rabat, Marrakesh and Tangier. They are, I must admit, rather challenging, in that Wolfert would have us actually make the couscous from scratch rather than buy the precooked version. Fair enough. But, looking at these and other recipes, they are for the dedicated only.

The publishers, in my view, have missed an opportunity in using no photographs. When I was in Marrakesh, the street food grilling amid charcoal smoke, the heaving markets, the souk and its characteristic embossed metalware, and the donkeys laden with bales of mint for the mint tea were wonderfully colourful and lively. Why not make the most of a country and its cuisine that demand to be illustrated?

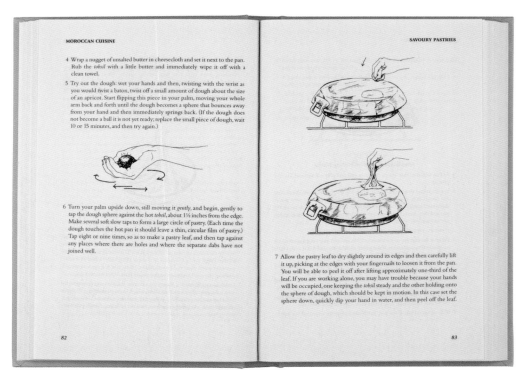

COUSCOUS RECIPES

Pumpkin Couscous

This is a superb lamb *couscous* and makes a brilliant follow-up to *djej mechoui* (Roasted Chicken, page 169). I like the fact that it is both ultra-refined and rustic at the same time: ultra-refined because its relatively few ingredients suggest a great purity of gastronomic thinking, and rustic because the inclusion of pumpkin is reminiscent of the earliest vegetable *couscous* preparations of the Berbers.

For 6-8 as part of a Moroccan dinner

90 g (3 oz) dried chick-peas or 300 g (10 oz) tin cooked chick-peas	1 teaspoon ground ginger
680 g (1½ lbs) *couscous*	2 pinches pulverised saffron
680 g (1½ lbs) lamb neck, cut into 5 pieces	½ teaspoon powdered turmeric
4 to 5 large Spanish onions	225 g (8 oz) unsalted butter
1½ to 2 teaspoons freshly ground black pepper to taste	450 g (1 lb) carrots
1 tablespoon salt	680 g (1½ lbs) pumpkin
	4 tablespoons granulated sugar
	225 g (8 oz) black raisins

1 Cover the dried chick-peas with water and soak overnight.

2 The next day, drain the chick-peas and cook in fresh water 1 hour. Drain, cool, and remove the skins by submerging them in a bowl of cold water and gently rubbing them between the fingers. The skins will rise to the top of the water – discard them. (If using tinned chick-peas, peel them and set aside.)

3 Prepare the *couscous* by following step 1 (first washing and drying of the *couscous*) in the master instructions (page 108).

4 To prepare the broth, place the lamb in the bottom of a *couscoussier*. Quarter and slice the onions lengthwise. Add to the lamb, along with the salt, spices, half the butter, 1.8 litres (3 pints) water, and the drained chick-peas. (Tinned chick-peas should not be added until 30 minutes

---

Lamb Tagine with Artichokes, Lemon, and Olives

The small artichokes found in Italian markets in the spring are especially good in this *tagine*. Note that tinned artichoke bottoms or frozen artichoke hearts will *not* produce a good dish.

For 4-6 people

Same as for *tagine makalli bil kerfas bil kreezoe* (Lamb Tagine with Carrots and Celery, page 206, but halve the amounts of black pepper, preserved lemons, lemon juice, and onions;	double the ginger and turmeric; substitute 8 to 10 small artichokes (about 1.15 kg /2½ lbs) for the celery and carrots; and leave out the green coriander

1 Follow step 1 on page 206.

2 Prepare the artichokes by removing the outside leaves and trimming the bases. Halve each one and remove the hairy choke. Place in acidulated water (water with 2 tablespoons of vinegar added) to keep from blackening while trimming the rest. Rinse and drain before using.

3 Place the artichokes over the pieces of meat after the meat has cooked 1½ hours. Place the rinsed preserved lemons, cut in quarters, on top. Cover tightly and cook 30 minutes. Sprinkle with lemon juice and olives and cook a few minutes all together.

4 Place the lamb in centre of the serving dish. Arrange the artichokes, flat side up, facing in one direction around the rim. By boiling rapidly, uncovered, reduce the sauce to a thick gravy. Adjust the seasoning of the sauce. Swirl the pan once to combine and pour over the meat. Decorate with preserved lemons and olives and serve at once.

Note: An alternative sauce includes a peeled and seeded tomato cooked with the sauce.

Lamb Tagine with Cardoons

Cardoons are domesticated thistles found in the spring, which have a taste similar to artichokes and an appearance similar to celery when all the stalks are tied together in a bundle. They make marvellous eating and should definitely be searched out and tried. They are not difficult to grow if you have a vegetable garden and can be bought throughout the Mediterranean.

For 6 people

Same as for *tagine makalli bil kerfas bil kreezoe* (Lamb Tagine with Carrots and Celery, page 206), but double the amount of lemon juice (cardoons need a great deal of lemon juice);	substitute 3 bundles of cardoons, cut into pieces, for the carrots and celery; add 6 tablespoons chopped parsley, and omit the green coriander

1 Remove the outer stalks and tough parts from the cardoons, separating the stalks, and cutting away the leaves. Wash the inner stem and bleached inner stalks well. With a paring knife, remove the strings and cut the stalks into 6 cm (3") lengths. Keep the cardoons in acidulated water (vinegar or lemon juice) to avoid blackening them.

2 Follow step 1 on page 206. After the lamb has cooked 1 hour, add the rinsed and drained cardoons, with enough fresh water to cover them in the casserole. (For the first 15 to 20 minutes of cooking, the cardoons must be covered by liquid.) Continue cooking for 40 minutes.

3 Follow step 5 on page 207, adding the lemon juice by tablespoons and tasting. Simmer gently, uncovered, to allow the sauce to reduce and flavours to blend.

4 Place the lamb in the shallow serving dish and cover completely with the cardoons. Decorate with the lemon peel and olives. Reduce the sauce, if necessary, over high heat to 300 ml (½ pint) and taste again for seasoning – add more lemon juice, if desired. Pour the sauce over and serve at once, or keep warm in a 130°C/250°F/Gas ½.

The Women's Institute
Poultry and Game

Edited by Rachel Ryan
National Federation of Women's Institutes,
London, 1960
56 pages
215 x 138 mm (8½ x 5⅜ in.)

Less lauded than Delia Smith, the Women's Institute has been publishing booklets of simple recipes, straightforwardly written, for decades. This particular booklet must be the first in my collection, bought because I had great need of it. My mother had been admitted to hospital for a simple operation, which meant an absence of about a week. She wanted to be sure that my father, a busy GP, would be properly fed. By me, who had done little more than boil an egg. I was sixteen.

My mother decided that I should give my father roast guinea fowl. I had no idea how this bird should be cooked (and she wouldn't tell me); indeed, I had no idea what sort of bird it was. Had I known it was native to the Guinea coast of Africa, I would have been even more alarmed. The WI's booklet came to my rescue. Treat it like chicken, with bacon to moisten the breast, and place some butter in the cavity with a few sprigs of parsley or tarragon. Roast for 45–60 minutes. Simple. I added green vegetables, and served.

My father was delighted; I had made no mistakes, I could cook. When my mother came home, I asked her how she normally cooked the bird. 'I've never tried guinea fowl', she confessed. Was this malice or a confidence-building exercise? I've never quite decided, but, thanks to the WI booklet, confidence was what I got.

Although more than fifty years old, Roger Nicholson's cover is not only accurate but striking. Compare and contrast with the dust jacket for *Good English Food* (page 204).

GOOSE

ROAST GOOSE

Mature geese weigh from about 10–14 lb. Like ducks, they are wasteful, so allow 1–1½ lb per person. A 10 lb goose should feed 8 people. The inside of the goose may be stuffed with either a herb, sage or apple stuffing (see page 25) or it may be rubbed over with lemon and peeled lemon placed inside (to absorb some of the fat) instead of stuffing.

Sprinkle the goose with flour and roast at 400° for 20 minutes. Then lower the heat to 350° and continue cooking. Allow 15 minutes to the lb (a 10 lb goose should take about 2½ hours to cook) but if there is reason to think the goose is on the old and tough side, give it 20 minutes to the lb and 20 over and cook more gently.

Apple sauce is usually served with goose, but all fruit goes well with it. Fried apple or pineapple rings make a good garnish for a roast goose and the gravy is improved if a sour apple is cooked in the pan with the goose.

ROAST GOOSE WITH MASHED POTATO STUFFING

Boil some potatoes, drain and make very dry, then mash and blend with 2 or 3 tablespoonsful of butter or thick cream. Add salt, pepper, a little sage and a finely chopped parboiled onion. This stuffing is used to fill the entire body of the goose.

Using up cold Goose

Devil the goose in the same way as turkey bones (see page 26).

Slice and eat cold with baked potato, a celery, apple and walnut (or beetroot) salad or a plain green salad and damson or quince cheese.

Mince and mix with pepper, salt, 1 teaspoonful curry powder, 1 dessertspoonful flour and enough gravy to moisten. Cook in a shallow greased dish in a fairly hot oven for about 25 minutes and serve with triangles of toast.

30

GUINEA FOWL

ROAST GUINEA FOWL

Young guinea fowl is tender but rather dry; the taste is something between that of a chicken and a pheasant. The breast must be covered with snipped bacon and it is advisable to put a little butter inside the bird. A few sprigs of parsley or tarragon may be put in with the butter. Stuff in the same way as chicken. Roast for 45–60 minutes in a moderately hot oven, basting well.

ROAST GUINEA FOWL WITH OLIVE STUFFING AND SOUR CREAM SAUCE

Peel and chop a dozen olives or 6 large ones, mix with pepper (no salt is needed) and a small teacupful of fine crumbs and bind with a beaten egg. Roast the guineas fowl in the usual way but instead of adding water or stock to the pan for gravy, add a cupful of sour cream or yoghurt, scrape the pan well and simmer for a minute or two.

Older guinea fowl may be casseroled in various ways (such as some of those given in the section on PIGEONS) and here is a very simple recipe from Norway.

NORWEGIAN METHOD OF DEALING WITH OLD GUINEA FOWL

1 guinea fowl
1 tin evaporated milk
½ pt stock or water
6 shallots
Seasoning

Brown the guinea fowl (whole) in a little fat or butter. Add milk, stock, shallots and seasoning. Bring to the boil. Stew gently until tender. Serve the bird with the liquid poured over it or if preferred carve it and re-heat in the sauce before serving. This method is equally good for any old game.

31

POTTED GROUSE

6 grouse (old or badly shot ones will do)
3 carrots
3 onions
Butter for frying
¼ lb bacon
Bouquet garni
Salt, pepper

Slice the vegetables and fry everything until brown. Cover with good stock and put in the oven for 2½ hours at gentle heat. Take all the meat from the bones and put everything *except the carrots* through a fine mincer and then pound or put through a fine sieve. Press the mixture into a shallow dish and cover with clarified butter.

Just a small glass of port added at the end is a great improvement. – Editor

BLACK GAME

Black Cock and Grey Hen

IN SEASON *20th August – 10th December*

These are a little larger than grouse and are very dry if not properly hung. They should not be washed but wiped inside and out. Cover the breasts with bacon and put a good nut of butter inside each bird. Roast in a fairly hot oven for 45–60 minutes (the hen is smaller than the cock), basting well. Dish on buttered toast.

ACCOMPANIMENTS: gravy, bread sauce, fried crumbs. Wafer potatoes and a salad.

CAPERCAILZIE

IN SEASON *1st September – 28th February*

This big and beautiful member of the grouse family is not often seen in shops. Each bird will feed 4 people. It should have slices of bacon tied over the breast and be roasted like grouse, but from 40–50 minutes. Same accompaniments as grouse.

36

PARTRIDGE

IN SEASON *1st September – 1st February*

Allow half per person.

ROAST PARTRIDGE

Cover the breast with bacon and roast in a fairly hot oven for 20–25 minutes. Baste with butter if possible. Split in two when serving and give half to each person.

ACCOMPANIMENTS: clear gravy, watercress garnish, wafer potatoes and a salad (apple and celery is good).

PARTRIDGE AND MUSHROOMS

Stuff the partridges inside with ¼ lb of mushrooms which have been sliced and cooked slowly in butter with seasonings. Cook in an open casserole in a rather hot oven until the birds are brown, then add the sauce and simmer for ¾ hour. Add an extra ¼ lb of mushrooms 15 minutes before the end of cooking.

GARNISH with watercress.

SAUCE 1½ oz flour, 1½ oz butter, ¾ pt stock, ½ tumbler sherry, salt and pepper.

37

Wyvern
Culinary Jottings

Higginbotham, Madras, 1891
(sixth edition; first published 1878)
620 pages
197 x 119 mm (7¾ x 4⅝ in.)

'Wyvern' was Colonel Arthur Robert Kenney-Herbert, who, while stationed in Madras at the height of the Raj, whiled away the hours writing about cookery for the *Madras Athenaeum and Daily News*. These 'jottings' were made into a book in 1878 (mine is the sixth edition, for it was enormously popular). A wyvern, a heraldic two-legged dragon with a barbed tail, formed part of the Herbert coat of arms.

The recipes, Elizabeth David said, are so 'meticulous and clear that the absolute beginner could follow them' (*Spices, Salt and Aromatics in the English Kitchen*; 1970). Riveting, too, is Wyvern's description of Anglo-Indian life. It is no good shouting at one's chef, says the colonel, remembering a mess president who, violet in the face with wrath, upbraided his Indian cook. 'The unhappy menial … had taken down that he was to boil the pâté de foie gras, and ice the asparagus.' On the other hand, his rice was superb: 'A sodden mass of "stodgy" rice as dressed by Mary Jane in England is a thing unknown to the Anglo-Indian exile.'

You might expect hot curries to make up most of the book, but you'd be wrong. Colonial India was all about keeping native ideas at bay. So curries come after chapters on savoury toasts, *réchauffés*, and eggs, macaroni and cheese. However, Wyvern does describe the definitive Indian curry powder, helpfully translated into Hindi – 9.3 kilograms (20½ lb) of nine spices. 'Do not be alarmed at the quantity … curry-powder *improves* by keeping, if carefully secured.' Slow cooking, he says, is the curry cook's secret: 'Is not this dish too frequently presented to us with the chicken like leather, and the gravy around it like oily water and snuff?' Jolly good show.

Right: Everyone who knows about Wyvern knows he was really Colonel Kenney-Herbert, who 'jotted' for the memsahibs of Madras – hence the note on the title page of my copy.

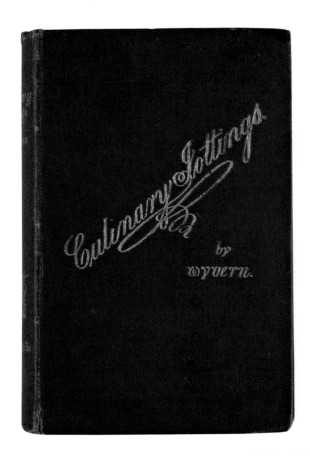

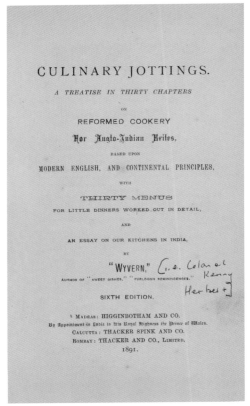

CHAPTER XXVII.

Curries—continued, and Mulligatunny.

THE outward bound passenger to India is generally very favourably struck by the curry presented to him at a Ceylon hostelry. Heartily weary of the *cuisine* on boardship, at that period of his voyage, he would probably welcome any change with thankfulness. The prospect of a little meal ashore, "be it ever so humble," is therefore especially enjoyable to him. It may, of course, be said that in such circumstances the traveller is predisposed to deliver a kindly verdict; and that if the dish that pleased him so much in the hour of his emancipation from cuddy barbarisms were placed before him after a proper course of civilized diet, it would, by no means, produce such an agreeable impression. It would, at all events, lack the charm of contrast, which, in the particular instance before us, could hardly fail to excite the warmest feelings of gratitude and satisfaction.

The nautical curry is not, as a rule, a *plat* to dream of, —a triumph to look back upon pleasurably, that is to say, with the half-closed eye of a *connoisseur*. A sea-faring friend with whom I once made a very cheery voyage, graphically described the composition as "yellow Irish stew." Those whose memory is retentive of trifles will no doubt call to mind without difficulty a bright saffron-tinted swill, covering sundry knotty lumps of potato and

a few bony atoms of mutton, with its surface beflecked, if I may so describe it, with glossy discs of molten grease. Not exactly the sort of dish to tempt a lady, still slightly affected by *mal-de-mer*, who has been urged by her stewardess to rouse herself, "poor dear," and try and eat something. Having had this mess thrust before him day after day for three weeks, no wonder that the "*vacuus viator*" finds something in the curry of Ceylon to delight him.

"Good! said I to myself, cheered at the sight" (a plump, freshly-roasted leveret), wrote Brillat Savarin concerning his experiences of a journey; "I am not entirely abandoned by Providence: *a traveller may gather a flower by the way-side.*"

Regarding the Ceylon curry, then, as a "flower by the way-side," let us proceed to consider its composition with all due attention. As I observed in my last chapter, the dish is quite a *spécialité*, peculiar originally to places where the cocoanut is extensively grown and appreciated. It is known by some as the "Malay curry," and it is closely allied to the *moli* of the Tamils of Southern India. Though best adapted for the treatment of shell-fish, ordinary fish, and vegetables of the *cucumis* or gourd family, it may be advantageously tried with chicken, or any nice white meat. We can describe it as a species of *fricassée*, rich with the nutty essence of the cocoanut, and very delicately flavoured with certain mild condiments. It ought to be by no means peppery or hot, though thin strips of red and green chilli-skin or capsicum may be associated with it. It therefore possesses characteristics very different from those of an ordinary curry. The knotty point is the treatment and application of the cocoanut, which should be as fresh and juicy as possible, and of which there should be no stint.

In places where cocoanuts cannot be readily procured, a very good "mock" Ceylon curry can be made with the

27

amongst it; dust a thick layer of grated cheese over the surface, and as soon as it browns nicely in the oven, send it to table. Maccaroni *au gratin* should be quite moist, and thoroughly impregnated with the flavour of cheese: the presence of mustard should also be perceptible.

IRISH STEW.

This homely yet excellent dish is so often mismanaged and improperly treated, that I think a recipe for it will be useful. The backbone of the composition is strong *mutton broth*, without which it is impossible to serve it correctly. My way, which differs from the ordinary one, is this:—

I take the whole of the neck of mutton, cut off the nice chops for the stew, and put the scrag-end and trimmings, with a couple of onions, black pepper, and salt to produce broth. This being ready, I strain and put the chops into it, with six Bombay onions, black pepper, and salt, close the stew-pan, and simmer slowly till the meat is very tender and parts easily from the bones. The potatoes I cook *separately*, boiling them till thoroughly done, then draining and mashing them, with a few spoonfuls of the broth, till a *purée* is obtained. The onions I mash with a silver fork, and mix with the potato *purée*; I then make this mixture hot, adding the rest of the broth, put the chops into it, and turn the whole out upon a very hot silver dish. Milk may be added with the broth to the potatoes. This stew has no lumps in it, the potatoes and onions being thoroughly mashed, and creamy.

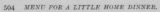

MENU NO. XXIV.

For a little home dinner.

Consommé de laitue.
Pomfret à la Normande.
Pièce de bœuf en aspic.
Courge-à-la-moelle au gratin.
Pain de groseilles.

1.—Make a clear *consommé* as usual, and treat the lettuce in this way:—Pick and wash one  large, or two small cabbage lettuces, dip them into boiling water for a few minutes, take them out, cut them into quarters: tie them together again: butter a stew-pan, place a couple of slices of bacon at the bottom of the pan, lay the lettuces on them, and cover them with stock: add two cloves, an onion, a tea-spoonful of sugar, and one of salt, and a tea-spoonful of dried herbs. Simmer the lettuces until done, take them out, drain them, and when dry, cut them into shreds with a dessert-knife: put the shredded pieces at the bottom of your tureen, pour the *consommé*, boiling hot, over them, and serve. One average lettuce will be found enough for four basins. The broth in which it is cooked must be strained, and added to the soup: see, however, that it is clear.

2.—Clean and trim a fine pomfret; draw off the skin and detach the flesh from the bone with a sharp knife: take the two sides so

---

* Lettuces cooked in this manner may be served as a vegetable, in which form they are delicious: omit the shredding and serve them with their broth poured over them.—W.

49

Yan-kit So

Yan-kit's Classic Chinese Cookbook

Dorling Kindersley, London, 1984
240 pages
233 x 190 mm (9⅛ x 7½ in.)

The combination of a scholarly, perfectionist Chinese historian, Dr Yan-kit So, and an innovative publisher, Dorling Kindersley, makes this book a classic in a number of ways. In Yan-kit's obituary in *The Guardian* (4 January 2002), Alan Davidson (page 68) called her work a brilliant example of 'cross-cultural communication'. This was the first English-language book to treat Chinese food and its complex ingredients, cooking methods and presentation seriously. A series of photographs at the beginning shows the difference between such vegetables as Chinese flowering cabbage and mustard greens, and between such noodles as cellophane and river rice. It was designed to help rootless overseas Chinese as much as Westerners.

Kitchen implements (then found only in Chinatown) are shown, as are the techniques of stir-frying, steaming and using a cleaver. I actually lunched with Yan-kit as her book was published, and was so excited I immediately rushed to Chinatown for my first wok and cleaver. An important scholar, she was born in China and brought up in Hong Kong, and later married an American historian who died tragically young.

This, Yan-kit's first book, was written after a breakdown brought on by grief. It was an immediate success, winning the Glenfiddich and André Simon awards for best food book when, as the writer and broadcaster Paul Levy said in Yan-kit's obituary in *The Independent* (3 January 2002), 'they still meant something'. Despite all the books on Chinese cooking currently on the market, this to me remains the clearest and the most inspiring.

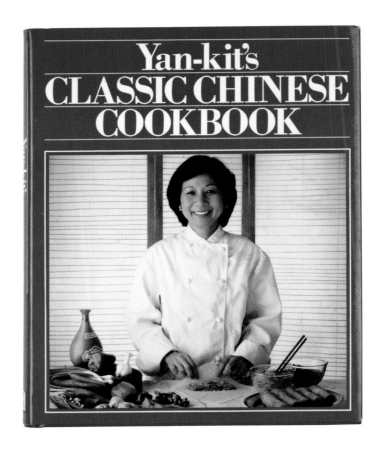

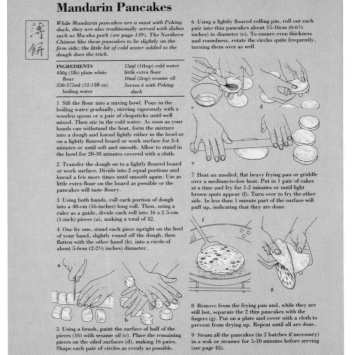

Cooks and Their Books

Darina Allen

Owner of Ballymaloe Cookery School in County Cork, Ireland, teacher, food writer, newspaper columnist and TV presenter.

Good Things
by Jane Grigson
(Michael Joseph, 1971)
This was given to me as a Christmas present by my husband, Tim, in 1971. I cooked virtually everything in it; I loved the drawings, too. For years I imagined that Jane Grigson looked just like the lady in the illustrations.

The Ballymaloe Cookbook
by Myrtle Allen
(Agri-Books, 1977)
I never tire of this book, which was written by my mother-in-law. I love the Mel Calman illustrations and the simple layout, with a recipe and story on each page. I read it over and over again.

French Provincial Cooking
by Elizabeth David
(Michael Joseph, 1960)
I came to Elizabeth David a little later than some. This is not a cookbook for total beginners; now, however, if I had to choose only one cookbook for my desert island, then it would have to be this one. Even though it was first published in 1960, it is timeless – as fresh and exciting as a newly published tome.

The Art of Simple Food: Notes, Lessons, and Recipes from a Delicious Revolution
by Alice Waters
(Clarkson Potter, 2007)
I think I own every single one of Alice Waters's books. I love them all, but this one might be my favourite.

Madhur Jaffrey's Indian Cookery
by Madhur Jaffrey
(BBC, 1982; see page 126)
I also own every cookbook written by Madhur Jaffrey, but it was the well-tested recipes in *Indian Cookery* that, by taking the mystery out of Indian food, gave me the confidence to explore the country's cuisine. I now travel to India every year, and continue to be amazed by what it has to offer.

Four Seasons Cookery Book
by Margaret Costa
(Thomas Nelson, 1970; see page 60)
My original copy of this book has long since lost its jacket. I have cooked every recipe between its covers, and many have now become a part of my repertoire.

A Book of Middle Eastern Food
by Claudia Roden
(Penguin, 1968; see page 168)
I also love Claudia Roden's food and prose. Which of her books to include here was a difficult choice, but every one has whetted my appetite for Middle Eastern food.

Mastering the Art of French Cooking, 2 vols, **by Simone Beck, Louisette Bertholle and Julia Child**
(Knopf, 1961 and 1970)
The first volume of this book was already a favourite in Myrtle Allen's kitchen when I arrived there, fresh from hotel school, in 1968. They are both astonishing books. The recipes can span from six to sixteen pages: exasperating but brilliant. Nothing is left to chance – not the size of the saucepan, nor the length of the wooden spoon – and there is no margin for error. If you follow a recipe exactly, the end result is perfection.

Maggie's Table
by Maggie Beer
(Lantern, 2005)
Maggie Beer is a beautiful cook from the Barossa Valley in Australia. She may not be as well known as Stephanie Alexander [see page 16], but I love her homely, simple, truly sophisticated food.

The Classic Italian Cookbook: The Art of Italian Cooking and the Italian Art of Eating
by Marcella Hazan
(Harper's Magazine Press, 1973; see page 114)
I bought my copy of this book in 1982, when I attended some cooking classes given by Marcella in Bologna. I can hear her speaking off every page. The recipes are minutely researched and really work.

Kind Cooking
by Maura Laverty
(Kerryman, 1946)
A social record of what the Irish were eating at the time. Laverty writes beautifully evocative prose with a truly Irish voice: I love this book.

Oops: I've just realized that all these books are by women. So, to redress the balance: **The River Cottage Cookbook** by **Hugh Fearnley-Whittingstall** (HarperCollins, 2001), **English Seafood Cookery** by **Rick Stein** (Penguin, 1988) and **Ottolenghi: The Cookbook** by **Yotam Ottolenghi and Sami Tamimi** (Ebury Press, 2008; see page 158). **The Times' Cookery Book** by **Katie Stewart** (Collins, 1972) is another favourite, but I must stop now. There are more than 2000 cookery books in my library …

Galton Blackiston

Chef at the Michelin-starred Morston Hall in Norfolk.

With any cookery book, the first section I turn to is the puddings; then I work backwards. Here are some of my favourites:

Roast Chicken and Other Stories
**by Simon Hopkinson with Lyndsey Bareham
(Ebury Press, 1994; see page 124)**

White Heat
**by Marco Pierre White
(Pyramid, 1990)**

Sauces: Sweet and Savoury, Classic and New
**by Michel Roux
(Quadrille, 1998)**

Pastry: Savoury and Sweet
**by Michel Roux
(Quadrille, 2008)**

La Potinière and Friends
**by David and Hilary Brown
(Century, 1990)**

The French Laundry Cookbook
**by Thomas Keller
(Artisan, 1999)**

New Classic Cuisine
**by Albert and Michel Roux
(Macdonald, 1983)**

Four Seasons Cookery Book
**by Margaret Costa
(Thomas Nelson, 1970; see page 60)**

Mrs Beeton's Dictionary of Every-day Cookery
**by Isabella Beeton
(S.O. Beeton, 1865)**

Geraldene Holt's Cake Stall
**by Geraldene Holt
(Hodder & Stoughton, 1980)**

Anything by Delia Smith
All her books have influenced me.

Mary Contini

Co-owner of Valvona & Crolla in Edinburgh, Scotland's oldest delicatessen, and one of the country's best-known cooks.

I was raised in an Italian kitchen, cooking with my mother and grandmother, whose daily purpose in life was to cook meals to please my father: familiar, seasonal and traditional recipes from the mountainous area of Lazio. The only cookery book in our house was a copy of *Be-Ro Home Recipes* [first published in 1923], which we turned to when making cakes and puddings.

Once I was married, I had to cook for my husband, who, with a Neapolitan father, preferred spicier recipes with more *peperoncini*, oil, fish and herbs. I was taught by my mother-in-law and my new Neapolitan grandmother, and still not a cookbook in sight.

The books I love today are scattered throughout my home: piled on my kitchen sideboard, behind and under my desk, beside the sofa and on my bedside table. My favourites are steeped in Italy, and almost all of them are written by women.

Amaretto, Apple Cake and Artichokes: The Best of Anna Del Conte
(Vintage, 2006)

Science in the Kitchen and the Art of Eating Well
**by Pellegrino Artusi
(University of Toronto Press, 2003; first published 1891)**

Honey From a Weed: Fasting and Feasting in Tuscany, Catalonia, the Cyclades and Apulia
**by Patience Gray
(Prospect Books, 1986; see page 96)**

The Classic Italian Cookbook: The Art of Italian Cooking and the Italian Art of Eating
**by Marcella Hazan
(Harper's Magazine Press, 1973; see page 114)**

La Potinière and Friends
**by David and Hilary Brown
(Century, 1990)**

Sunday Roast: The Complete Guide to Cooking and Carving
**by Clarissa Dickson Wright
(Headline, 2002)**

Cooking Weeds: A Vegetarian Cookery Book
**by Vivien Weise
(Prospect Books, 2004)**

Chez Panisse Café Cookbook
**by Alice Waters
(HarperCollins, 1999; see page 200)**

Paul Bocuse's French Cooking
**by Paul Bocuse
(Pantheon, 1977)**

Be-Ro Home Recipes: Scones, Cakes, Pastries, Puddings, **18th edn
(Thomas Bell & Son Ltd, 1930)**

Tom Jaine

Owner of Prospect Books, which specializes in books about cookery and food history.

My top-ten cookery books are as follows, with a few words to justify each choice:

The Accomplisht Cook
by Robert May
(London, 1660)
The big one for the seventeenth century and beyond.

The Closet of Sir Kenelm Digby Knight Opened
by Sir Kenelm Digby
(London, 1669; see page 76)
Perhaps the most enjoyable cookery book of all time.

The Country Housewife's Family Companion
by William Ellis
(London, 1750)
One of the few early authors to pay attention to the common people.

Fish, How to Choose and How to Dress
by Piscator
(Longman, Brown, Green and Longmans, 1843)
The first English fish cookbook.

Maison rustique des dames
by Cora Millet-Robinet
(Librairie Agricole de la Maison Rustique, 1859)
Here's how to be a proper French housewife.

Culinary Jottings
by Wyvern
(Higginbotham, 1878; see page 212)
If memsahib is more your style, this will explain haute cuisine as well as curries.

Gastronomie pratique
by Ali-Bab
(Ernest Flammarion, 1907)
The greatest French culinary instructor of all time.

French Provincial Cooking
by Elizabeth David
(Michael Joseph, 1960)
David's best book.

The Fruit Book
by Jane Grigson
(Michael Joseph, 1982)
Similarly, this is Grigson's finest work.

Honey from a Weed: Fasting and Feasting in Tuscany, Catalonia, the Cyclades and Apulia
by Patience Gray
(Prospect Books, 1986; see page 96)
A modern classic.

Paul Levy

Journalist and author, former Food and Wine Editor of *The Observer*, and the recipient of many prizes for food writing and journalism.

How do I organize my cookery books? First, I don't know how many there are – although the number is in the high thousands, as I receive review copies of most of the serious ones published in Britain. I also buy food-related books in France and the United States. And the late Alan Davidson [see page 68] and I amassed a collection of late 1970s Chinese cookery books. Before the Cultural Revolution (1966–76), recipes in China were passed on orally, even in professional kitchens. By the time of our arrival in the country in 1980, a lot of elderly chefs had been called back from working in the fields to teach their now-forgotten recipes to young apprentice-chefs. So our books represent the first recipes published in China. Unfortunately, neither of us could read any form of Chinese, and these books contain not a word in any other language. Alan's have been split up and sold. Mine, meanwhile, moulder on the shelves – divided roughly by national or regional cuisine – that line one-third of my kitchen; or in my book-lined study; or on shelves in the ground-floor corridor; or throughout the entirety of the second floor; or in one of two glory holes, one on the mezzanine, the other in the attic. So how do I find anything? By country. By chance. Or by asking my wife.

Michael Mina
Award-winning American chef, restaurateur and
food writer.

The French Laundry Cookbook
by Thomas Keller
(Artisan, 1999)

Alinea
by Grant Achatz
(Ten Speed Press, 2008)

Modernist Cuisine: The Art and Science
of Cooking
by Nathan Myhrvold *et al.*
(Cooking Lab, 2011)

The Professional Chef, 9th edn,
by The Culinary Institute of America
(Wiley, 2011)

Culinary Artistry
by Andrew Dornenburg and Karen Page
(Wiley, 1996)

Jasper White's Cooking from New England:
More Than 300 Traditional and
Contemporary Recipes
by Jasper White
(Jessica's Biscuit, 1998)

Jean-Louis: Cooking with the Seasons
by Jean-Louis Palladin
(Lickle Publishing, 1989)

The Greens Cookbook: Extraordinary
Vegetarian Cuisine from the Celebrated
Restaurant
by Deborah Madison
(Bantam, 1987)

Le Bernardin Cookbook: Four-Star
Simplicity
by Eric Ripert and Maguy Le Coze
(Clarkson Potter, 1998)

Jeremiah Tower's New American Classics
by Jeremiah Tower
(Harper & Row, 1986)

Anton Mosimann
Former head chef at the Dorchester hotel, London,
TV presenter, and founder of a number of business
ventures in the hospitality industry.

Adelrich Furrer, whose cookery book collection forms the basis of my own, was unwittingly responsible for the turning point in my life. After I was awarded the first ever Nestlé Toque d'Or (an annual award for catering students) in 1974, he sent me a letter of congratulations and mentioned that he had enjoyed reading my first press interview. He also invited me to dinner at his Zurich home. I was stunned, as Furrer was a famous figure, renowned for the elaborate butter sculptures that formed the centrepieces of his magnificent cold buffets. He worked for Hilton Hotels, and was responsible for all its grand openings. I was terrified by the idea that such a formidable chef should contact me, and it took me six months to accept the invitation. My then fiancée, Kathrin, and I finally went along to his house, and during dinner Furrer showed me his collection of cookery books. Naturally I was enchanted, and because I was so enthusiastic, he commented to his wife: 'Darling, when I am in heaven, he should have first refusal.' Three months later Furrer received a call from Eugène Käufeler, the doyen of London's Dorchester hotel, asking if Furrer could recommend his successor as maître chefs des cuisines. Furrer mentioned that we had met and warmly endorsed me; consequently, I was appointed at the Dorchester. It does not end there, as six months after arriving in London I received a call from his wife. Sadly, Furrer had passed away, but true to that first conversation she offered me his library. I was newly married and certainly did not have any money, but found a friendly bank manager who agreed to lend me the 20,000 Swiss francs I needed in order to purchase Furrer's collection of 800 books. These, when added to the dozen or so books I had already acquired, became the core of my collection.

Without doubt, the book I treasure most is *Opera dell'arte del cucinare* (1570) by **Bartolomeo Scappi**, chef to two popes in the sixteenth century. I already owned an edition of the book from 1605, and when I heard that a first edition was coming up for auction, I was on tenterhooks. The book features numerous illustrations of kitchen equipment, much of which is still used today.

The book that really got me started is a handwritten, leather-bound volume from 1737. It was authored by an anonymous lady cook who was in the employ of an aristocratic family. The calligraphy alone is a work of art, not to mention the recipes, which include cheesecake and a chocolate sorbet; it is hard to believe that such dishes were being served in the stately homes of the eighteenth century. There are also remedies for a variety of everyday ailments.

It is difficult for me to select the next eight books as I have a great attachment to about three hundred. I suppose I would select the works of the French chef **Auguste Escoffier**, who, through his books, was able to demonstrate the art of cooking in a five-star hotel. Years later, my experience at the Dorchester was probably similar to his at the Savoy.

Elizabeth David's books inspired the British nation at a time when olive oil was still purchased from the chemist. So, for her courage in publishing something so groundbreaking, I choose *Italian Food* (Macdonald, 1954; see page 66). I also enjoyed meeting her on many occasions, and fondly remember taking afternoon tea at her home in Chelsea.

Jill Norman

Creator of the Penguin Cookery Library, and editor of Elizabeth David's books.

Modern Cookery for Private Families
by Eliza Acton
(Longman, Brown, Green and Longmans, 1845; see page 14)
The best nineteenth-century book on English cooking. Acton's recipes are a model of sensible instructions written in elegant prose.

French Provincial Cooking
by Elizabeth David
(Michael Joseph, 1960)
The descriptions of the French provinces, the quotations from literature and the well-researched recipes inspired me to cook.

Good Things
by Jane Grigson
(Michael Joseph, 1971)
A collection of recipes for all the things I like to cook, from scallops to rabbit, leeks to walnuts.

Simple French Food
by Richard Olney
(Jill Norman & Hobhouse, 1981)
Mostly Provençal recipes, elegantly and precisely described. Richard was a very fine cook.

A Book of Middle Eastern Food
by Claudia Roden
(Penguin, 1968; see page 168)
My introduction to the wonderful cooking of the region.

Roast Chicken and Other Stories
by Simon Hopkinson with Lyndsey Bareham
(Ebury Press, 1994; see page 124)
Inspirational recipes for dishes to cook at home.

Thai Food
by David Thompson
(Pavilion, 2002)
The history and culture of Thai food with excellent recipes.

Lebanese Cuisine
by Anissa Helou
(Grub Street, 1994)
In my opinion, the best collection of authentic Lebanese dishes.

Moro: The Cookbook
by Sam and Sam Clark
(Ebury Press, 2001; see page 52)
The Clarks' dishes from Spain and North Africa are simple and good.

Plenty
by Yotam Ottolenghi
(Ebury Press, 2010)
Modern vegetarian food at its best.

Thane Prince

Former food columnist for the *Daily Telegraph*, author of several cookery books and a highly regarded cookery teacher.

My top-ten cookery books? Well, I must start with **Margaret Costa**'s *Four Seasons Cookery Book* (Thomas Nelson, 1970; see page 60) and **Robert Carrier**'s *Cooking for You* (Hamlyn, 1973). Both these books had a profound influence on me when I was learning to cook – the Carrier as there was a picture for each dish, and the Costa because there wasn't. With *Four Seasons* I could picture for myself what was wanted and learned not to follow recipes slavishly.

Marcella Cucina by **Marcella Hazan** (Macmillan, 1997) is my Italian bible. Hazan is very strict and makes me cower a little, but everything is perfectly explained and reasoned. For things Near Eastern I turn to **Claudia Roden**, and here I choose her *Tamarind and Saffron: Favourite Recipes from the Middle East* (Viking, 1999) for the sheer 'cook now' quality of the recipes.

Madhur Jaffrey taught me all things Indian, and her *Eastern Vegetarian Cooking* (Jonathan Cape, 1981) is a classic. **Jill Norman** gathered together some wonderful cooks for the essential *Cook's Book: Recipes and Step-by-Step Techniques for Success Every Time from the World's Top Chefs* (Dorling Kindersley, 2005), which I refer to when in need of technical advice. *Moro: The Cookbook* by **Sam and Sam Clark** (Ebury Press, 2001; see page 52), **Martha Stewart**'s *Baking Handbook* (Clarkson Potter, 2005), *Plenty* by **Yotam Ottolenghi** (Ebury Press, 2010) and **Jamie Oliver**'s *Jamie at Home: Cook Your Way to the Good Life* (Michael Joseph, 2007) are all well thumbed.

A Book for Cooks

Mitch Tonks

Award-winning food writer, restaurateur and fishmonger, and one of the leading seafood chefs in the United Kingdom.

The Harry's Bar Cookbook
by Arrigo Cipriani
(Smith Gryphon, 1991)

Provence: The Beautiful Cookbook
by Richard Olney
(HarperCollins, 1993)

Preserving
by Oded Schwartz
(Dorling Kindersley, 1996)

Week In, Week Out
by Simon Hopkinson
(Quadrille, 2007)

A Book of Mediterranean Food
by Elizabeth David
(John Lehmann, 1950)

Fish Cookery
by Jane Grigson
(David & Charles, 1973)

The Best of Indonesian Cooking:
A Selection of Popular Indonesian Recipes
by Sri Owen
(Centurion, 1992)

Nose to Tail Eating: A Kind of British
Cooking
by Fergus Henderson
(Macmillan, 1999)

British Seasonal Food: A Year Round
Celebration of the Finest Produce
by Mark Hix
(Quadrille, 2008)

Chez Panisse Café Cookbook
by Alice Waters
(HarperCollins, 1999; see page 200)

Phil Vickery

Former chef at several Michelin-starred restaurants in the United Kingdom, and now a well-known TV presenter.

The following books have really changed the way I think about cooking and food in general:

The Oxford Companion to Food
by Alan Davidson
(Oxford University Press, 1999)

Food from Your Garden: All You Need to
Know to Grow, Cook and Preserve Your
Own Fruit and Vegetables
(Reader's Digest Association, 1977)

English Food: An Anthology
by Jane Grigson
(Macmillan, 1974)

European Peasant Cookery
by Elisabeth Luard
(Bantam, 1986; see page 138)

The Modern Housewife
by Alexis Soyer
(Simpkin, Marshall, 1849)

Great Chefs of France
by Anthony Blake and Quentin Crewe
(Mitchell Beazley, 1978)

Mrs Beeton's Household Management
by Isabella Beeton
(S.O. Beeton, 1861; see page 32)

El Bulli 2003–2004
by Ferran Adrià *et al.*
(Ecco Press, 2006)

The Constance Spry Cookery Book
by Constance Spry and Rosemary Hume
(J.M. Dent, 1956; see page 190)

Spices, Salt and Aromatics in the
English Kitchen
by Elizabeth David
(Penguin, 1970)

Bibliography

Julian Barnes
The Pedant in the Kitchen
London (Atlantic) 2003

Ann Barr and Paul Levy
The Official Foodie Handbook:
Be Modern – Worship Food
London (Ebury Press) 1984

Lisa Chaney
Elizabeth David: A Biography
London (Macmillan) 1998

Elizabeth David
An Omelette and a Glass of Wine
London (Robert Hale) 1984

Nicola Humble
Culinary Pleasures: Cook Books and
the Transformation of British Food
London (Faber and Faber) 2005

Eric Quayle
Old Cook Books: An Illustrated History
London (Studio Vista) 1978

Jeffrey Steingarten
The Man Who Ate Everything
London (Headline) 1998

Index

Acknowledgements

Merrell Publishers should like to thank Anton Mosimann for allowing us to reproduce parts of his copy of *The Art of Cookery Made Plain and Easy* by Hannah Glasse (page 94); particular thanks go to Elizabeth St Clair George at Mosimann's Academy for granting us access to Mr Mosimann's library. We should also like to thank Grub Street for kindly allowing us to reproduce parts of the following titles:

Colman Andrews
Catalan Cuisine: Europe's Last Great Culinary Secret (see page 24)

Lindsey Bareham
The Big Red Book of Tomatoes (see page 26)

Glynn Christian
Real Flavours: The Handbook of Gourmet and Deli Ingredients (see page 46)

Sally Clarke
Sally Clarke's Book: Recipes from a Restaurant, Shop and Bakery (see page 54)

Margaret Costa
Four Seasons Cookery Book (see page 60)

Anne Dolamore
The Essential Olive Oil Companion (see page 80)

Nathalie Hambro
Particular Delights: Cooking for All the Senses (see page 110)

Elisabeth Luard
European Peasant Cookery (see page 138)

Lyndsay and Patrick Mikanowski
Potato (see page 148)

Janet Ross and Michael Waterfield
Leaves from Our Tuscan Kitchen; or, How to Cook Vegetables (see page 176)

Constance Spry and Rosemary Hume
The Constance Spry Cookery Book (see page 190)

Paula Wolfert
Moroccan Cuisine (see page 208)

The Author

After a day at the coalface of various newspapers – the *Northern Echo*, the *Sunday Times*, the *Daily Telegraph* – Leslie Geddes-Brown cooked for relaxation (and collected old cookery books). Following a stint as deputy editor of both *Country Life* and *World of Interiors*, she ran a weekly column on food for *Country Life* and wrote for *Observer Food Monthly*, to which she still contributes articles on food and reviews of cookery books. This has resulted in a cookery book collection numbering in the thousands, and strong views about which are the best. She has houses in London and Suffolk, and recently sold a third in Tuscany.

The Illustrator

Chloë Cheese is known for her lithographs, many of which are of domestic interiors, and is the illustrator of several cookery books, including Anne Willan's *Desserts and Pastries* (1988), Antonio Carluccio's *Passion for Pasta* (1993) and *Big Flavours and Rough Edges* by David Eyre and the Eagle chefs (2001), later published as *The Eagle Cookbook* (2009; see page 86). She lives in London and collects kitchen paraphernalia.

First published in 2012 by Merrell Publishers, London and New York

Merrell Publishers Limited
81 Southwark Street
London SE1 0HX

merrellpublishers.com

British Library Cataloguing-in-Publication Data:
Geddes-Brown, Leslie.
A book for cooks : 101 classic cookbooks.
1. Cooking – Book reviews. 2. Cookbooks – History.
I. Title
641.5-dc23

ISBN 978-1-8589-4579-8

Produced by Merrell Publishers Limited
Designed by Nicola Bailey
Cover and text illustrations by Chloë Cheese
Project-managed by Mark Ralph
Indexed by Vicki Robinson

Printed and bound in China

With the exception of *The Art of Cookery Made Plain and Easy* by Hannah Glasse (see page 223), all the books reproduced in this volume are from the library of the author.

Picture Credits

Dale Cherry: page 221 (right); Mina Group: page 219 (left); Mosimann's: page 219 (right); Nick Atkins Photography: page 218; Chris Terry: page 221 (left)

9 781858 945798